W9-BNC-199

AN ABC OF WITCHCRAFT
PAST AND PRESENT

An
ABC
of Witchcraft
Past & Present

DOREEN VALIENTE

NEW YORK
ST. MARTIN'S PRESS

133
.403
V172a

Affiliated Publishers: Macmillan & Company Ltd, London
also at Bombay, Calcutta, Madras and Melbourne—The
Macmillan Company of Canada, Limited, Toronto

CONTENTS

ILLUSTRATIONS

ALPHABETS, MAGICAL. Examples of alphabets from *The Magus*
by Francis Barrett   *Page 20*

(between pages 192 and 193)

ATHO, the Horned God of Witchcraft, as shown in a painting by
the author

BAPHOMET, the god of the Knights Templars, from Eliphas Lévi's
Transcendental Magic

BELLARMINE JUGS. One example

BROCKEN, THE. An old engraving, "The Spectre of the Brocken"

CATS AS WITCHES' FAMILIARS. "A Male Witch and his
Familiar", a print after the seventeenth-century picture attributed
to Jordaens

CIMARUTA. This Italian witch amulet, representing a sprig of
rue, surrounded by other amulets from the author's collection

DEVIL. Two woodcuts illustrating conceptions of the Devil. An
old engraving of the Wild Hunt riding the night wind at the full
moon

ESBAT. The Witches' Frolic, from an engraving by the nineteenth-
century artist, George Cruikshank

EVIL EYE. Witch amulets against the Evil Eye: *mano in fica* and
mano cornuta

FLAGELLATION. A miniature from a fifteenth-century French
manuscript of St Augustine's *Civitas Dei*

FOSSILS. Some examples from the author's collection

GARDNER, GERALD. "Witch on a Broomstick", a plaque made
by Gerald Gardner

INCUBI AND SUCCUBI. A drawing from a book by the nineteenth-
century French occultist, Jules Bois

LOVE CHARMS. A young witch performs a love spell in "The
Charm of Love" by the Master of Niederheim, an unknown Flemish
artist of the fifteenth century

ACKNOWLEDGEMENTS

The author wishes to thank the following for the provision of illustrations: *Radio Times* Hulton Picture Library; the Mansell Collection; The Bodleian Library; Mrs M. Caine; and particularly Mr Colin Harris for photographing the remaining items listed above which are in the author's own library and collection.

INTRODUCTION

Yes, this is a biased book about witchcraft; but it is biased in the opposite direction to that of most books on the subject. This book is on the side of the witches.

The reason is that the writer is a witch herself. Three hundred years ago that statement could have brought me to the gallows. But times have changed. Today, the Craft of the Wise has to a certain extent come out into the open as a pagan faith in which those who practise it can find enjoyment and fulfilment.

It has been argued by sceptics that witchcraft cannot possibly be a genuine religion, because it has no sacred book, no sacred liturgy, nor anything which identifies it with the other religions of mankind. The reason, however, why witchcraft has none of these things, is that it is older than these things. Witchcraft is as old as mankind itself; and it does not begin from books. It begins in the heart. Anyone who has a sense of wonder, an imagination that can respond to the moods of nature, who is not satisfied with the glib answers of the intellectual and materialist, who has curiosity and awareness—that person has the beginnings of witchcraft.

I became a witch many years ago. That is, I was initiated into one of the various branches of the witch cult in Britain today; and since that time I have made contact with other sections of the cult and been initiated into some of those also.

I have danced at the witches' Sabbat on many occasions, and found carefree enjoyment in it. I have stood under the stars at midnight, and invoked the Old Gods; and I have found in such invocations of the most primeval powers, those of Life, Love and Death, an uplifting of consciousness that no orthodox religious service has ever given me.

I found, however, that apart from a small band of writers such as Charles Godfrey Leland, Margaret Murray, Gerald Gardner and Robert Graves, nearly everyone who wrote books about witches presented them as being either crazily evil celebrants of the Black

Mass and confederates of Satan, or else as pathetically deluded victims of mass hysteria.

So I wrote a book called *Where Witchcraft Lives* (Aquarian Press, London, 1962 and Wehman, 1962), about witchcraft in the county where my present home is, Sussex; and I brought into it some of the things I had been taught about what witches really did and believed. At that time for personal reasons I was not able to come out openly and say I was a witch. Instead, I described myself as a student of witchcraft.

In fact, I still am such a student. I do not profess to tell all, because, unlike some writers on the subject, I do not profess to know all. Witchcraft is a big subject—as old as the human race and as deep as the human mind. I can only shed light on some aspects of it in a book like this. There are many realms still to be explored, and doubtless many discoveries still to be made.

By 'witchcraft' I mean the remains of the old religion of Western Europe, driven underground by the rise of Christianity and compelled to organise itself as a secret cult in order to survive; a cult which spread to North America and elsewhere, carried there by European immigrants.

I have not touched upon so-called African 'witchcraft', or the 'witchcraft' of any other of the peoples that we are pleased to regard as primitive; because 'witchcraft' in all these cases is the white man's opprobrious or patronising word for what these people believe and do. It is not what such people themselves call it.

Magic, both black and white, is a world-wide heritage. All over the world, in every society, occult powers have been used—and sometimes misused. Witchcraft is an Anglo-Saxon word, coined at a period when the old pagan faith and the new Christian faith were overlapping each other; when a king's warriors might submit to being baptised because their liege lord was baptised, but would still call on Thor when they went into battle; and when the Christian missionary priests were trying to persuade the 'heathen'—the people of the heaths—that their old gods were devils. It is a very old word: witchcraft—the craft of the wise. And yet it keeps cropping up in the most unexpected places; even in this slick, new world of space flight and computers. People can laugh at it; they can be afraid of it; they can denounce it; they can deny that it exists; but somehow man cannot seem to get away from it.

Moreover, with regard to psychic powers and happenings, from my own experience and conversations with others, I believe that these things are actually far more common than people realise. The reason people believe them to be something rare and bizarre, is that those who experience something of this nature are afraid to talk about it, because they are worried about what others might think. People's minds have been literally bedevilled by fear of the unknown.

Today a great many taboos are being swept away. The frank discussion of the occult and the supernormal is going hand-in-hand with a franker attitude towards sex, nudity, and other previously banned subjects. People are beginning to say what they really think and feel about these matters, instead of what hitherto they have imagined that they ought to think and feel in order not to offend society. The wind of the Age of Aquarius is rising.

In these extraordinary days, it is no wonder that anything so apparently extraordinary as a revival of witchcraft should be taking place in Europe and America. People are not trying to put the clock back, however. They are advancing towards a new society, of which a regenerated and enlightened paganism is going to be part.

Many wild guesses have been made at the actual number of practising witches in Britain today. None of them are or can be accurate, because the Craft of the Wise is not all organised under the same leadership. There are covens which seek publicity; there are others which abhor it. There are covens which insist on the old concept of ritual nudity; there are others which do not. There are covens which are devoted mainly to the moon goddess Diana; there are others which give the greater importance to the Horned God—call him Pan or what you will; and there are other covens which invoke both the male and female aspects of Divine Nature equally. However, in spite of this apparent diversity, there is a certain basic feeling and attitude to life which is common to all who have any real knowledge of witch lore.

There is a general belief among witches in the invocation and worship of the forces of life, the male and female aspects of nature, through which all manifestation takes place. These powers are personified as the Horned God and the Moon Goddess. They have a great many names, because of their great antiquity. Witches believe that ancient works of art, dating back to the Stone Age, depict the same deities which they worship today; and therefore, they say, witchcraft is the oldest religion in the world.

The cult group of thirteen, called a coven, is generally, though not invariably, adhered to. Coven meetings take place every month, at or near the full moon. These monthly meetings are called Esbats.

In addition to these, there are the more religiously important Sabbats, of which there are four Greater Sabbats and four Lesser Sabbats. The Greater Sabbats are Candlemas, May Eve, Lammas and Halloween. The Lesser Sabbats are the Equinoxes and the Solstices.

The means of invocation are simple, such as dancing, chanting or sitting cross-legged in meditation. There are other techniques in the more advanced stages of the cult, and these sometimes involve trance. These practices take place within the magic circle, which is drawn to concentrate the power that is raised, and to exclude any hostile forces. The circle is lit by candlelight if the rite takes place indoors. Outdoors, a bonfire is often lit. The burning of incense is involved whenever possible, and the ritual black-hilted knife, called an Athame, is used to draw the circle. The participants may be nude, or they may wear cloaks and hoods.

It has been suggested that witchcraft is connected with drug-taking. I have never seen this happen in any circle I have ever attended; and I do not believe it plays any significant part in modern witchcraft. In the old days, witches undoubtedly had a great knowledge of the safe use of vegetable drugs; but a good deal, though not all, of this has been lost.

There is a general belief that initiation should always pass from a man to a woman, and from a woman to a man. In other words, initiation into witchcraft must be given by a person of the opposite sex. The exception to this rule is when a witch initiates his or her own children.

There is also a general belief in the world of spirits, both human and elemental. Those who have been powerful witches in the past are believed to be still able to aid and counsel their descendants in the present day, if rightly invoked to do so.

Another general tenet of belief is in reincarnation, and the destiny involved therein. Many members of the witch cult today feel that they have been members in the past also; and there is a saying, 'Once a witch, always a witch'.

Contrary to popular belief, witches' attitude towards Christianity is not particularly hostile. I have heard of one witch who put a portrait of Jesus in her private sanctuary because, she said, he was a great white witch and knew the secret of the coven of thirteen. However, witches have little respect for the doctrine of the churchs, which they regard as a lot of man-made dogma; and they can scarcely be expected to remember kindly the years of Church-directed witch-hunting, torture and death.

Witches do not claim that the rites they use today have descended unchanged from the Stone Age. Could any living religion of any antiquity claim that its rites today are precisely the same as those used when it was founded? If it did, it would not be a living religion; it would be fossilised. On the contrary, what modern witches practise is a present-day version of a very old faith, of which the basic essence has remained unchanged.

With regard to black magic and Satanism, two things often confounded with witchcraft in the popular mind, these are in fact nothing to do with the Craft of the Wise, nor do modern witches wish to have anything to do with them or those who practise them. To say that black magic and Satanism do not exist, in view of the desecrations of churches and graveyards that have made the headlines in recent years, would be to ignore a good deal of disturbing evidence. Nevertheless, witches were not the culprits.

I have written this book as it stands because I wanted it to be not just another book about witchcraft but something different. That I am inclined to favour the Old Religion I do not deny; but is it wrong for me to write in this way, when so much has been published that is prejudiced against it?

Let me assure the reader, however, that I am not seeking to convert anyone; merely to present a different point of view. If he or she can find interest and pleasure in the savour of this cauldron I have brewed, from so many and varied ingredients, I shall be content.

So with the little rune that Charles Godfrey Leland learned from the witches of Italy:

> May Diana the Queen of the Moon,
> The Sun and the Stars,
> Earth and Sky,
> Send you fortune!

DOREEN VALIENTE

Brighton, 1972

A

AIRTS, THE FOUR

This is an old Gaelic term for the four points of the compass, north, south, east and west. They are important in magic, as the magic circle should always be orientated to them. Early Christian churches were also carefully orientated, with the high altar in the east; though in modern days this custom is not invariably observed, probably because present-day scarcity of land compels church architects to build as best they can on the ground available. The Great Pyramid is orientated with remarkable accuracy.

The magic circle usually has a candle or lamp at each of the four quarters. The powers of the Four Elements are naturally connected with the Four Airts. Different exponents of magic have differing attributions of these; but the most usual one in the Western magical tradition is air at the east, fire at the south, water at the west, and earth at the north.

This attribution is based on the quality of the prevailing winds. In Britain the south wind brings heat and dryness, while the west wind usually brings warm rainy conditions. So these quarters are regarded as the places of fire and water respectively. The wind from the east is cold, dry and bracing, so this is the place of the powers of air. The north wind is cold and freezing, coming from the place of eternal snow. It represents the darkness of earth.

In other parts of the world, of course, these conditions will not apply; so the truly talented magician, unlike one who has merely read the subject up in books, will note the prevailing winds of his own country, and invoke the Four Elements accordingly.

The Gaelic Airts had a traditional association of colours attributed to them. The east took the crimson of dawn; the south the white light of high noon; the west the brownish-grey of twilight; and the north the black of midnight.

It is notable in this connection that the song "Black Spirits" referred to in Shakespeare's *Macbeth* was not written by him, but occurs in another old play, Middleton's *The Witch,* and may well have been an old folk-rhyme. It runs as follows:

> "Black spirits and white,
> Red spirits and grey,
> Mingle, mingle, mingle,
> You that mingle may!
> Firedrake, Pucky,
>   make it lucky.
> Liard, Robin,
>   you must bob in,
> Round, around, around
>   about, about!
> All ill come running in,
>   all good keep out!"

In fact, it is calling upon the spirits from the four cardinal points, by the colours of the old Gaelic Airts, and was thus singularly appropriate to the Scottish witches Shakespeare was depicting. Firedrake, Puckey, Liard and Robin were the names of the witches' familiars.

A present-day witches' version runs as follows:

> "Black spirits and white,
> Red spirits and grey,
> Come ye and come ye,
> Come ye that may!
> Around and around,
> Throughout and about,
> The good come in
> And the ill keep out."

The magical ideas of dancing or circumambulating *deaseil* or *tuathal,* are connected with the Four Airts. *Deaseil,* or sunwise, is fortunate, and a movement of blessing; but *tuathal,* or widdershins, is generally a movement of adverse magic and cursing. These names come from the Scots Gaelic words for the cardinal points; *tuath,* north; *aiet,* east; *deas,* south; and *iar,* west. *Airt* was the starting-point of invocations; so one turned right-handed to *deas,* or left-handed, literally the sinister side, to *tuath.*

ALPHABETS, MAGICAL

It is probable that all alphabets were originally magical. Only in later times did they come to be reduced to the more prosaic transactions of mere record and trade.

The names which the letters were given often concealed some religious secret, which they enshrined in an abbreviated form. Also, the number of the letters, and their divisions into consonants and vowels, had an inner and arcane meaning. A frequent proportion found in old alphabets, is that of twenty-two letters, whereof seven are vowels. This conceals, in a rough approximation, the relation of the diameter of a circle to its circumference, which is today mathematically expressed by the Greek letter Π.

Moreover, before numeral figures were invented, the letters of the alphabet also served for the figures of numbers, such as $A = 1$, $B = 2$, and so on. In this way, a word or a name was also a number. Hence the study of what is today called numerology is a very time-honoured practice.

The Hebrew alphabet in particular contains mystic meanings in this way; and the study of these, and the use of numbers to express transcendental ideas, a kind of spiritual algebra, is called the Qabalah, meaning 'traditional knowledge'. This word is sometimes spelt Cabala, or Kabbala. It has become an important part of the mystic and magical tradition of the West.

The Arabic alphabet, too, is used in this way, by the Sufis and other arcane brotherhoods of the Near East. The Greek alphabet also lent itself to such use and interpretation, in ancient times.

In Britain, the Celtic Druids made use of the Ogham alphabet, which had several forms. These have been studied extensively in our day by Robert Graves, in his now famous book, *The White Goddess* (Faber and Faber, London, 1961). He found them to throw a flood of new light upon the religion of Ancient Britain, and to show among other things that Britain was by no means a benighted and savage region, as often previously taught, but a country in touch with the philosophy and religion of the greater part of the ancient world.

When the Angles and Saxons and the rest of the northern invaders settled in these islands, and Celtic Britain became Anglo-Saxon England, another magical alphabet found its way to this country. This was the Runic alphabet, or Futhork (so-called from its first six letters).

ALPHABETS, MAGICAL. Examples of alphabets from *The Magus* by Francis Barrett.

This alphabet has given us the word 'rune', meaning a magical rhyme. Originally, the Runes were the letters it was written down in. Each of the Runic letters had a magical meaning. Runic inscriptions were cut upon the hilt of a warrior's sword, to make it powerful and victorious in battle; and this may be the origin of the 'magical weapons', knives and swords with mystic sigils and inscriptions upon them, which play such an important part in medieval magic. The magician uses such weapons to draw the magic circle, and to command spirits. (Though the witches of ancient Thessaly also used short swords as magical weapons. *See* ATHAME.)

It was because of their connection with pagan magic that the old Ogham and Runic alphabets were regarded with disfavour by the Christian Church. With the spread of Christianity, these old alphabets fell into disuse and were replaced by the Latin alphabet, upon which our present-day alphabet is based.

The use of Ogham, however, was continued by the Bards of Wales, in order to write down the traditional knowledge they claimed to have received from the Druids. They also evolved their own Bardic Alphabet, for the same purpose.

The Middle Ages saw the invention of a number of secret alphabets, which were used by magicians and witches exclusively for magical purposes. These were mostly based upon the twenty-two-letter Hebrew alphabet; though there is one, the so-called Theban Alphabet of Honorius, which is based upon the Latin alphabet (i.e. that one in general use). Consequently, this is a favourite magical alphabet of the witches, whose magic generally is not Qabalistic; and the Theban alphabet is often used by them today. It takes its name from a legendary great magician of the past, Honorius the Theban.

To write something down in a magical alphabet, serves two purposes. Firstly, it conceals the secret of what has been written, and hides it from the uninitiated. Secondly, it compels the magician or the witch to concentrate more upon what he or she is writing, because they have to use unfamiliar characters to express it. Hence, more power of concentrated thought goes into an inscription so written, and makes it more magically potent.

The magical alphabets reproduced as an illustration in this book are those given in *The Magus,* by Francis Barrett (Lackington and Allen, London, 1801, and University Books, New Hyde Park, New York, 1967). He in turn copied them from older books of magic.

AMULETS

An amulet is a magical object the purpose of which is to avert danger
and evil influence from its possessor. It is a protection device, as
distinct from a talisman. The latter is intended to attract some benefit to its possessor, whereas the amulet acts as an occult shield to
repel.

Pliny tells us that *amuletum* was the country folk's name for the
cyclamen, which people planted near their homes in the belief that
its magical influence prevented any poisonous drug from having
power to harm. Amber was anciently called *amuletum* also, because
it was believed to be an averter of evil influence and infection.

The word amulet is probably derived from the Latin *amolior*,
meaning "I repel, or drive away".

All kinds of things have been, and still are, used as amulets, all
over the world. That which they are most called on to drive away
is evil influence of an occult nature, bad luck generally, or the much-
dreaded Evil Eye. (*See* EVIL EYE.)

Brightly-polished horse-brasses are amulets for this purpose.
So are the bright blue beads popular in the Near East. In fact the
colour of pure, bright blue is much esteemed in the East as an
averter of evil, perhaps from its connection with heaven.

The charm bracelet, so popular today, was known in Ancient
Greece. A beautiful example of such a bracelet, delicately fashioned
in solid gold, and over 2,000 years old, was shown in Brighton
Museum in 1960 as part of the collection of the late Mr Moyshe
Oved. It was of exactly the same type as those worn today, consisting
of a number of 'charms' hung from a gold chain which fastened
round the wrist.

The word 'charm' is usually applied to these little amulets of silver
or gold; but this word is actually derived from the Latin *carmen,*
a song, and originally meant the incantation which was chanted over
an amulet or talisman, to consecrate it and endow it with magical
power. The word became transferred to the object itself, which had
been 'charmed'.

The idea that an amulet needs to be consecrated in order to be
really effective, is behind the belief that a 'lucky charm' which someone gives you is more potent than one which you buy for yourself.
The thought of goodwill behind the gift has in a sense consecrated it.

Many of the ancient magical symbols are regarded as being both
amulets and talismans, able to attract good fortune as well as repell-

ing bad luck. Such, for instance, are the swastika, the Ankh Cross, the five-pointed star or pentagram, and the six-pointed star or Solomon's Seal. These symbols are so old that their actual origin is hidden in prehistory, and the changing fortunes of nations have carried them all over the world.

The usual practice of witches, when giving someone an amulet, is to choose some small object which is strange or unusual, which makes a strong impression on the mind of the recipient. They will then charm the object with some ceremony or formula of words, and give it to the person, usually telling them to keep it secret and not show it to anyone else. This involves practical psychology. People can often think themselves into being lucky or unlucky. If they have accepted the idea that nothing they do will ever prosper, that they are doomed to misfortune, then they are in effect beaten before they start in whatever they undertake. Life being what it is, everyone at some time or other encounters adverse conditions, and becomes a prey to depression and negative thinking. Acquiring an amulet can change the direction of their thought, restore their self-confidence, and so really and effectively change their luck.

ANTIQUITY OF WITCHCRAFT

Witchcraft is as old as the human race. It dates from the days when, by the flickering light of a clay lamp, a Stone Age artist worked in the silent depths of a cave sanctuary, drawing upon the walls the great beasts he hunted for his food.

Sometimes he depicted the beasts with arrows and spears in them, in order to gain power over them by sympathetic magic. Sometimes he showed them in sexual union; because unless they mated freely and had abundant young the herds would diminish and he would be hungry.

Fertility of animals and humans was all he knew; farming had not yet been evolved. The mysterious principle of life worked in Nature, and carried on the world; a world of forests and plains, of chasing great beasts more powerful than himself, of the safety of the dark cave and the warmth of the blazing fire; a world where fire, water, the season-changing earth and the wide air, full of stars at night, were indeed the elements of life.

For him the moon waxed and waned, filling the night with ghosts and shadows, and manifestly ruling women in the cycle of their creative life, bringing each month either the magic moon-blood or a waxing of their womb, until a new baby appeared.

Woman was the vessel of fertility, the vessel of life. The first known artistic works of humanity are little figurines representing a nude and pregnant woman. Some of them are carved from mammoth ivory, others from stone. They are beautiful, dignified, remote. Beside them the Pyramids are things of yesterday. They are not portraits. They represent rather the abstract principle of fertility, of life itself; a goddess of fertility, man's most primeval object of worship.

Because woman contained life, she also contained magic. From Algeria comes a very interesting Paleolithic drawing on stone. One might even call it the earliest known picture of a witch. It depicts a woman standing with upraised arms, in an attitude of invocation. From her genital region a line runs across to the genitals of a man; he is shown half-crouched, and in the act of releasing an arrow from a bow. Around him are animals, and the arrow is being aimed at a large bird which looks like an ostrich.

This is obviously a scene of hunting magic; the woman at home in her cave or hut, practising witchcraft to enable her man to kill game for their food. The drawing, though primitive, is done with a true artist's hand. The tension in the man's figure, the cautious hunter closing in for the kill, and the woman's earnest invocation, are well conveyed. She is depicted rather larger than the man, to give her importance, and seems to be wearing some magical jewellery, a girdle and some dangling amulets on either arm. Upraised arms as an attitude of prayer and invocation are frequently seen in very ancient art.

Another remarkable picture that has come down to us from those twilight centuries of Stone Age time, is the famous 'Sorcerer' from the Caverne des Trois Frères, in Ariège, France. This depicts a dancing figure, half-man, half-beast, with the spreading horns of a stag. Some authorities regard this as a masked man, others as a Horned God. Margaret Murray describes this picture as "The earliest known representation of a deity"; but I believe the fertility goddess figurines, referred to above, are now thought to be older.

The naked goddess of life and fertility, and the Horned God, are still the deities worshipped and invoked by witch covens today. Of course, this does not prove a direct inheritance from Stone Age times, except that which we all bear in the deepest levels of our minds. Nevertheless, witchcraft is certainly not the invention of superstitious churchmen in the Middle Ages, as some writers would have us think. (*See* CAVE-ART, RELIGIOUS AND MAGICAL.)

Witches very like those of the Middle Ages were known to the Ancient Greeks and Romans. Lucius Apuleius wrote about them. (*See* APULEIUS, LUCIUS.) So did Virgil, Pliny, Theocritus, Petronius Arbiter, Horace, Lucan and Tibullus. Medea and Circe were regarded as witches. Ovid describes Medea as using wax images to cause harm to the people they represented, and Diodorus calls her Hecate's own daughter. (*See* HECATE.)

Hecate was the Ancient Greek goddess of witchcraft. (How could the Ancient Greeks have had a goddess of something which did not exist until the Middle Ages invented it?)

However, by the time of the classical writers, witchcraft had come to be feared as something rather uncanny, and not respectable to meddle with. It belonged to an older stratum of society, before the polished urban civilisation of Rome; even though the latter, in popular orgiastic rites such as the Floralia and the Lupercalia, retained distinct traces of more primitive times.

Witchcraft belonged to the old half-forgotten days of the primeval matriarchy, when woman who tended the hearth-fire and stirred the cooking-pot was the first 'wise one', the seeker of herbs and binder of wounds, the seer of pictures in the fire, the hearer of voices in the wind, the interpreter of dreams and the caster of painted stones for divination, the worker of magic for hunting, and of the greatest magic of all, the magic of life.

Witches were the descendants of the Wild Women who had sacrificed the Divine King, when his term of office was fulfilled, so that his blood might fertilise the land. Their magic was both dark and bright, like the Moon Goddess they served. But the time came when the masculine idea and the male gods began to rise and challenge the supremacy of the Goddess Mother of Nature.

Kings began to insist on ruling in their own right, instead of by favour of the goddess; nor would they accept a sacrificial death. Descent began to be traced through the father, instead of through the mother. Men began to arm themselves with stronger weapons, and war and conquest were glorified. Laws and customs that tended to repress the dangerous powers of the feminine side of things came into existence. Men took over the chief places of the priesthood, and organised religions that exalted the male side of deity.

The older, deeper things of religion found their way into the Mystery Cults. These endured because they appealed to something within the human soul that felt a kinship with magic and mystery; for the same reason that witchcraft and the fascination of the occult endure today.

With the coming of Christianity according to St. Paul, the take-over was complete. Women were told to keep silent in church, that they should be ashamed to be female, that sex was unclean. The pagan Mysteries were forbidden in the fourth century A.D., and their priests and priestesses denounced as sorcerers. From then onwards, the underground organisation of witchcraft began to take shape. So too did the various abominations witches were accused of.

Black witchcraft had always existed. Lucan's Erichtho, and Horace's Canidia and Sagana, are terrifying hags who take part in horrible rites involving blood sacrifice and desecrated graves. But now came the complete refusal to recognise any other side of the coin. All witchcraft was declared to be black, because the old gods were devils; so their servants must be devil-worshippers. (One finds the same outlook among some writers today.)

The common people, however, tended to cling obstinately to the old ways; and there was a long transition period in Europe before the Christian Church finally gained the upper hand, which it did more by force than by popular vote.

The first English writer to recognise that the witches' Sabbats were simply the continuation of the old popular Nature worship, more or less clandestinely, into Christian times, was the distinguished antiquarian, Thomas Wright. In 1865 a new edition, privately printed, was published of Richard Payne Knight's *Discourse on the Worship of Priapus,* to which was now added another essay, "On the Worship of the Generative Powers during the Middle Ages of Western Europe".

Owing to Victorian prudery, the book had to be privately printed; and Wright, remembering the storm of denunciation which had broken on the head of Payne Knight when his first book appeared in 1786, prudently refrained from adding his name to the work. The book was for many years classed as something to be sold under the counter, and only recently has it begun to receive the recognition it deserves, as an original piece of research. Meanwhile, all the old fables of hell-fire and devil-worship continued to be told about witchcraft. People did not mind hearing about Satan; but sex was *really* something terrible!

Briefly, the thesis contained in these two essays is that the worship of the powers and means of fertility by the ancient peoples of the world was in reality neither obscene nor depraved. It was the worship of the fundamental power of Life itself, animating the universe, and bringing forth all the things of Nature in their wonderful beauty and diversity. When the early Christian Church came under the influence of fiercely sex-hating puritans and ascetics, this old worship and its rituals, dear to the common people, were driven underground, and gave rise to the cult of witchcraft as we know of it today.

Historically and psychologically, this theory makes sense. We have to remember that people died because they would not renounce the 'heresy' of witchcraft. When people die for a faith, that faith exists. We know that in the full hysteria of witch-hunting that gripped men's minds in the Dark Ages, many people perished who were not witches at all; but this was not always so.

Nor did people risk persecution and even death to attend the Sabbats, if the Sabbats were the impossible farrago of horrors that official propaganda represented them to be. People went to the Sabbats for a perfectly understandable reason; they enjoyed them. They carried on the witch cult for a perfectly understandable reason; it was a different religion from orthodox Christianity, with a very different outlook, and they preferred it.

Thomas Wright regarded the witches' Sabbat as being mainly derived from the Roman traditions of the Priapeia and the Liberalia, festivals of orgiastic Nature worship. Today, however, we have a wider knowledge of ancient religions; and we know that in fact the ideas behind the worship of the Life principle are fundamental to them all, in both East and West.

The Chinese formulated their philosophy of the interplay of Yang and Yin, the masculine and feminine principles of Nature. The original Shiva of the Hindus was an ithyphallic horned god, whose representations, found in the prehistoric city of Mohenjo-daro, bear a curious resemblance to the Celtic horned god, Cernunnos. In some of them, he even has something which looks like a candle or torch between his horns, the very attribute of the Devil of the Sabbat.

Margaret Murray, in her famous book *The Witch Cult in Western Europe* (Oxford Paperbacks, 1962), draws an important distinction between Operative Witchcraft and Ritual Witchcraft. Under Operative Witchcraft she classes charms and spells of all kinds; but Ritual Witchcraft is witchcraft as a system of religious belief and ceremony.

The very fact that witchcraft needs to be so divided is another pointer to its great antiquity. In the beginning, religion and magic were two aspects of the same thing, the belief in numinous, unseen powers, both inherent in Nature and transcending Nature. Only slowly and lately did the division between religion and magic take place. The original priest was also a magician; and before the priest was a priestess, who was also a witch.

APULEIUS, LUCIUS
Lucius Apuleius is best known to us as the author of *The Golden Ass,* one of the most famous romances in the world, containing as it does the story of Cupid and Psyche. His importance to the study of witchcraft rests on the fact that *The Golden Ass* is a romance of witchcraft, and illustrates the beliefs which were held about witches in the pre-Christian world.

This work of Apuleius proves that witchcraft was not, as some modern writers have claimed, an invention of the Middle Ages. On the contrary, witchcraft was known, feared and respected in Ancient Greece and Rome.

Lucius Apuleius was a priest of Isis, who was born at Madaura, a Roman colony in North Africa, early in the second century A.D. His family was wealthy, and he travelled quite extensively for those times, in search of education and insight into religious mysteries. He was once himself accused of practising black magic. He had married a wealthy widow, older than himself, and the widow's jealous family brought an accusation against him of having bewitched her into matrimony. However, Apuleius successfully defended himself in court by a brilliant and witty speech, which was later published under the title of *A Discourse on Magic* (*Apulei Apologia sive pro se de Magia Liber,* with introduction and commentary by H. E. Butler and A. S. Owen, Clarendon Press, Oxford, 1914).

His book *The Golden Ass* has been translated into English by William Adlington in 1566 (Simpkin Marshall, London, 1930 and AMS Press, New York, 1893), and in our own day by Robert Graves in 1950. It pretends to be an autobiography, telling how Lucius as an adventurous young man found himself in Thessaly, a region in Greece notorious for witchcraft. After hearing from his travelling companions various hair-raising tales about the dark powers of Thessalian witches, he determined to pry into witchcraft himself. His cousin, Byrrhaena, warned him that his host's wife, Pamphile, was a most dangerous witch; but her words of caution only made his curiosity keener.

He resolved to seduce Pamphile's maid, Fotis, and thus gain entry into the secrets of Pamphile's witchcraft. As Fotis was quite willing to be seduced, Lucius' plan at first appeared to prosper. He persuaded the girl to let him secretly watch her mistress anointing herself with a magic unguent, which transformed her into an owl and enabled her to fly through the night in that shape.

However, when Lucius got the girl to steal a pot of the witch's unguent for him, it changed him not into an owl, the bird of wisdom, but into an ass. Fotis told him that the counter-magic which would restore him to human shape was to eat roses; but before he was able to do this he passed through one wild adventure after another, until the goddess Isis took pity on him and helped him to regain his humanity.

The witches in *The Golden Ass* have many of the characteristics attributed to those of the Middle Ages. They can change their shape by means of magic unguents; they steal parts from corpses to use in their spells; they bewitch men by obtaining pieces of their hair; they can cast a glamour over the senses, and charm people asleep; they can pass through a hole in a door by changing themselves into a small animal, or even an insect; and they can transform others into animal shape.

However, Apuleius as a priest of Isis shows both sides of the cult of the moon goddess, the right- and left-hand paths. He recognises Isis as the Queen of Heaven, yet identical in her dark aspect with Hecate and Proserpine, the Queen of the Underworld. The roses which redeem Lucius from the shape of an ass are the symbol of the Mysteries; an idea which in later years was repeated in the occult emblem of the Rosy Cross.

William Adlington, the sixteenth-century translator of Apuleius, recognised that this magical romance had an inner meaning, and that "this booke of Lucius is a figure of man's life", conveyed in the form of a picaresque novel.

ARADIA

Aradia, or the Gospel of the Witches is the title given by Charles Godfrey Leland to the important collection of witch-lore that he published in 1899 (David Nutt, London). He tells us that as far

back as 1886 he learned from his acquaintances among the witches
of Italy that there was a manuscript in existence setting forth the
doctrines of *La Vecchia Religione,* the Old Religion of witchcraft.
He urged his friend, Maddalena, to obtain it for him. (*See* LELAND,
CHARLES GODFREY.)

Eventually, at the beginning of 1897, he received a manuscript
from her; and this formed the basis of his book *Aradia,* which was
published in London by David Nutt. It is one of the most important
pieces of evidence for the survival of the Old Religion into modern
times, and also for the fact that the beliefs of the witches do constitute a religion, however fragmented by the passing centuries.

It is the more convincing in that it is, as it stands, obviously mud-
dled and incomplete. In fact, in my own opinion, the text of *Aradia*
has been deliberately 'pied', because the witches, although they regarded Leland as one of themselves, indeed as a veritable *stregone,*
or powerful wizard, did not really want their secrets published in
plain terms. In order to sort out the text of *Aradia,* one needs to be
a witch oneself, and also to be able to compare Leland's English translation with the Italian original. It so happens that this writer possesses both these qualifications.

Aradia seems, curiously enough, to have been bypassed by most
writers on witchcraft. At the time when Leland published it, most
of its contents would undoubtedly have been considered 'not quite
nice'. Its sexual frankness—which Leland has toned down in his translation—its attacks on the Christian Church, its anarchistic attitude
towards the social order, all contributed to make it a book that was
pushed aside. Moreover, it did not fit in to any recognised category.
People simply did not know what to make of it.

In those days, the study of folklore had not progressed very far.
Such ideas as those advanced today, of the ancient matriarchal system
which preceded the patriarchal society as we know it, of the worship
of the Great Mother Goddess throughout ancient Europe and the
Near East, even of witchcraft as the remains of an ancient religion,
were then something quite novel, and little, if at all, regarded. Sir
James Frazer's famous book, *The Golden Bough* (Macmillan and
Co, London, first published 1890), had started people thinking
about the implications of the Sacred Divine King; but such thought
had not ventured very far into these implications.

Yet the cosmogony of *Aradia,* this fragmentary collection of spells and stories received from illiterate Italian peasant women, is of this ancient matriarchal kind. Leland says of it:

> To all who are interested in this subject of woman's influence and capacity, this Evangel of the Witches will be of value as showing that there have been strange thinkers who regarded creation as a feminine development or parthenogenesis from which the masculine principle was born. Lucifer, or Light, lay hidden in the darkness of Diana, as heat is hidden in ice. But the regenerator or Messiah of this strange doctrine is a woman —ARADIA, though the two, mother and daughter, are confused or reflected in the different tales, even as *Jahveh* is confused with the *Elohim*.

Because of this feature of the *Vangelo delle-Streghe,* or Gospel of the Witches, Leland thought that it might have originated in the writings of "some long forgotten heretic or mystic of the dark ages". Today, however, we know that the ancient matriarchy underlies all the later religions and social structures that have grown above it, as the deep dark earth itself underlies all, whether forest or city.

The actual text of the *Vangelo* was too short and fragmentary to make a book of. So Leland supplemented it with some similar stories, involving witchcraft and the worship of Diana, which he had gathered during his travels in Italy, and which are additional evidence of his central thesis. This is, that witchcraft was still surviving in his day, as a living though clandestine religion; and that it was not, as the Catholic Church asserted, the invocation of Satan, but something much older, namely the cult of the moon goddess Diana and the semi-religious, semi-magical practices associated with her.

This, then, is the doctrine of the *Vangelo delle-Streghe:* "Diana was the first created before all creation: in her were all things; out of herself, the first darkness, she divided herself; into darkness and light she was divided. Lucifer, her brother and son, herself and her other half, was the light". (This is a concept paralleled by some of the religious thought of the East, particularly that of the religion of Shiva and Shatki, from which the Tantric beliefs and practices arise.)

The *Vangelo* goes on to tell how Diana, seeing the beauty of the light, trembled with desire, longing to receive it back again into her darkness. But Lucifer, the light, fled from her, like the mouse which flees before the cat. (This is another echo of very ancient things. One of the titles of the Greek Sun-God was *Apollo Smintheus,* 'Apollo the Mouse'; and sacred white mice were kept in some of his temples.)

So Diana went in search of counsel, "to the fathers of the Begin-

ning, to the mothers, the spirits who were before the first spirit".
Now, who were these mysterious primeval powers, both male and
female? It seems from the foregoing that they were the unmanifest
aspects of Diana herself—what C. G. Jung has called the Ouroboros,
the male-female foundation of Nature.

The counsel Diana received was that "to rise she must fall; to become the chief of goddesses she must become a mortal". So in the
course of the ages, when the world was made, Diana descended to
earth, "as did Lucifer, who had fallen".

Now, as the god of the sun, Lucifer 'falls' in the course of every
year, as the sun declines into winter. Then he becomes the Lord of
the Underworld, as did the Egyptian sun god Osiris. This also has
a more esoteric meaning, when the light 'falls' by becoming enmeshed
in the world of manifestation.

So, continues the *Vangelo*, Diana prevailed upon Lucifer by the
first act of witchcraft. Her brother had a beautiful cat, which slept
upon his bed every night. Diana spoke to the cat, because she could
perceive that it was really a fairy spirit in the form of a cat; and she
persuaded it to change forms with her. So she lay upon her
brother's bed, and in the darkness, while he slept, she resumed her
own form, and made love with him in his sleep. Thus she became
pregnant by her brother, and eventually gave birth to her daughter
Aradia.

When he awoke in the morning, Lucifer was angry to discover how
"light had been conquered by darkness". But Diana sang to him a
song of fascination, a powerful spell of enchantment, and Lucifer
fell silent and yielded to her. "This was the first fascination; she
hummed the song, it was as the buzzing of bees (or a top spinning
round), a spinning-wheel spinning life. She spun the lives of all men;
all things were spun from the wheel of Diana. Lucifer turned the
wheel". (Once again, we are back in the realms of very ancient
myth—the myth of Fate, the spinner, the great goddess who spins
human life. The function of the male is merely to "turn her wheel",
after a love-chase in which the female is the pursuer, and he the
pursued.)

Then follows the story of how Diana, by an act of witchcraft, created the round heaven above, peopled it with stars, and made rain
fall upon the earth. "And having made the heaven and the stars and
the rain, Diana became Queen of the Witches; she was the cat who
ruled the star-mice, the heaven and the rain".

The image of the moon as "the cat who rules the star-mice" is a striking and poetic one. It reminds us of Diana's transformation into a cat in order to seduce Lucifer, and of the way in which cats have long been considered sacred and magical animals, and the companions of witches. As the moon, Diana is the natural ruler of water and rain.

The *Vangelo* tells of Diana's daughter, Aradia, born by her to her brother Lucifer. Diana took pity upon the sufferings of the poor, whom she saw oppressed by their rich feudal masters. She observed how they suffered from hunger and constant toil, while the wealthy, supported by the Christian Church, lived well and safely in their castles.

She saw, too, how many of the oppressed were driven by their wrongs to become outlaws, and to take to crime because they had no other resource. She saw the Jews and the gypsies, whom their sufferings made into criminals. She decided to send upon earth her daughter Aradia, to be the first witch, and give to the poor and powerless some refuge and resource against their oppression by Church and State.

So Diana instructed Aradia in witchcraft and told her to found on earth the secret society of witches. She would show the men and women who followed her how to strike secretly at the "great lords" with the weapon of poison, and "make them die in their palaces", how to conjure up tempests to ruin the crops of those peasants who were rich and mean and would not help their poorer brothers. Moreover, when the priests of the Christian Church threatened her, or tried to convert her, she should tell them, "Your God the Father, Son, and Mary are three devils. The true God the Father is not yours".

Diana instructed her daughter in all that she knew of witchcraft, and Aradia in her turn went on earth and taught it to her followers, the witches. Then Aradia told them that she was going to leave the world again; but that when she was gone they should assemble every month at the full moon, meeting together in some deserted place, or in a forest. There they should adore the spirit of Diana, and acknowledge her as their queen. In return, Diana would teach them all things as yet unknown.

They should feast and drink, sing and dance; and as the sign that they were truly free, all of them, both men and women, should be naked in their rites. "All shall sit down to the supper all naked, men and women, and, the feast over, they shall dance, sing, make music, and then love in the darkness, with all the lights extinguished for it is the Spirit of Diana who extinguishes them; and so they will dance and make music in her praise."

Aradia told the witches that at the supper they should eat cakes made from meal, wine, salt and honey, cut into the shape of a crescent moon, and then baked; and when the cakes were made, an incantation should be said over them, to consecrate them to Diana. (In the *Vangelo*, there are three confused incantations, supposedly given for this purpose, which in my opinion are among the things that have been put in to mislead. The real incantation appears later, if one reads the text carefully: "I do not bake the bread, nor with it salt, nor do I cook the honey with the wine; I bake the body and the blood and soul, the soul of great Diana. . . .")

So it came to pass that Diana recalled her daughter Aradia, after the latter's mission on earth was accomplished; but she gave Aradia the ability to bestow upon the witches who invoked her, certain powers, which the *Vangelo* proceeds to enumerate:

> To grant her or him success in love.
> To bless or curse with power friends or enemies.
> To converse with spirits.
> To find hidden treasures in ancient ruins.
> To conjure the spirits of priests who died leaving treasures.
> To understand the voice of the wind.
> To change water into wine.
> To divine with cards.
> To know the secrets of the hand.
> To cure diseases.
> To make those who are ugly beautiful.
> To tame wild beasts.

Once again, there is a subtlety in the text; the second in this list is really two powers, to bless and to curse. If one counts the powers with this in mind, they come to thirteen, the witches' number. These powers may, moreover, be taken literally or symbolically.

The *Vangelo* continues with incantations to Diana and Aradia (who is really a younger version of Diana herself); spells for various purposes, such as to obtain a familiar spirit—*il folletino rosso,* the Red Goblin who dwells in a round stone; the conjuration of the lemon stuck with pins, to make either a charm for good fortune or a curse of malediction; a spell to enjoy a girl's love in a dream; incantations for good luck, to bring good fortune to one's vineyard, and so on; as well as a number of strangely enchanting stories, not all of them actually from the MS. that Leland received; but, as mentioned above, included by him because they obviously belonged to the same body of myth and legend.

Evidently not all the stories are of the same age. The beginning of the *Vangelo,* which I have described in detail above, seems to be the oldest part. All, however, will repay study. Leland realised the importance of what he had discovered; but he was aware of his advancing age, and the lack of sympathy in his own day for such ideas. He appeals at the end of his book, for any who possess information confirming what is set forth therein, to communicate it or publish it in some form, so that it may not be lost. However, many years were to pass before the Old Religion could come further out of the darkness.

ARTEMIS

This is the Greek version of the classical moon-goddess, whom the Romans called Diana. Like the moon, she changes her form. Sometimes we see her as the 'huntress chaste and fair', the young girl, ever virgin, bearing the silver bow of the new moon. But at Ephesus, which was a leading centre of her worship in ancient times, she appeared as a great mother, many breasted, and surrounded by figures of living creatures.

The Ephesian Artemis wears a necklace of acorns, perhaps to convey her association with forests. Her crown is in the shape of a tower, like that of the great mother goddess Cybele. Altogether, she is very different from the usual conception of the virgin huntress Diana, so beloved of Elizabethan poets. Also, as Artemis Eileithyia, she was the patroness of childbirth, a characteristic which seems strange for an ever-virgin goddess.

In Sparta, an ancient wooden image called Artemis Orthia (Upright Artemis), was worshipped with rites which involved ritual flagellation. The legend of this image stated that it had been found hidden in a thicket of willows, a tree sacred to the moon. One day two young princes entered the thicket, and found the image held upright by the willow branches which had grown around it; the circumstance from which the name of 'Upright Artemis' was derived. The boys were so terrified at the sight of this image that they went mad.

Once a year the Spartan boys contended before the image of Artemis Orthia, as to who could bear the most blows of ritual scourging. This is probably connected with the ancient magical idea that scourging was a means of purification, and the driving out of evil spirits, which were long believed to cause madness. It is not so very long ago in historical time that whipping was a regular means of treating 'lunatics', so called because their affliction was believed to be connected with the influence of the moon.

However, the legends also state that this image was of the dark form of the goddess, which demanded human sacrifice; and which in the terrible form of Taurian Artemis, she had received. At first, a human sacrifice was made each year to Artemis Orthia, until the more humane King Lycurgus abolished the practice, and substituted ritual flagellation. This is an interesting example of the way in which flagellation became a substitute for the more barbaric forms of sacrifice. (*See* FLAGELLATION.)

Taurian Artemis was identified with Hecate, who was the goddess of witchcraft. It is not difficult to see in these different forms of the goddess the ancient triplicity of the moon: the young girl of the waxing moon, the fertile bride and mother of the full moon, and the weird and terrifying old crone of the waning moon.

The derivation of the name Artemis is doubtful; but it may mean 'High Source of Water', as the moon was anciently supposed to be the source and ruler of all waters. She ruled the tides, not only of the sea, but also the mysterious ebb and flow of psychic power, and the monthly phases of women's fertility. Hence the moon goddess, by whatever name she was known, was the mistress of magic, enchantment and sorcery.

Upon the original statue of Artemis at Ephesus were engraved certain mysterious writings or characters. These appeared in three places, upon the feet of the statue, upon the girdle, and upon the crown. Their meaning was unknown, but copies of them were carried by people for good luck. They were regarded as containing very potent magic, and were known as Ephesiae Literae, or Ephesian Letters.

The great Temple of Artemis at Ephesus, once numbered among the Seven Wonders of the ancient world, has long fallen into ruins, and only the site remains. But a version of the mysterious inscription upon the statue of the goddess has been preserved by Hesychius. It reads:

ASKI. KATASKI. HAIX. TETRAX. DAMNAMENEUS. AISION.

This has been interpreted as: "Darkness-Light-Himself-the-Sun-

Truth"; but the interpretation is doubtful. These words were used by magicians in ancient days, to cast out evil spirits.

ASTRAL PLANE, THE

Belief in the astral plane is part of the common heritage of occult philosophy which is shared by witch and ceremonial magician alike. The word 'astral' is derived from the Latin *astrum,* a star. It was used by medieval occultists to designate that super-physical medium by means of which the influence of the heavenly bodies was conveyed to the earth, and affected all things upon it.

In brief, the astral plane is part of the super-physical world, a world composed of finer essence or of energy at a higher rate of vibration, than that of the physical world. It is not higher in the sense of being above in heaven. On the contrary, everything in the visible world of matter is surrounded and permeated by its astral counterpart. Occultists see the universe as a great scale of vibrations, of which our physical plane is only one; the one to which our physical senses respond.

Because the writings of such nineteenth-century Theosophical authors as Madame Blavatsky, and the many books on modern Spiritualism, have tended to familiarise readers with the idea of the astral plane, it is not always realised that this is in fact a very old magical concept. Nevertheless, Francis Barrett in *The Magus,* published in 1801 (one of the classics of ceremonial magic), explains it as one of the fundamental ideas upon which magical practice depends. Eliphas Levi, another great nineteenth-century magus, treats extensively of this concept, which he calls 'the Astral Light'.

One of the chief claims made by occultists about the substance of the astral plane is that it is responsive to thoughts and emotions. Hence the astral body of man, the double, *doppelganger* or 'fetch', is called by the Hindus the *Kama Rupa,* or 'desire body'. It is a remarkable fact that all ancient occult philosophers, even though they lived continents and centuries apart, have had these ideas and beliefs. The Ancient Egyptians, too, believed in the human double, which they called the *Ka.* Old Norse legends tell of the *Scin Laeca,* or 'shining body', the apparition of the human being surrounded by ghostly light. If the beliefs of occultism are a mere chimera, why does the *same* mythical beast gallop through the minds of men, from one race and one time to another?

The astral body is the means by which man functions upon the

astral plane, and which survives the death of the physical form. He
can, however, visit the astral plane, and perceive visions in the astral
light, while still incarnate upon this earth. This clairvoyant travel
is one of the attainments sought by the witch. It is the reality behind
the wild stories of witches flying through the air. The flying witch
is not in her physical, but her astral form.

This was realised by Henry More as long ago as 1647. More was
a Platonist and a student of occult philosophy. In his *Poems* (University of Manchester, 1931 and AMS Press, New York, 1878) published in that year, when witchcraft was still a capital offence in
Britain, occurs the following significant passage:

> And 'tis an art well known to Wizards old
> And wily Hags, who oft for fear and shame
> Of the coarse halter, do themselves withold
> From bodily assisting their night game.
> Wherefore their carcasses do home retain,
> But with their souls at these bad feasts they are,
> And see their friends and call them by their name,
> And dance about the Goat, and sing har, har,
> And kiss the Devil's breech, and taste his deadly cheer.

More, as a Christian, regarded the witches' Sabbat as being diabolical but his occult studies had enabled him to penetrate to the
truth behind the tales of popular fantasy, namely that astral projection
is one of the secrets of witchcraft.

This is also the explanation of the old belief that a witch or wizard
casts no shadow. If one saw them in their astral form, of course the
double, not being of physical matter, would cast no shadow; and
such was the superstitious terror engendered by the Church's ban on
any use of psychic powers, that a person who could project their astral
body was automatically regarded as a witch.

The astral plane and its related phenomena constitute such a vast
subject that whole books could be and have been written about it.
Any brief sketch such as this must necessarily omit many interesting
and important points. Many occultists divide the astral plane into
seven gradations, or sub-planes, from the lowest to the highest; though
it must be remembered that in this connection the terms 'lowest' and
'highest' do not refer to position in space, but to different states of
being.

The higher gradations of the astral plane are regions of beauty

transcending that of earth; they are the 'Summerland' of the Spiritualist. The lowest regions of the astral, on the contrary, are the dwellings of spiritual darkness; but this darkness proceeds from the
debased and vicious souls of their dwellers. The mind creates its own
surroundings; this is even true of the physical world, and still more
so of the astral. Like attracts like; and the soul after death is drawn
to that region which is its natural affinity.

These ideas are by no means the invention of modern Spiritualists
or Theosophists. They are as old as Ancient Greece and Ancient
Egypt, and probably older. Even Neanderthal Man buried his dead
with grave-goods, indicating a belief in a continuing life in the
Beyond.

Beside the discarnate human souls who dwell upon the astral plane,
there are many orders of other spirits which are not human. There
are the souls of animals, some of whom have achieved individuality,
while others belong to a group soul of their species. There is the
vast kingdom of nature-spirits, which contains many ranks, some
lower than humanity and some much higher. The nature spirits were
divided by medieval occultists according to that element of Nature
with which they had affinity. The earth spirits were called gnomes, the
water spirits undines, the air spirits sylphs, and the fire spirits salamanders.

These spirits of the elements should not be confused with the
semi-intelligent entities called artificial elementals. The latter are
formed from the elemental essence of the astral plane, by the power
of human thought and desire acting upon that essence. Hence they
may be beautiful or hideous, protective or menacing. Their life depends upon the power of the thought which calls them forth. Most
people are quite unconscious of the power of their thought, and what
it can do; but the occultist uses this power deliberately, to create
artificial elementals and thought-forms. This power of thought is another of the fundamentals of magic, which have been known all over
the world, throughout the ages. It is known in the East as *Kriyashakti*.

Artificial elementals and thought-forms may be perceived by one
whose power of astral vision is opened, intentionally or otherwise.
They account for many of the fantastic visions seen by people who
rashly experiment with so-called 'psychedelic drugs'.

Beyond the astral plane are still higher and more spiritual levels
of being. To attain these is the goal of the true occultist and magician,
so that he may master the astral light, instead of being mastered by it.

ASTROLOGY

Astrology, the study of the influence of the stars and planets upon
life on this earth, is another of the fundamentals of magic. It is studied by witch and magician alike. In the past, it was as important to
the village witch in her lonely cottage, as it was to the wealthy and
learned man who practised magic behind the locked doors of his
study.

The basic premise of astrology is contained in the famous sentence
from the Emerald Tablet of Hermes Trismegistus: *"Quod est inferius
est sicut quod est superius, et quod est superius est sicut quod est
inferius, ad perpetranda miracula rei unius."* ("That which is below
is like unto that which is above, and that which is above is like unto
that which is below, for the performing of the miracles of the One
Thing.")

In other words, the universe is a unity. Vibrations thrill throughout it, manifesting upon different planes as different effects, material
or non-material. These vibrations basically correspond to the sacred
number, seven; hence they are sometimes called the Seven Rays.

In our solar system the planets and luminaries have been named
after the gods who rule these Seven Rays, who are known to us as
Saturn, Jupiter, Mars, Sol, Venus, Mercury and Luna. The actual
planets and luminaries visible to us in the sky are the physical manifestations of these influences, and the means whereby they are transmitted to the earth.

Beyond Saturn, the farthest planet visible to the naked eye, are
Uranus, Neptune and Pluto. These are regarded generally by astrologers as higher and more spiritual versions of the planetary influences
of Mercury, Venus and Mars, rather like a musical note being repeated an octave higher. Paracelsus, the great occultist of the Middle
Ages, predicted the discovery of other planets, telling his contemporaries that "there were some stars that had not yet cast their rays".

It has been objected to astrology that it is founded upon the ancient ideas of astronomy, which pictured the earth as the centre of
the universe, and the sun and all the planets and stars as revolving
around it. Today, the critics say, these notions are all exploded; so
astrology must perish with them.

However, astrology always has been based upon the *apparent*
motions of the heavens, as seen by us on earth. For us as human
beings, for our practical purposes, the earth under our feet *is* the
centre of the universe; and the sun *does* rise in the east and set in

the west. Astrology, witchcraft and magic are often most misunderstood precisely when they are most down-to-earth and practical.

A horoscope is a chart of the heavens *as they appear to a person on earth at a particular place and a particular time.* The so-called 'horoscopes' which often appear in the popular press are not really horoscopes at all; they are brief, generalised readings from the current positions of the planets as they affect the twelve different signs of the zodiac.

There are really two zodiacs, the zodiac of the constellations which can be seen in the night sky, and the zodiac which is the plane of the ecliptic. The former is called the Sidereal Zodiac, and the latter the Tropical Zodiac. The astrologers of India and the East generally, still use the Sidereal Zodiac; but those of the West mostly use the Tropical Zodiac.

The latter is the apparent path of the sun in a year, as it appears to circle the earth. Like any other circle, this has 360 degrees. These are divided into twelve signs of 30 degrees each, and these twelve signs are named after the shining constellations of the Sidereal Zodiac.

The Tropical Zodiac commences at the spring equinox, when the sun appears to enter the sign of Aries, the Ram, and day and night are equal. But owing to the phenomenon called the precession of the equinoxes, this point no longer coincides with the constellation Aries. It is the constellation Pisces, and slowly moving backwards towards Aquarius. It does in fact pass very slowly backwards through all the constellations, in a cyclic movement which is called the Great Year of Twelve Ages, a span of time lasting over 25,000 earthly years.

These Twelve Ages actually reflect the characteristics of each zodiacal sign, and this can be traced in world history, as Vera W. Reid has shown in her book *Towards Aquarius* (Riders, London, 1944). We are now in the transition period between the Age of Pisces and the Age of Aquarius; hence the world unrest and breakdown of the old forms of society, and of old-established ideas, manners and moral codes, which so alarms many of the older generation. But together with this breaking-down process, a building-up is also going on, of the ideas and ideals characteristic of the Aquarian Age which is coming; an age which, occultists believe, will be a happier and more enlightened one than the Age of Pisces, which is now crumbling to decay.

On 5th February 1962 an unusual astrological event occurred. All seven of the oldest-known planets, Mars, Saturn, Sol, Luna,

Mercury, Venus and Jupiter, in that order, were gathered in the Sign of Aquarius. Astrologers regarded this as of great significance; some said that it might indicate the birth of some great soul, who would further the ideals of the Age of Aquarius, which is the sign of the brotherhood of man. We can only hope that they might be right.

The twelve signs of the zodiac are ruled by the planets and luminaries, called for convenience the seven planets. (The ancients were perfectly well aware that the sun and the moon are not planets; but it was needlessly awkward to keep making this distinction.) This sacred seven extend their rulership over everything upon earth; the day of the week, the colours of the rainbow, minerals, metals, jewels, plants, trees, animals, fishes, birds; everything in Nature has its astrological correspondence and rulership.

The great importance of these rulerships in practical magic can easily be seen. If, for instance, a witch wants to select a herb to use for a magical purpose, she has to use one whose astrological rulership is correct for the work in hand. Love charms, for instance, will call for herbs ruled by Venus. The moon rules psychic things, and a herb of the moon, mugwort, or *Artemisia vulgaris,* is used to make an infusion or tea which many believe is an aid to clairvoyance. (*See* HERBS USED BY WITCHES.) One of the tasks of the would-be magician is learning astrological correspondences, and the signs and symbols relating to them, from such books as Aleister Crowley's 777 (*777 Revised: A Reprint with Much Additional Matter,* The Neptune Press, London, 1956), or *The Magus,* by Francis Barrett (London, 1801). (This latter book was a favourite of 'Cunning' Murrell, the famous wizard of Hadleigh, in Essex.)

All the older herbals, such as the original seventeenth-century Culpeper's *Herbal* (*Culpeper's English Physician and Complete Herbal,* Nicholas Culpeper, first published London, 1652, and Wehmann, 1960), contain the astrological rulerships of the herbs they recommend. Old Nicholas Culpeper himself gives many dissertations about the importance of astrology in treating diseases, saying that physic without astrology is like a lamp without oil. His *Herbal,* together with William Lilly's *Introduction to Astrology* (London, 1647), were part of the stock-in-trade of many of the later village witches.

Lilly gives many examples of horary astrology; that is, answering questions, discovering stolen goods, etc, by means of an astrological figure set up for the time of the question or the event inquired about. This was and still is an important branch of magical practice, though often brought into disrepute by charlatans.

At the present day, a witch known to me, who is the leader of a coven, makes practical use of astrology in selecting suitable members. If anyone wants to join her coven, she asks them for their time, place and date of birth, and casts their horoscope. From this she deduces whether or not they will make good witches, and if they will be able to work in harmony with other members of the coven.

ATHAME
The black-handled knife that is the traditional witches' weapon. It is used for drawing the magic circle and for controlling and banishing spirits.

The use by witches of a magical weapon of this kind is very ancient. A picture upon a Greek vase of circa 200 B.C. shows two naked witches engaged in 'drawing down the moon', that is, invoking the powers of the moon to aid in their magic. One holds a wand and the other a short sword. Evidently the magical knife could have evolved from this sword.

An engraved gem from ancient Rome shows Hecate, the goddess of witchcraft, in triple form. Her three pairs of arms bear the symbols of a burning torch, a scourge, and a magical dagger; once again, this appears to be a prototype of the Athame.

An early edition of the grimoire called the *Clavicle of Solomon,* dated 1572 and now in the British Museum, mentions the magical knife by the name *Arthana.* A woodcut which illustrates Olaus Magnus' *Historia de Gentibus Septentrionalibus (History of the Northern Peoples),* published at Rome in 1555, shows a witch controlling a phantasmagoria of demons which she has conjured up, by brandishing an Athame in one hand and a bunch of magical herbs in the other. One of the fantastic witchcraft pictures of the Dutch artist Teniers depicts a similar scene of a witch controlling spirits by means of her Athame.

The use of a consecrated dagger to control spirits is also known in Tibet. These weapons, known to Westerners as 'devil-daggers', have a triangular blade and a haft in the shape of the dorje, or thunderbolt. It is curious how such a magical belief should be found in places so far apart.

ATHO, A NAME OF THE HORNED GOD

Atho is the name given to a carved head of the horned god of witch-craft, owned by Mr. Raymond Howard of Norfolk. In 1930, when Mr. Howard was a boy, he lived with relations on a farm in Norfolk. Here he met an old lady called Alicia Franch, who lived with the Gypsies or Romanys. She took an interest in the boy, whom she first met when he was playing by a roadside pond on the day of the summer solstice.

Old Alicia apparently took this meeting as a sign, and she taught him some of the traditions of witchcraft that she knew. She told him that when she died she would leave him a legacy; and she kept her word. In due course, Mr. Howard inherited from Alicia Franch a number of magical objects, among which was the head of Atho.

I have met Mr. Howard and seen this carved head myself. It is a very impressive carving, having a crude strength and power which make it a remarkable work of primitive art. It is fashioned from a solid trunk of dark oak, evidently very old. The head is adorned with two bulls' horns, and inset in various places with silver and jewels. It is covered with mystic symbols, representing the beliefs of the followers of Atho.

Mr. Howard allowed the head to be photographed by the press, and shown on television. He now feels this was unwise, as in April 1967 the head was stolen from Mr. Howard's antique shop in Norfolk. Despite police enquiries, the mystery of the theft remains unsolved. The thief evidently came specially for the statue, as other valuables and a cash-box containing money were ignored. We can only hope that this remarkable relic of the witch religion will one day come to light again and be restored to its rightful owner.

It was characteristic of pagan Celtic Britain to carve sacred heads of deities. These were usually of stone, whereas the head of Atho is of oak. Nevertheless, the idea may have survived and been handed down. With widening archaeological discoveries, we know today that the worship of the Celtic horned god Cernunnos was widespread throughout Ancient Britain; many representations of him have been found. The name Cernunnos is really a title, and means 'The Horned One'. He was one of the many versions of the horned god of the witches.

My own painting of the head of Atho is reproduced as an illustration to this book. It is as precise a copy of the details of the original as the limits of my talent will allow.

The horns are ornamented with the signs of the zodiac. On the forehead are the five rings of witchcraft, the five different circles which are cast by witches. The nose is a wine-cup, which holds the Sabbat wine; it is ornamented with a pentagram, the sign of magic. The mouth is shaped like a bird, the messenger of air. The chin is a triangle, with the various magical meanings of the Triad.

Below are the twin serpents, representing positive and negative forces. The other symbols depicted around the head are actually carved upon the original. The sprouting and twining foliage of the background represents the forces of life and fertility, which Atho personifies.

The name Atho is evidently a Sassenach version of the Old Welsh *Arddhu*, 'The Dark One'.

ATLANTIS, TRADITIONS DERIVED FROM

The late Lewis Spence, who was an authority on Ancient Mexico and also on the subject of Atlantis, made an extraordinary discovery, relevant to the history of the witch cult, in a pre-Columbian manuscript. This native Mexican painting, known as the Codex Fejervary-Mayer, shows quite unmistakably, a picture of a naked witch wearing a pointed hat and riding on a broomstick.

Spence stated in his *Encyclopaedia of Occultism* (George Routledge, London, 1920, and University Books, New Hyde Park, New York, 1959), that he had found good evidence for the existence of a witch cult similar to that of Europe, in pre-Columbian Mexico. He remarks that this seems to indicate a very ancient origin for what he calls "the witch-religion".

How could the unknown artist of a picture painted in Mexico before Columbus discovered the Americas, have possibly depicted this very distinctive figure? There are witches in Mexico today; but their existence can be accounted for by the beliefs brought to the New World by the Spanish Conquistadores. Nevertheless, before the European conquest of Mexico, followers of a cult that worshipped a lunar goddess and the god of the Underworld, of death and the world of spirits, used to meet at crossroads, as European witches did.

The pointed cap worn by the pre-Columbian witch in the picture mentioned above, is of course the ancient original of the pointed 'witch's hat' worn by the sorceresses of popular fairy tales. It probably represents the 'Cone of Power' that witches seek to raise by their ritual. It appears also in an even older painting, one in fact dating from the Stone Age, at Cogul in north-eastern Spain.

Robert Graves in *The White Goddess* (Faber, London, 1961 and Farrar, Straus and Giroux, New York, 1966), describes this latter picture as "The most ancient surviving record of European religious practice". It appears to depict a dance of witches, a group of women dancing in a circle round a naked man. The women are wearing pointed caps and the man something that looks very like the ritual garters which are traditionally a mark of rank in the witch cult. (*See* CAVE-ART, RELIGIOUS AND MAGICAL.)

We may then at least speculate, on the evidence, that the witch-cult is of very ancient origin, and that in some remote period of antiquity there was some contact between its devotees in Europe and Central America. The means of that contact may have been the lost continent of Atlantis.

At least one of the surviving branches of the witch-cult in Britain definitely claims to derive its traditions from Atlantis or, as it calls it, 'The Water City'. Orthodox historians may scoff at the whole idea of the sunken continent, and dismiss it as legendary. For many years, the city of Troy was dismissed in the same way, until Heinrich Schliemann dug it up.

AUSTRALIA, WITCHCRAFT IN PRESENT-DAY

When modern Australia came into being, peopled by emigrants from Europe, it was natural that the old beliefs of witchcraft should have travelled with them.

Nevertheless, a considerable sensation was created when a well-known Australian artist, Rosaleen Norton, publicly admitted to being 'The Witch of King's Cross', the Bohemian quarter of Sydney. Lurid and sensational allegations were made against her and her associates, which led to her arrest in 1956; but at her subsequent trial she was acquitted.

In previous and subsequent interviews with the Press, Rosaleen Norton spoke frankly of her life as a witch. She was born in Dunedin, New Zealand. Her father, a captain in the Merchant Navy, was a cousin of the composer, Vaughan Williams. From her earliest years, she felt herself to be somehow different from most other people. Being a witch came to her naturally. At the age of 13 she took a private and personal "Oath of allegiance to the Horned God", in a ceremony which involved the burning of a joss stick, and the use of some wine, a little of her own blood and some green leaves. She had never been taught this ritual; it came to her instinctively.

Miss Norton's own description of herself contains certain small but significant physical peculiarities which in former days would have been regarded as evidence of the Devil's mark. These include two small blue dots on her left knee, which appeared when she was 7 years old; a pair of unusual muscles down her sides, which are not normally found in the human body; a rare formation of the upper ears, known as 'Darwin's Peak'; and the ability to see clearly in semi-darkness, like a cat.

Add to these an extraordinary talent for drawing and painting the fantastic and weird conceptions of her own inner mind, from the beautiful to the horrific, and it is easy to see how she caused consternation among the respectable bourgeoisie of Australia. An exhibition of her pictures was alleged to be 'obscene'; but again she fought the case and was acquitted.

She said in 1955 that her coven in Sydney consisted of seven persons; but that it was only one of half a dozen covens in that city, and she knew personally about thirty people, men and women, who were witches. They met at various places, sometimes outdoors.

Witchcraft was known as 'The Goat Fold'. Her coven invoked the pagan gods, who were sometimes called Pan and Hecate. A splendid mural painting of Pan presided over a little altar in her Sydney flat, with a motto written across the lower part: "I 'Psi' with my little 'I'." ("Psi" is the psychic researchers' term for supernormal faculties.)

Like modern witches in Britain, Rosaleen Norton denied being a Satanist or devil-worshipper. For her, she said, the God Pan was the spirit of this planet Earth, and of all aspects of Nature which pertain to it. His name in Greek means 'All'. His horns and hoofs are emblems of "natural energies and fleet-footed freedom"; his pipes "a symbol of magic and mystery". Only people who projected on to him their own malice and frustration regarded him as the Devil.

Her coven sometimes worked naked, and sometimes wore robes and hoods. They also made use of masks, representing various animals; a practice that was found in some of the old European covens. Each initiate took an oath of allegiance to the deities of the coven in an old ceremonial posture, kneeling with one hand on the crown of the head and the other beneath the sole of one foot. A new name was given to the initiate, together with a talisman to wear, and a cord known as 'The Witches' Garter'.

Incense was used freely in the ceremonies, and sometimes infusions of herbs were prepared and drunk. An invocation of the Four Elements, earth, water, air, and fire, also had a place in the ritual.

Pictures of Pan's altar in Rosaleen Norton's flat showed it decorated with stag's antlers and pine cones, and bearing candles, incense, ritual vessels, and a spray of green leaves in a vase. Miss Norton, slim, dark and attractive, was posed beside it.

Witchcraft was in the Australian news again in 1961, when another coven led by Anton Miles was described and pictured in the press. Miles was stated to be an Englishman, who had come to Australia after travelling in Asia and the Middle East, where he had studied magic and the occult. In 1959, according to Miles, he had been initiated as a witch while on a visit to Britain, in a coven that met in the Watford area, north of London. He returned to Australia, and started his own cult in Sydney.

His coven danced in the nude round a candle-lit altar. Wine and cakes, as symbols of the gifts of Nature, were placed on the altar, and incense was burned. Music was provided by a record player as an accompaniment to the dancing. The object of the rites was to bring the participants into harmony with Nature. The male aspect of Nature was called Pan, and the female Diana.

This coven practised a kind of pagan marriage ceremony, called a 'pairing rite', in which a man and a girl, both nude within the magic circle, would leap hand in hand over a broomstick, which was held by two other members of the coven.

Anton Miles admitted that his rites were newly imported into Australia; but Rosaleen Norton and her associates claimed that their basic rituals had come to Australia in the nineteenth century, with early immigrants from the country districts of England.

AVALON, THE ANCIENT BRITISH PARADISE

Avalon, where the dying King Arthur found rest at the end of his epic story, has been identified with the present-day Glastonbury. Many legends cling to this ancient place, among the green hills of Somerset. Even today it is a land of enchantment.

Rumours of witchcraft meetings at midnight on Glastonbury Tor have been current for many years. This was mentioned in *Focus on the Unknown,* by Alfred Gordon Bennett (Riders, London, 1953). Today, a number of occult societies, quite unconnected with the witch cult, regard the Tor as an ancient sacred place, and occasionally meet there.

Glastonbury is sacred to both pagan and Christian. An old poem called the "Prophecy of Melkin, or Maelgwyn", tells us that Avalon was the great burial-place of pagans, before Joseph of Arimathea came there and founded the first British Church of Celtic Christianity. Glastonbury Tor was the haunt of Gwyn ap Nudd, the King of the Fairies and an ancient Celtic God of the Dead. Gwyn ap Nudd survives to this day as the Wild Huntsman, who rides on dark windy nights over the hills of Wales and the West Country. (The Saxons called him Woden.)

The presence of the pagan powers is the reason for the church which was built on the summit of the Tor, and dedicated to St. Michael. It was an attempt to counteract their lingering and insidious influence. Some years ago, most of this church was destroyed by a landslide, and today only the tower remains, a conspicuous and dramatic landmark on the Glastonbury scene.

Archaeologists are interested in the curiously terraced appearance of the Tor. It has been suggested that this is the remains of a processional way, by which pilgrims climbed the Tor in a spiral or maze-like ascent, as a ritual of spiritual cleansing and purification.

Chalice Well, at the foot of the Tor, is built inside with massive stones, which the late Sir Flinders Petrie believed to be Neolithic, and fitted together in a way that reminded him of the stones of the Pyramids. Its water has for many years been credited with supernormal properties of healing.

Another local tradition declares that there is a secret cave within the Tor, which long ago was a shrine or sanctuary of some kind.

The names of Chalice Well, and nearby Chalice Hill, recall the association of Glastonbury with the mystical stories of the Holy Grail, which is said to be buried somewhere in the locality. However, some of the oldest Grail legends make it clear that the Grail was not always a chalice. This was only one of its forms; and it has a good deal in common with the Sacred Cauldron of Cerridwen, the goddess of Nature, of the moon, and of poetry, who was invoked by the Druids.

The cauldron so frequently associated with witches as one of their ritual objects, is really another version of the miraculous Cauldron of Cerridwen, as Lewis Spence has pointed out in his book *The Mysteries of Britain* (Riders, London, 1928). It may be a surprising and even shocking thought to some, that the Holy Grail and the cauldron of the witches have a common origin in ancient Nature worship; but the evidence is strongly indicative of this. (*See* CAULDRON.)

The name of Avalon means 'The Place of Apples'. Somerset is still the county "where the cider apples grow"; and real old-fashioned Somerset cider is a very potent drink indeed. It may well have been associated in the past with orgiastic rituals in honour of the pagan gods. Apple trees have been growing in Britain since very early times. According to Stuart Piggott's *Ancient Europe,* apples were being cultivated in Britain around 3,000 B.C.

The tree or plant which gives an inebriating, and therefore magical product, has always been regarded as sacred and magical itself. To this day, in the West Country, some people regard strong cider as a witches' brew.

There is another reason for the fruit of the apple tree being regarded as sacred. It has the magical symbol of the pentagram, or five-pointed star, naturally imprinted within it. If one slices an apple across, the shape made by its core is a five-pointed star.

In witchcraft rituals today, the priestess stands with feet together and arms crossed upon her breast, representing the skull and cross-bones, the sign of the God of Death and the Beyond. Then she opens her arms, and stands with arms outstretched and feet apart, representing the pentagram, the sign of the Goddess of Life and Rebirth.

The pagans believed in reincarnation; and so Avalon, the Place of Apples, was the place of death and rebirth. This is borne out by the inscription said to have been placed upon the tomb of King Arthur: *"Hic jacet Arthurus, rex quondam, rexque futurus* ("Here lies Arthur, the once and future King"). (*See* REINCARNATION.)

B

BAPHOMET

This name was given to the statue of a mysterious deity alleged to be worshipped by the Knights Templars. The latter, although a powerful and wealthy order of chivalry, came to be distrusted by Church and State at the beginning of the fourteenth century, and were disbanded. They were accused of heresy, of worshipping the Devil in the guise of Baphomet, and of practising homosexuality. The order was put down with the utmost severity, and its Grand Master, Jacques de Molay, burned at the stake.

It has been suggested that the word Baphomet was really a version of 'Mahomet', and that the Templars, from their connections with the East, had secretly become Mohammedans. This widely-accepted explanation is, however, absurd. Nothing could be more repugnant, nor more strictly forbidden, to anyone who had really embraced Islam, than to make a graven image of either Allah or the Prophet Mohammed.

The accounts given of this mysterious statue, by the accused Templars when they were brought to trial, are confused. Some of their evidence was extracted under torture, by people who were determined to get evidence that the Templars were secret devil-worshippers. Sometimes the image was said to be simply a head but of terrifying aspect, and sometimes merely a bare skull; but another account told of the figure being worshipped by kissing its feet. Sometimes it is described as bearded, and "like a demon"; but it is also described as being like a woman. It was generally agreed, however, that the image, or what it represented, was worshipped, and that it was regarded as the giver of abundance and fertility.

In 1816 a distinguished antiquarian, Baron Joseph Von Hammer-Purgstall, published a book entitled *Mysterium Baphometis Revelatum,* in which he gave his opinion that the Knights Templars really were secret heretics, or "Gnostics" as he called them. He based this opinion upon certain very curious relics of thirteenth-century art, consisting chiefly of statuettes, coffers and cups or goblets. These contained mysterious figures, which are evidently pagan, and correspond to the descriptions of 'Baphomet' secretly worshipped by the Templars. That is, the figures are androgynous, bearded but with female breasts, or otherwise showing the characteristics of both sexes, and often with a skull at the feet, and displaying the magical sigil of the pentagram. Sometimes inscriptions in Arabic accompany the figures; but their sense is deliberately obscure.

These images have certain things in common with the deities of the witches. They are sources of life and fertility, and they are associated with the symbols of the skull and the five-pointed star. Their sexual characteristics are emphasised, as were those of Pan and the goddesses of Nature. Their generally pagan appearance would certainly have caused the medieval Church to regard them as devils.

Thomas Wright, in his *Essays on the Worship of the Generative Powers during the Middle Ages of Western Europe* (in Payne Knight's *Discourse on the Worship of Priapus,* privately printed, London, 1865), gives his opinion that:

> the comparison of facts stated in the confessions of many of the Templars, as preserved in the official reports, with the images and sculptured cups and coffers given by Von Hammer-Purgstall, leads to the conclusion that there is truth in the explanation he gives of the latter, and that the Templars, or at least some of them, had secretly adopted a form of the rites of Gnosticism, which was itself founded upon the phallic worship of the ancients. An English Templar, Stephen de Staplebridge, acknowledged that 'there were two professions in the order of the Temple, the first lawful and good, the second contrary to the faith'. He had been admitted to the first of these when he entered the order, eleven years before the time of his examination, but he was only initiated into the second or inner mysteries about a year afterwards.

The existence of an inner circle within an order or society of some kind, is a frequent means of occult organisation. Many such 'orders within orders' exist at the present day.

In medieval times, the Devil was often regarded as being androgynous. The card called 'The Devil' in the old pack of the *Tarot de Marseilles* represents him thus; and the Old English word *'scrat'* meant both a devil and a hermaphrodite. 'The Old Scrat' is still a dialect term for the Devil.

The distinguished nineteenth-century French occultist, Eliphas

Lévi, declared Baphomet of the Templars to be identical with the god of the witches' Sabbat; it was not the figure of a devil, however, but of the god Pan, or rather a pantheistic symbol of the whole of Nature.

The word Baphomet, when written backwards "Kabbalistically", reveals three abbreviations: TEM, OHP, AB, which stand for *Templi omnium hominum pacis abbas,* "The father of the temple of universal peace among men." This explanation may sound somewhat far-fetched; but Eliphas Lévi was in touch with secret occult fraternities which preserved traditional knowledge, though he often wrote in an obscure and devious style, being anxious not to give too much offence to the Catholic Church.

There is a very curious and interesting carving in the church of Saint-Merri in France, which is traditionally said to be a representation of Baphomet. It is a horned and winged figure, bearded but having female breasts; and it sits cross-legged, rather like the old Gaulish figures of the Celtic Horned God, Cernunnos.

The idea that God, containing all things, was therefore androgynous, is a very ancient and widespread one. It occurs in the collection of magical legends of the witches of Italy, which Charles Godfrey Leland published as *Aradia: The Gospel of the Witches.* (*See* ARADIA.) In this, the legend of Diana states: "Diana was the first created before all creation; in her were all things; out of herself, the first darkness, she divided herself; into darkness and light she was divided. Lucifer, her brother and son, herself and her other half, was the light."

The same idea occurs in the mystical symbolism of the Qabalah. The Sephiroth, or Divine Emanations from the Unmanifest, which are arranged as the Qabalistic Tree of Life, represent the attributes of God; and of these some are male and some female. S. L. Mac-Gregor Mathers, in *The Kabbalah Unveiled* (Routledge & Kegan Paul, London, 1957), has pointed out how the translators of the Bible have "smothered up" and glossed over every reference to the fact that God is both masculine and feminine. This was, of course, done to establish the patriarchal conception of God the Father, with femininity regarded, after the Pauline fashion, as something inferior if not actually evil.

However, in the Ancient East the highest deities were sometimes represented in androgynous form. Such figures were called Brahma Ardhanarisa, or Shiva Ardhanarisa. The Syrian god Baal was sometimes represented as double-sexed; and old accounts tell us that his worshippers called upon him thus: "Hear us, Baal! Whether thou be god or goddess!" Mithras was sometimes referred to as androgynous; and the Greek Dionysus even more frequently so. One of his titles was *Diphues,* meaning 'double-sexed'. The Orphic Hymns sing of Zeus, the supreme god of nature, in the same way; as man and as virgin eternal.

Goddesses, too, were sometimes regarded in the ancient world as double-sexed; in particular, the most supposedly feminine of them all, Venus or Aphrodite. In Cyprus, a strange image of Venus was worshipped, bearded and masculine, but dressed in female attire. At the festivals of this worship, transvestism was practised, women wearing men's clothes and men dressing as women. Similar festivals honoured the goddess Astarte; and it is interesting to note that transvestism was condemned by the Christian Church, which associated it with witchcraft.

There seems no particular reason why transvestism should be regarded as wicked, when one comes to think of it. It is probable that the real cause of the Christian and Old Testament denunciations of the practice, lies in the fact that it was a custom carried out in honour of pagan deities.

The figure of Baphomet, therefore, is connected with worship of great antiquity, the depth and widespread nature of which have been little realised, on account of the veil which has been drawn over these matters. Only in the present day has this veil of *pudeur* begun to be lifted, when people have come to realise that the 'obscenity' of the old Nature worship was mostly in the eye of the beholder.

BASIC BELIEFS OF WITCHES

One of the witches' most important basic beliefs, obviously, is the reality and possibility of magic. (*See* MAGIC.) This involves the idea that the physical world is only part of reality, the part that we are able to apprehend with our five senses. Beyond are vaster realms; and in these the witch seeks to venture. This, again, involves a further belief, namely that human beings have more senses than the usual reckoning of five. By means of these innate psychic capacities, the realms beyond the physical are contacted. These powers, say the witch, are perfectly natural; but latent and inactive in the majority of people. They are powers that have become overlaid and hidden by the artificialities of civilisation; but they can be reawakened.

This is one of the matters that have brought witches so often into conflict with the priests of orthodox religions. The established religion of a country does not find it acceptable for people to have their own contact with the Beyond, independently of orthodox priests and their rules and sacraments. This may well have been the reason why the so-called Witch of Endor had to live in hiding. (*See* BIBLE, REFERENCES TO WITCHCRAFT IN THE.) The Establishment does not like having its authority weakened.

Witches reject the masculine, patriarchal concept of God, in favour of older ideas. They do not see why a rigid monotheism should necessarily be a sign of human advancement, as it is generally taken to be. It seems more reasonable to them to conceive of divinity as being both masculine and feminine; and as evolving moreover a hierarchy of great beings, personified as gods and goddesses, who rule over the different departments of nature, and assist in the evolution of the cosmos.

If witches' concept of God were to be more precisely defined, it could perhaps best be called Life itself—the life-force of the universe. This, it seems to witches, must be basically benign, however apparently destructive and terrible some of its manifestations may be; because if this is not so, then Life is divided against itself, which is absurd. Moreover, it must be supreme wisdom, because of the wonder and beauty manifested in its myriad forms. Its tendency is to evolve forms capable of expressing ever higher degrees of intelligence; so we who are its children should seek to live in harmony with nature, which is the visible expression of cosmic life, and in doing so find true wisdom and happiness.

Witches do not believe that true morality consists of observing a list of thou-shalt-nots. Their morality can be summed up in one sentence, "Do what you will, so long as it harms none." This does not mean, however, that witches are pacifists. They say that to allow wrong to flourish unchecked is *not* 'harming none'. On the contrary, it is harming everybody.

This bears some resemblance to Aleister Crowley's law for the New Aeon: "Do what thou wilt shall be the whole of the law. Love is the law, love under will." People often quote the first part of Crowley's dictum, and claim that he advocated universal licence. They forget the second part of his words. Centuries before, Saint Augustine said something very similar: "Love God, and do what you will."

The idea of reincarnation seems to witches to be not only much older, but more reasonable and right, than the concept of only one short life, to be followed by heaven for the righteous and hell for the wicked; or that the materialist's idea that when you're dead you're finished. They quote the statement of the old occult philosophers—which I believe modern science supports—that nothing in this universe can be destroyed; it can only change its manifestation. Descartes said, "I think, therefore I am." Human individuality and intelligence exist. Through the physical body, they manifest. When the body wears out, or is damaged beyond repair, the person is said to be 'dead'. But it is the body which is dead. You cannot bury or cremate people—only bodies. In so far as a person is an individual intelligence, *can* that individuality be destroyed?

The testimony of all ages and countries says, "No." But at the same time, nothing can stand still. Everything is constantly changing and evolving. To be imprisoned in the personality of John Smith or Jane Brown for all eternity, is no more consonant with cosmic law than being annihilated. Here we may notice the derivation of the word 'personality'. It comes from *persona,* a mask. There is that in us which truly says, "I am." The personality is the mask it wears—a new one for each incarnation. (*See* REINCARNATION.)

Between earthly incarnations, witches believe the soul rests in the Land of Faery, a pagan paradise like the Celtic *Tir-Nan-Og,* the Land of the Young. Many references to this pagan otherworld can be found in British and Celtic legend. It is a very different place from the Christian heaven, involving no harps, haloes nor golden gates, but a country like the old dreams of Arcady. It is conceived of as being, not somewhere 'up above', but in another dimension co-existing with the world we can see with mortal sight. Sometimes, say witches, we visit this other dimension in our dreams, and can bring back fragmentary recollections of it.

Another implicit belief is the power of thought, for good or ill. Truly, thoughts are things, and the realisation of this is one of the fundamentals of magic. We have become accustomed to this idea as it is put forward in the modern world by the exponents of various movements, such as the so-called 'New Thought', practical psychology and so on. But as long ago as the beginning of the fourteenth century, Robert Mannying of Bourne wrote of the power of thought in his tale "The Wicche, the Bagge and the Bisshop", an episode in his long poem *Handlyng Synne.*

This story tells of a naughty witch who made a magic bag of leather, that went about of its own accord and stole the milk from people's cows. Eventually she was arrested and brought before the bishop, together with the magic bag. The bishop ordered her to give him a demonstration of her witchcraft, and she obliged by making the bag rise up and lie down again.

The bishop thereupon tried the charm for himself, doing and saying just as the witch had done; but the bag never moved. He was amazed, and asked the witch why the magic would not work for him. She replied, "Nay, why should it so? Ye believe not as I do," and explained to him that "My belief hath done the deed every deal." Whereat the bishop, rather set down, "commanded that she should naught believe nor work as she had wrought".

This story is notable in that it ascribes the powers of witchcraft, not to Satan, as it would certainly have done in later centuries, but to the hidden abilities of the human mind; and the bishop, instead of ordering the witch to be burned at the stake, simply tells her to go away and not do this again. In 1303, when this poem was commenced, the great illusion of 'Satanism' had not yet bedevilled men's minds to the exclusion of reason.

Practitioners of magic have always emphasised that, although there are techniques to be acquired and the uses of magical accessories to be learnt, in the last resort it is the mind that holds the power of magic. Paracelsus and Cornelius Agrippa, two famous adepts, said this in the sixteenth century; and at the end of the nineteenth century Miss Mary A. Owen, telling of her investigations in America in *Among the Voodoos* (International Folk Lore Congress, London, 1891); said: "'To be strong in de haid'—that is, of great strength of will—is the most important characteristic of a 'conjurer' or 'voodoo'. Never mind what you mix—blood, bones, feathers, grave-dust, herbs, saliva, or hair—it will be powerful or feeble in proportion to the dauntless spirit infused by you, the priest or priestess, at the time you represent the god or 'Old Master'."

This is the same as the witch belief, although it comes from the other side of the world.

There are two museums in Britain today which are devoted to showing the beliefs and practices of witches. One is at Boscastle in Cornwall, and is run by Mr Cecil H. Williamson. The other is at Castletown, Isle of Man, and is run by Mr and Mrs Campbell Wilson.

BELLARMINE JUGS, THEIR CONNECTION WITH WITCHCRAFT

The so-called Bellarmine jugs, bottles, and drinking-mugs were produced by the potteries of the Rhineland area, from the sixteenth century onwards. They were exported in large numbers to this country, where they became very popular.

These handsome stoneware vessels take their name from the fierce, bearded face embossed upon them, which was supposed to be that of Cardinal Bellarmine. They are also sometimes called greybeard jugs, on account of this typical decoration.

As well as being in general use as a household article, Bellarmine bottles were remarkably popular for the purpose of casting spells and counterspells, especially in London and the eastern counties of England.

They have often been unearthed from the ruins of old English houses dating from the sixteenth and seventeenth centuries, in circumstances which point to their connection with witchcraft. The typical Bellarmine bottle has a large body and a narrow neck, which can be tightly stoppered. When used as a witch-bottle, these vessels have been found with highly unpleasant contents, such as human hair entangled with sharp nails, cuttings of human finger-nails, a piece of cloth in the shape of a heart and pierced with pins; and sometimes human urine and salt. The bottle was well sealed up, and then buried in some secret place, or thrown into a river or ditch.

One of these bottles was recovered from the mud of the Thames in fairly recent years; and the frequent post-war demolition works of the 1950s produced a number of examples of these mysterious vessels, brought to light when the foundations of old houses were revealed. All had typically sinister contents as described above.

Whether the witch-bottle was a spell or a counterspell is not always clear. One theory is that it was a form of self-defence, used by people who believed themselves to be 'overlooked' by the Evil Eye, to get back at the person who was bewitching them. Believing that a magical link existed between the witch and themselves, they tried to put the magic into reverse, and turn it back upon the sender.

They used their own hair, nail-clippings, urine, etc., as the magical link; and a heart, cut probably from red cloth, to represent the witch's heart, which they pierced with pins. Sharp nails were added, to nail the witch; and salt, because witches were supposed to hate it. Then the whole thing was buried in some dark and secret place, in the hopeful belief that it would cause the witch to decline and perish.

However, this spell could be used offensively also, if the practitioner got hold of someone else's hair, nail-clippings, etc., to form the necessary magical link. Nor, in those days when sanitation was decidedly primitive, and the chamber-pot a very necessary and often handsome article of furniture, would it be too difficult to obtain some of the hated person's urine. The pin-pierced hearts which have been recovered from these witch-bottles, seem to be going rather far for self-defence; and the very nastiness of the spell would give satisfaction to a hate-filled mind.

But why the choice of a Bellarmine bottle for this uncanny business? What had Cardinal Bellarmine to do with witchcraft? The answer, most probably, is nothing; because the face on the bottle does not represent the Cardinal at all, but something much older. Some of the earliest examples of this ware have a triple face on them; that is, three faces combined into one symbolic countenance. This bearded, triple face dates back to pre-Christian times in Celtic Europe, and represented an ancient god of Nature.

In Christian times, sculptors tried to work it into Church decorations by calling it a symbol of the Holy Trinity; but in the sixteenth century it was banned by the Council of Trent, who declared it to be pagan. It is in fact one of the ways in which the Celtic Horned God, Cernunnos, is depicted. Probably because of its old associations with paganism, the triple face was one of the attributes often given in medieval art to the Devil. Dante in his *Inferno* portrays the great Devil in Hell, whom he calls 'Dis', in this way; a typical instance of the god of the old religion becoming the devil of the new.

The complicated design of the triple face on the greybeard bottles, etc., became simplified into a single powerful-looking countenance bearded and virile; but it was still the figure of the old pagan god, and hence a suitable vessel for mischief and forbidden arts. But who knew that it was? Who recognised it?

The historical fact that these bottles, with their ancient design, were used for witchcraft, is a pointer to the underground survival of pagan tradition, to a far later date than is generally attributed to it.

BIBLE, REFERENCE TO WITCHCRAFT IN THE

The best-known Biblical text referring to witchcraft is verse 18 in the twenty-second chapter of *Exodus,* which states: "Thou shalt not suffer a witch to live." It is printed on the title-page of *The Discovery of Witches* by Matthew Hopkins, the notorious Witch-Finder General. His book was published in 1647, "For the Benefit of the Whole Kingdome".

This supposed portion of the word of God has been the pitiless death-warrant of thousands. Yet it is nothing but a false translation.

The Authorised Version of the Bible was produced in the time of King James I, a monarch who fancied himself as an authority on witchcraft, while at the same time being much afraid of it. To gratify the King, numerous references to witchcraft were worked in to the translation, which the original does not justify.

This particular text, the most useful of all to the witch-hunters, does not in fact refer to witchcraft at all. The word translated as 'witch' is the Hebrew *chasaph*, which means a poisoner. In the Latin version of the Bible called the Septuagint, this word is given as *veneficus*, which also means a poisoner.

Another well-known supposed reference to witchcraft in the Bible is the story of the so-called 'Witch of Endor' (I Samuel, Chapter 28). However, the actual text refers to her simply as "a woman that hath a familiar spirit". She seems to have been a clairvoyant or medium, and a genuine one; though we are not told precisely how the apparition of the deceased prophet Samuel took place.

Apparently the woman saw him first, and then his message was conveyed to Saul; but it is not clear whether Saul could see him too, or whether he "perceived that it was Samuel" from the woman's description. The whole episode is reminiscent of Spiritualistic practices today.

It is notable that the woman had been driven into hiding, and was in fear of persecution, when Saul consulted her. She may have been a priestess of an older, pagan faith, outlawed by the monotheistic, patriarchal creed of the followers of Yahweh.

Hence the two most famous references to witchcraft in the Bible, though often quoted, do not in fact have quite the meaning usually given to them.

BLACK FAST, THE

This ritual was one of fasting to aid concentration, for some particular purpose. It was alleged to have been used by Mabel Brigge, who was executed for witchcraft at York in 1538.

The fast involved abstaining from meat, milk and all food made with milk. During the period of the fast the witch concentrated all her mental energy and will-power upon some particular object. This was usually to cause misfortune or death to some person; hence the rite was feared and called the Black Fast.

Mabel Brigge protested at her trial that she had only used this method to compel a thief to restore stolen goods, and hence its purpose was a righteous one. However, a witness against her claimed that she had admitted using the Black Fast to bring about a man's death, and that the man had broken his neck before the period of the fast was completed.

She was accused of attempting the lives of King Henry VIII and the Duke of Norfolk by this means; and she was found guilty and executed. This case is interesting, because it shows that witchcraft has always involved practices which are not mere mumbo-jumbo, but are based upon the power of thought, and the occult potentialities of the human mind.

BLACK MASS, THE

Popular belief credits the Black Mass with being the central rite of witchcraft, and the very ultimate in horror and abomination. As a matter of fact, however, the Black Mass is not a witchcraft rite at all.

The whole point of the Black Mass is to pervert and insult the highest Christian sacrament. Therefore, one has to accept the validity of the Mass as the highest Christian sacrament, and to believe in its efficacy, before one can pervert it; and people who believe this are Christians, not witches. They may be bad Christians, but they are certainly not pagans. In fact, they are really playing Christianity, by their very laboured efforts at blasphemy, a sort of back-handed compliment.

The Christian Mass is a ritual involving bread and wine, which the Christian believes to be changed mystically into the Body and Blood of Christ; but the pagan does not believe this. Indeed, to celebrate the Black Mass, one has not only to be a Christian, but a Roman Catholic, who believes in the real Mass. Otherwise, as Gerald Gardner has pointed out, one is going to a great deal of trouble to insult a piece of bread.

The stories about the Black Mass have had a number of different sources; but they are not all fiction. Black Masses of various kinds have taken place, and probably still do. Where they are genuine, they arise mainly from a revolt against Church oppression, and the frustration of those who have to submit to it.

In the Middle Ages the Church ruled public and private life with an iron hand. The feudal system, which the Church supported, was a heavy yoke upon men's necks. Under the surface, resentment smouldered, and sometimes burst forth into flame, only to be stamped out with pitiless severity. The lords ruled in their castles, while the serf had no future but constant toil, in order to make them richer.

In these circumstances, Satan in medieval France acquired a significant title, *Le Grand Serf Revolté*, 'The Great Serf in Revolt'; and the stage was set for probably the only circumstances in which real devil-worship manifests itself. Not because people choose to worship evil; but because everything they can enjoy or hope for in this world, they have been told belongs to the Devil. Freedom is of the Devil; sexual enjoyment is of the Devil; even music and dancing are of the Devil. Very well—then let us invoke the Devil!

But how can we invoke the Devil? What other means than by reversing the forms of Christianity? Remember, the Mass in those days was always said in Latin; the Lord's Prayer was the *Paternoster*. These were the sonorous incantations which invoked the Christian God. Reversed, would they invoke the opposite forces to those of Christendom—the forces of joyous and unbridled lust, of naked freedom, such as the serfs had once known at the old pagan festivals, of which folk-memory still held a far-off echo, a warmth of remembered fire? There may well have been people who thought like this, in those Dark Ages.

Nor was this mental climate confined to those countries ruled by the Roman Catholic Church. John Buchan, in his novel *Witch Wood*, has vividly depicted the oppressive atmosphere of Puritan Scotland, under extreme, narrow-minded Protestantism; and the means which the people found of relieving their frustrations, in either a genuine or an imitation witches' Sabbat.

However, the Black Mass does not belong to genuine witchcraft, because the latter has its own traditions and rituals. The real witch is a pagan, and the old Horned God of the witches is much older than Christianity or the Christian Devil or Satan. Though it will be seen from the foregoing how the Horned God can have come to be united in the popular mind with the Devil; especially as the Church had impressed upon everyone that the old pagan gods were all really devils. The only reason people ever worshipped the Devil was that the image of the Christian God was made so harsh and cruel that the Devil seemed pleasanter.

The witches today have a ceremony of wine and cakes, which is described in Charles Godfrey Leland's *Aradia: the Gospel of the Witches*. (*See* ARADIA.) Wine, or ale or cider when wine could not be had, was (and still is) used to drink the health of the Old Gods. But this is not done in mockery of the Christian Mass or anything else. The wine is consecrated to the Horned God and the Moon Goddess, the deities of the witches. The Sabbats and the Esbats always involve a ritual feast, or at least some eating and drinking; and in the heated imagination of anti-witch writers, this nearly always becomes a Black Mass, even though it bears no resemblance to the Christian sacrament.

Apart from the foregoing influences in the story of the Black Mass, there is the fact that some Christian, or nominally Christian, priests perverted their saying of the Mass to the purposes of baleful magic; and this practice, too, is very ancient. As early as the seventh century A.D. the Council of Toledo denounced the practice of saying the Mass for the Dead in the name of a living person, so that the person named should sicken and die.

There are also in existence magical grimoires which require that the instruments of magic, the wand, the knife etc., should be laid upon an altar and a Mass said over them.

The story of the notorious Abbé Guibourg, who said Mass upon the naked body of the King's mistress, Madame de Montespan, as she lay upon a secret altar, is a well-documented historical fact. The object of this ritual was that Madame de Montespan should retain Louis XIV's fickle favour, and with it her position as queen in all but name. The rite not only invoked the perversion of sacred things, but ritual murder. The blood of a sacrificed baby was mingled in the chalice.

But the whole point of this Black Mass was that it had to be performed, not by a witch, but by an ordained Christian priest, who had the power to consecrate the elements of the Mass; and this still holds good (or should we say bad?) today. The Black Mass is a perversion of a Christian rite. Its connection with witchcraft, historically speaking, is comparatively recent.

Moreover, the highly-sophisticated Black Mass, so beloved of films and books designed to thrill as they horrify, is mainly of literary origin. The Marquis de Sade included descriptions of it in his notorious novels, *Justine* (Paris, 1791) and *Juliette* (Paris, 1797). These descriptions may have been inspired by stories in French high society about the secret activities of Madame de Montespan. De Sade's books had an extensive circulation 'under the counter', in spite of

efforts to suppress them. Forbidden fruit is always attractive, hence
the idea of the Black Mass gained status, especially when suitably
decorated with beautiful, nude women.

In Britain, the famous Hell Fire Club, or the Monks of Medmen-
ham, organised by Sir Francis Dashwood, had been staging something very similar, though much more light-hearted. There were in
fact a number of Hell Fire Clubs in the eighteenth and early nineteenth centuries; but their object was more daring debauchery than
serious black magic. Like some similar organisations today, if their
'invocations of the Devil' had actually produced some manifestation,
no one would have been more terrified—or surprised—than themselves.

Nevertheless, within the late and literary Black Mass, with its
theatrical trappings, there is one genuinely ancient figure—the naked
woman upon the altar. It would be more correct to say, the naked
woman who *is* the altar; because this is her original role, not that
of sacrificial victim (whom the hero of the thriller rescues just in
time from the black magician's knife, as so often seen in films). This
use of a living woman's naked body as the altar where the forces of
Life are worshipped and invoked, goes back to before the beginnings of Christianity with its dogmas about Satan; back to the days
of the ancient worship of the Great Goddess of Nature, in whom all
things were one, under the image of Woman.

BONFIRES

The most likely derivation of the word 'bonfire' is that it was a 'boon-
fire'; that is, a fire for which the materials had been begged as a boon
or gift. We still see this taking place in the weeks before our present-
day bonfire celebrations on 5th November, when children come round
seeking fuel for their bonfires. The latter, in commemoration of the
Gunpowder Plot, have taken the place of the old Halloween bonfires, which from time immemorial had blazed at the end of October
and beginning of November.

A ritual bonfire was a favourite pagan method of celebrating a
festival. The four great feast-days of the Celtic year, which have
become the four Great Sabbats of the witches, were always occasions
of ritual fire in one form or another. The Celtic names for these feasts
were Imbolc, Beltane, Lughnasadh and Samhain. They were held at
the beginning of February, the beginning of May, the beginning of
August, and the beginning of November, respectively. The Midsummer festival was also called Beltane, meaning 'bright fire'.

In later years, these occasions became known as Candlemas (2nd February), May Eve (30th April), Lammas (1st August) and Halloween (31st October). (*See* SABBAT.)

There is something very magical about a bonfire, which somehow seems to invite people to dance round it. The flickering of the flames, the crackling of blazing twigs, the showers of golden sparks, the pungent scent of the wood-smoke, all evoke an atmosphere of cheerfulness and excitement.

Also, the glowing fires in times past served the practical purposes of warmth, light and facilities for cooking and roasting. The latter were necessary and doubtless welcome, when people had come to the Sabbat from considerable distances, bringing provisions with them. In the thinly-populated countryside of olden times, big fires could be built in remote places, that provided enough heat for the traditional naked dances of the Sabbat, which so scandalised the Church.

Old place-names often recall the sites of pagan bonfires. There are quite a number of Tan Hills or Tain Hills in Britain, deriving their name from the old Celtic *teinne,* meaning 'fire'. Sometimes these sites, as in the case of the one near Avebury, have been Christianised as 'St Anne's Hill'; but the fair that was held on this hill was still called Tan Hill Fair, thus preserving the older name.

Scottish place-names yield such examples as Ard-an-teine, 'the light of the fire'; Craig-an-teine, 'the rock of the fire'; Auch-an-teine, 'the field of the fire'; Tillie-bet-teine, 'the knoll of the fire'; and so on.

In Cornwall, we find Lantinney, meaning 'the enclosure of the fire'. The great time for bonfire festivals in Cornwall was Midsummer Eve, the second 'Beltane' in the Celtic year.

Fires were lit from one end of the Duchy of Cornwall to the other, and the country people, old and young, danced merrily round them. Midsummer Eve was called 'Witches' Night'; but the pagan nature of the celebration was disguised by saying that the fires were built to protect against evil.

For a time, the old bonfire celebrations in Cornwall were allowed to fall into disuse. However, in modern days people and societies interested in preserving old Cornish customs and the Cornish language, have revived them, and Midsummer Beltane blazes again from hill to hill. The Cornish word for it is Goluan, which signifies both 'light' and 'rejoicing'.

The custom of the Midsummer bonfires was formerly kept up all over Britain, and recognised as having its origin in pagan fertility rites.

Thus in Langley's version of Polydore Vergil (1546), we find the following: "Oure Midsomer Bonefyres may seme to have comme of the sacrifices of Ceres Goddesse of Corne, that men did solemnise with fyres, trusting thereby to have more plenty and aboundance of corne."

Midsummer bonfires were popular throughout Europe, and indeed still are in many places; though today they are officially held to celebrate St John's Eve, which takes place on 23rd June.

The purpose of many bonfire rituals was distinctly magical, apart from rejoicing. Thus in Hereford and Somerset the Midsummer bonfires were lit to bless the apple trees; and the old country folk feared their crops might fail if they omitted this ceremony. In many places, the smoke from a bonfire kindled in the ancient way, by the friction of two pieces of wood, was a remedy against sickness among cattle, which were driven through the smoke for this purpose. Ritual fire produced in this way was called need-fire, from the old Saxon *niedfyr,* meaning 'forced fire', that is, fire produced by friction.

The ashes of ritual bonfires were lucky and protected against evil and ill-wishing. They were gathered up after the ceremonies, and mixed with the seed when it was sown, or scattered over the fields where the young plants were beginning to appear. The essential meaning of these old bonfire rites derives from fire as a symbol of life. (*See* FIRE MAGIC.)

BOOK OF SHADOWS

This is the name given by modern witches to the book in which they write their rituals, invocations and charms. Witches copy from each others' books that which appeals to them, and things which have been learned from experience; so that in practice no two books are exactly alike.

An old rule of the covens, with regard to written material of this description, is that when anyone died his book was to be burned. (*See* WITCHCRAFT.) The reason for this, from the old days, was to save embarrassment to the person's family. A written book was proof positive to accuse a person of witchcraft; and as the latter was popularly supposed to run in families, the discovery of such a thing might make the position of a witch's surviving relatives very difficult.

Such a writing is called a Book of Shadows, because its contents can only be this world's shadow of the realities of the Other World; the world of magic and the Beyond, the world of gods and spirits.

Even so, I am told, do Freemasons regard their ceremonies; which they preserve "until time and circumstance shall restore the great originals".

BROCKEN, THE

The Brocken, also called the Blocksberg, was the most famous meeting-place of witches in Europe. An old-fashioned poet, Matthison, wrote of it with gruesome awe:

> The horn of Satan grimly sounds;
> On Blocksberg's flanks strange din resounds,
> And spectres crowd its summit high.

One wild story even claimed that here on Walpurgis Night (30th April or May Eve), was held the Grand Coven of all the witch-leaders of Europe.

Because in Germany the activities of the witch-hunters, both Catholic and Protestant, reached a degree of frightfulness which exceeded that of anywhere else in Europe, the name of the Brocken as an alleged site of witches' Sabbats became notorious. In later years Goethe brought the tradition of the Brocken into his famous work *Faust,* describing a fantastic Sabbat upon its haunted heights.

In the eighteenth century German map-makers usually added to any map of the Hartz Mountains, of which the Brocken is the highest peak, a few witches flying on broomsticks towards its summit. One of these old maps, drawn by L. S. Bestehorn and published at Nuremberg in 1751, is particularly interesting. This map also contains a short description of the Brocken, which states that at the summit of the mountain is the famous 'Witches' Ground', where the Sabbats take place, and close to it is an altar, which was formerly consecrated to a pagan god. There was also a spring of water here, and both the spring and the altar were used in the witches' ceremonies.

This explains why the Brocken was so famous as a witches' meeting-ground. It is evidently an old sacred mountain, on the summit of which pre-Christian rites took place. The scenery in the Hartz Mountains is among the wildest and most beautiful in Germany. Hence the Brocken's remoteness added to its aura of mystery and terror.

The famous 'Spectre of the Brocken', though a natural phenomenon, was frightening enough to deter a lonely traveller. When the atmospheric conditions are right, the 'Spectre' will appear, as a huge shadowy giant, looming up before one. Actually, it is caused by the climber's own shadow being projected by the sun's rays upon a bank of mist. On paper, this examination sounds very matter-of-fact and reassuring; but to be confronted, in the silence of some lonely mountain, with this gigantic apparition, can still send a shiver down one's spine.

A curious episode took place on the Brocken in June, 1932, when the late Harry Price staged a reconstruction of an alleged black magic ritual there. Accounts of what, if anything, happened are hazy and contradictory. Apparently a goat was involved, which was supposed to turn into a human being at midnight, but failed to do so. This was certainly one of the oddest phases in the controversial career of this famous psychical researcher.

The Brocken in the Hartz Mountains was not the only witches' meeting-place which was known as the Blocksberg. Other hills and mountains which bore a similar reputation, also acquired the same name. In Pomerania, there were several high places known as the Blocksberg; and the Swedish witches called their meeting-place Blocula.

BROOMSTICK OR BESOM, THE

The broomstick has come to be the traditional companion to the witch, and the enchanted steed for her wild and unholy night-flights through the air. Even Walt Disney paid tribute to its legendary magical character, in his film *Fantasia,* when he drew Mickey Mouse as the Sorcerer's Apprentice, with a bewitched broomstick that did its work only too well.

However, the broomstick was only one of the means witches were supposed to use for the purpose of flight. (*See* BUNE WAND.) Its frequent occurrence in folklore points to the fact that it possessed some special significance.

This significance is in fact a phallic one. In Yorkshire folk-belief, it was unlucky for an unmarried girl to step over a broomstick, because it meant that she would be a mother before she was a wife. In Sussex, the May-Pole, which was itself a phallic symbol, used to be topped with a large birch broom. A 'besom' is a dialect term for a shameless, immoral female.

'To marry over the broomstick', 'jump the besom', was an old-time form of irregular marriage, in which both parties jumped over a broomstick, to signify that they were joined in common-law union.

At gypsy wedding ceremonies, the bride and groom jump backwards and forwards over a broomstick; further evidence of the broom's connection with sex and fertility.

In a curious and interesting old book, *A Dictionary of Slang, Jargon, and Cant,* by Albert Barrère and Charles Godfrey Leland (London, 1899 and 1897, also Gale Detroit, 1889), we are told that a slang term in those days for a 'dildo' or artificial penis was 'a broomhandle'; and the female genitals were known vulgarly as 'the broom'. To 'have a brush' was to have sexual intercourse. This throws considerable light on the real significance of the broomstick in witch rituals, and in old folk-dances, in which it often plays a part.

The original household broom was a bunch of the actual broom plant, *Planta genista,* tied round a stick. "Broom! Green broom!" was an old street cry, used by vendors of broom-bunches for this purpose. The *Planta genista* was the badge of the Plantagenet family, who derived their name from it. They were rumoured to favour the Old Religion. (*See* ROYALTY.)

At one time of the year, the broom plant was unlucky. The old saying goes: "If you sweep the house with blossomed broom in May, you will sweep the head of the house away." This could perhaps have some connection with old sacrificial rites at the commencement of summer.

Sometimes the broomstick was regarded as having power to repel witches; perhaps with the idea of turning their own magic against them. At any rate, a broomstick placed across the threshold of a house was supposed to keep witches out.

A broomstick could also be a luck symbol. When alterations were being made to an old house at Blandford in Dorset in 1930, a broomstick was found walled up in the structure. It was recognised as having been put there for luck, and it was allowed to remain in its hiding-place.

These additional meanings of the broomstick are in accord with its phallic significance. Things which are sex symbols are life symbols, and hence luck bringers and protectors against the Evil Eye.

In Reginald Scot's *Discoverie of Witchcraft* (London, 1584, and, edited by Hugh Ross Williamson, Centaur, Southern Illinois University Press, 1964), he says of the witches' Sabbats: "At these magicall assemblies, the witches never faile to danse; and in their danse they sing these words, Har, har, divell divell, danse here danse here, plaie here plaie here, Sabbath, sabbath. And whiles they sing and danse,

everie one hath a broome in hir hand, and holdeth it up aloft." He
was quoting from the descriptions of witch rites given by a French
demonologist, Jean Bodin. It appears from other old descriptions that
witches also performed a kind of jumping dance, riding on staffs;
and if broomsticks were used for this purpose, too, it is easy to see
how this dance, combined with the witches' experience of wild visions
and dreams of flying while in a stage of magical trance, gave rise to
the popular picture of broomstick-riding witches in flight though
the air.

When broomsticks or besoms began to be made of more durable
materials than the broom plant, the usual combination of woods
for them was birch twigs for the brush, an ashen stake for the handle,
and osier willow for the binding. However, in the Wyre Forest area
of Worcestershire, the traditional woods are oak twigs for the sprays,
which is the makers' term for the broom part; hazel for the staff;
and birch for the binding. All of these trees are full of magical meanings of their own, and feature in the old Druidic tree alphabets of
Ancient Britain. The ash is a sacred and magical tree; the oak is the
king of the woods; the hazel is the tree of wisdom; the willow is a
tree of moon-magic; and the birch is a symbol of purification.

BUNE WAND

This is the old Scottish name given to anything a witch used to fly
on. Contrary to popular belief, the instrument of the witches' legendary flights through the air was by no means always a broomstick.
The earliest accounts often refer to a forked wand, or simply a staff,
which is given to the witch when she is initiated, together with a vessel
of ointment, the witches' unguent; and it is the latter which enables
the witch to fly. (*See* FLYING OINTMENTS.)

One of the earliest writers on witchcraft whose book was printed,
was Ulrich Molitor, a Professor of the University of Constance. His
book, *De Lamiis* (*Of Witches*), was published in 1489, and contains six very quaint and rather attractive woodcuts. One of them is
the earliest known picture from a printed book of witches in flight.
It depicts three witches, wearing fantastic animal masks, and sharing
the same forked staff, on which they are soaring over the countryside.

The incidence of this forked staff as a bune wand is interesting,
when we remember that Diana and Hecate, the classical moon goddesses of witchcraft, were both given the title Trivia, 'of the three
ways', and their statues stood at places where three roads met. The

forked staff could well symbolise this, and hence be used in witches' ritual. It also resembled the horns of the Horned God.

Long-stalked plants were often believed to be bune wands for witches, especially such plants as grew in wild and desolate places. The yellow ragwort is one such; and there is a saying in the Isle of Man, "As arrant a witch as ever rode a ragwort."

Isobel Gowdie, that young Scottish witch whose detailed confession has an air of wild poetry about it, spoke thus of her witch flights: "When we would ride, we take windle-straws, of beanstalks, and put them betwixt our foot, and say thrice:

> Horse and Hattock, horse and go,
> Horse and pellattis, ho! ho!

And immediately we fly away wherever we would."

If the witches were well rubbed with the intoxicating ointment before they performed this ritual, it might well serve the purpose of fixing their minds on the idea that they were flying on a wand or a broomstick; so that their subsequent visions in drug-induced trance would take that form.

BURNING AT THE STAKE AS PUNISHMENT FOR WITCHES

Contrary to popular belief, witches were not burned at the stake in England, after the Reformation. Instead, death sentences were carried out by hanging.

In Scotland, however, the sentence of burning was still inflicted; but if the witches had confessed what they were ordered to confess, they were accorded the mercy of being strangled before being burnt. If they refused to confess, they were burnt alive. This custom was followed upon the Continent also, and accounts for many of the fantastic 'confessions' recorded as having been made by witches. Knowing that they had no hope of escape, they confessed whatever was required—however much their alleged crimes were an affront to anyone's intelligence—in order to obtain a more merciful death. (*See* LAWS AGAINST WITCHCRAFT.)

The record of witch-burning in Europe as a whole is a sickening one. How many people actually perished in the years of witch-hunting can only be guessed at. It is a story which shames Protestant and Catholic alike; because, although the persecution of witches started under the Catholic Church, the Protestants carried it on with equal inhumanity.

The American authority, George Lincoln Burr, from his studies of the history of witchcraft, has given his opinion that a minimum of 100,000 men, women and children were burned for witchcraft in Germany alone. It is true that Germany was a country in which the mania for persecution raged with particular fierceness. Even so, when we read of such things as the Frenchman Nicholas Remy, the Attorney-General of Lorraine, boasting that he had been personally responsible for the burning of 900 persons for witchcraft in ten years, from 1581 to 1591, we may guess and shudder at the unknown total of Europe's victims.

Witch-hunting established itself as a profitable business; because not all witches were poor people by any means, and the property and estate of a convicted witch were confiscated, sometimes by the Church authorities, sometimes by the State, or even by the local feudal overlord, depending upon individual circumstances. All the costs of the trial and execution were charged against the witch's estate; and grisly documents setting out the actual tariffs for burning witches in Scotland and elsewhere still exist.

The last witch-burning in the United Kingdom took place in Scotland in June 1722, when an old woman called Janet Horne was burned at Dornoch on a charge of having lamed her daughter by witchcraft. At least, this is the last Scottish witch-burning of which we have definite historical record. There are rumours of later executions in Scotland; but by this time in history not the quality of mercy but eighteenth-century scepticism and rationalism were putting the curb on the witch-hunters.

In 1736 witchcraft ceased to be a capital charge, in Scotland as well as England; and in 1743 this fact was publicly denounced by certain Scottish Churchmen, as being contrary to the express Law of God!

Before the Reformation in England, witches had been treated as heretics, and could be burned under the statute *De Haeretico Comburendo*, passed in 1401. But before this date, witch-burnings were already being carried out in the British Isles, as in the case of Petronilla de Meath of Dame Alice Kyteler's coven in Ireland in 1323. (*See* KYTELER, DAME ALICE.)

Looking back at the horrifying records of the burning of witches, one is compelled to wonder how the human mind could consent to such cruelty. The answer seems to be that fear played a large part in it; the terror of black magic. The Christian Church did not invent the punishment of death by burning. There is the case of Theoris, a Greek woman of Lemnos, mentioned by Demosthenes, who was publicly tried in Athens and burned for sorcery. It is certain that people came to believe that a witch's influence could only really be destroyed by her body being burnt.

In our own times, the remains of Rasputin, the occultist who was regarded as the evil genius of the Tzarist Court of Russia, were torn from their tomb and burned by the revolutionaries—an act that may have been something more than an expression of hatred alone. Furthermore, on several occasions in the last twenty years, disturbing stories have leaked out of Mexico, of women being killed and their bodies burned, because they were believed to be witches. The body of the revolutionary, Che Guevara, was burned and the ashes scattered, by order of the authorities.

There were occasions in England when women were publicly burned at the stake, after the Reformation. If a woman were found guilty of witchcraft which involved treason, for instance using occult means for an attempt upon the life of the sovereign, this was punishable by burning at the stake. Also, for a woman to kill her husband, by witchcraft or any other means, was regarded as 'petty treason'; and this too was punishable by burning at the stake.

Incredible as it appears, this sentence was actually carried out twice in Sussex as late as the eighteenth century. In 1752 a woman called Anne Whale was publicly burned at the stake at Horsham for poisoning her husband. Again in 1776, another woman, a Mrs Cruttenden, was found guilty of killing her husband by cutting his throat as he lay in bed; and she, too, was publicly burned at Horsham.

There was no mention of witchcraft in either case; but this kind of execution, which as we have seen survived to an astonishingly late date, has often been mistaken for a witch-burning.

It is a psychologically interesting fact that it was not equally punishable for a man to kill his wife. This was murder, but not 'petty treason'; so it carried only a normal death sentence. The horrific punishment of burning at the stake was in this instance meted out solely to women. It seems likely that it was in some deep and unconscious way related to the old practice of burning witches.

C

CANON EPISCOPI

This important document in the history of witchcraft is at least as old as the beginning of the tenth century A.D. and may be older. It was published by Regino (circa A.D. 906) in his *De Ecclesiastica Disciplinis* (quoted in *The Geography of Witchcraft* by Montague Summers, Kegan Paul, London, 1927), as being part of the Canon Law of the Church. Regino ascribed it to the Church Council of Ancyra, which met in A.D. 314; but modern authorities doubt this. At any rate, the *Canon Episcopi*, as it was known, was for centuries the official teaching of the Christian Church about witchcraft.

Its importance lies in the fact that it describes witches as deluded heretics, who worship "Diana, the goddess of the pagans"; *not*, as the Church later alleged, the Devil or Satan. However, says the *Canon Episcopi*, it is the Devil who seduces them into doing this. Furthermore, the witches' meetings, and their supposed flying by night to such meetings, are all mere hallucinations.

This is the exact opposite of what the Church later taught, in such literature as the notorious *Malleus Maleficarum* (translated by Montague Summers, Pushkin Press, London, 1948), the witch-hunters' handbook published in 1486. The previous dogma evidently had not availed to root out the heresy of witchcraft; so the Church had to change it and bring in all the horrific allegations of devil worship and of real Sabbats where all sorts of horrors and abominations took place, in order to light the fires which would effectively, as the witch-hunters thought, burn out witchcraft for ever.

From the first, the Church persecuted witches, not because they were wicked but because they were heretics. The *Canon Episcopi* shows plainly that the witches were accused of being pagans; and it is also evidence of their devotion to Diana, the moon goddess, just like that of the pre-Christian witches described in classical literature, and those of *La Vecchia Religione* whom Charles Godfrey Leland found in modern Italy. (*See* ARADIA.)

The following is an extract from the *Canon Episcopi*. Its description of witches has a certain echo of poetry, as if the good Churchman who wrote it had himself felt the dangerous glamour of the moonlight and the night wind:

> It is also not to be omitted that some wicked women perverted by the devil, seduced by illusions and phantasms of demons, believe and profess themselves, in the hours of night, to ride upon certain beasts with Diana, the goddess of pagans, and an innumerable multitude of women, and in the silence of the dead of night, to traverse great spaces of earth, and to obey her commands as of their mistress, and to be summoned to her service on certain nights. But I wish it were they alone who perished in their faithlessness, and did not draw many with them into the destruction of infidelity. For an innumerable multitude, deceived by this false opinion, believe this to be true and, so believing, wander from the right faith and are involved in the error of pagans when they think that there is anything of divinity or power except the one God. Wherefore the priests throughout their churches should preach with all insistence to the people that they may know this to be in every way false and that such phantasms are imposed on the minds of infidels and not by the divine but by the malignant spirit.

In some later versions of the *Canon Episcopi*, the name of Herodias is given, as well as that of Diana. This again links this very old document (whatever its actual date) with Charles Godfrey Leland's discoveries; because Aradia and Herodias are evidently one and the same. Herodias may be simply a monkish rendering of Aradia, confusing her with the Herodias of the Bible. It may be also, that the name Herodias is in fact the name of an ancient goddess, similar to Lilith, after whom the lady who enchanted King Herod was named.

CATS AS WITCHES' FAMILIARS

The cat, especially the black cat, is a creature of witchcraft, in all popular belief. No artist's conception of a witch's cottage of the olden time could possibly be complete without Baudrons or Grimalkin, sleek and purring by the fire, watching with glowing eyes over all that takes place.

The witch's cat, however, did not have to be black in colour. In *Macbeth* it is a brindled cat which mews significantly, and the name

'Grimalkin' means a grey cat. Indeed, the whole royal feline race of cats have something about them which is magical and uncanny.

They probably inherit this quality from Ancient Egypt, where they were sacred beasts. The Egyptian cat goddess Bast seems to have been a feline form of Isis. Bubastis was her sacred city; and there and at other places in Egypt thousands of carefully mummified and reverently interred bodies of cats have been found. The British Museum possesses a number of beautiful relics of the cat cult of Ancient Egypt; notably the hollow sarcophagi, or statues in the life-like forms of cats, inside which the mummified bodies of deceased pets were placed.

Cats have been known in Britain from early times. The domesticated cat was brought from Ancient Egypt and introduced to Britain by the Romans. A certain Welsh prince, Hywel, passed special laws for the protection of cats. He was evidently a cat lover; but the cats depicted in old churches are usually of sinister aspect. Feline demons carved in stone glare grotesquely at the worshipper, especially in some of our churches which date from the Norman period. This is another instance of the gods of the old religion becoming the devils of the new.

A famous weird carving connected with witchcraft is the one in Lyons Cathedral, which depicts a naked witch holding up a cat by its back legs, as she rides upon a goat, which has formidable horns but a human face. Her only garment, a cloak, streams behind her in the wind; with one hand she clings to the goat's horns, while she grasps the cat in the other.

Witches were often accused of changing themselves into cats for the purpose of molesting people, or for running swift-footed by night upon some uncanny errand. The cat's nocturnal habits, its moon-like eyes and horrid midnight caterwauling, all contributed to its sinister reputation. So also did the electric nature of its fur, from which visible sparks of static electricity can sometimes be stroked in a dark room.

The Devil was sometimes said to appear at the Sabbat in the form of a huge black cat. One wonders whether this was a far-off reminiscence of ancient cat worship. The pagan gods were sometimes believed to appear as animals. Diana took the form of a cat, and Pan of a goat. The deities of the witches were in fact aspects of Pan and Diana, the Horned God and the Moon Goddess; and the cat and the goat are the animals most associated with witchcraft, in popular legend and belief.

To this day, there are people who fear to have a black cat cross their path; though they probably do not realise the origin of this belief, namely that the animal might be a witch in cat form. Others, however, regard the black cat as a symbol of good luck. The old folk rhyme tells us:

> Whenever the cat of the house is black,
> The lasses of lovers will have no lack.

People wear black cat charms and brooches; and in the nineteen-twenties and thirties there was quite a vogue for teapots in the form of black cats, as there is today for table-lamps in the same shape.

There are innumerable stories of cats being able to see things which are invisible to human eyes. Indeed, there is hardly a confirmed cat lover to be found, who cannot tell some anecdote of their pet having psychic or telepathic powers. The writer has heard of two cases (one observed by her own mother) of cats which were capable of astral projection; that is, their forms were seen in one place when it was proved that their sleeping bodies were in another.

It has also been a matter of my own observation, that cats definitely enjoy Spiritualist seances. A Spiritualist friend of mine tried her best to exclude her cat from the room where seances were held, because she believed that the cat 'took the power'. I am not quite sure what she meant by this; but the cat refused to accept this exclusion, and would try every trick he knew (and cats know plenty) to slip into the room and take part in the sitting.

Some other Spiritualist friends, however, accepted their cat's desire to be present at seances; and this particular cat, a huge black neutered tom, would stalk majestically into the seance room and preside over the meeting. Either of these cats, had they lived a few centuries ago, would have been highly valued as witches' familiars. The belief in occult powers associated with the cat is one of the strongest survivals of the old witch lore.

CAULDRON

The cauldron, like the broomstick and the black cat, is one of the features of any scene of witchcraft as pictured in the popular mind. Some of the belief derives from Shakespeare's play *Macbeth,* where the witches' cauldron is introduced on the stage, with its accompanying dances and incantations. Actors regard *Macbeth,* because of the witch-scenes in it, as an unlucky and uncanny play.

However, the connection between the cauldron and witchcraft dates back to a long time before *Macbeth;* back, in fact, to the days of Ancient Greece. Greek legend contains the story of Medea, the witch of Colchis, whom Jason married in the course of his search for the Golden Fleece. Medea was a priestess of Hecate, the goddess of the moon and of witchcraft; and not only did she have a cauldron, she had a coven too. According to Robert Graves in his *Greek Myths* (Penguin Books, London, 1957 and Baltimore, Maryland, 1955), Medea was attended by twelve Phaeacian bond-maidens, who assisted her in her horrible plot to kill King Pelias with the aid of her magic cauldron.

In Ancient Britain and Ireland magical cauldrons featured largely in religious mysteries. Heroes went into strange enchanted realms of the Other World to win a wonderful cauldron as a prize for their adventures. It is the writer's belief that a far-off echo of this survives in folk-memory as the custom of giving ornamental cups, usually of gold or silver, as the reward for sporting contests. The delirious excitement of the Cup Final, when the victorious team raises the great, shining, hard-won Cup to the cheering crowd, has its origin far off in ancient myth.

The transformation of the cauldron into a cup is evidenced by the legends of the Holy Grail, which has its roots in pre-Christian Celtic myth. With the coming of Christianity, the Cauldron of Inspiration and Rebirth, for which Arthur and his followers sought in perilous and uncanny realms of the shades, as sung of in bardic poetry, became the Holy Grail, for which the Knights of the Round Table rode forth upon the quest.

The witches, however, kept the old pagan version, and the cauldron, originally that of the Druidic moon goddess Cerridwen, became their symbol. A cauldron is an all-embracing symbol of Nature, the Great Mother. As a vessel, it represents the feminine principle. Standing upon three legs, it recalls the triple moon goddess. The four elements of Life enter into it, as it needs fire to boil it, water to fill it, the green herbs of earth to cook it, and its fragrant steam arises into air.

The cauldron in fact represented a great step forward in civilisation. Before men were able to make metal cooking pots, which would withstand fire, they had to be content with thick earthenware pots, which were heated by the laborious process of dropping very hot stones into them. The metal cauldron, over which the woman as head of the household presided, gave men better cooked food, more plentiful hot water to cleanse themselves, and herbal medicines which could be decocted by boiling or infused in boiling water. Hence the cauldron became an instrument of magic, and especially of women's magic.

The cauldron also took on a sexual significance, as evidenced in the saucy old ballad about the lady and the wandering tinker, who offers to "clout her cauldron", should she stand in need of his services.

Such have been the transformations of that which is itself the vessel of transformation, because it takes raw uneatable things and transforms them into good food; makes herbs and roots into medicines and potent drugs; and is the emblem of woman as the greatest vessel of transformation, who takes the seed of man and transforms it into a child. In a sense, to the pagans all Nature was a cauldron of regeneration, in which all things, men, beasts, plants, the stars of heaven, the lands and waters themselves, seethed and were transformed.

"We claim the cauldron of the witches as, in the original, the vase or urn of the fiery transmigration, in which all things of the world change." (Hargrave Jennings, *The Rosicrucians, Their Rites and Mysteries,* London, 1870.)

The ancient British goddess Cerridwen, whom the Druids regarded as presiding over the Mysteries, brewed a Cauldron of Inspiration with magical herbs, which had to boil and bubble for a year and a day. At the end of that time, out of it flew the Three Drops of Wisdom, the mystical Awen. This word is pronounced AH-OO-EN, which is reminiscent of the Eastern Aum. The Three Drops are identical with the Three Rays, or Tribann, which is one of the most important symbols of Druidic lore, and means Divine Inspiration. (*See* DRUIDS.)

CAVE ART, RELIGIOUS AND MAGICAL

The depths of a cave were man's first sanctuary. In deep, silent inaccessible places, away from the surroundings of their everyday life, the Stone Age hunters worshipped and practised magic.

We know this today, because the carvings and paintings of those men of the dawn, men separated from us by a veritable gulf of time, have been found in caves which were evidently chosen for their secrecy. The art of the painted caves of France and Spain, from which we have gained a certain insight into the mind of Stone Age man, is a religious and magical art.

Painted caves have been found which were far from the places actually inhabited by primitive man, and which were evidently set apart as shrines. Some of them display such a variety of art that they seem to have been used in this way for several thousand years.

Among the great beasts depicted on their walls some are shown wounded, or being struck by weapons. A figure of a mammoth has a heart indicated by a blob of red ochre, within its outline. By drawing the pictured 'heart', perhaps man could, in his belief, gain power over the mighty beast, and slay it. By carefully representing a bison struck by spears, the artist intended not only a picture, but a magical ritual to ensure that his hunting would be fortunate, and his spears hit their target. This was the beginning of sympathetic magic.

The magic of the caves was concerned with primal things: life and death. In order to live, primitive man had to master the great beasts, to hunt and kill them. But unless there were many young born to the beasts, the herds would fail, and man would go hungry. Unless the women of his tribe were fertile, in those days when life was precarious and its expectation short, man's species too would lose its hold upon the world.

So man made magic for life as well as hunting. For instance, he fashioned figures of animals mating. Two clay figures of bison, a bull and a cow, were found in a deeply hidden cave at Tuc d'Audoubert, near St. Girons in France. Nearby were found interlacing footmarks on the floor of the cave, thought to be the traces of ritual dancing. This cave had been blocked by a landslide untold centuries ago; and the traces of primordial magic had lain hidden here, in the silence and the darkness, until three young men in 1912 took a boat up a subterranean river and explored through caverns of stalactites until they found another way in, and stood beside the prints of naked feet that had been dust since the dawn of time.

Some of the most remarkable and beautiful of early man's works of art are his figures of women. They are not portraits, but impersonal characterisations of female fertility, of woman as the vessel of life, with pregnant womb and swelling breasts. Some of these so-called 'Venus figures' are quite small, beautifully carved from soapstone or mammoth ivory. Other larger figures of the same kind are drawn or sculpted on the walls of caves. A particularly interesting find is that made at Angles-sur-l'Anglin, of a triple representation, three life-size goddesses, at a place significantly named Roc aux Sorciers, 'Witches' Rock'.

A wonderful Palaeolithic carving, which is certainly fit to represent a goddess, is the so-called 'Venus of Laussel'. This was carved in bas-relief on the wall of a rock shelter in the Dordogne, and it also showed traces of red pigment, symbolic of blood to give it life. The figure is that of a naked woman with long hair hanging over her shoulders, holding in one hand a drinking horn. The latter is perhaps a very early version of the Horn of Plenty.

Male figures are sometimes depicted also. The ones given most importance are those of men wearing a ritual disguise, the skin and horns of a bull or a stag. In Britain, a small example of such a figure has been found, in the Pin Hole Cave at Cresswell Crags on the border of Nottinghamshire and Derbyshire. A bone was found, beneath 3 inches of stalagmite deposit, and on it was carved a little figure of a man, ithyphallic, and wearing an animal mask. Incidentally, the Pin Hole Cave got its name because it contained a water hole into which people dropped pins to gain wishes—a long continuity of magical use which seems almost incredible but is nevertheless true.

The most numinous of these male maskers is the famous 'Sorcerer', or Horned God, of the Caverne des Trois Frères, in Ariège. This cave was found by the same three intrepid brothers, the sons of Count Bégouen, who discovered Tuc d'Audoubert, and it is named after them. The figure is that of a dancing man wearing an animal's skin and tail, and a mask crowned with the antlers of a stag. The impression of movement, and of the human limbs beneath the animal skin, is skilfully conveyed.

It is a very fortunate thing that this masterpiece of Stone Age art was not discovered until the beginning of the twentieth century. Had it come to light in the days of the great witch persecutions, the Church would have ordered its destruction, as a figure of the Devil, and sprinkled the place with holy water afterwards.

Undoubtedly, in these motifs of Stone Age art, the Naked Goddess and the Horned God, we have the very deities of the witches. The claim of the witch cult to be the oldest religion in the world is justified.

Not only the deities, but the ritual of the witches is depicted, in the round dance of women portrayed in a cave-painting from Cogul in Spain. Also, it is evident from the foregoing that the processes of imitative or sympathetic magic, 'raising the power and showing

it what to do', are of great antiquity. Yet magic on these lines is still
practised today. The unknown person who nailed two thorn-pierced
human effigies, and a sheep's heart also transfixed with thorns, to the
door of the old castle at Castle Rising, Norfolk, in September 1963,
was attempting the same sort of magic as was used by the shamans
of the Stone Age. This is only one of many such evidences of magic
ritual that have been found in Britain in recent years.

The cave itself conveys to man's mind the idea of the womb of
the great Earth Mother; the place of birth and also, as a sepulchre,
the place of death. It represents the Round of Life: birth, death and
the possibility of rebirth. Thus the dead were ceremonially interred
in a way that would aid the great magic of rebirth. Bones found in
caves where Stone Age man buried his dead have been stained with
red ochre, showing that this was sprinkled abundantly over the dead
to simulate blood, the fluid of life. Shells have often been found buried with the dead, as a female symbol, the emblem of the portal of
birth. Cowrie-shells, which especially resemble this, were possibly
man's oldest talisman; and they are still valued in Africa today. Even
though the graves were many miles from the sea-coast, the body
would still be accompanied by shells.

Other valuable things, such as flint tools, would also be buried
with the dead; the archaeological term for these deposits is 'grave
goods'. Even Neanderthal Man, the mysterious primitive species now
vanished from the earth, buried his dead ceremonially, with grave
goods. It is strange that this creature, with receding forehead and
body matted with hair, should have had more faith in his own im-
mortal soul than many civilised men today. He sent his dead into the
Beyond with tools and weapons and with meat for their journey. The
bones of food animals have been found in Neanderthal graves, as in
those of other types of primitive man.

A very old practice which definitely connects with the magic of
rebirth is that of so-called 'crouched burial'. This means that the
body was buried in a position like that of a child in the womb, lying
on its side with knees drawn up. In dying, man returned to the womb
of the Great Mother, his first idea of divinity; in due course, he
would be born again. The cave was his shelter, his birth-place, his
dwelling, his temple and his sepulchre.

The tradition of sacred caves still survives all over the world;
sometimes in connection with witchcraft. Wookey Hole in the West
Country is famous as the legendary dwelling-place of the 'Witch

of Wookey'; and remains found there, including a primitive gazing-crystal, confirm that it was in times long past inhabited by a woman recluse who practised magic. Deep caves at Eastry, in Kent, have in one part a kind of chapel, ornamented with pairs of stags' antlers, evidently of considerable age; and vague stories claim that this was once the scene of secret rituals.

Present-day witch covens sometimes use caves for their rites. The occult magazine, *New Dimensions,* published in November 1964 a remarkable article called "Witches' Esbat", by a coven leader who used the pen-name of 'Robert Cochrane'. It gave a vivid description of a rite in a West Country cave, when chanting and dancing took place round a fire, until a spiritual presence, that of a master witch of long ago, manifested itself. The identity of the author of this article is known to the writer.

In modern times also, the aborigines of Australia have used caves as the scene of magical and religious art. They paint figures of deities whom they invoke to send rain, and they also depict animals whose numbers they hope to increase. If a painting becomes dimmed with the passage of time, they touch it up with fresh colours, in order to maintain its magical potency. By our observation of how living tribes of primitive people do things like this, we can achieve some further insight into the thoughts and feelings of the artists of the Palaeolithic days.

So far as our present knowledge goes, the time-span covered by Palaeolithic art in Western Europe extends over some 18,000 years, from about 30,000 B.C. to about 12,000 B.C. After that time, man's culture merged into the Middle Stone Age conditions, when the climate became warmer, and he became more a food-gatherer and fisherman, and less dependent upon hunting; and the brilliance of cave art seems to have died away. In the New Stone Age, man discovered agriculture, and evolved new kinds of magic connected with the growth of crops and the fertility of the earth. But the Horned God and the Naked Goddess, the magical images of the primordial cave, continued to appear and reappear in man's religious conceptions, and to be invoked in his magic.

CEREMONIAL MAGIC, ITS DIFFERENCE FROM WITCHCRAFT

It is the custom of some writers upon the occult, notably the late Montague Summers, to lump together indifferently both witchcraft and ceremonial magic, and to label them both as 'devil worship'. This is completely misleading.

The magic of the grimoires, such as the *Key of Solomon,* the *Lemegeton,* the *Sixth and Seventh Books of Moses,* etc., is something entirely different from the old pagan traditions of witchcraft. Ceremonial magic is the magic of learned men, and even of priests. It has a strongly religious tinge, of both Christianity and Judaism, and has mostly been derived from the Hebrew Qabalah and given a Christian veneer.

Its method of working is to control the powers of nature, which are conceived of as being either angelic or demonic, by the powerful Divine Names which form the words of conjuration. Such words, for instance, as Agla, Adonai, Tetragrammaton, Sabaoth, Anaphaxeton, Primeumaton, Sother, Athanatos; words which are a mixture of Hebrew and Greek, and are all names of God.

Its instructions are usually complicated and exacting, and require the magician to purify himself by fasting, taking baths, and dressing in clean and consecrated robes before he enters the magic circle. He uses pentacles and consecrated tools, as does the witch, but all of a more elaborate kind. He prays at length, in the forms of either Judaism or Christianity, for power to perform this magical operation, by compelling the spirits of either heaven or hell to do his bidding.

The witch's method of proceeding is simpler and more direct. In fact, the people who practised witchcraft could be and often were illiterate; while the ceremonial magician had to be more or less a 'learned clerk'.

His arts were officially forbidden by the Church, but not in practice with such severity as those of the witch; because the witch was a pagan heretic, while the ceremonial magician, even when he set out to evoke demons, considered himself to be within the Church's pale.

He would indignantly deny that he was a Satanist or a devil worshipper. Indeed, the alleged cult of Satanism is, in the writer's opinion, something of fairly modern and mainly literary origin. The Black Magic novels of Mr Dennis Wheatley, while first-rate entertainment as imaginative thrillers, bear little relationship to the real traditional practices of either ceremonial magicians or witches.

The witch's origins and practices go back to the dawn of time. She keeps pagan festivals and invokes pagan gods; and while there is much common ground between witchcraft and ceremonial magic, this is the main and essential difference.

CHANCTONBURY RING

In England Chanctonbury Ring is one of the time-honoured meeting-places of the Sussex witches. A well-known landmark and local beauty-spot, it is a green, rounded height, crowned by a fine clump of trees.

Newcomers often believe these trees to be the 'ring' of Chanctonbury. However, they were planted in the eighteenth century; the real 'ring' is a prehistoric bank and ditch, of which traces can still be found.

Many legends cluster round Chanctonbury. The local people call the spot 'Mother Goring'; and at one time there was a custom of coming up to the Ring to see the sun rise on the morning of May Day. The Ring is said to be haunted by the apparition of a man on horseback. Ghostly hoofbeats are heard, and then the rider comes galloping past—and vanishes.

The main local legend, however, is the one that connects Chanctonbury with witchcraft. Go to the Ring at midnight, says the story, and run round it seven times. Then the Devil will appear, and offer you something to eat or drink. "A bowl of soup," says one version; which sounds rather prosaic, unless the contents of the witches' cauldron are intended. But if you accept what the Devil offers, you are his for ever.

It will be seen how this legend, and the custom of seeing the sun rise from the Ring on May morning, both tie up with the Ring's being used for the witches' Sabbats. To see the sun rise on May morning means that you have been out all night on May Eve, the old Walpurgis Night and one of the four Great Sabbats.

In modern days, archaeologists have examined Chanctonbury Ring, and found it to be the site of a Romano-British temple. So the old sacred place of the pagan gods became the meeting-place of the witches.

CIMARUTA

The *cimaruta*, or *cima di ruta*, is an unusual and beautiful amulet, pertaining to Italian witch lore. A fine example of the *cimaruta* is reproduced as an illustration in this book.

The name of this amulet means 'a sprig of rue'. The herb rue (*Ruta graveolens*) is sometimes called Herb of Grace; and rue and vervain are supposed to be the two plants most pleasing to the goddess Diana, the queen of Italian witches.

The *cimaruta* must be made of silver, because that is Diana's metal.

As well as the representation of the sprig of rue, it also contains the five-petalled flower of vervain, the waning moon to banish evil, the key which is the attribute of Hecate, and a fish, which is a phallic symbol.

Fairly common in the nineteenth century, the *cimaruta* is not so well known in modern Italy. At least, the writer has shown this example of it to Italians, and they did not know what it was; though perhaps they did not care to identify it, on account of its association with witchcraft, '*La Vecchia Religione*', or the 'Old Religion'.

The purpose of the *cimaruta* is to show oneself a votary of the witch goddess, by wearing her favourite herbs; and in general, to bring good luck and ward off evil. It also protects against the much-dreaded *malocchio,* or power of the Evil Eye, a matter which is seldom discussed, but still strongly believed in.

CIRCLE, MAGIC

The circle has long been regarded by occult philosophers as being the perfect shape. It is the symbol of infinity and eternity, because it has neither beginning nor ending. The early astronomers were much misled by their idea that the heavenly bodies must move in circles, on account of the circle's meaning as the figure of perfection.

The magic circle is part of the general heritage of magical practice, which is world-wide and of incalculable age. Magic circles have varied from the elaborate spiritual fortress of divine names, which may be used by the ceremonial magician, to the simple round drawn by the witch.

One sometimes sees dramatic pictures made by artists, depicting magical ceremonies, which show an impressively-robed magus raising a spirit within a circle, while he himself stands outside it. This is, however, quite the reverse of the real way in which a magical circle is used.

The circle is drawn to protect the operator from potentially dangerous or hostile forces without, and to concentrate the power which is raised within. The latter, arising from the magic circle, is called the Cone of Power. It is this Cone of Power that the traditional pointed hat of the witch, or the tall pointed cap of the magus, is symbolical of. People who are clairvoyant have claimed to be able to see the Cone of Power arising from the magic circle in the form of silvery-blue light.

The magic circle is carefully orientated to the cardinal points, by having a light, or some symbolic object, placed at the east, west, south and north. For white magic in general, movements within the circle should always be *deasil,* that is, sunwise. The widdershins movement, or *tuathal,* is a movement of averse magic and cursing.

The circle may be drawn upon the ground in various ways; e.g., marked out with chalk. But in order to give it power, it has to be traced round with the Athame, or consecrated ritual knife. Ceremonial magicians sometimes use a sword for this purpose. Very precise details about making a magic circle may be found in Gerald Gardner's occult novel *High Magic's Aid* (Michael Houghton, London, 1949), and in Aleister Crowley's *Magick in Theory and Practice* (privately printed, Paris, 1929, and Castle books, New York).

In order to have a permanent magic circle in a convenient form, some magical practitioners make use of a large square of plain carpet or felt, upon which the circle has been painted. This can be rolled up and hidden when not in use. Occult lodges often adopt this method; though of course the circle should be ceremonially reconsecrated with the magical weapon, as described above, each time it is used.

A small table or pedestal stands in the centre of the circle, to serve as an altar. On it are placed the various requirements of the ritual, such as a lighted candle, a censor of incense, etc.

According to tradition, the most effective size for a magic circle is one having a diameter of 9 feet. Outside this is sometimes drawn another circle, one foot larger all round; and between the two circles, at the four cardinal points, pentagrams are drawn. The lights, etc., which mark the four quarters, are placed within these pentagrams. However, some magicians have used much more elaborate circles than this, of which many illustrations can be found in the old books of magic called grimoires.

The great age of the concept of the magic circle is shown by the fact that it is described in the writings of the ancient Assyrians, which have been translated from their tablets of baked clay. The magicians of Assyria called the magic circle *usurtu.* In ancient India also, the practitioners of magic made use of consecrated circles, which they marked out in red lead or black pebbles.

It will be seen that the figure of the magic circle, oriented to the four cardinal points and with the altar in the middle, is precisely similar to that of the mandala, which Carl Gustav Jung regards as of deep significance to the collective unconscious of mankind. Jung has written extensively of the symbolism of the mandala, as an archetypal figure which conveys the idea of spiritual balance, and right relationship between God, Man and the universe. According to the theory of high magic, it is only when such balance and relationship exist that man can become a true magician.

COTSWOLDS, WITCHCRAFT IN THE

The area of the Cotswold Hills has long been famous as a centre of witchcraft lore. In modern days two events have brought this fact to notice: the so-called 'Witchcraft Murder' on Meon Hill in 1945, and the opening of Mr. Cecil H. Williamson's witchcraft museum at Bourton-on-the-Water at Easter 1956, which aroused considerable controversy in the area at the time. The museum closed about ten years later, Mr. Williamson having opened another at Boscastle in Cornwall.

During the years it remained at Bourton-on-the-Water, this witchcraft museum, arranged in a picturesque fifteenth-century Cotswold stone house, provided a fascinating panorama of objects connected with magic and witchcraft. When I visited it in 1961, it contained, among innumerable other exhibits, an indoor shrine used by a witch for thanksgiving to the Old Gods in recognition of spells successfully accomplished, and a life-size representation of a scene in an old-time witch's cottage, showing how a 'divining familiar' worked.

A wax figure of a witch sat before a big old-fashioned table, on which was a skull draped with a black shawl; also on the table were a black-hilted knife, and four candles in crude, home-made candlesticks of bone. Specimens of different herbs were displayed before the familiar, a small animal (a weasel, I think). It was explained that the animal became possessed by a god or a spirit, and indicated the right herb to use in a particular case.

This was in fact a correct representation of a 'divining familiar'. I have known a cat to be used in the same way, to divine by selecting cards from an outspread pack with its paw.

The exhibit which aroused most controversy, however, was a life-size wax figure of an almost nude witch-priestess lying upon an altar. She was described as a priestess of Tanat, the Phoenician moon goddess, whose worship, it was claimed, was still carried out in Cornwall and the West of England, being celebrated by ritual bonfires on the old pagan festival dates.

In June 1956 someone hanged a cat from a beam outside the

museum. Mr. Williamson interpreted it as a 'death warning', from one who objected to the museum's being opened.

Mr. Williamson's museum would have been controversial anywhere. It was doubly so in the Cotswolds, where fear of witchcraft as a sinister influence is still lively today. The events of the Meon Hill murder have not been forgotten; nor how the famous anthropologist, the late Dr. Margaret Murray, spent a week in the area of the murder, ostensibly as an artist with a sketch-book, but actually carrying out her own investigation. Later, she stated publicly that she believed the murder victim, an old man named Charles Walton of the village of Lower Quinton, had been killed because of the local belief in witchcraft.

Walton was found dead under a tree on Meon Hill, on 14th February, 1945. His body was pinned to the ground by a hayfork, and his throat and chest had been slashed in the form of a cross. Police investigating the murder came up against a wall of silence, and no arrest was ever made. February 14th is Candlemas by the Old Calendar, which is twelve days behind the present dating; and Candlemas is one of the Great Sabbats of the witches.

Recently another investigation into this mysterious killing has been carried out by Donald McCormick, who published his findings in his book *Murder by Witchcraft* (John Long, London, 1968). Mr. McCormick has uncovered new facts about the man who was killed, which have convinced me personally that witchcraft, or rather the fear of witchcraft, was the motive for this murder; Charles Walton was slain because someone feared his powers as a witch.

He was slain bloodily, because to spill a witch's blood destroyed their influence. In 1875 an old woman named Anne Turner had been killed in a similar manner, in another Cotswold village, Long Compton, by a man who believed her to be a witch. He was influenced by an old local saying: "There are enough witches in Long Compton to draw a waggon-load of hay up Long Compton Hill."

The traditional meeting-place of the Cotswold witches is the Rollright Stones, a prehistoric stone circle between Long Compton and Chipping Norton. Outside the circle and across a road is a big standing stone called the King Stone, strangely weathered by the passing centuries; and nearby in a field is a cromlech of big stones called the Whispering Knights.

On 12th May 1949, a witches' Sabbat was held at the Rollright Stones which was observed by two independent witnesses, whose stories got into the local and national press. It was the night of the full moon, and May Eve by the Old Calendar. The latter, as stated above, is twelve days behind the New, or Gregorian Calendar, which was adopted in Britain in 1752; but traces of the old reckoning can still be found in custom and folklore.

The man who witnessed the rites had gone there because he had heard rumours of witch meetings there before, and curiosity attracted him. He was unable to get very close, but he saw a number of people, both men and women, performing a ritual round the King Stone, with chanting and dancing. The leader wore a disguise, which the observer thought was a goat-headed mask. The other eye-witness, a woman, was afraid to remain, and fled from the scene.

Since this time, traces of bonfires have been found at the Rollright Stones on various occasions; but since the newspaper publicity, witches have tended to avoid using the Stones for their meetings. However, the magazine *Life International,* in its issue dated 18th May 1964, carried a detailed article about witchcraft in Britain, which included photographs of a special meeting at the Rollright Stones organised by a London coven under the leadership of Mrs. Ray Bone, whose witch-name is Artemis.

She invoked the Old Gods of the witches, and the coven joined hands to dance round a bonfire lit within the circle of stones. Then the witches jumped over the flames of the fire, which according to their ritual symbolised the life-giving properties of the sun. The rite was held to celebrate May Eve, the traditional beginning of summer.

A remarkable historical novel, based upon fact, and dealing with witchcraft in the Cotswolds in the seventeenth century, is *The Silver Bowl,* by Hugh Ross Williamson, first published in 1948 (Michael Joseph, London). It deals particularly with Chipping Campden, and the strange events known as the Campden Wonder, when three witches, Joan Perry and her two sons, were hanged for the supposed murder of a man who had disappeared, but who later returned alive to the village. It mentions Seven Wells, within a circle of trees on a hill south of Chipping Campden, as the meeting-place of the seventeenth-century coven, and contains many unusual details about witchcraft, which it calls "the Craft of the Wise".

I can add to the evidence of witchcraft in the Cotswolds a story of my own. About fifteen years ago an uncle and aunt of mine came to see me, and talked about a motoring tour they had enjoyed. They had passed through the Cotswolds, and been to see the Rollright

Stones. They were very conventional people, who knew nothing about witchcraft or my interest in it.

My aunt said that they had seen a woman dancing slowly round the King Stone, "waving her hands in strange gestures". Then she had knelt down in front of the stone and seemed to be praying. My uncle had been inclined to jeer, but my aunt had restrained him; because, she said, "You could see she was quite serious, and believed in what she was doing." They hadn't known what to make of it; and I didn't tell them.

At the old Fleece Inn at Bretforton, near Evesham, on the edge of the Cotswolds, the custom is kept up of drawing three white circles on the hearth, "to stop witches from coming down the chimney". This derives from the old idea that the influence of witchcraft could enter a house through the windows, the doors, or the chimney; and protective amulets were hung or placed in these locations to prevent it. The number three has always been sacred and magical, while the circle was anciently regarded as the symbol of perfection and eternity, and whiteness as the colour of purity. Hence the protective magic of this traditional rite.

COVEN

The traditional number of persons to form a witches' coven is thirteen. Ideally, they should consist of six men, six women and a leader.

This does not mean, however, that a witches' cult-group cannot function unless it comprises thirteen persons. Less than this number can form a coven; but the members of a coven should not *exceed* thirteen. When the membership goes above this figure, the coven should divide itself, and form a new coven. Thus the Craft spreads and continues.

There is an old witch law that the meeting-place of a coven should be at least a league (3 miles) from the meeting-place of any other coven, to avoid any clashes of interest. It is also a traditional rule that covens should not know too much about the private business of other covens or their members. Only the leaders should keep in touch with each other. The reason for this was, that in the times of persecution, what people did not know they could not be made to tell.

The practice of using 'eke-names', or nicknames, for members of the coven, arose partly from the same source; though this is also an old and world-wide custom, that people going through a significant religious ceremony take a new name, to signify a permanent change of personality. We can even see a reminder of this in the Christian Church, where people are allowed to change their Christian names at Confirmation, if they wish to do so.

The coven of thirteen is the best-known of the witches' cult groups; but there is also a lesser-known coven of eight. This consists of more experienced initiates than the coven of thirteen. In fact, the latter might be called the fertility coven, invoking and worshipping the powers of life and luck in a general way; whereas the coven of eight is the magical coven, which concentrates on deeper things, and is especially interested in achieving the higher states of consciousness. The people comprising a coven of eight are likely to be generally older, and much more reserved and secretive, than those who belong to a coven of thirteen.

Apart from these two kinds of coven, there are individual witches who are not organised into any coven, and prefer to work on their own. Such witches are generally elderly, and often possess a good deal of experience, and more potent occult powers than those who are members of covens. It will generally be found, however, that they have been trained in a coven in their earlier years; and they usually know the whereabouts of other witches, and will occasionally join forces with them for some special purpose.

In recent years various estimates have been made of the number of witch covens operating in the British Isles. Most of these have been merely fanciful guesses; as not all witches by any means belong to the same rule of witchcraft. Owing to the years of persecution, the craft has become fragmented, and different branches of it follow their own ramifications, 'keeping themselves to themselves'.

The well-meaning activities of the late Gerald Gardner, in publicising witchcraft, aroused strong indignation among many of the old practitioners. In fact, they would agree with the person who said that today there were three kinds of witches—white witches, black witches, and publicity witches! They regard the activities of people who call themselves 'Kings' and 'Queens' of the witches as being just showmanship. Nor do these oldsters view with favour the version of witchcraft practised in the covens Gerald Gardner founded, which they feel to be more 'Gardnerian' than traditional.

To this, the 'Gardnerians' retort that Gerald Gardner's motives for publicising witchcraft were good and sincere, and that thanks to him the old Craft of the Wise has experienced a veritable renaissance in the present day. They claim that their practices are as traditional as anyone else's, and that their beliefs and philosophy have brought happiness to many people, who, were it not for Gerald Gardner, would never have heard of witchcraft as a religion and a way of life.

They agree that publicity was a break with the old custom; but they say that times have changed, and that public discussion of witchcraft has enabled old traditions to be gathered together and preserved, that might otherwise have died out and been lost.

They agree, too, that the renewal of public interest in witchcraft and the occult generally has brought a good deal of highly dubious activity in its train. However, they point out that this is a perennial problem for all serious occultists, and that time eventually sorts out the good from the bad, and the genuine from the bogus.

The number thirteen has long been regarded as having peculiar magical properties, which are reflected in the cult-group of twelve people and a leader. In astrology, which goes back far into the pre-Christian era, we have the sun and the twelve signs of the zodiac. Also, and this is the thing which most probably applies to witchcraft, there are thirteen *lunar* months to the year; an older time measure than the twelve calendar months we now have. Thus there were thirteen full-moon Esbats to each year, as celebrated by the witches.

Throughout history, we find cult groups of thirteen people; that is, twelve and a leader. Romulus, the hero who founded Rome, had twelve companions, called lictors. The ancient priesthood of the Arval Brethren were twelve, who danced round the statue of Dea Dia, representing the thirteenth. The Danish hero Hrolf, was followed by his twelve Berserks. Some versions of the Arthurian legends say that King Arthur's Round Table consisted of the king and twelve of his principal knights. In medieval legend, King Charlemagne had his twelve Paladins. Robin Hood's band in Sherwood Forest, according to some stories, consisted of twelve men and one woman, Maid Marian.

The old Celtic stories tell us of the Thirteen Treasures of Britain, which Merlin the wizard took with him when he vanished from among men. The same concept of the sacred thirteen appears in the legends of the Northmen, who pictured Odin as ruling in Asgard over a company of twelve principal gods and goddesses.

We have a survival of the sanctity and potency of thirteen in our system of trial by jury, which calls for twelve people, presided over by the judge, to return their verdict. There is also the old belief, often encountered in English ghost lore, that twelve clergymen acting together could banish a troublesome spirit, or at any rate, bind it to trouble the living no more. In this case the ghost is the thirteenth.

From its associations with witchcraft, the number thirteen came to be called the 'Devil's Dozen'. Old pictures of witches' meetings often depict twelve people and a thirteenth. There is, for instance, a very charming fifteenth-century French miniature from the Rawlinson MS in the Bodleian Library, which depicts a witches' meeting just outside a village. In the foreground, three women and a man are adoring a goat, with lighted candles in their hands. Behind them, two couples are embracing. Three witches mounted on broomsticks fly merrily overhead, and another witch is just emerging from the chimney of the nearest house. Thus there are twelve witches in the picture, and the Goat God is the thirteenth.

Margaret Murray, in her book *The God of the Witches* (Faber, London, 1952), reproduces a picture of a witches' dance from an old black-letter ballad of "Robin Goodfellow". There are shown eleven witches dancing in the ring, man and woman alternately. Outside the circle of dancers, a twelfth witch plays on some musical instrument, probably a recorder. The thirteenth figure is Robin Goodfellow, dancing in the circle, horned and hoofed, and carrying a lighted candle and a broomstick. He is either the Old God himself or his earthly representative in ritual disguise. There is another version of this picture which shows six men and six women in the circle, plus the figure of Robin Goodfellow and the musician outside the circle. It is curious that these two versions exist and it may have some significance.

One of the earliest witchcraft trials in the British Isles of which full details have survived, is that of Dame Alice Kyteler of Kilkenny in 1324. The names of the accused are recorded, and they total twelve. The thirteenth was one Robin Artisson, the 'Devil' of the coven, who escaped (as eventually did Dame Alice). (*See* KYTELER, DAME ALICE.)

Two more covens of thirteen are described by Joseph Glanvil in his *Sadducismus Triumphatus,* published in 1681. Glanvil was Chaplain to King Charles II, and he deplored the growing scepticism of the times, or 'Sadducism' as he called it, and he wrote his book to confute it. He recounts a number of interesting tales to prove the reality of witchcraft and the supernatural. Among them is the story of the Somerset witches who were tried in 1664. There were two covens of thirteen people each, one at Wincanton and the other at

Brewham. They were governed by a mysterious 'Man in Black', whose identity was never revealed. Again, this is a case in which the actual names of the two covens of thirteen are preserved in legal records.

A Scottish witch, Isobel Gowdie of Auldearne, for some reason gave herself up to the authorities in 1662 and made the longest and most detailed confession which has come down to us from a witch trial in Britain. In the course of this, she stated that the witches were organised in covens, and that there were thirteen people in each coven.

Dr. Rossell Hope Robbins, in his *Encyclopaedia of Witchcraft and Demonology* (Crown Publishers Inc, New York, 1959), scorns the idea of the real existence of witch covens, and says that the word 'coven' first appeared in 1662, as a result of Isobel Gowdie's confession, which he calls "these meanderings of an old woman". But according to Christina Hole, in her *Witchcraft in England* (Batsford, London, 1945 and Collier Macmillan, New York, 1966), Isobel Gowdie was "a pretty, red-haired girl, the wife of a farmer", and her name is still remembered among the people of Morayshire. She was hanged at the West Port of Elgin, and her body was afterwards burned to ashes, in the belief that this was the only way a witch's power could be really banished. Why she sacrificed herself has never been discovered.

Chaucer uses the word 'covent' in his *Canterbury Tales,* meaning an assembly of thirteen people. It is actually a variant of the word 'convent', and survives to this day in London in the name of Covent Garden. The Latinised spelling 'convent' was introduced about 1550, and gradually superseded the older form. A poem of the early fourteenth century, called "Handlyng Synne", tells of a 'coveyne' of thirteen people who impiously held a dance in the churchyard while the priest was saying Mass, and were duly punished for their sinful ways.

Evidently the 'covent', 'coveyne' or 'coven' (there are a number of variant spellings) was a group of thirteen people. They might be Christians, as in a book of *Ecclesiastical Memorials* (quoted by the *Oxford English Dictionary,* Clarendon Press, Oxford, 1933), written in 1536, which speaks of houses of religion "whereof the number in any one house is or of late hath been less than a covent, that is to say under thirteen persons". But the naughty people of the 'coveyne' who danced in the churchyard were certainly not religious persons.

Eventually, the word 'coven' came to be used exclusively of the witches' cult group; and so it has come down to our day.

The traditions of heraldry embody much curious lore and symbolism, some of which contains hints of the occult. It is notable that the old constitution of the College of Heralds consists of thirteen persons: three Kings of Arms, namely Garter, Clarencieux and Norroy; six Heralds, Somerset, Richmond, Lancaster, Windsor, Chester and York; and four Pursuivants, called Rouge Dragon, Blue Mantle, Portcullis and Rouge Croix.

CROSSROADS AS WITCHES' MEETING PLACES

Ever since the days of Diana Trivia, or Diana of the Three Ways, crossroads have been traditional meeting-places of witches. This may be the origin of the custom, observed up to comparatively recent years, of burying the bodies of suicides and executed criminals at the crossroads, with a stake through the heart. The latter was to prevent the ghost from walking. The body, having been denied Christian burial, was symbolically abandoned to the pagan powers.

Statues of Diana Trivia, or of the triple moon goddess Hecate, both of whom were divinities of witchcraft, were erected by the Greeks and Romans at places where three or more roads met. This is why, in later years, witches chose crossroads for their rendezvous. It was a place sacred to the moon goddess of witchcraft.

In Ashdown Forest, Sussex, there is a place where three roads meet, called Wych Cross. In past years, this place-name was spelt 'Witch Cross', bcause it was the meeting-place of the local witches.

Another forest crossroads where witches used to meet is Wilverley Post, in the New Forest in Hampshire, near the old oak-tree called the Naked Man.

CROWLEY, ALEISTER

Aleister Crowley earns a place in this book, not because he was a witch, but because he was not! This, of course, does not stop Crowley's name being dragged into every Sunday newspaper's latest "Exposure of Witchcraft and Black Magic" (they seldom know the difference). But perhaps if a brief sketch of Crowley's life is given here, it may help to a better understanding of what this very remarkable man really stood for.

Crowley was a pagan, a poet, a mountaineer, a magician and a prophet. He was also a world traveller and an all too daring explorer of the dangerous inner world of hallucinatory drugs. But the magic he practised—or 'Magick' as he preferred to call it—was the Qabalistic magic taught by the Order of the Golden Dawn, the famous occult brotherhood which claimed descent from the original Rosicrucians. In Crowley's eyes at any rate, it was very definitely white 'Magick'; and it was not witchcraft of any description.

As a matter of fact, Crowley was rather afraid of witchcraft, judging from some of the references to it in his works. This was probably because he recognised the strong feminine influence in witchcraft; and Crowley distrusted and professed to despise women. There was a pronounced homosexual bias in his nature, and his deepest and most significant relationships were with men.

As a poet, Crowley has never yet received the recognition he deserves. Like Oscar Wilde, his love of shocking the smug *bourgeoisie* rebounded upon him, to rob his work of the praise it merited. Today, however, in more broad-minded times, more and more of Crowley's books are being reprinted and made available, so that people can appreciate his strange genius for themselves, instead of only being able to read shocked (and usually inaccurate) accounts of how 'wicked' he was.

For such a flamboyant character, Crowley had a surprising home background. He was the son of two devout members of the Plymouth Brethren sect, a wealthy brewer called Edward Crowley and his wife Emily. They lived at Leamington Spa, Warwickshire, in the utmost Victorian respectability; and there Aleister Crowley was born, on 12th October 1875.

Perhaps they were rather too devout and respectable. Their talented little son stifled and suffered in an atmosphere of narrow-minded creedalism; and when he rebelled, his mother told him that he was as bad as the Great Beast in the Book of Revelations! This seems to have stuck in Crowley's mind; because when he became a man he took the title of the Great Beast—even to the extent of having it printed on his visiting cards.

His whole life was a revolt against his parents and everything they stood for. They must have made him very unhappy—no doubt with the best of intentions.

Crowley inherited a substantial fortune from his father. He went to Trinity College, Cambridge; and having utterly rejected his parents' religion, he became interested in the occult. Eventually he joined the Hermetic Order of the Golden Dawn, which numbered many distinguished people among its initiates. He also travelled extensively in the East, learning Eastern systems of Yoga and occultism.

The leader of the Golden Dawn was another remarkable personality, S. L. MacGregor Mathers; and he and Crowley ended by quarrelling bitterly. Crowley thereafter went his own way and founded his own order, the Argentinum Astrum or Silver Star, abbreviated to A.A.

Crowley had married Rose Kelly, the sister of Sir Gerald Kelly, the artist. While on holiday in Egypt with his young wife, Crowley took part with her in magical rituals, as a result of which he received what he considered to be a message from the gods who rule the destiny of this planet. This message was dictated to him by what he called "a praeter-human intelligence". He wrote down three chapters of a manuscript, which he named *Liber Legis*, the *Book of the Law*.

From the *Book of the Law* Crowley took his famous dictum: "Do what thou wilt shall be the whole of the Law. Love is the Law, Love under Will". Upon this manuscript Crowley based all of his subsequent life and teachings.

Liber Legis is an extraordinary document. However much it may be argued that it actually emanated from Crowley's subconscious mind, nevertheless it is undeniable that this book contained prophecies, both about Crowley's own personal life and about world events, which have been fulfilled.

Crowley received the *Book of the Law* in April 1904. The world was then in the palmy days of the British Empire, the lower classes knew their place, and all was peace, prosperity and croquet on the lawn. The *Book of the Law* proclaimed that all this was going to dissolve into war and chaos, out of which a new Aeon was to arise. The orthodox religions of the world would become discredited; the accepted moral codes would be despised. A new order of things had begun. It was the Equinox of the Gods.

The new Aeon would be called the Aeon of Horus, because it was going to be an Aeon of youth. Horus is the Egyptian god who was the child of Isis and Osiris. The law set forth in *Liber Legis* would be the guiding light of the new Aeon; and Crowley was to proclaim it.

Crowley has often been called a charlatan; but he undoubtedly devoted the rest of his life to playing out his role of the Logos of the Aeon of Horus. He believed in what he was doing; and no amount of personal misfortune, loss, or the alienation of his friends and those dear to him, would turn him from his path. Crowley was a figure of fate; he has made his mark upon the world, and particularly the world of the occult.

The press denounced him as "The Wickedest Man in the World", because of what they alleged went on in his notorious 'Abbey of Thelema' which he established at Cefalu in Sicily. It is now known that a good deal of the allegations made were false. However, Mussolini, who was then ruler of Italy, expelled him from Sicily, and he returned to Britain.

Here he became involved in a famous and sensational libel case. He sued Nina Hamnett, the sculptress, alleging that in her book of reminiscences, *Laughing Torso* (Constable and Co., London, 1932), she had libelled him by saying that he practised black magic. The case was heard in April 1934 before Mr. Justice Swift. The other side was able to produce such extraordinary evidence of Crowley's bizarre life and scandalous writings, that the judge was horrified. Of course, Crowley lost the case, amid a new furore of press publicity, and was forced into bankruptcy.

A number of disciples, however, remained loyal to him and helped him in his declining years. He ended his stormy life quietly in retirement at Hastings, in Sussex; unrepentant and unbowed. He died peacefully in his bed on 1st December 1947.

His remains were cremated at Brighton, and the ashes sent to his disciples in America. To the horror and indignation of Brighton councillors, Crowley's "Hymn to Pan" had been proclaimed from the pulpit of the crematorium chapel, with other extracts from his writings, instead of the usual religious service.

The worst charge that can be levelled against Crowley concerns the effect that he had upon some of his close associates. There were cases of mental collapse, alcoholism, broken lives and suicide among his devotees. His 'Magick' was strong and dangerous stuff. But he meant it to be white Magick; and although it was paganism, it was not witchcraft.

An excellent biography of Aleister Crowley is *The Great Beast* by John Symonds (Riders, London, 1951 and St. Martin's Press, New York, 1972). A shorter, but also very enlightening book about him, is *Aleister Crowley* by Charles Richard Cammell (New English Library, London, 1969, and by Hill and Wang, New York, 1970). Still more recently, Dr. Francis Israel Regardie, who at one time was Crowley's personal secretary, has written *The Eye in the Triangle; An Interpretation of Aleister Crowley* (Llewellyn, U.S.A., 1970).

D

DANCING, ITS USE IN WITCHCRAFT

Dancing is one of the activities, like poetry and music, which are essentially magical. All primitive people have ritual dances, not only for enjoyment, but with some purpose behind them. They dance for life, and they dance also for death; as the Irish still do for 'wakes', to give the deceased person a good send-off on their journey to the Other World.

Dancing is very often imitative magic. The witches danced on riding-poles, leaping to make the crops grow tall. The riding-pole between the legs was a phallic symbol, a bringer of fertility and continuer of life. The witches of Aberdeen in 1596 were accused of gathering upon St. Katherine's Hill, and there dancing "a devilish dance, riding on trees, by a long space". Much earlier, in 1324, an Irish witch, Dame Alice Kyteler, was accused of having "a pipe of ointment, wherewith she greased a staff, upon the which she ambled and galloped through thick and thin, when and in what manner she listed". This kind of dancing helped to give rise to the legend that witches rode through the air on staffs or broomsticks.

Another kind of witch dance is the round dance, performed around a person or around some object such as a tree or a bonfire. The aim of the round dance is to raise power. When it is done with some person, probably the leader of the coven, in the middle, then that person is directing the 'Cone of Power' that is being raised. The Stone Age witch dance depicted in the cave-painting at Cogul is of this type. When done around a tree, a bonfire, or perhaps an old sacred stone, it can be simply for enjoyment and exhilaration, and for invocation and worship of the Old Gods by this means. Witches have the idea that the gods enjoy seeing people happy, and this is therefore an acceptable form of worship.

A third kind of witch dance is a spiral, which is danced into the centre and out again. This symbolises penetration into the mysteries of the Other World. It is sometimes called 'Troy Town', after the old maze pattern, which was supposed to resemble the walls of Troy. Britain has a number of turf-cut mazes scattered throughout the countryside, mostly of unknown date but certainly very old. They are connected with the ancient British Mysteries. The dwelling-place of dead heroes, and of the Cauldron of Inspiration, was called Spiral Castle by the old Bards.

The idea of using a maze to represent penetration into another world was taken up by Christianity, and the maze-pattern can sometimes be found in old churches, with 'Heaven' or 'Zion' in the centre.

So much did the ring dance come to be associated with witchcraft, that in Sussex the 'fairy-rings' found upon the grassy Downs are called 'hag-tracks', from the belief that they are formed by the dancing feet of witches. They are regarded as natural magic circles, and used to this day by country folk for various private magic; though this is done in a very quiet and secret manner.

Witches are traditionally supposed to dance back to back. This seems to have been mainly a kind of frolic. The author of *A Pleasant Treatise of Witches* (London, 1673), says: "The dance is strange, and wonderful, as well as diabolical, for turning themselves back to back, they take one another by the arms and raise each other from the ground, then shake their heads to and fro like Anticks, and turn themselves as if they were mad." This sounds like a very fair description of some of our present-day dancing: the Jive, Rock and Roll, the Twist, and so on!

In fact, the witch-dancing he is talking about was probably very much like our young people's dancing today, free and uninhibited. Respectable folks in those days danced very formal and courtly dances, and thought any other style of dancing vulgar and immoral.

It may well have been the witches who founded modern dancing; because Reginald Scot quotes Bodin as saying that "these night-walking or rather night-dancing witches brought out of Italy into France, that dance which is called *La Volta*". La Volta is the dance that is believed to be the origin of the waltz, whose exciting rhythms gradually superseded the old stately minuets and pavanes, and paved the way for the livelier dances we know today.

Dancing has a very important magical effect upon people. It unites them in unison, by the rhythm of the beat of the dance. A group of people dancing in harmony together are of one mind, and this is essential to magical work. Their mood can be excited or calmed, by varying the pace of the dance. In fact, a state of light hypnosis can be induced by magical forms of dancing; or people can achieve a state of ecstasy, which in its original form is *ex-stasis,* 'being outside oneself'.

That is, the everyday world is left behind, with its squalor and cares; and the magical realms open. The old witch dances helped people to attain this experience, and it was the excitement and enjoyment of the wild dancing, by night in the open air or in some deserted ruin or secret rendezvous, that was one of the main attractions of the Old Religion, and made it so difficult for the Church to extirpate it.

It put colour and enjoyment into the common people's lives, when they had little enough to look forward to but a life of hard toil and submission. Many of its ceremonies and usages have spilled over into folk custom that is still alive and vigorous today; such as, for instance, the famous Horn Dance at Abbot's Bromley in Staffordshire. In fact, a great many of our colourful and time-honoured folk-customs have something of the old nature-worship and wisecraft at the heart of them.

The round dance is an imitation of the circling stars, the movement of the heavenly bodies. Consequently it is a kind of imitation of the universe. It is the wheel of the seasons, the wheel of life itself, of birth and death and rebirth. To dance it is to enter into the secret and subtle harmonies of Nature, and become one with the Powers of Life. Something of this is what the witches felt, and still feel, when they dance. A dance can be a prayer, an invocation, an ecstasy, or a spell. It is world-old and world-wide magic.

DEE, DR. JOHN

One of the most famous names in English occultism is that of John Dee. He was born in London in 1527; but his family came from Wales, and claimed to be descended from Roderick the Great, one of the native princes of Wales.

Dee was educated at Cambridge, where he eventually became a Fellow of Trinity College. From his earliest years, he was devoted to occult researches, being particularly interested in alchemy. He was a notable mathematician, and a collector of books and manuscripts. One of the cruellest blows of his life was when, on a journey abroad, he learned that an ignorant, bigoted mob had broken into his house at Mortlake and pillaged his library, because they believed him to be a worker of black magic.

Most of Dee's works have still never been published; but one, *The Hieroglyphic Monad*, was translated from the Latin by J. W. Hamilton-Jones, and published in 1947 by John M. Watkins. This extraordinary book gives an insight into Dee's strange and brilliant mind; as does a less accessible book, *A True and Faithful Relation of what passed for many years between Dr John Dee and some Spirits*, by Meric Casaubon, published in 1659.

Under the rule of the Catholic Mary Tudor, Dee came dangerously near to being burned as a heretic and "a conjurer, a caller of devils". Somehow he managed to clear himself of this charge, though he spent some time in prison. On the accession of Elizabeth I, he was received favourably by her at Court. He was responsible for selecting by astrology the most fortunate day for her coronation.

We now know that Dee was much more than Queen Elizabeth I's occult adviser. In his frequent journeys abroad, he acted as a secret agent for the Queen; and by a curious coincidence, his code-name was '007'. Whether Ian Fleming, the creator of the present-day '007', James Bond of Her Majesty's Secret Service, was aware of this, is unknown; but some of Dee's adventures were in stranger realms than Bond ever knew.

It has often been alleged by writers on the occult that witches have a secret language. It is true that a magical language exists; though witches are not the only occult practitioners who study and sometimes use it. This language is called Enochian; and we owe it to the researches of Dr. John Dee and his associate Edward Kelley.

The Enochian language was obtained by the clairvoyance of Edward Kelley, using a crystal or 'shew-stone' as a scrying instrument. (*See* SCRYING.) By this means, Kelley obtained a number of large charts divided into squares, each square having a letter of the alphabet. These charts or 'tablets' were copied out, and then Kelley would describe how he saw in his vision an 'angel' or spirit pointing to one letter after another, to spell out a message. Dee, who acted as recorder at these seances, would note the message down from his copy of the chart. Sometimes the messages were given backwards, because the spirits said that the sacred names and invocations transmitted in this rather complicated way were so potent that their straightforward recitation could raise powers too strong to handle, and the magical operation of transmission might be upset.

Aleister Crowley, who was very interested in the Enochian language, endorses this view in his *Magick in Theory and Practice*. He says that use of the magical Enochian words requires prudence, because when they are used things happen—for good or ill. He notes also, as others have done, that this mysterious tongue really is a language, and not just a farrago of strange words. It definitely possesses traces of grammar and syntax. It also possesses a distinctive alphabet; though the Enochian words resemble Hebrew, in that they mainly consist of consonants, and the vowels have to be supplied by the speaker, according to certain rules.

The Enochian language is a complete philological mystery. It has been suggested that it is the remains of the speech of ancient Atlantis; perhaps because it seems to be named after the mysterious patriarch Enoch, who lived before the Flood, and who "walked with God, and he was not, for God took him" (*Genesis,* Chapter 5, verses 21-4). There exists a strange old volume, *The Book of Enoch,* which purports to tell the story of those 'Sons of God' who came down from heaven and mated with the daughters of men, and thereby gave forbidden knowledge to mankind, including the knowledge of magic. (*See* DEMONOLOGY.)

A memory of John Dee lingers on the borders of Wales, where between Knighton and Beguildy is a hill called Conjurer's Pitch. According to local tradition, this is a place where Dee, when visiting Wales, used to perform magical rites.

Elizabeth's successor, James I, looked upon Dee with less favour than had the Virgin Queen; and he ended his days in comparative poverty and obscurity, dying at Mortlake in 1608. In his time, however, John Dee had been the friend of men like Sir Francis Bacon and Sir Walter Raleigh. He was a member of the circle called 'The School of Night', which met secretly at Sir Walter Raleigh's house at Sherbourne in Dorset, for the purpose of discussing occult and scientific subjects. Sherbourne is not far from the area of the Glastonbury Zodiac, so it may have been here that Dee learned of this. (*See* ZODIAC.)

DEMONOLOGY

A knowledge of demonology, or the supposed science of the study and classification of demons, was considered in times past to be essential to the investigation of witchcraft. This followed logically upon the Church's doctrine that all witchcraft, and indeed all rival cults to that of Christianity, were inspired and directed by Satan.

This attitude is exemplified by the fact that in medieval times *Mahound,* a popular form of Mohammed, the founder of Islam, was another name for the devil.

The whole doctrine rested upon the Biblical references to the fallen angels, who were supposed to have been cast out of heaven, together with their leader, Satan or Lucifer, and thereafter to have become the implacable enemies of God and mankind. It is doubtful, however, if the ancient Hebrews originally meant anything like this by their references to Satan. In the Book of Job Satan figures as a sort of heavenly *agent provocateur,* employed by God to test people's faith. He enters boldly into heaven among the sons of God, a term used in Genesis to refer to the angels. The word *satan* means an adversary.

An echo of this doctrine is found in the Lord's Prayer, in the rather puzzling words "and lead us not into temptation". The famous French occultist Eliphas Lévi has pointed out that if the Devil exists, he must be a Devil of God. Lévi had to write in an obscure manner to avoid offending the Catholic Church, of which he was a member; but he protests in his chief work, *Dogme et Rituel de la Haute Magie* (Translated as *Transcendental Magic* by Arthur Edward Waite, George Redway, London, 1896), against the ideas of the demonologists. He accuses them of setting up Satan as a rival to God, and derives their beliefs from the Eastern doctrines of Zoroastrianism rather than from true Christianity. Zoroaster postulated two great powers, one of light and one of darkness, between which the rulership of the universe was divided.

The identification of Satan with Lucifer rests upon a text in Isaiah, Chapter 14, verse 12: "How art thou fallen from heaven, O Lucifer, son of the morning! How art thou cut down to the ground, which didst weaken the nations!" Early Biblical scholars connected this with the story in Revelations about the great star that fell from heaven, and with the words of Jesus in the Gospel of St Luke, Chapter 10, verse 18: "I beheld Satan as lightning fall from heaven." Yet it is obvious from the context of this passage from Isaiah that the prophet is not referring to Satan at all, but to a proud and oppressive king of Babylon. The Hebrew word translated as 'Lucifer' means 'shining one', one of the stars of heaven. Out of such doubtful beginnings did religious doctrines grow, with the assistance of pious and semi-literate demonologists.

One of the chief source-books for the story of the fallen angels is *The Book of Enoch,* a collection of pre-Christian fragments which enlarge upon the strange story about the sons of God who "came in unto the daughters of men, and they bare children to them, the same became mighty men which were of old, men of renown" (Genesis, Chapter 6, verses 1-4). *The Book of Enoch* tells how, in the days before the Flood, some 200 'angels' descended upon Mount Hermon, and took wives from among earthly women. The 'angels' not only interbred with the people of earth, but also taught them all kinds of knowledge they had never possessed before. For this, they were punished with great severity, and God sent the Flood to destroy the dangerous hybrid race of 'giants' which had resulted from this forbidden mating. (*The Book of Enoch,* translated by R. H. Charles, S.P.C.K., London, 1970.)

In the days when these accounts were written, the earth was thought to be the centre of the universe, the only place inhabited by men; and any other beings who descended from heaven could only be either angels or devils. Today, with our beginning of space travel and our knowledge of other possible worlds inhabited by intelligent beings, perhaps more advanced than ourselves, we can see quite a different explanation for these traditions.

Some extra-terrestrial beings may have come to this earth in the far-distant past, sufficiently like ourselves to mate with human women and produce children, yet more advanced in knowledge and civilisation. The ordinary men of earth would naturally have been jealous and suspicious of these interlopers, and when the flood that drowned Atlantis took place—an event of which there are many traces in legend—they would have blamed it on the newcomers, with the old argument of *post hoc, ergo propter hoc.*

However, to the demonologists of the Middle Ages, the subject of the fallen angels was of great importance. In the notorious grimoire called *The Goetia, or Lesser Key of Solomon,* we are given the names and descriptions of seventy-two fallen angels, each of whom is a ruler over legions of spirits. We are told that King Solomon, by his command of magic, confined these demon rulers within a vessel of brass, which he then sealed with a magical seal and cast into a deep lake. Unfortunately, the people of Babylon, thinking the vessel contained treasure, drew it out and broke it open, so that all the demons escaped again. Nevertheless, by means of the magical sigils and instructions derived from Solomon, the magician may command these spirits and make them obey him. The same theme is repeated in other grimoires.

Another view of demons is that they are not fallen angels, nor created wicked, but rather the personification of blind forces of nature. Alternatively, they may be regarded as non-human spirits of a violent, capricious nature, often hostile to man, but of inferior mentality to him, and therefore able to be commanded by a powerful magician. This latter concept of demons is one which prevails among practitioners of magic all over the world.

The Victorian novelist Bulwer Lytton, who was the leader of a secret magical circle, tells us in his occult novel *A Strange Story:*

> In the creed of the Dervish, and of all who adventure into that realm of nature which is closed to philosophy and open to magic, there are races in the magnitude of space unseen as animalcules in the world of a drop. For the tribes of the drop, science has its microscope. Of the hosts of yon azure Infinite magic gains sight, and through them gains command over fluid conductors that link all the parts of creation. Of these races, some are wholly indifferent to man, some benign to him, and some deadly hostile.

Such is an initiate's view of demons, namely that some spirits may be dangerous for man to meddle with, not because they have been created for the purpose of tempting and tormenting, but in the same way that a wild animal is dangerous.

This is a dark and difficult subject. Nevertheless, demonologists in years gone by undauntedly drew up the most precise, detailed and fantastic list of demons, and their various powers and offices. The legions of hell were believed to be everywhere, and witches were their agents. These beliefs undoubtedly contributed much to the panicking of public opinion, until people unthinkingly acquiesced in the cruellest persecutions of the days of witch-hunting. (*See* DEVIL.)

DEVIL

This word of fear to the superstitious, and of profit to the sensational reporter, is generally taken to mean the personified principle of evil. However, the doctrine of the existence of a personal Devil has of late years been dropped by many leading churchmen. The belief in a rebellious Satan as the Power of Evil has always been contrary to the text in Isaiah, Chapter 45, verse 7: "I form the light, and create darkness: I make peace, and create evil: I the Lord do all these things."

Some religious people need the concept of the Devil; it comes in extremely useful. For one thing, the idea that man is responsible for his own evils is distasteful to him. He likes to have something, or someone, to blame. The pattern was laid down very early, according to the story of the Garden of Eden; Adam blamed the woman, and the woman blamed the serpent. In the eyes of the early Church, which was markedly anti-feminist, woman and the Devil had been responsible for all mischief ever since.

Also, the story of the Devil, ever seeking and plotting for man's damnation, has been a powerful weapon of fear, to be used to keep people in line. When the very successful film, *Rosemary's Baby* (which deals with the alleged diabolical activities of some modern witches), was first shown in America, it was condemned by the National Catholic Office for Motion Pictures. The plot of the film concerns a girl who has a baby by the Devil; and Mia Farrow, who starred in this part, spoke up in reply to the Catholic Office's ban.

She was quoted as saying that she did not see what grounds they had for condemnation of the picture, because it was the Catholic Church itself which had "invented the Satan figure" and it was they who were trying to hold masses of people together by the fear of hell.

Miss Farrow could have added that it was the Catholic Church which laid down the dogma that, because all the gods of the older religions were really devils, all pagans were devil-worshippers, and therefore fair game for any treatment, however bad. This attitude appears still to be maintained today, in certain sections of the Press.

Yet the very fact of the enormous success of *Rosemary's Baby*, both as a book and a film, indicates the ambivalent attitude of society towards the concept of the Devil. He is supposed to be the personification of evil, and yet he fascinates. Why?

The statement that "the god of the old religion becomes the devil of the new" is something which anthropologists, and students of comparative religion, have found to be literally true. For instance, 'Old Nick' as a name for the Devil is derived from Nik, which was a title of the pagan English god Woden. Sometimes the Devil is simply called 'the Old 'Un', another name full of meaning in this respect. (*See* OLD ONE, THE.)

The conventional representation of the Devil is that of a being with horns upon his head, and having a body which terminates in shaggy lower limbs and cloven hoofs. Again why? Is there any text in the Bible which describes 'Satan' or 'the Devil' in this manner? None whatever. Yet this is the picture which a mention of 'the Devil' conjures up.

In fact, it is simply a representation of Pan, the goat-footed god of nature, of life and vitality; and the Great God Pan himself is just

another version of the most ancient Horned God, the deity whom
the cave-men worshipped.

"Beloved Pan, and all the other gods who haunt this place, give
me beauty in the inmost soul; and grant that the outward and the
inward may be as one." Such was the prayer of Socrates. Was he a
devil-worshipper?

Certainly the pagans had some gods of terrifying aspect. But these
gods were not fallen angels, who plotted hideously to encompass
man's misery and perdition. They were the personification of destroying natural forces: the storm-wind, the darkness, the plague.
The people who really worshipped Nature knew that she was not
all pretty flowers and charming little birds and butterflies. The forces
of creation were counter-balanced by the forces of destruction; but
the Great Mother destroyed only to give rebirth in a higher form.

The word 'Devil' is of uncertain derivation. In my opinion, its
most likely origin is the same as that of *Deus,* God; namely the
Sanskrit *Deva,* meaning 'a shining one, a god'. The Gypsies, whose
Romany language is of Indo-European origin, call God *Duvel.* Truly,
Demon est Deus Inversus, "the Demon is God reversed", as the old
magical motto has it.

The word 'demon' itself comes from the Greek *daimon,* which
originally meant a spirit holding a middle place between gods and
men. Only later, in Early Christian times, was it taken to mean an
evil spirit.

The spirits of Nature which the pagans sensed as haunting lonely
places, were neither good nor evil. They were simply different from
man, not flesh and blood, and therefore best regarded with caution
and respect. People of Celtic blood in the lonelier parts of the British
Isles take this attitude to this day towards the fairies, whom they
call the Good Neighbours or the People of Peace.

The Devil is that which is wild, untamed and unresolved—in nature,
and in human nature. He is the impulses in *themselves,* which people
fear and which they dislike to admit the existence of. Hence these
impulses become exteriorised, and projected in the form of devils
and demons. No wonder that in the Middle Ages, when the Church
ruled with an iron hand, the Devil appeared everywhere! He was the
projected image of the natural desires, especially sexual desires, which
would not be denied, however much the Church denounced them
as sin.

The Devil as the personification of the mysterious and untamed forces of nature, appears all over the British Isles in place-names, applied to things which seemed extraordinary and inexplicable. There is the great gash in the South Downs, near Brighton, called the Devil's Dyke. Hindhead, in Surrey, has the Devil's Punch Bowl, and there are two more in the Scilly Isles and in Eire. There are two Devil's Glens, one in Wicklow and another in the Vale of Neath. A curious pinnacle of rock in the witch-haunted Cotswolds is called the Devil's Chimney. On the bank of the River Wye, opposite Tintern Abbey, is the Devil's Pulpit, from which he is said to have preached in defiance of the Church.

There are the Devil's Cheese-Wring, a strange heap of rocks near Liskeard in Cornwall; the Devil's Frying-Pan, in the same county; the Devil's Jumps, a series of low hills near Frensham in Surrey; and so on and on, all over the map.

Curious old buildings often have the Devil's name attributed to them. There is a Devil's Tower at Windsor Castle, and a Devil's Battery in the Tower of London. Prehistoric stone monuments have been called the Devil's Arrows or the Devil's Quoits; and one legend ascribes the building of Stonehenge to the Devil. Anything which was felt to be beyond human ingenuity or comprehension, belonged to the realm of the Devil. He was the personification of the Unknown.

He was the rebel; he was everything which would not conform. He was the spirit of the wild, the darkness, the storm, the Wild Huntsman riding the night wind. He was the forbidden, yet dangerously attractive; the secret, which allured while defying one to find it out. He put the spice into life, in a situation where goodness had become synonymous with dullness and respectability. He was the enemy of the negative virtues.

As such, the Devil has played an important part in the psychological development of mankind. The corruption of man's heart has been projected on to him. People have accused his supposed servants, the witches, of doing the forbidden things they wanted to do themselves, in the dark deep hells of their own souls, and then tortured and burned the witches for being so 'wicked'. It is significant that the word 'hell' comes from the same root as the Anglo-Saxon *helan,* 'to conceal, to cover over'. The real powers of hell come not from external devils, but from the unacknowledged contents of man's own mind.

To what extent, then, is the Devil the god of the witches? The answer is that the Church, and not the witches, identified the old

Horned God with the Devil, precisely because he stood for the things the Church had forbidden—especially uninhibited sexual enjoyment and the pride that will not bow down and serve. So determined were they upon this identification, that in the old accounts of witch trials nearly every mention by the witches of a non-Christian deity is set down as 'the Devil' by those recording the proceedings. The male leader of the coven, also, was so persistently described as the Devil that some witches actually began to call him this—though the term is seldom used by witches today.

In fact, the Horned God of the witches is far, far older than Christianity; and he only began to be identified with the Devil when the Church branded nature itself as 'fallen', and natural impulses as 'sin'. This identification was not only a deliberate matter of dogma; it was a psychological process, which in some places is still at work.

It was this deep-seated emotional drive which gave the witch-hunts of olden days their horrific impetus, their pitiless and obscene cruelty, their element of nightmare unreasonable. In those days, the dark forces were indeed released; but the hell they came from was of man's own making, not God's or the Devil's.

DEVIL'S MARK

The Devil's mark was supposed to be the mark placed upon a witch by the Devil at the time of his or her initiation. It was also called the *sigillum diaboli* or Devil's seal.

It might have been argued by any reasonable person that it was surely very unwise of the Devil to be obliging enough to mark witches in this way, so that they could be the more easily detected. To counter this argument, the witch-hunters asserted that this mark was of a very specialised nature, and it took great skill and experience to find it.

Consequently, a veritable guild of witch-prickers, as they came to be called, at one time existed in Scotland. These men spread the belief that witches were marked in a very subtle, often *invisible* manner; but that nevertheless, the Devil's mark could be detected by them, because it was insensible, and when a pin was driven into it it would not bleed.

A suspected witch would therefore be handed over to the witch-pricker, who would strip her naked, sometimes in public, and proceed to search her for the Mark of the Devil. As these men were paid by results, and made a livelihood of their trade, one may be confident that they would not fail to find something which they would say was the Devil's mark; unless, of course, they were well bribed not to do so.

Some of them made use of a trick bodkin, which would only *appear* to penetrate the skin, when in fact the point was retracted inside the hilt. So by means of a simple conjuring device they seemed to the horrified onlookers (who, impelled by religious duty, had flocked to see a naked woman being tortured), to have driven a point into her flesh, without her feeling anything or any blood issuing forth. If they had previously been using a real bodkin, which caused sufficient agony and flow of blood to convince the spectators of the seriousness of the trial, and then by sleight of hand switched to the fake one, the effect was very striking and realistic.

Eventually, after they had caused many executions, the cheats of these rogues became so notorious that in 1662 the practice of 'pricking for witchcraft' was forbidden by law, unless it was done by special Order in Council; and when some of the men concerned received prison sentences for their frauds, the practice died out.

However, in the days of witch-hunting, almost any natural mark or peculiarity could be passed off as the Devil's mark, if someone was determined to convict a person as a witch. The descriptions of this supposed *sigillum diaboli* were vague and variable. Sometimes it was said to be a blue spot, sometimes something like the print of a toad's foot, sometimes a physical peculiarity of almost any kind. Thus, when King Henry VIII had fallen out of love with Anne Boleyn, he accused her among other things of witchcraft, and declared that a certain natural oddity of her person was the Devil's mark.

There are various traditions of what this peculiarity was. One account says that Anne Boleyn had a rudimentary extra finger on one hand; another states that she had an extra nipple on one breast. Whatever it was, Henry seized on it to declare that "he had made this marriage seduced by witchcraft; and that this was evident because God did not permit them to have any male issue".

The extra nipple or 'witch's teat' was supposed to be a particularly certain and damning mark of the Devil; because this was bestowed upon a witch in order that she could give suck to her familiar, when the latter took animal or reptile form. Sometimes even male witches were accused of maintaining familiars in this way. 'Evidence' of this nature was particularly frequent in witch trials in Britain. The Act of Parliament of King James I against witchcraft specifically mentions those who "consult, covenant with, entertain, employ, feed, or reward any evil and wicked spirit to or for any intent of purpose"; making it an offence punishable by death.

Now, the fact is that the occurrence of extra nipples on the human body is quite well known to medical science. It is not common; but it is by no means such an unheard-of thing as people might suppose, and it is a perfectly natural phenomenon.

Such supernumerary nipples, as doctors term them, usually occur on what is called 'the milk line', an imaginary line running through the normal location of the breasts on either side, up past the armpit to the shoulder, and downwards from the breasts towards the pelvic region. However, in some cases, though more rarely, such nipples are found in other places on the body also. Medical authorities have estimated that supernumerary nipples can be found in from one to two per cent of the population.

A famous case in medical history is that of a woman called Thérèse Ventre, who was written about by two French scientists in 1827. Madame Ventre not only had two normal breasts, but an extra breast on the outside of her thigh, which was sufficiently developed to give milk. A contemporary picture shows her holding a baby in her arms and feeding it in the normal way, while another small child is taking milk from the breast on her thigh. If this lady had lived a couple of centuries previously, she would certainly have been condemned as a witch.

DIANA

Diana is the Roman name of the goddess of the moon, whom the Greeks called Artemis. (*See* ARTEMIS.) Her temple at Ephesus was one of the Seven Wonders of the ancient world.

The name Diana comes from the Indo-European root *Di,* meaning 'bright, shining', as befits the lady of the bright lamp of heaven. Under this name, she would have been equally acceptable to the people of the Celtic provinces of Rome, as the Celtic words *dianna* and *diona* also mean 'divine' or 'brilliant'.

Perhaps this is one reason why the worship of Diana was so widespread and long-enduring. We have seen how the very early Canon Law of the Christian Church denounced women who continued to worship Diana by night. (*See* CANON EPISCOPI.) Charles Godfrey Leland tells us how in nineteenth-century Italy he found people who

had insufficient education to know anything about the classical goddess Diana, who were yet perfectly well aware of her as queen of the
witches. (*See* LELAND, CHARLES GODFREY.)

The beautiful invocations to Diana, which Leland collected from
Italian witches and published in *Aradia, or the Gospel of the Witches
of Italy* (London, David Nutt, 1899), are proof of the surviving cult
of Diana and its importance to the understanding of what witchcraft
really is. (*See* ARADIA.)

Jerome Cardan, who wrote of witches in his book *De Rerum
Varietate,* published in Basle in 1557, says: "They [witches] adore
the *ludi Dominam* [the Lady of the Games] and sacrifice to her as
a god." This 'Lady' was Diana, and the "games" were the full-moon
Esbats, which take their name from the Old French *s'esbattre,* meaning to frolic. In Italy, these witch frolics were sometimes called 'the
game of Benevento', after a district notorious as a witches' meeting-
place.

Other names which the goddess acquired during the Middle Ages
were Dame Habonde, Abundia, Satia, Bensozia, Zobiana and Herodiana. In Scotland she was called Nicneven, who rode through the
night with her followers "at the hinder end of harvest, on old Halloween", as an old Scots poet describes it.

Some of these names are evidently descriptions of her attributes.
Abundia, for example, is connected with 'abundance', and Satia with
'satisfaction'. Herodiana is a combination of the names of Diana and
her witch-daughter Herodias. Bensozia could mean 'the good neighbour', an expression which was a name for the fairies. Many of the
Old Gods became associated with the fairies in the popular mind,
after the coming of Christianity. Shakespeare's Queen of the Fairies,
Titania, bears what is actually an old name of the Moon Goddess. In
Ireland, the *Sluagh Sidhe,* or Fairy Host, was led by the beautiful and
shining figures of the old Celtic gods and goddesses.

Fairyland, in fact, was simply the pagan Other World, to which
the souls of pagans went when they died; and Diana was its queen.
This was quite in accordance with classical myth, which gave to the
triple goddess of the moon rulership over three realms; that of
Heaven, Earth and the Other World, the dwelling-place of the dead.
As the divinity of the moon, she was Selene; as the goddess of the
woodlands and the wild things, she was Artemis; as the queen of the
mysterious Beyond, she was Hecate.

The poet John Skelton describes her three-fold divinity:

> Diana in the leaves green,
> Luna that so bright doth sheen,
> Persephone in Hell.

As a universal goddess, Diana had many forms and many names. In fact, it would be more correct to say that there was a universal goddess, of whose myriad names Diana was one. Naturally, the cult of a goddess so widely worshipped was carried on all over the ancient Roman Empire, where it mingled with those of native goddesses like Dana, Briginda and Cerridwen.

The cult of Diana was particularly important to Ancient Britain, because, according to legend, it was she who had directed the Trojan Prince Brutus, the founder of the royal line of Britain, to take refuge here after the Fall of Troy. The descent of British royalty from the Trojans was accepted without question in olden times and was a matter of pride. Britons called themselves Y Lin Troia, 'The Race of Troy'.

The place where Brutus landed, at Totnes in Devon, is still shown; and London was called Troy Novaunt, or New Troy, because Brutus had founded it.

The sacred relic of London, London Stone, which is still preserved, is said to have been the original altar which Brutus raised to Diana, in gratitude for his kingdom. On its safety the fate of London is supposed to depend.

The temple of Diana founded by Brutus is said to have occupied the site of the present St. Paul's Cathedral. This may be the real origin of a strange medieval custom which was formerly kept up at the cathedral on St. Paul's Day, 25th January. In 1375 a certain Sir William Baud had been permitted to enclose 20 acres of land belonging to the cathedral, on condition that he presented annually to the clergy of the cathedral a fat buck and a doe. These animals were brought into the cathedral, when the procession was taking place, and were offered at the high altar.

> The buck being brought to the steps of the altar, the Dean and Chapter, apparelled in copes and proper vestments, with garlands of roses on their heads, sent the body of the buck to be baked, and had the head and horns fixed on a pole before the cross, in their procession round about the church, till they issued at the west door, where the keeper that brought it blowed

the death of the buck, and then the horns that were about the city answered him in like manner.

So says Robert Chambers in his *Book of Days* (2 vols, W. & R. Chambers, London and Edinburgh, 1869; also Gale Detroit, 1886), quoting from an old author. In fact, this ceremony is in keeping with a pagan rite associated with a pagan site, upon which the original cathedral was built. Then the old rite continued in a Christianised form; and in 1375 a man was given some land on condition that he supplied the annual sacrifice of the horned beasts of Diana.

The alchemists sometimes used figures of Diana as a symbol of silver, the moon's metal. The old belief in turning your money over for luck, when you first see the new moon, is a relic of the worship of Diana. It should, of course, be silver money which you are asking her to increase.

Diana's crescent moon and blue robe of stars were directly taken over by artists, and bestowed as attributes of the Madonna, when she is represented as Queen of Heaven. The beauty of medieval Madonnas is the loveliness of a goddess, who was anciently Diana, and before that Isis, and before that the Divine Woman of the dark and secret sanctuaries of the cave men.

DIGITALIS

This drug, the active principle of the foxglove plant, was first introduced into general medical practice by a doctor who bought its secret from a witch.

He was Dr. William Withering (1741-1799), who was born at Wellington in Shropshire. He published *An Account of the Foxglove and Some of its Medical Uses* in 1785.

Withering discovered in his practice in Shropshire that people resorted to village wise women, or white witches, for cures; and he was intrigued to find that such cures were sometimes successful. There was one old lady in particular, who had a herbal medicine which benefited certain heart conditions.

Having established this as a fact, Withering went to see the old witch-wife, and bought the recipe from her. He found that the most important ingredient was foxglove, and this started him on his own study of the properties of this plant.

He became famous during his lifetime as a result of his contribution to medicine; and his monument in Edgbaston Old Church was ornamented with carvings of foxglove, in tribute to his discovery.

The foxglove plant has for a very long time been associated with witches, and is sometimes called witches' glove or witches' thimble. Its name is really nothing to do with foxes; but was originally folks' glove, 'the glove of the good folk, or fairies'.

Digitalis is in regular use in medical practice today. This proves that the traditional lore of the witches was not all superstitious nonsense; especially in the department of 'wortcunning', or knowledge of the properties of herbs.

DIVINATION

Divination is the name given to the art of foretelling the future, or discovering hidden things, by magical means.

It is a practice as old as the human race itself, and innumerable means have been used, and still are used, for this purpose. Cards, teacups and crystal gazing are resorted to, often by people who would indignantly deny that they were practising witchcraft, or even magic. Nevertheless, divination in all its forms has always been an important part of the witch's craft.

It is difficult to say what is the oldest form of divination; probably seeing pictures in the fire, or listening to the voice of the wind, or the sound of a running stream or waterfall. Even a very 'civilised', intellectual person today—by quieting the thinking mind and attuning himself or herself, in the right atmosphere, to the subtler forces of Nature—can achieve a certain message, a perception of the inner mind, by these means.

Many people have the erroneous idea that clairvoyance necessarily involves going into a trance; but this is not so. It means a degree of quietness, attunement and perception; the ability to lay aside for a while all the jumble and chatter of everyday life and allow the inner mind to speak, and tell what it perceives, either by means of symbolic vision, an inner voice, or simply by intuitive impression.

Because clairvoyance so often conveys its meaning by symbols, one finds so many lists of symbols and their meanings connected with, for instance, tea-cup reading. However, one does not need to learn a list of this kind, and stick to it by rote, although it may be helpful to the beginner to do so; because *what really matters is what a symbol means to the person who is doing the reading*.

For instance, the figure of a dog is usually given in these lists as meaning "a faithful friend". But suppose the person reading the cup disliked dogs, and was frightened of them? This meaning would hardly apply in such a case. Therefore the individual element always enters into the interpretation of any divinatory symbols, and should be allowed for.

However, as psychologists are finding out in their interpretation of dreams, there are many symbols which do have a more or less universal meaning; and anyone who wants seriously to practise divination will benefit by a study of symbolism in all its many manifestations.

The writer can testify from personal experience that if divination is practised seriously it will give worthwhile results. If, however, it is done 'just for a laugh', or in the spirit of, 'Oh, well, we'll try it, but of course it won't work', then naturally no good results can be expected.

Sometimes ready-made sets of symbols are used for divination. The painted pebbles which are often found in the caves once inhabited by Stone Age man, were probably used for this purpose. Later, as civilisation advanced, man evolved much more sophisticated methods; for instance, the *I Ching* of Ancient China, the Tarot cards of mysterious and unknown origin, or the sixteen symbols used in the Western system of geomancy.

The essential thing is that the diviner should have some basic set of symbols which he is thoroughly familiar with, and which convey a definite meaning, but that is nevertheless elastic enough to give full play to the powers of psychic perception. It is necessary also that the question should be precisely formulated and concentrated on, with real desire for a true answer. Furthermore, the selection of the meaningful symbols must be at random, left to be carried out by the subconscious mind. There must be no attempt to force or twist the answer.

The most difficult thing for a diviner to establish is time; that is, *when* the thing will happen. Some rules about this are usually laid down in the method of divination adopted. In reading the symbols formed by the tea-leaves, for instance, the ones nearest the rim of the cup are supposed to be near at hand in point of time, especially those closest to the handle by which you are holding the cup, because that represents the person you are reading for. The ones in the bottom of the cup are fading away in the distance, into the future. But in the last resort, the diviner's own *feeling* about a particular manifestation is the most important thing.

Various little ceremonies are associated with divination, to attract the right influences and make it fortunate. For instance, in tea-cup reading we are told to swirl the remainder of the leaves three times round the cup, then up-end it in the saucer and give three slow taps on the base, before attempting to read it. What this actually does is to distribute the leaves well, and allow time for the liquid to drain away, so improving the chances of the reading.

People may jeer at the simplicity of tea-cup reading; but it is in fact a very practical means of divination. The random shapes of the leaves give the inner mind something from which to form meaningful pictures; rather like the ink-blot test, which is a standard method of psychological testing. Also, the fact that a person has just drunk from the cup, and has thus been in intimate contact with it, has put that person's influence momentarily upon the cup and its contents.

The methods used for divination in all ages and countries are legion; but the basic principles which have been explained in this article underlie them all. One should distinguish, however, between divination by the use of some method of signs, such as a spread of Tarot cards for instance, and divination by omens which happen without being sought for. To know the meaning of the latter is an occult study in itself.

While long scoffed at as mere superstition, the observation of odd and curious events has today been restored to respectability by psychologists of the school of C. G. Jung, who have given it the name of 'synchronicity'. It is wonderful what a long, high-sounding word will do! The study of witchcraft is often frowned upon; but the study of extrasensory perception, hypnosis, psychic phenomena, astral projection, telepathy etc., is today carried on by learned professors at many universities. Yet all these things in the old days were part of witchcraft, and were generally included under that heading. (*See* TAROT CARDS AND SCRYING.)

DORSET OOSER

This is the name given to a very curious horned mask, with a still more curious history attached to it. It is certainly connected with the Old Religion, and that from a long way back.

The particular mask known by this name to students of folklore was first written about in *Somerset and Dorset Notes and Queries,* in 1891. Fortunately, it was not only described but photographed; because, like the head of Atho, it has since disappeared in mysterious circumstances. Margaret Murray reproduced this photograph in her famous book *The God of the Witches,* as an example of the long-surviving customs connected with the worship of the Horned God.

The mask was hollow, and made of painted wood. It was trimmed with hair, and bearded, and also provided with a fine pair of bull's horns. Its peculiarly vivid expression, lively and fear-inspiring, made it a splendid example of folk-art in itself, apart from its strange and secret associations.

The lower jaw was movable, and worked by pulling a string; and a very remarkable feature of this mask was that in the centre of the forehead it bore a rounded boss, exactly in the place which the Eastern yogis and lamas call 'the Third Eye', regarding it as the seat of psychic powers.

At the time when it first came to be noticed by writers on folk-lore, the Dorset Ooser was in the possession of the Cave family, of Holt Farm, Melbury Osmond, in Dorset. They knew that its traditional name among local people was the Ooser; but do not seem to have been too sure of its real significance, except that it was associated with village revels.

Further research has shown that it was formerly worn at the Christmas festivities, by a man dressed in animal skins. He was known in Dorset as 'the Christmas Bull', the 'Ooser', or 'Wooser'; and a similar figure used to accompany the Christmas Wassailers at Kingscote, in Gloucestershire.

This is interesting; because a very old book of Church ordinances, called the *Liber Poenitentialis* of Theodore, who was Archbishop of Canterbury from 668 to 690 A.D. sternly castigated those heathenish people who kept up this very custom; "Whoever at the Kalends of January goes about as a stag or a bull; that is, making himself into a wild animal and dressing in the skin of a herd animal, and putting on the heads of beasts; those who in such wise transform themselves into the appearance of a wild animal, penance for three years because this is devilish." ("The Kalends of January" is the beginning of the month, which was within the old Twelve Days of Christmas during which the festivities were kept up.)

In *Dorset Up-Along and Down-Along,* a collection of Dorset folk-lore collected by members of the Women's Institutes and published in 1951, it was stated that the appearance of the Wooser was a recognised Christmas custom "up to forty years ago"; that is, to about the turn of the century at least. So the particular mask belonging to the Cave family must have been only one of a number. Evidently the people of Dorset down the centuries cared little for the Archbishop's wrath or penances, but retained their pagan customs just the same. Perhaps they cared more about keeping the luck of the Old Gods than they did for the threats of the Archbishop and his successors.

As late as 1911, a Dorsetshire newspaper carried a report of a man being charged with frightening some girls by chasing them when he was "dressed in a bullock's skin and wearing an ooser".

This word 'ooser' as the dialect term for a horned mask, has intrigued philologists. It is pronounced ooss-er, with a short 's' sound; not ooze-er, as it might appear to those not of Dorset. This may derive from a medieval Latin word *osor,* as a synonym for the Devil, as F. T. Elworthy suggested in his book *Horns of Honour* (John Murray, London, 1900). However, the writer would like to advance another suggestion: namely, that 'Ooser' comes from the Old English *Os,* meaning a god. This word survives in such names as 'Oswald', meaning 'God-power'; 'Osmund', meaning 'God-protection', and so on. It is notable that the village where the Caves lived is called Melbury *Osmund.*

The circumstances in which the Dorset Ooser disappeared are as follows. Its owner, Dr. Edward Cave, left Holt Farm for Crewkerne, in Somerset, and took the mask with the rest of his goods. In 1897 he moved his residence again, from Crewkerne to Bath. This time, the mask was left behind at Crewkerne, stored with some other property in a loft, in the care of the family coachman. When Dr. Cave enquired for the Ooser, it could not be found. A groom admitted that he was responsible for letting it go. He said that a man from "up Chinnock way", had called one day and asked to buy it; and the groom, thinking it of no particular value, had sold it to him.

When one recollects that this horned mask had been in the possession of the Cave family for 'time out of mind', the groom's story sounds rather thin; though of course possible. At any rate, all enquiries for the mysterious stranger from "up Chinnock way" proved fruitless. Neither he nor the mask was ever seen again.

Perhaps someone didn't like the Dorset Ooser being taken out of Dorset? There may have been some idea that its removal was taking away luck or protection. It is possible also that a coven of witches saw a chance to obtain possession of something which would have been of great significance to them. To date, the mystery remains unsolved.

DRAKE, SIR FRANCIS

Sir Francis Drake is known in all English history books as the man
who delivered England from the Spanish Armada. Not so well known
is the fact that in his native Devonshire he is reputed to have belonged
to the witch cult.

During the Second World War, at the time when England seemed
in imminent danger of invasion, a large gathering of witches took
place in the New Forest, to work a rite to protect the country. It
was recalled then that similar rituals had been carried out in past
years against Napoleon, and before that against the Spanish Armada. (The ceremony against Hitler took place at Lammas 1940;
and the writer has known personally two people who took part in it.)

Many legends have gathered about Drake and his defeat of the
Armada. That of Drake's Drum is well known; and its ghostly beat
is said to have been heard during both the First and the Second World
Wars. In the West Country, Drake is told of, in winter evening fireside
tales, as a particularly active ghost, who has been known to lead the
Wild Hunt on dark nights of wind and storm.

This identification of Drake with the leader of the Wild Hunt is
interesting, because the Wild Hunt is definitely connected with the
Old Religion. Other stories say that, because he practised witchcraft
in his lifetime, Drake's soul cannot rest. This is why his ghost drives
a black coach and four about the Devonshire lanes on stormy nights.

Another version of the story says that Drake sold his soul to the
Devil in return for the defeat of the Spaniards, and this is why his
spirit is doomed to wander. Both tales are basically versions of the
same thing, that Drake belonged to the Old Religion.

There is a headland at Plymouth, to the west of the docks and over-
looking the entrance to Devonport, which is called Devil's Point. It
was here that Drake is said to have foregathered with the witches, in
order to raise the storms that harried the Spanish ships and played
a large part in the Armada's defeat. This headland is still believed to
be haunted as a result of the witchcraft that took place there in olden
times.

DRUIDS, THEIR LINKS WITH WITCHCRAFT

The question of what links, if any, Druidism had with witchcraft is
a difficult one, because our knowledge of Druidism is very incomplete.

However, we do know that there were Druidesses as well as

Druids; and when Druidism was suppressed these women may well have joined the cult of witchcraft. Lewis Spence, in his book *The Mysteries of Britain* (Riders, London), regards witchcraft as "a broken-down survival of Iberian-Keltic religion."

He points out that there is a likeness between the traditional cauldron of the witches and the Sacred Cauldron of Inspiration presided over by the Goddess Cerridwen, who was revered by the Bards and the Druids.

In fact, says Spence, the Mysteries of Cerridwen were still being celebrated in Wales in the twelfth century A.D. Hywel, Prince of North Wales, was initiated into the Lesser Mysteries of Cerridwen in 1171. The goddess was addressed as "the moon, lofty and fair", just as the goddess of the witches was. And, again like the witch-goddess, she had a dark as well as a bright aspect, as indeed any goddess of Nature is bound to possess, if she is to be a true deity and not a mere sentimental picture.

I have been told by a present-day Chosen Chief of a Druid Order that Druidism is not in fact a religion, but rather a philosophy and a way of life. If this viewpoint is accepted, then there is no reason why the Druids should not have respected the pagan religion of their day, much as the Greek philosophers did that of their country, while reasoning among themselves as to the true nature of the gods and goddesses whom the common people worshipped.

From the surviving relics which we have of Druid philosophy, handed down by the Bards of Wales and from other sources of Celtic tradition, we find that they had an important belief in common with witches, namely that of reincarnation.

The Druids taught that the human soul had to pass through a number of existences in Abred, the Circle of Necessity, before it could attain to Gwynvyd, the Circle of Blessedness. Abred was the condition of earthly life; but once it had been transcended, and its lessons learned, the soul would return to it no more. Three things hindered the soul's progression, and caused it to fall back into the changes of Abred: namely, pride, falsehood and cruelty.

When Charles Godfrey Leland was carrying on his researches into the witch lore of Italy in the late nineteenth century, he found the idea of reincarnation cherished among the witches of the Romagna as a secret and esoteric doctrine, which was believed in but not much talked about. He testifies to this in his *Etruscan-Roman Remains in Popular Tradition* (Fisher Unwin, London, 1892).

The belief in reincarnation was widespread in the ancient world; so it is not really surprising that witches and Druids should have it in common, nor by any means impossible that it should have been transmitted by them to the present day. (*See* REINCARNATION.)

What is perhaps a closer link is the fact that the Great Sabbats of the witches are identical with the four great yearly festivals of the Druids in Celtic countries; namely Beltane (30th April), Lughnassadh (1st August), Samhain (31st October) and Imbolc or Oimelc (2nd February).

April 30th is of course May Eve, the witches' Walpurgis Night; Lughnassadh is Lammas; Samhain is Halloween; and Imbolc is Candlemas.

The four lesser Sabbats of the equinoxes and solstices were also observed by the Druids. Their Druidic names are Alban Arthan for the winter solstice; Alban Eilir for the spring equinox; Alban Hefin for the summer solstice; and Alban Elfed for the autumn equinox.

These eight ritual occasions divide the year like the spokes of a great wheel; and they are in fact the natural progress of the seasons. The Celts very sensibly regarded the British Isles as having only two real seasons, namely summer and winter. Summer began on May Day, and was welcomed with the fires of Beltane, Maypole dancing, and the singing of May carols. Six months later, on 31st October, came Samhain, meaning 'summer's end'; and all the witchery of Halloween, when the forces of winter, dark and mysterious, gained the ascendancy.

Both May Eve and Halloween are still sometimes called Mischief Night in various parts of Britain, on account of the pranks and revelry enjoyed on these occasions. They were the in-between times, when the year was swinging on its hinges, the doors of the Other World were open, and anything could happen.

Parallels between the old Druidism and the religion of the witches are certainly there. However, in the opinion of the writer they are really indicative of a common origin in ancient nature worship, rather than meaning that either cult is derived from the other.

As well as the moon goddess Cerridwen, the Druids also reverenced a version of the Horned God. This was Hu Gadarn, who was associated with the cult of the bull. The name Hu meant that which is all-pervading. The bards used it as a title meaning the divine omniscience and omnipresence. In other words, Hu was the personification of certain attributes of deity, rather than a personal god.

Hu Gadarn was a god of fertility. According to the Bardic Triads, he was the first who taught men to plough and cultivate the land. His worship survived to a startlingly late date.

The historical evidence of this is in a letter from Ellis Price to Cromwell, secretary to Henry VIII, dated 6th April, 1538, referring to pagan survivals to the Diocese of St. Asaph, in Wales:

> There ys an Image of Darvellgadarn within the said diocese, in whome the people have so greate confidence, hope, and truste, that they comme dayly a pilgramage unto hym, somme with kyne, other with oxen or horsis, and the reste withe money; in so much that there was fyve or syxe hundrethe pilgrimes to a mans estimacion, that offered to the said image the fifte daie of this presente monethe of Aprill. The innocente people hath ben sore aluryd and entised to worship the saide image, in so much that there is a commyn sayinge as yet amongst them that who so ever will offer anie thinge to the saide Image of Darvellgadarn, he hathe power to fatche hym or them that so offers oute of Hell when they be dampned.

The authorities took action upon this information. In the same year the image was taken to Smithfield and burned. With it was burned also a man, described as a "friar", who bore the same name as the image. He was evidently a priest of the cult of Darvellgadarn; and the latter name was a combination of part of the name of Hu Gadarn and—what? Could "Darvell" have been the Welsh-speaking countryside version of Devil, or even the Romany Duvel? He seems to have been a lord of the Other World, as well as a bestower of good fortune, to whom people made offerings for that reason.

For many years, Druidism was neglected and frowned upon because of its pre-Christian origin. Today, however, with a general widening of religious tolerance, and the renaissance of occult studies generally, people are beginning to look again at native Celtic traditions. There are a number of circles today which hold regular Druidic meetings, beside the well-known annual gathering at Stonehenge for the summer solstice.

Although we know that the Druids whom Caesar, Pliny and other classical writers described (and sometimes slandered), were not the actual builders of Stonehenge, nevertheless the ideas of the Druids, and their system of philosophy from Nature are in harmony with the beliefs that inspired the erection of the great stone circles and menhirs that enrich our landscape. The spirit of the old mystic sense of beauty, and faith in the unseen, overshadows both Druidic philosophy and the Craft of the Wise alike.

Wordsworth, a poet of Nature, wrote:

> Though in the depths of sunless groves, no more
> The Druid priests the hallowed oak adore;
> Yet, for the Initiate, rocks and whispering trees
> Do still perform mysterious offices.

The old paganism arose from a sense of the numinous, immanent in all Nature. If we follow all religion back far enough, we shall find its common source in this. (*See also* STONES AND STONE CIRCLES.)

E

EASTERN LINKS WITH EUROPEAN WITCHCRAFT

It has not been generally realised by writers on witchcraft, that some very interesting links exist between European witchcraft and the Arabic and Near Eastern countries. However, some information about this has been published by Idris Shah Sayid, in his remarkable book *The Sufis* (W. H. Allen, London, 1964). Further details have appeared in *A History of Secret Societies* by Arkon Daraul (Tandem Books, London, 1965 and Citadel Press, New York, 1962).

We may never know the full story of what communications there were between the secret mystics of the East and those of the West. However, two points of contact certainly did exist in medieval times. One was the Moorish kingdom in Spain, which lasted from A.D. 711 until 1492. The scholarship of the Moorish doctors was far in advance of that of most of Europe. They gave us the Arabic number signs which we still use today, a great advance upon the clumsy Roman numerals; and many terms in astronomy and chemistry, such as 'azimuth', 'alcohol' and so on, are derived from Arabic. So are the astrological terms 'zenith' and 'nadir'.

It was natural that men of such comparatively advanced scientific learning should be accused of sorcery. However, the Moors also had a considerable interest in occult philosophy, alchemy, astrology, and magic generally. The city of Toledo in Spain became notorious all over Europe as a place where the magic arts were studied; so much so that the word 'Toledo' was used as a cryptic password among occultists. Its apparently casual mention in conversation was a clue that the speaker was interested in occult matters, and sought fellow students.

Saragossa and Salamanca also had a reputation for magical studies and practices. The name of the wizard Michael Scot was associated with Salamanca; and while many of the stories told about him are legendary, nevertheless he seems really to have existed. To have studied among the Moors was a necessary preliminary to achieving mastery of the occult arts, according to many old tales. Christian Rosenkreutz, the supposed founder of the Rosicrucians, was said to have journeyed to Fez in Morocco, and there to have acquired some of his learning.

The other point of contact between East and West was the Order of the Knights Templars. One of the reasons why this very important and powerful order of knighthood fell out of favour with the Church, and was suppressed, was that they were getting altogether too friendly with the Saracens instead of slaughtering them as became good Christian men.

The contrast of character between the noble and chivalrous Saladin, the Saracen leader, and the venal, squabbling chiefs of the Crusaders, had not been without its impression upon thinking people; all the more so as the Crusades, in spite of fierce fighting and bloodshed, had most undeniably failed.

The Knights Templars were accused of heresy, and of worshipping a deity called Baphomet, who bore a strong resemblance to the god of the witches. (*See* BAPHOMET.) Idris Shah Sayid has suggested that his name is derived from the Arabic Abufihamat, meaning 'Father of Understanding'.

The Arabic words for 'wisdom' and for 'black' closely resemble each other; hence to the Arabic mystics 'black' became a synonym for 'wisdom'. This is based upon the Arabic Qabalah, which, like the Hebrew Qabalah, derives occult meanings from the numerical values of the letters of words.

The most famous order of Arabic mystics is that of the Sufis. This order still exists today, and claims to date back to before the time of Mohammad and the foundation of Islam, although its members respect Islam in their practices. The late Gerald Gardner, who contributed so much to the present-day rebirth of witchcraft, was also a member of a Sufi order, and had travelled extensively in the East.

The suggestion had been made that the triumph of Islam, and the rapid spread of the Mohammadan creed, caused a number of people in the affected Near Eastern countries, who adhered to older faiths, to become somewhat insecure, and to leave their native lands and travel Westward. It also caused some of the devotees of older faiths to go underground, even as the spread of Christianity had done, and to form secret societies and cults. Thus an Eastern version of witchcraft sprang up; and eventually there was a certain infiltration, and exchange of ideas, between the Wise Ones of the East and those of the West.

Hugh Ross Williamson based his fascinating historical novel, *The Silver Bowl,* first published by Michael Joseph (London) in 1948, upon the idea that there was an Eastern as well as a European version of the Craft of the Wise, and that some communication had taken place between the two.

Some writers have gone so far as to suggest that the *medieval* version of witchcraft in Europe, with its organisation of Sabbats, covens of thirteen and so on, was actually a Saracenic import, grafted on to the old moon-magic cult of Diana and Herodias. How much truth there is in this it is hard to say; because it is the old question of finding resemblances between two things, and then asking, "Is this evidence that the one was derived from the other, or is it evidence that both had a common origin in the distant past?" The writer inclines to the latter view, upon the present state of our knowledge.

However, it certainly does seem possible that the European witch cult, languishing under the increasing power and influence of Christianity, received a transfusion of new life and new ideas from the East. The possibility of such communication, as we have seen, was there. Also, as Gerald Gardner mentioned in *Witchcraft Today* (Riders, London, 1954), the witches have a tradition among themselves that their cult came from the East.

Idris Shah tells us of the Aniza Bedouin, whose great Sufi teacher was Abu el-Atahiyya (A.D. 748–*circa* 828). His circle of disciples were called The Wise Ones; and they commemorated him by the symbol of a torch between the horns of a goat. The tribal name Aniza means 'goat'.

After the death of Abu el-Atahiyya a group of his followers migrated to Spain, which was then under the rule of the Moors. The Maskhara Dervishes, called 'The Revellers', are connected with this teacher and with the Aniza tribe.

However, this symbol of a horned head with a torch between the horns is much, much older than the time of Abu el-Atahiyya. It can in fact be traced back to Ancient India. (*See* ANTIQUITY OF WITCHCRAFT.) It also bears some resemblance to the horned headdresses of Ancient Egyptian gods and goddesses. These often take the form of two horns with a shining disc between them, which the torch or candle is a substitute for. The god Amoun, the god of mystery and the infinite, was represented as a ram, with an elaborate horned head-dress. At Mendes an actual sacred ram was adored with strange rites, described by Herodotus. Amoun was the primeval god of the Egyptians. He was believed to be able to take any form that he wished; all other deities were his various forms. Therefore his names were many; but his real name was secret. He was especially associated with all the gods of fertility, because he was Life, the Life Force itself.

The representations of Amoun as Harsaphes, the ram-headed god of the Faiyum district, are particularly beautiful and interesting, in this respect. They show a man with a ram's head (or mask) having a disc between the horns, probably representing the sun, and also the Atef Crown of Osiris; one of the most splendid and impressive versions of the Horned God, an example of which can be seen in the British Museum.

It seems probable that the Aniza Bedouin were named after one of the ancient North African representations of the Horned God; and that Abu el-Atahiyya's followers, the Wise Ones, adopted this symbol of a horned head with a light between the horns, because it not only commemorated their master and teacher, but also had an older and deeper meaning for them.

The Maskhara Dervishes, who, as we have seen, are connected with this great Sufi teacher, have given us the two words, 'masquerade' and 'mascara'. They conducted wild dances dressed in animal masks; and they also used a cosmetic to blacken their faces in the course of some of their rituals. Hence the 'mascara' that women use today for eye-paint. The purpose of this may have been the ritual connection between 'black' and 'wisdom', noted above.

In Britain, there are the Morris Dancers, today as British as roast beef, but their name means the 'Moorish dancers', because they used to black their faces when they danced, so that they should not be recognised. Their dancing is believed to bring luck by its performance; and it is certainly a splendid and exciting thing to see, and very much alive today. Some historians think that the Morris Dance was brought to Britain from Spain, probably by John of Gaunt and his followers in the time of Edward III. John of Gaunt, the brother of the Black Prince, spent much time in Spain, and had some hopes of becoming King of Castile.

Arkon Daraul, in his book on *Secret Societies,* previously referred to, tells of a very curious secret cult, of a mystical and magical nature, called 'The Two-Horned Ones' or Dhulqarneni. This arose in Morocco, and crossed into Spain as had the Aniza cult. The Moslem authorities frowned upon it, and tried to put it down; but nevertheless it became fairly widespread.

Its devotees believed that they could raise magical power by dancing in a circle. They had some association with moon worship; and they said the Moslem prayers backwards and invoked El Aswad, the 'Black Man', to help them. Both men and women were admitted to this cult, and they were marked at their initiation with a small wound from a ritual knife, called Al-dhamme, the 'blood-letter'. This word resembles the witches' Athame.

They met by night at the cross-roads; and their meetings were called the Zabbat, meaning 'the Forceful or Powerful One'. The circle of initiates was called the Kafan, which is Arabic for winding-sheet, because each member wore nothing but a plain white robe over his naked body. Thus attired, they would have looked like a company of ghosts, and probably scared off any intruder. The witches adopted frightening disguises for this purpose also.

The Dhulqarneni carried a forked staff, the symbol of horns, the sign of power. Early representations of witches show them riding upon forked staffs. The name 'Sabbat' for witch-meetings of special importance has never been satisfactorily explained; but 'coven' is a word which is connected with the Latin *conventus,* and meant a cult-group of thirteen people. (*See* COVEN.)

However, the circle of the Dhulqarneni was a circle of twelve people with a leader; and so are the circles of the Sufis at the present day.

The leader of the circle of the Horned Ones was called Rabbana, 'Lord'. He was also called the 'Black Man' or the 'blacksmith'. Blacksmiths have always been supposed to have magical powers; and the old ballad of "The Coal-Black Smith" is regarded as a witches' song. It is also called "The Two Magicians", and tells how a blacksmith and a witch had a magical contest, which ended with them becoming lovers. Robin or Robinet is a name which was sometimes given to the 'Devil' of a witches' coven, and it bears a resemblance to Rabbana. It is also an old word for phallus. The terms the 'Black Man' or the 'Man in Black' were also used of a male coven-leader.

The cult of the Horned Ones continued among the Berber people of North Africa up to comparatively recent times, and may still exist. There are stories of followers of this cult dancing round lighted bonfires, carrying a staff which they call 'the goat'. They have a secret

Grand Master called Dhulqarnen, the 'Two-Horned Lord', who is reincarnated upon earth every 200 years.

It is remarkable from our point of view that this cult should flourish among the Berbers; because the Berbers are racially akin to the small, dark, long-headed people who inhabited Britain in the Neolithic period, and who migrated from North Africa. The people of pre-dynastic Egypt are also racially related to them.

The Berbers are regarded in North Africa as a race of sorcerers, whose outward submission to Islam covers the hidden practice of strange and heretical creeds. They hold women in great esteem, as repositories of ancestral wisdom and magic. This is in marked contrast to the usual Arabic attitude of contempt for women, as the inferior sex. Many strange travellers' tales of Berber magic have come out of North Africa. They are said to have a secret language, in which, and only in which, magical matters can rightly be discussed.

The relationship between such Eastern seekers of wisdom as the Sufis, and the European witches, or devotees of wise-craft, is a subject of which we know all too little. Future study may, we hope, reveal more.

One belief the Sufis and the witches have in common is that of *baraka,* meaning 'blessing' or 'power'. This is not a mere metaphysical abstraction, but something that can be actually raised and transmitted. The Sufi utterance, *"Baraka bashad"*, "May the blessing be", is very similar to the greeting of the witches, "Blessed be". It also resembles the time-honoured Word of Power, 'Abracadabra', meaning *Ha Brachab Dabarah,* 'Speak the blessing'. The essential meaning of these concepts is practically the same, and can be paralleled by the *mana* of the Kahunas of Hawaii.

The Jewel in the Lotus, by Allen Edwardes (Tandem Books, London, 1965), gives an extraordinary insight into the sexuality of the East, which is inextricably bound up with Eastern religion. It describes some of the Eastern holy men, and the way in which sexual intercourse with them was regarded as a privilege conferring sanctity. This is reminiscent of the way in which medieval witches are said to have regarded their Devil, the 'Man in Black', when he presided over the coven wearing his ritual grand array, the horned mask, animal skins, etc.

It is implied in many of the accounts of old-time witchcraft that the Devil of the coven had a kind of *droit de seigneur* over the young girls and women who joined, which they probably found agreeable rather than otherwise. We find, in the very detailed accounts of the confessions of witches, preserved by Pierre de Lancre (*Tableau de l'Inconstance des Mauvais Anges,* Paris, 1613), the allegation that the Devil *"oste la virginité des filles"* at the time when he joined male and female witches in marriage.

Some holy men of the East regarded it as a sacred duty to do the same thing, namely to deflower virgins. Some Western critics have jeered at Eastern religions for this reason, regarding them as a mere hypocritical cloak for the activities of shameless libertines. In doing so, they have completely failed to understand the ideas and emotions of Eastern people, who regarded sex as a most sacred manifestation of the Life Force, and therefore of the Creative Divinity behind it. There was nothing hypocritical, or to them immoral, in the phallic and sexual rites of Eastern people; rites which, in fact, were practised all over the world in bygone days.

This regard for sexual contact with the persons of holy men, as conferring sanctity and blessing, throws a new light upon the many stories of the *Osculum infame,* or so-called 'obscene kiss', supposed to have been conferred upon the Devil of the coven by his followers on ritual occasions.

The Jewel in the Lotus tells us that in many areas the wandering holy man, the Dervish or Sufi, was greeted by devotees with an extraordinary token of respect. This consisted of kissing him upon the lips, then lifting his robe and kissing him successively upon the navel, the penis, the testicles, and the buttocks.

This is the exact way in which Jeanette d'Abadie, a young witch of the Basses-Pyrenees, confessed to greeting the Devil in 1609; *"que le Diable luy faiscoit baiser son visage, puis le nombril, puis le membre viril, puis son derrière",* says Pierre de Lancre (op. cit.). ("The Devil made her kiss his face, then the navel, then the virile member, then his backside".) This charge of 'obscene homage' was often made against witches.

In 1597 Marion Grant of the Aberdeen witches was accused of rendering homage to the Devil; who, it was said, "causit thee kiss him in divers parts, and worship him on thy knees as thy lord". And earlier, in 1303, no less a person than a Bishop of Coventry was sent to Rome to face a similar accusation, the Devil in this case having been in the shape of a "sheep" (probably a ram is meant, or a man wearing a ram's head mask). The Bishop managed to clear himself of the charge.

This latter case, according to Margaret Murray, is the earliest recorded one in Britain, of this kind of worship of the Horned God or his representative. It may therefore give some indication, if the theory of Eastern influence is correct, of at what period this influence began to show itself upon the Old Religion in Britain.

The Knights Templars also were accused of having a ritual kiss of this kind, demanded by the initiating Master from the men who were newly admitted to the order. This may be another indication of their absorption of Eastern religious ideas and customs, probably from the Sufis. "According to the articles of accusation, one of the ceremonies of initiation required the novice to kiss the receiver on the mouth, on the *anus,* or the end of the spine, on the navel, and on the *virga virilis.*" (*Two Essays on the Worship of Priapus,* Richard Payne Knight and Thomas Wright, London, 1865.)

The exact similarity of this very extraordinary ritual act, in the case of the Knights Templars, the witches and the devotees of certain Sufi holy men, seems beyond coincidence. It is a clue to the real meaning of the notorious *Osculum infame,* and to the strange and secret links between the occult circles of the East and those of Europe in past centuries.

ELEMENTS, SPIRITS OF THE

Occultists of olden time regarded the spirits of Nature as being divided into four groups, according to the Four Elements of Life. The spirits of earth were called gnomes; those of water were called undines; the unseen inhabitants of air were named sylphs; and the spirits of fire were known as salamanders.

These names are traditional; however, 'gnome' seems to be derived from the Greek *gnoma,* meaning 'knowledge'. So the gnomes are 'the knowing ones'. 'Undine' is from the Latin *unda,* a wave; they are 'the creatures of the waves', the nymphs of the waters. 'Sylph' is from the Greek *silphe,* a butterfly; they are depicted as beautiful, delicate forms with butterfly wings.

The word 'salamander' is less certain in origin; but it may be connected with the Greek word *salambe,* a fireplace. The salamander was visualised as being like a lizard or small dragon; and there is a kind of lizard called by naturalists a salamander, perhaps after this old belief. However, the salamander of the old occultists was a spirit which dwelt in fire. The old Christmas game of 'Snapdragon', played by snatching raisins from a dish of burning brandy, may take its name from this old idea of the fire-elemental as a dragon-like creature, or 'fire-drake'.

Benvenuto Cellini, in his memoirs (*The Life of Benvenuto Cellini, Written by Himself*) claimed to have seen one when he was a little boy. (He lived between 1500 and 1571.) It was a very cold day, he tells us, and a big fire of oak logs was burning in the room. His father was sitting by the fire, amusing himself by playing a viol and singing. "Happening to look into the fire, he espied in the middle of the most burning flames a little creature like a lizard, which was sporting in the core of the intensest coals." Benvenuto's father promptly called him and his sister to see this strange sight, and gave young Benvenuto a good box on the ear to make him remember it, on account of the great rarity of such a thing being seen. (Though Cellini grew up to have even stranger occult experiences, if we are to believe all the stories he tells in his colourful memoirs.)

Friendly elementals are believed by many occultists and witches to assist them in their magical work. The sign of the pentagram or five-pointed star, is potent to control elementals. It should have one point above, when used for this purpose; because then it represents Spirit ruling over the kingdoms of the Elements.

Some magical practitioners regard the Four Elements as being literally kingdoms. They give the names of the elemental kings as: Paralda, the King of the Sylphs; Niksa, the King of the Undines; Djin, the King of the Salamanders; and Ghob, the King of the Gnomes. (The latter may be the origin of the word 'goblins' for small, tricksy spirits.) (*See* FAMILIARS.)

ESBAT

The Esbat is the monthly meeting of a witches' coven. It takes place at the time of full moon.

The full moon is not only the flood-tide of psychic power. In the olden days, before the introduction of street lighting and paved roads, it was the most practicable time for people to travel about the countryside.

Those who made their way to witches' meetings would wear a black cloak with a hood, and this has become a traditional part of a witch's attire. Its original purpose was camouflage. A person dressed like this can quickly merge into the shadows on a moonlit night. Also, if they do happen to be seen, one cloaked and hooded figure looks very much like another. It is difficult even to tell if it is a man or a woman; let alone recognise someone, perhaps as a fellow villager.

To a witch today, the traditional black cloak and hood symbolise night and secrecy. This attire has no particular connection with black magic, except in the imaginations of thriller writers.

The Esbat is a smaller and less solemn occasion than the Sabbat. For the latter, several covens might foregather but the Esbat is a local affair. It may be held for some particular coven business, or simply for fun and enjoyment. The word 'Esbat' comes from the Old French s'esbattre, meaning to frolic and amuse oneself.

Because there are thirteen *lunar* months in a year, there are generally thirteen full-moon Esbats. This is the probable origin of the magic of the number thirteen.

Some old writers on witchcraft had the idea that the Esbat was held on a particular day of the week. This, however, is not so; its date is dependent upon the moon.

The rites that take place vary somewhat, from one coven to another. Basically, however, they consist of dancing, of invoking the Old Gods, and of partaking of wine and probably a small feast as well, in the gods' honour.

The Great Old Ones, the souls of great witches who have passed beyond this earth, are also remembered. Thanks are given for past favours, and prayers may be said for something that is needed, or some particular magic worked for it. News is exchanged; magical objects consecrated; sometimes, some divination is performed for the future. Full moon is a particularly good time for the latter, or for the exercise of any kind of psychic power.

Sometimes a man and a woman who wish to be partners in magic, are joined together ceremonially by the leader of the coven. They are then regarded by the rest of the coven as being married according to the laws of the Craft. This ceremony, like that of initiation, may take place at either an Esbat or a Sabbat. Contrary to popular belief, witches are not sexually promiscuous people. In fact, if the full truth were known, they are probably less so than some of those who write lurid articles denouncing them.

Another thing which may happen at an Esbat is the presentation of a baby to the Old Gods. This is done by its parents, when the latter are members of the coven. It is the witch equivalent of baptism.

This is the truth behind the horrid old stories of babies being offered to the Devil. In the old days, it would have been very dangerous for parents to fail to get their child baptised. When church-going was compulsory by law, as it was in times past, those who failed to observe the ordinances of the Church immediately put themselves under suspicion. So, of course, the witch parents would have to present the child ultimately for Christian baptism; but they dedicated it to the Old Gods first.

This compulsory baptism into the Christian Church was some-times bitterly resented; and this fact is the explanation of another old story, namely that when people were initiated as witches, they denied their Christian baptism. If they came from witch families, and knew that their parents had been forced to have them baptised, they quite probably did make a formal denial of this kind, simply for their own satisfaction.

At the Esbat also, ideas can be exchanged and instruction in witch-craft given. Old magical legends are recited, and songs are sung. There are some old ballads that are traditionally associated with witchcraft. "Greensleeves" is one of them. The lady dressed in "the fairies' fatal green" is the goddess herself. Another song is "Hares on the Mountain"; the hare is traditionally associated with the moon and with witches. The old ballad of "The Coal-Black Smith" is gen-erally regarded as a witches' song also.

In fact, the music of the witches' Esbats and Sabbats was mainly the popular tunes of the day. In the accounts of Scottish witchcraft, there is mention of a number of lively and bawdy old ballads being sung and danced to, much to the displeasure of the Kirk; and else-where it was probably much the same. The instruments played were the old pipe and tabor, the bagpipes in Scotland, the fiddle, the tam-bourine and the recorder.

Today the recorder has all too often been exchanged for the tape-recorder when witch-meetings are held indoors; although the battery-operated portable tape-recorders and record players have been quite a boon to modern witches, in providing music for their meetings, indoors or out.

EVIL EYE

The idea of the Evil Eye is one of the world's most time-honoured and widespread magical beliefs.

Old John Aubrey, in his *Miscellanies* (London, 1696), summed it up very briefly and to the point: "The glances of envy and malice do shoot also subtilly; the eye of the malicious person does really infect and make sick the spirit of the other."

To be able to put the Evil Eye upon a person is one of the main powers attributed to black witchcraft. People capable of this were called 'eye-biting witches'. Their victims, who pined away or suffered misfortune by reason of this deadly glance, were said to be 'overlooked', 'fascinated', 'eye-blighted'; and one curious English dialect term calls them 'owl-blasted', perhaps from the idea of the owl's staring eyes.

The effects of the Evil Eye might be felt in two ways: either by physical or nervous illness or by a run of bad luck and unfortunate events. The belief in the possibility of this is still almost as lively as it was in the Middle Ages. We often hear people saying of someone that they "put the mockers on it"; meaning that their influence ruined something—or somebody. This is really only another way of saying 'They put the Evil Eye on it'.

When certain 'labour rackets' were being investigated in New York in 1957, the investigating committee found that a man reputed to possess the Evil Eye had actually been hired by an employer to intimidate his staff. The man would come in once or twice a week, and stare fixedly at the men, in order to keep them in fear; and apparently he succeeded in doing so.

This story, fantastic as it sounds, proves one thing; namely, that human nature and the human mind are basically the same beneath the sky-scrapers of New York in modern times, as they were centuries ago, in narrow medieval streets or remote villages.

A few years ago in Britain, a society lady whose tennis and garden parties were persistently spoiled by rain, told a gossip columnist: "I am going to get myself a string of blue beads. Someone is putting the Evil Eye on me."

Bright blue beads as a preventative of the Evil Eye are popular in the Near East. They may be of glass or pottery; it is the brightness and clarity of the colour that matters, not the expensiveness or otherwise of the necklace.

Amulets against the Evil Eye are of very many kinds, and are often attractive and artistic in their form. The Hand of Fatima, for instance, is frequently made of silver-gilt, jewelled with semi-precious stones. This representation of a hand is named in this way today out of compliment to Fatima, the daughter of the Prophet Mohammed; but the figure of a hand as symbolic warder-off of evil is very old indeed. In fact, the prints of hands found on the painted walls of Stone Age caves may have had this significance.

This amulet derives from man's instinctive gesture of putting up his hand before his face, to ward off the baleful glance of the Evil Eye. Bronze figures of hands, called the *mano pantea,* stood in Roman houses in ancient days, for the same purpose. They were encrusted with many other amuletic figures, such as serpents, lizards, acorns, pine-cones, horns and so on. The position of the fingers on these pre-Christian amulets is the same as that used today for blessing, namely with the thumb and first two fingers upright, and the other two fingers closed.

Two other finger gestures against the Evil Eye are the *mano cornuta,* or 'making horns', and the *mano in fica* or 'the fig'. These are very popular in Latin countries, but are fairly well known almost everywhere. The *mano cornuta* consists of lifting up the first finger and the little finger, while folding the other two fingers and the thumb into the palm. The *mano in fica* is made by closing all the fingers into a fist, and thrusting the thumb between the first and second fingers. 'The fig' is a synonym for the female genitals. Both these gestures are signs used by witches, as well as being defences against the Evil Eye.

Little amulets of hands making these signs can still be bought in Britain and on the Continent. These gestures are of very great antiquity. Ancient Egyptian examples of the *mano in fica* have been found; and the paintings in Etruscan tombs show dancers holding up their hands in the position of the *mano cornuta.*

The *mano in fica* was known in Britain too, as the old folk-rhyme shows:

> Witchy, witchy, I defy thee!
> Four fingers round my thumb,
> Let me go quietly by thee.

Dean Ramsay, writing about his schooldays in Yorkshire between about 1800 and 1810, told how he and his classmates "used to put one thumb between the first and second finger, pointing it downwards, as the infallible protection against the evil influences of one particularly malevolent and powerful witch".

Another means of baffling the Evil Eye was by means of twining and interlacing knots. It was thought that the malicious glance, on being confronted by a pattern like this, was caused to wander and lose its force. A relic of this belief can be found in the elaborately patterned silver buckles sometimes worn on their belts by nurses.

In olden days a good deal of sickness was blamed on to the Evil Eye; so a nurse in particular had to be able to protect herself. Hence the custom arose of wearing buckles of this kind; though present-day nurses may not realise the origin of it.

The elaborate interlacings and intertwinings of Celtic and Saxon decorative art probably arose from the same idea. Such decoration protected against the Evil Eye; so it was fortunate and good to enrich things with.

Another remedy against the Evil Eye was to have something to outstare it. So representations of eyes were worn, in particular the so-called 'eye-beads' made of black and white onyx, cut and polished so as to resemble an eye. Brooches, rings and men's cuff-links are also seen today made from this semi-precious stone. In Ancient Egypt the amulet called the Eye of Horus was worn for the same purpose.

Bright, shining witch-balls were hung in the windows of old houses, to reflect the sinister looks of dangerous passers-by back upon themselves. (*See* WITCH-BALLS.)

The tremendous number of different amulets against the Evil Eye, of practices and ceremonies to avert it and of various names for it in different languages, all show the universality of this belief. The Ancient Romans called it the *oculus fascinus;* the Greeks knew it as *baskania.* In Italian, it is *malocchio,* or *la jettatura.* Germany calls it *böse blick;* Spain *mal ojo;* France *mauvais oeil.* In far-off India, it is feared as *drishtidosham.* Old-time Gaelic-speaking Scotland called it *chronachaidh,* and to the Irish it was *droch-shuil.*

And an old Gaelic charm, to be spoken over one who had been 'overlooked', ran like this:

> The eye that went over,
> And came back,
> That reached to the bone,
> And reached the marrow,
> I will lift from off thee,
> And the King of the Elements
> Will aid me.

Of course, all charms have to be spoken three times; and this one was supposed to work best on a Thursday or a Sunday.

But how was the Evil Eye supposed to be *put on?* Innumerable are the remedies against it; but information about how it casts its evil spell is scanty. Very often people are believed to be born with this power; and frequently without any wish for it on their part.

A number of famous people have been credited—or should one say discredited?—with possessing this malign power. Lord Byron, the poet, was one. So was the late King of Spain, Alfonso XIII, and Napoleon III, the Emperor of France. Even Pope Pius IX, and his successor, Pope Leo XIII, were believed to have the Evil Eye; not because they were wicked, but simply because they had been born with this fatal gift, whether they wanted it or not.

The person who is *different* is the one whom human nature fears. Thus, among the generally fair-haired and blue-eyed English, it is the dark, flashing eye of the Gypsy, the Latin or the Oriental that raises fearful thoughts of fascination and sorcery. But among the Spaniards, *blondes* are feared! "Las rubias son venenosas", "Blondes are poison", runs the old Spanish proverb. The dark Moroccans think that people with *blue* eyes are the ones to beware of.

"The eyes are the windows of the soul", says the old proverb; and this can be interpreted for good or evil. The silent curse of the Evil Eye, *which came from the soul within,* was more dreaded than openly-spoken maledictions. Its very silence gave it the pent-up concentration of something formulated with one's whole being. And if a truly deep and burning anger were behind it—who knows?

In 1616 a woman called Janet Irving was brought to trial in Scotland on charges of witchcraft. It was stated in evidence that "the Devil" had told her: "If she bore ill-will to any body, to look on them with open eyes, and pray evil for them in his name, and she should get her heart's desire".

"The Devil" may have meant the leader of the coven, who instructed her in magic, or perhaps 'Old Hornie', the god of the witches himself. But this description is the only one I know of the real laying-on of the Evil Eye.

For after all, if witchcraft had no teeth and claws to defend itself, would it have endured through centuries of persecution?

The effect of the belief in the Evil Eye in Scotland (and elsewhere) was sometimes turned to good account by cunning old ladies, who would otherwise have lived in dire poverty. As the old Scots song tells us:

> Kimmer gets maut, an' Kimmer gets meal,
> And cantie lives Kimmer, right couthie an' hale;
> Kimmer gets bread, an' Kimmer gets cheese,
> An' Kimmer's uncannie een keep her at ease.

And good luck to the "pawkie auld dame"! The lot of the poor

and the unfortunate, in the days before the Welfare State, was often
pitilessly hard. They can scarcely be blamed for turning popular beliefs to their advantage.

The harried and hounded gypsies do the same thing today. How
many people have bought something off a gypsy, not because they
wanted it but because 'you never know'?

EVOCATION

One often finds the words 'evocation' and 'invocation' used in writings about the occult, as if they both meant more or less the same
thing. To a practical occultist, however, this is not so. It is only the
lower orders of spirits which can be evoked; the higher spirits and
the gods are invoked. One invokes a god to the magical circle; one
evokes a spirit into the magical triangle.

This principle holds good both for the craft of the witch and for
ceremonial magic of the kind taught by the books of magic called
grimoires. Most of the latter give directions for forming the magic
circle, protected by sigils of occult potency and by Words of Power;
and outside the circle they depict the triangle of evocation, protected
in a similar manner and drawn in the place where the spirit is expected to appear.

Sometimes a censer of incense is placed within the triangle, so
that the spirit can make itself a body, so to speak, out of the curling
and wavering smoke arising from the censer. This process is helped,
so magicians aver, by blending with the incense a herb called Dittany
of Crete (*Origanum dictamnus*).

Probably the best description in print of what really happens at
a serious attempt at magical evocation, is given in Gerald B. Gardner's historical novel *High Magic's Aid* (Michael Houghton, London,
1949).

The witch, or the white practitioner of the craft at any rate, seldom
meddles with evocation of the type described in the grimoires. (By
'white' in this context, I refer to the type of magic involved, not the
colour of the operator's skin.) The magic of the grimoires, by its own
admission, consists of evoking highly dangerous forces, which are
controlled and compelled by the Names of Power and by the magical
sigils, and made to do one's bidding. These Names of Power are a
strange mixture of Hebrew, Greek and sometimes unknown tongues,
and they usually mean some attribute of God, or some Qabalistic
formula. AGLA, for instance, means *Ateh Gibor Leolam Adonai*,

"Unto Thee be Power for Ever, O Lord"; TETRAGRAMMATON means the Holy Name of four letters, whose true pronunciation was only known to the High Priest of Israel; and so on.

The evocations described in the grimoires are performed by rites which are within the framework of either Judaism or Christianity, however unofficial those rites may be. In the same way, a Mohammedan magician will use the Holy Names of Allah and recite verses from the Koran, in order to make the spirits obey him. Magic has been practised, and continues to be practised, in a thousand forms, all over the world; but its basic principles remain the same.

On this point, the anonymous author of a very rare and remarkable old book, *Art Magic* (Progressive Thinker Publishing House, Chicago, Illinois, 1898), had this to say:

> Let it be borne in mind . . . that such features of each system are but the exoteric forms in which the esoteric principles are wrapped up. They have no real potency beyond the satisfaction they procure to pious minds, that they are engaged in no ceremonials displeasing to their Gods, or contrary to their forms of worship.
>
> Provided always that the magician is duly prepared by fasting, abstinence, prayer, and contemplation—provided that his magnetism is potent and his will all-powerful—the spirits will obey and answer him, whether he conjures them in the name of Buddha, Osiris, Christ or Mahomet. The true potency resides in the quantity and quality of the Astral fluid, by which the operator furnishes means for the use of the spirits, and the power of the will, by which he compels beings less potent than himself to obey him.

This passage illustrates also the essential difference between evocation and invocation. Evocation seeks to *compel* a discarnate entity, presumed to be of a lower order, to obey our summons. Invocation calls upon a spiritual being, which we feel to be at least our equal (as in the case of a human spirit) or our superior; and solemnly *asks* that spirit, angel, or god to grant us the favour we seek.

The endeavour to communicate with spirits of departed human beings is usually a matter of invocation, of providing the necessary conditions and atmosphere and then inviting friendly spirits to communicate. However, attempts at evocation of discarnate humans are sometimes made; for instance, in the case of a malignant haunting, or an unwanted obsession by such a spirit, some magical practitioners would seek to compel the spirit to manifest, and then order it to depart to its proper sphere. In general, however, the spirits summoned by processes of evocation are not human spirits but those of the many orders and types of elementals. (*See* ASTRAL PLANE, THE.)

We find the belief that:

> Millions of spiritual creatures walk the earth
> Unseen, both when we wake and when we sleep

is shared by people of all times and all races. Even today, in our world of motor cars, moon-flights, and television, we still get curious and inexplicable tales of poltergeist disturbances, for instance, or of queer things happening when a fairy rath is disturbed in Ireland.

We also have many eye-witness accounts from people who have seen non-human spirits, such as are usually called elementals. These may be beautiful or hideous, friendly or horribly malignant. Furthermore, the belief that such non-human spirits may become the familiars of magicians, and be commanded by them, is also world-wide. We find it among the occultists of the East, as much as among those of the West.

In general, however, the witch avoids the types of evocation which seek to compel spirits to do one's bidding and seeks the aid only of friendly spirits who willingly lend their assistance.

There is this to be said, nevertheless, about some of the old forms of evocation; namely that they have an extremely potent effect *upon the operator*. They serve to raise the mind of the magician to a magical fever-pitch, in which the inner eye of the mind may open and things be perceived which were veiled before. The rhythmic chanting of some old form of evocation, by its insistent beat, puts the mind into a receptive state.

This is the reason why there is so much stage superstition about Shakespeare's play *Macbeth*. Actors, being sensitive people, regard *Macbeth* with a certain timidity, because they have found that the witches' incantations in the play have a real effect, even if only to cause a shiver. The intensity with which they are uttered, the strangeness of the words, the cumulative rhythm of the chanted spell, all work upon the suggestibility of the person who says them, in the right atmosphere of shadowy, uncanny, anything-may-happen weirdness.

There is an old magical dictum: *"Change not the barbarous names of evocation"*; "the long strings of formidable words which roar and moan through so many conjurations", as Aleister Crowley called them. A basic teaching of witchcraft, as the writer has received it at any rate, is that the real powers of magic are within the magician, and that the purpose of magical ritual with all its adjuncts is to bring them out, to awaken them and set them working. Then things start to happen!

Sometimes, indeed, more starts to happen than the operator is prepared for, or is able to handle. Hence the subject of evocation is one to be approached cautiously and handled with care; as indeed is all practical occultism.

F

FAIRIES AND WITCHES

The relationship between the world of witchcraft and the world of Faerie has always been close; so close, indeed, that it is not easy to draw a precise boundary in these enchanted lands, and to say where one world ends and another begins.

Some writers, notably Margaret Murray, have advanced the theory that the 'fairies' were actually the aboriginal people of these islands, the Little People of the Hills. These small, dark people, displaced by the waves of incoming Celtic settlers from the Continent, took refuge in remote places. They lived in huts roofed over with green turf, an effective form of camouflage which made their dwellings seem at a distance like little hills. They feared the iron weapons of their conquerors, and would flee at the sight of them. But they had subtle and deadly weapons of their own; small, sharp arrowheads of flint, poisoned so that even a slight wound from one of them could be fatal; and, even more dreaded than their 'elf bolts,' the powers of their heathen magic, the uncanny and unholy glamourie that their conquerors feared.

Their friendship was capricious; but, once bestowed, they were faithful, and would work hard for those they liked, seeking no more reward than bowls of simple food, left out for them overnight. However, they had two characteristics which their Celtic neighbours found strange and disconcerting. They were people of the night, who would move and work in darkness, or by moonlight; and they preferred to wear little or no clothing, or the least that the climate would permit.

Respectable housewives who tried to get their small, dark servants to wear decent clothes, were rewarded by 'Brownie' spurning their well-meant gifts of wearing apparel, and going off in a huff.

It is a remarkable fact that in the Ashdown Forest area of Sussex, as late as the nineteenth century, there were, according to local traditions certain small, dark forest-dwellers, clannish, reserved and odd in their ways; and one of their oddities was that they wore little or no clothing when in their own environment. People were afraid to pass through the forest alone, especially at night, on account of these 'yellow-bellies', or 'pikeys', as they were called.

The 'pikeys' were certainly not supernatural beings, however. They were perfectly material humans; and there were certain public houses in the forest they were known to frequent. They had a sort of 'bush-telegraph' among themselves, and the presence of any stranger was immediately noted and intelligence passed around, with remarkable quickness. People were rather afraid of the 'pikeys'. They were also known as 'diddikais'; and this word really means a travelling person with some Romany blood. However, these people did not travel; they were forest-dwellers and always had been.

Their descendants are still to be found in the Ashdown Forest area; though now more or less absorbed into the rest of the community. People like this, living in isolated parts of the country, must have been very much like what Margaret Murray conjectures the fairies to have been.

There are many stories contained in the evidence given in the old witch trials, especially in Scotland, of association between witches and fairies. Some of these stories are very circumstantial. Someone goes to a fairy hill and is welcomed inside. They meet the fairy king and queen and are given food; though the presence of small cattle, 'elf bulls', running around at the entrance to the fairies' dwelling, is rather disconcerting.

Inside, they see people making the deadly 'elf bolts', the flint arrowheads to be dipped in poison. They also see the fairies concocting herbal salves and medicines. They are given instruction in the fairies' herbal cures; but they are threatened that if they talk too much, and betray their hosts' confidence, it will be the worse for them.

There are also strange hints they hear, that every seven years the fairies "pay a teind to hell"; that is, one of their number dies as a human sacrifice. There are even whispers that a 'mortal' may be kidnapped and used for this purpose, instead of one of their own.

The fairy women give birth to children; and a mortal midwife is sometimes called on, in these circumstances, to render aid. Nursing mothers are kidnapped, to be wet-nurses to fairy children; and pretty, fair-haired mortal babies are stolen, and a wizened dark-faced changeling left in their place.

People are thoroughly afraid of the fairies, and propitiate them by calling them the 'Good Neighbours', the 'Good Folk', or the 'People of Peace'. About all these features of fairy-lore, there is nothing necessarily supernatural. They could all refer to members of another race, small indeed in comparison to the rest of the population, but not too small to intermarry with them. There are a number of stories of mortals who married fairies; though the marriages seldom lasted, because the wild Little People of the Heaths refused to adapt themselves to the others' ways.

It is interesting in this connection to note the actual derivation of the word 'heathen'. It means, in fact, the People of the Heath; just as 'pagan' derives from *paganus,* a countryman, a rustic. The original heathens and pagans were people who kept to the old lore of the countryside, and the old gods and spirits of Nature, while the more sophisticated town-dwellers had adopted more 'civilised' forms of religion.

An important source of information about Scottish witch trials in which fairies are mentioned, is Sir Walter Scott's *Letters on Demonology and Witchcraft* (John Murray, London, 1830). From this book we see that association with the fairies featured in the accusations made in the trials of Isobel Gowdie (1662), Bessie Dunlop (1576), Alison Pearson (1588), and John Stewart (date not given). One Andro Man was also accused of associating with the Queen of Elfin, "who had a grip of all the craft"; and Thomas the Rhymer, the famous prophet, gained his psychic powers by favour of the Queen of Faerie, as the old ballad tells us.

In fact, the leading female witch of a Scottish coven was evidently called the Queen of Elphame; a word which is simply the Scottish version of the Old Norse *Alfheim,* the country of the elves, or Fairyland.

The word 'fairy' itself derives from the Old French *faerie,* meaning 'enchantment'. The Realm of Faerie is the realm of enchantment and magic; hence another reason for its association with witches.

It is evident that the fairy lore of the British Isles is made up of a number of different strands. There are actual memories of the Little People of the Hills, as described above; but there is also the fairy who is quite evidently a spiritual creature, a spirit of Nature, and the story of an adventure in the Realm of Faerie which is actually a description of a vivid psychic experience.

In addition to these features of fairy lore, there is the idea of the

Fairy Host as being composed of the souls of the unbaptised, or of those who were 'too good for hell, but too bad for heaven'. Such hosting fairies, who rode past on the rushing wind, were the spirits of the pagan dead, and they were led by gods and heroes of the past.

The Realm of Faerie is often conceived of as being a beautiful but uncanny place which is underground, actually within the earth. It is curious in this respect to compare this belief with the Eastern stories of Agharti.

The antiquarian Thomas Wright, in his essay "On the National Fairy Mythology of England" (in Essays on England in the Middle Ages, Vol I, John Russell Smith, London, 1846), tells us:

> The elves have always had a country and dwelling under ground as well as above ground; and in several parts of England the belief that they descend to their subterraneous abodes through the barrows which cover the bones of our fore-fathers of ancient days is still preserved. There were other ways, however, of approaching the elves' country, and one of the most common was by openings in the rocks and caverns, as we find in the poem of Sir Orfeo, and in the tale of Elidurus, told by Giraldus. The great cave of the peak of Derby was also a road thither, and Gervase of Tilbury has preserved a tale how William Peverell's swineherd ventured once to descend it in search of a brood-sow; and how he found beneath a rich and cultivated country, and reapers cutting the corn. The communication, however, has long been stopped up; and those who go now to explore the wonders of the cavern find their progress stayed by the firm impenetrable rock.

Sometimes, however, stray beings from this underground country appeared in the world of men. Such, for instance, as those described in the weird tale of the Green Children, which is averred as truth by two old English chroniclers, William of Newburgh and Ralph of Coggeshall; though the first-named says it happened in the reign of King Stephen, and the latter that it took place in the reign of Henry II. Gervase of Tilbury also mentions it.

The story goes that two mysterious children, a boy and a girl, were found by peasants at a place called Wolfpitts, in Suffolk. They were lost and weeping; they wore strange garments; and their skin was green. They could speak no English, nor at first would they eat anything except green beans. They were taken to the house of Sir Richard de Calne and cared for. However, the boy sickened and died; but the girl accustomed herself to eating earthly food, and gradually lost her green colour, took on human colouring and learnt our speech.

She said that they came from an underground country, where all the people were green-skinned like themselves. No sun was perceived there; but the land was lit by "a brightness or shining, such as would happen after sunset". She and her brother had been following some sheep or small cattle, and arrived at a cavern. They were lured onward by a sweet sound, like the ringing of bells, and wandered on through the cavern until they came to its end. "Thence, emerging, the excessive brightness of our sun and the unwonted, warm temperature of our air astonished and terrified them. And for a long time they lay upon the edge of the cave." There they were found as aforesaid.

The girl was baptised, and remained as a servant in the house of Sir Richard de Calne. "She showed herself very wanton and lascivious"; but eventually settled down and married a man at King's Lynn, in Norfolk. A strange tale of unsolved mystery!

The wanton young lady from this underground Elfland was only following the traditionally amoral nature of the fairies. The Reverend Robert Kirk, Minister of Aberfoyle in Scotland, also wrote of their naughtiness: "For the Inconvenience of their Succubi, who tryst with Men, it is abominable".

Robert Kirk's book, *The Secret Commonwealth of Elves, Fauns and Fairies* (Scotland, 1691; reprinted with introduction by Andrew Lang, David Nutt, London, 1893), is one of the most curious works to be met with on this subject; the more so as its author was reputed, in the next year after its publication, to have been carried away by the fairies himself. He was walking one evening upon a fairy hill near the manse, when he fell down in a fit or swoon, and was taken for dead. He was accordingly buried in the churchyard of Aberfoyle; but after the funeral his ghost appeared to one of his relations and said that he was not really dead, but a captive in Fairyland. He gave directions as to how he could be liberated. His ghost, he said, would appear at the christening of his posthumous child; and if his cousin Grahame of Duchray would throw his dirk over the head of the appearance, Robert Kirk would be restored to the world of the living. The ghost was indeed seen at the christening; but his cousin was so astonished that he failed to throw the dirk, and the Minister remained in the fairies' power.

Given Mr Kirk's known interest in fairies, and in the second sight, with which his book also deals, it was inevitable at that place and period that such eerie tales should be told of him. However, his book certainly exists; and written as it was only twenty-nine years after the trial of Isobel Gowdie, the Scottish witch whose testimony about her association with the fairies has so intrigued many writers on this subject, it seems to tell against the theory that the fairies were an actual race of aboriginal people.

Robert Kirk's fairies are definitely spiritual beings, "of a middle Nature betwixt Man and Angel". Their bodies are made of "congealled Air", which can be made to appear or disappear at pleasure, and are most easily seen at twilight. He calls the fairies "that abstruse People", and refers to them as "Subterraneans". Those who have the second sight can see the fairies, especially at "the Beginning of each Quarter of the Year", at which time the fairies change their habitations, and travel abroad.

The quarters of the year to which Mr Kirk refers are the old Celtic divisions of the year, Candlemas, May Eve, Lammas and Halloween, when all kinds of uncanny beings were abroad, and when the witches held (and still hold) their Great Sabbats. This belief in fairy activity at these times is also found in Ireland.

He notes that the fairies have tribes or orders among themselves, and live in houses, which are sometimes visible and at other times not so. "They speak but little, and that by the way of whistling, clear, not rough." They had births, marriages, and deaths among them; and even sometimes fought among themselves.

"They live much longer than wee; yet die at last, or at least vanish from that State. 'Tis ane of their Tenets, that nothing perisheth, but (as the Sun and Year) every Thing goes in a Circle, lesser or greater, and is renewed and refreshed in its Revolutions; as 'tis another, that every Bodie in the Creation moves (which is a sort of Life); and that nothing moves, but has another Animal moving on it; and so on, to the utmost minutest Corpuscle that's capable to be a Receptacle of Life." How Mr Kirk obtained this strange glimpse into the secrets of the fairies, he does not tell us; but one receives the impression from his book that he was deeper in mystic things than he cared to state plainly.

About actual witchcraft, he tells us discreetly little; but he says, "The *Tabhaisver,* or Seer, that corresponds with this kind of Familiars, can bring them with a Spell to appear to himself or others when he pleases, as readily as Endor Witch to those of her Kind."

A man called John Walsh, of Netherbury in Dorset, confessed to having converse with the fairies when he was examined upon accusations of witchcraft in 1566. He made a detailed and interesting confession, containing many particulars about his magical practices, which was printed under the title of *The Examination of John Walsh* (John Awdeley, London, 1566). It refers to his relations with the fairies as follows: "He being demanded how he knoweth when any man is bewitched, he saith that he knew it partly by the fairies, and saith that there be three kinds of fairies, white, green and black, which, when he is disposed to use he speaketh with them upon hills whereas there is great heaps of earth, as namely in Dorsetshire. And between the hours of twelve and one at noon, or at midnight, he useth them, whereof, he saith, the black fairies be the worst."

My own opinion is that the fairy creed is a composite of several factors: actual spirits of nature whose presence can sometimes be perceived, but who usually share this world invisibly with humans; souls of the pagan dead, who take the third road that the Fairy Queen showed to Thomas the Rhymer, "the road to fair Elfland," away from either the Christian heaven or the Christian hell; and folk-memories of aboriginal races, now mostly vanished. There may be a fourth factor, the very old and apparently world-wide belief in a hidden land or underworld within the earth.

All these different strands have become intertwined, until they are like the twisting magical knots upon some old Celtic or Saxon carving, with strange faces and forms peeping out between. And because they were of the pagan and forbidden side of things, the old gods of paganism and witchcraft became their natural rulers. Hence, as King James I noted in his *Daemonologie,* the goddess Diana was regarded as Queen of Faerie; and the witches of Italy in their magical legends recorded in *Aradia,* sometimes called the goddess Fata Diana, 'Fairy Diana'.

Her personal representative, the high priestess of a witch coven, was called after her 'the Queen of Elphame'. Hence it is not always easy to distinguish in these old tales between the Queen of Elphame who is a mortal woman, and the visionary lady on a milk-white steed that True Thomas saw as he lay on Huntlie Bank.

FAMILIARS

Witches' familiars may be of three kinds. The first kind is that of a discarnate human being or, in other words, the spirit of a dead person. The second kind is that of a non-human spirit, an elemental. The third kind is that of an actual material creature, a small animal such as a cat or a ferret, or a reptile such as a toad.

Familiars of the second kind, the elementals, sometimes indwell a particular object; and these serving spirits have been attributed to ceremonial magicians in the past, as well as to witches. The famous occultist Paracelsus, for instance, was said to have a familiar which dwelt in a large precious stone, probably a crystal, which was set in the pommel of his sword. In old books of magic, one often finds rituals for attracting a spirit and binding it to a crystal or a magic mirror, in order to serve a magician. By the agency of such a spirit, visions would be seen in the crystal or mirror.

The idea of a spirit ensouling some object, generally a statue, is also found among the magicians of primitive races. Anthropologists have named such a statue a 'fetish'.

Among witches in Britain, the kind of familiar most frequently met with is the third; that is, a small living creature of some kind, kept as a pet. Witch-hunters usually insisted on describing these familiars as 'imps', and alleged that the witch fed them on her own blood.

There is a shred of truth in the latter allegation, although misunderstood as usual. The imagination of witch-hunters is often much nastier than that of witches.

What really happened was that the witch gave the creature from time to time a spot of his or her blood, or if the witch were a woman and a nursing mother, a little of her milk. The object of this was to make a psychic link between the witch and the familiar, and to continue that link. Otherwise, the familiar would be fed on whatever food was normal for it to eat.

Many animals have acute psychic perceptions, and by observing their behaviour the presence of unseen visitants, friendly or otherwise, can be divined. The utter refusal of dogs to go into a place which is the scene of a genuine haunting is a fact frequently attested by experience. Cats, on the other hand, seem rather to enjoy ghostly company. (*See* CATS AS WITCHES' FAMILIARS.)

The toad is a remarkably intelligent creature, and easily tamed. The natterjack, or walking toad, was the type specially favoured as a witches' familiar; but all toads make quite good pets, if they are kept in suitable conditions. They must have water available, as they breathe partly through their skin, and if this gets too dry they will die. They feed upon insects; so the cottage garden was an excellent habitat for them and some old-fashioned gardeners kept toads simply for this purpose, to keep down the insects that menaced the plants.

The toad is also generally harmless. He cannot bite, because he has no teeth; and the old story that he spits poison is a libel. What really happens is that the toad, when angry, frightened or excited will exude poison through his skin, from certain glands in the region of his neck. If you do not frighten or injure him, he will remain harmless; and he has the most wonderful, jewel-like eyes of any creature in the reptile kingdom. (As the reader may have gathered, the writer *likes* toads.)

This substance exuded by the skin of the toad has a milky appearance, and consequently it received the name of toads' milk. Witches who kept toads as pets had certain ways of obtaining the toads' milk without injuring or upsetting the toad—a good familiar was too valuable for that. Toads' milk was used in some of the witches' secret brews; and modern scientists have discovered that it contains a substance they have named *bufotenin,* which is an hallucinogenetic drug.

It is also an extremely deadly poison, when used in the wrong way. The writer, therefore, does not feel that it would be in the public interest to disclose too many details on this subject. The present irresponsible attitude towards hallucinogens, unfortunately displayed by many people today, precludes it.

This, however, was one of the reasons for the popularity of the toad as a witch's familiar. The other reason is that toads, like cats, are very psychic creatures, and will react to ghostly influences.

The animal familiar was used for divination. The method was to set before it within the magical circle a number of objects representing different divinatory meanings, and see which one it selected. The painted pebbles mentioned in the entry on divination would be very suitable for this; or sprigs of different herbs or twigs of trees could be used. Before the divination started, the witch would have to cast the magic circle, and invoke the Gods to send a spirit to possess the familiar and inspire it to give the right answer.

Another way in which the animal familiar was used was to convey a magical influence, for good or ill, to another person. An instance of this is contained in the confession of Margaret and Philippa Flower, who were hanged for witchcraft at Lincoln in 1619.

These two sisters had been employed at Belvoir Castle by the Earl and Countess of Rutland. For some reason, one of them, Margaret, was dismissed. Feeling that she had been unjustly treated, she applied to her mother, Joan Flower, for revenge. Joan Flower was already reputed to be a witch, and she had a familiar, a cat called Rutterkin. Margaret Flower managed to steal a glove belonging to Lord Rosse, the heir of the Earl and Countess; and this glove was used to make the magical link for the ritual of revenge.

The witch-mother, Joan Flower, rubbed the glove upon Rutterkin the cat; and she must have pronounced a curse upon Lord Rosse as she did so. Then the glove was dipped into boiling water—doubtless the cauldron was bubbling nearby. It was taken out again, pricked either with pins or with the magical knife, and finally buried. Lord Rosse became ill and eventually died.

The Flowers continued to practise witchcraft against the family of the Earl and Countess, until rumours got about locally, and they were arrested and taken to Lincoln for examination. The mother, Joan Flower, fell down and died as she was being taken to Lincoln Jail; after which the two sisters confessed and were hanged. What happened to the cat is not recorded; but this case is interesting as one of the rare instances in which we have some actual details of how familiars were really used. The cat evidently acted as a sort of medium for the powers of witchcraft.

Witches acquired well-trained familiars from each other. They might be given at initiation, or passed on between members of a family, or inherited as a legacy. The familiar was given a name, and well cared for. Sometimes the names were curious and fanciful.

Some recorded names of witches' familiars in Britain are Great Tom Twit and Little Tom Twit (these were two toads); Bunne; Pyewacket; Elimanzer; Newes (a good name for a divining familiar); Elva (which was also the name of a Celtic goddess, sister-in-law to the sun god Lugh); Prickeare; Vinegar Tom; Sack and Sugar; Tyffin; Tissey; Pygine; Jarmara; Lyard (a word meaning 'grey'); Lightfoot; Littleman; Makeshift; Collyn; Fancie; Sathan; Grissell and Greedigut. From the Continent come names like Verdelet, Minette, Carabin, Volan, Piquemouche, and so on. Cornelius Agrippa, a famous writer on occult philosophy and magic, was supposed to keep a familiar in the shape of a little black dog called Monsieur.

A curious sidelight on the belief in the efficacy of animal familiars is the fact that, during the Civil War in England, the supporters of Cromwell quite seriously accused the Royalist Prince Rupert of having a familiar. Apparently the Prince had a little white dog called Boye; and the Puritans' accusations were ridiculed in contemporary Royalist pamphlets, which improved on the original story by suggesting that Boye was really a beautiful Lapland witch, who had changed herself into a dog in order to keep the gallant Cavalier company.

But to the Puritans, witchcraft was no subject for jest. It was during the Civil War that the notorious Witch-Finder General, Matthew Hopkins, carried on his reign of terror in East Anglia. Many elderly people were bullied and tormented into 'confessions', and ultimately hanged, for no other crime than keeping a pet animal or bird that their persecutors had decided was a familiar.

At the present day, there are some extreme Protestant congregations which forbid their members to keep pets. This may be an unacknowledged survival of the old fear of witchcraft and the familiar.

The word 'familiar' comes from the Latin *famulus,* meaning an attendant. The most detailed story from the British Isles of such an attendant in the form of a human spirit is that of the Scottish witch Bessie Dunlop of Ayrshire, who was condemned and executed in 1576. Her familiar was the ghost of a man called Thome Reid, who had been killed at the Battle of Pinkie in 1547.

She described his appearance as that of "a respectable elderly-looking man, grey-bearded, and wearing a grey coat, with Lombard sleeves, of the auld fashion. A pair of grey breeches, and white stockings gartered above the knee, a black bonnet on his head, close behind and plain before, with silken laces drawn through the lips thereof, and a white wand in his hand, completed the description of what we may suppose a respectable-looking man of the province and period." So says Sir Walter Scott, who, in his *Letters on Demonology and Witchcraft* (London, John Murray, 1830), gives full particulars of this case.

Thome Reid was evidently no mere dubious wraithlike phantom. Furthermore, he gave proof of his identity:

> More minutely pressed upon the subject of her familiar, she said she had never known him while among the living, but was aware that the person so calling himself was one who had, in his lifetime, actually been known in middle earth as Thome Reid, officer to the Laird of Blair, and who died at Pinkie. Of this she was made certain, because he sent her on errands to his son, who had succeeded in his office, and to others his relatives, whom he named, and commanded them to amend certain trespasses which he had done while alive, furnishing her with sure tokens by which they should know that it was he who had sent her.

Thome Reid advised Bessie upon how to treat the sick, both humans and cattle, and her treatments were generally successful. He also helped her to divine the whereabouts of stolen property. On one occasion, she said, perhaps too bluntly, that the reason some stolen plough-irons had not been recovered was that a certain sheriff's officer had accepted a bribe not to find them. This cannot have been pleasing to the authorities concerned; and one wonders whether this was why she fell foul of the law, as she was never alleged to have done harm to anyone. Nevertheless, as Sir Walter Scott says, "The sad words on the margin of the record 'Convict and burnt' sufficiently express the tragic conclusion of a curious tale."

It is notable that Spiritualist mediums of the present day claim to be aided by spirits whom they call 'Guides'; that is, spirits who particularly attach themselves to a medium for the purpose of assisting in the production of phenomena, and of advising the medium. Without wishing in any way to give offence to Spiritualists, this is exactly what the human familiar of the witches did and still does.

One of the objects of present-day witches' rites is to contact the spirits of those who have been witches in their past lives on earth, and who have thus acquired wisdom both on earth and in the Beyond. The witches' procedure, while not precisely the same as that of Spiritualists, is nevertheless very similar in many respects. The Spiritualists' practice of sitting in a circle, and of having men and women seated alternately, is precisely the same as that of witchcraft; as is their belief that power is latent in the human body, and that under the right conditions this power can be externalised and used by discarnate entities to manifest.

Witches also believe, in common with Spiritualists, that a person of the right temperament can enter into a state of trance, during which a spirit can make use of that person's mind and body in order to speak, write, or perform actions; in other words, they believe in mediumship. This may be one reason for some Churchmen's implacable opposition to Spiritualism—that they recognise in it many of the beliefs and phenomena of witchcraft.

The witch maintains, however, as does the Spiritualist, that these powers and phenomena are perfectly natural ones; that they are within the framework of natural laws, even though the materialist may not understand the working of such laws; and that it is the way in which these powers are used that makes them good or evil, and not the essential nature of the powers themselves.

With regard to the witch's familiar which is a non-human discarnate entity, a nature-spirit, this is a belief not confined to witches. It can be found in the East also, where many fakirs and magicians claim to produce marvellous phenomena by means of their alliance with the spirits of the elements. (*See* ELEMENTS, SPIRITS OF THE.)

In the West such nature-spirits were accepted by people of all races. The Greeks and Romans felt the presence of the nymphs of river and mountain, the tree-nymphs and the goat-footed fauns of the forest; and to them they raised altars in lonely places of the wild. Such an altar, inscribed *Diis campestribus,* is described by Sir Walter Scott as being preserved in the Advocates' Library in Scotland. It was discovered near Roxburgh Castle; and the old gentleman in charge of the library used to translate its inscription as "The Fairies, ye ken."

After the coming of Christianity, all these nature-spirits were regarded as belonging to the world of Faerie, of which Diana, the goddess of the woodlands and of the moon, was queen. They were "The Secret Commonwealth", as old Robert Kirk of Aberfoyle described them in 1691; and association with them was banned by the Church as a thing of witchcraft. Even today, some of the more severe Irish clergy tell their flock that the little leprechauns are 'divils'.

Respect for the fairies, however, has by no means died out, especially in the more Celtic parts of the British Isles. In the Isle of Man, for instance, it is usual for people to salute the Good Folk when they pass by the Fairies' Bridge; and this custom was observed even by Royalty, on a visit to the island in recent years. To many, it is simply a colourful piece of local folklore; but frequent also are the tales of people who have treated the fairies with discourtesy, and have experienced inexplicable breakdowns of their cars, or other misfortunes thereafter.

However, any intimate friendship between mortals and the fairies was regarded, generally rightly, as a sign of witchcraft in bygone days. The records of this are so extensive and curious that they require an entry to themselves. (*See* FAIRIES AND WITCHES.)

Belief in the fairy familiar is still sufficiently alive to have been perpetuated by Hollywood. That very funny film *Harvey,* starring James Stewart, was actually about a familiar of this kind; and it stuck very close to tradition in the way it described 'Harvey', the *pooka* or fairy spirit in animal form, and his prankish powers.

FAMOUS CURSES

Can a curse really work? The answer of world-wide and age-old experience says that provided the curse is justly deserved, it can and does.

This might seem to classify a curse as an example of black magic; but this is by no means necessarily so. Records show that the curse which works with deadliest effect is that which is addressed to the powers of fate and justice, in vengeance for a wrong that human law cannot or will not right.

It may be argued that superstitious fear and a troubled conscience, on the part of the person who has been cursed, will account for the curse's apparent working. This can, indeed, account for some famous curses taking effect; but not for all. It could not, for instance, explain the working-out of the Tichbourne Curse, which was laid upon a noble English family in the reign of Henry II, and came true in precise detail centuries afterwards.

The originator of this curse was a pious and strong-minded woman, Lady Mabell de Tichbourne, who wished to leave an annual gift or 'dole' to the poor. Knowing the mean disposition of her husband, she told him on her death-bed that if he or his descendants ever stopped this charity, great misfortune would fall upon the family, their name would be changed and their race die out. As a sign that their doom was impending, there would be the birth in one generation of seven sons and in the next of seven daughters, and the family home would fall down.

For hundreds of years the Tichbourne Dole, in the form of a yearly free distribution of bread, was given to the poor. Then in 1796 the seventh baronet, Sir Henry Tichbourne, decided that the event had become a nuisance, and stopped it.

In 1803 a large part of the old mansion collapsed. The seven sons, followed by seven daughters, were duly born; and a series of family misfortunes, including the notorious law-case of the Tichbourne claimant, convinced the descendants of Lady Mabell that their ancestral curse was a fact. The family, whose name had been changed to Doughty-Tichbourne by circumstances of inheritance, decided that the dole should be resumed. It is given out yearly to this day, though now in the form of flour instead of bread.

Another famous curse which worked out over the centuries was the Doom of the Seaforths. This is an example of those curses which take the form of a fatal prophecy. Scotland seems to be the particular home of them, probably because of its long tradition of the second sight. The Doom of the Seaforths was pronounced by Kenneth Odhar, known as the Brahan Seer. He was condemned to death as a witch by the Countess of Seaforth, and publicly burned at the stake in the latter part of the seventeenth century. When on his way to execution, he solemnly pronounced these words: "I see a chief, the last of his house, both deaf and dumb. He will be the father of four fair sons, all of whom he shall follow to the tomb. He shall live careworn and die mourning, knowing that the honours of his house are to be extinguished for ever, and that no future chief of the Mackenzies shall rule in Kintail."

The seer went on to describe in detail what misfortunes would overtake the family; and he said that when four great lairds were born "one of whom shall be buck-toothed, the second hare-lipped, the third half-witted, and the fourth a stammerer", the Seaforth then holding the title would be the last of his line. This prophecy, made publicly in such dramatic form, was long remembered; and in 1815 the line of the Seaforths became extinct, in the exact circumstances the Brahan Seer had pronounced.

Both of the above stories are well-founded upon historical fact. A number of similar tales could be added from old English and Scottish family records.

In 1926 the Reverend Charles Kent, Rector of Merton in Norfolk, revealed that he had held a public religious service in an attempt to lift the famous 'Curse of Sturston', a Norfolk village that was cursed in the time of the first Queen Elizabeth. He used an old altar tomb in the ruined churchyard as a lectern from which to read the service; and people gathered from miles around. He believed that his action had at last laid the curse; but subsequent events proved him wrong.

The curse had been pronounced upon the Lord of the Manor of Sturston, one Sir Miles Yare, by an old woman reputed to be a witch. Exactly why she should have cursed her landlord is not clear; but she uttered a malediction upon him and his house and lands, and said that the place should go to ruin until not one stone remained upon another. The area has indeed steadily declined. The old manor became a farmhouse, and eventually stood empty, falling to pieces, and believed to be haunted.

The Rector had been asked to lay the curse, because of the district's long history of ill-luck and decay. For a time, things did seem brighter after his service; but with the coming of the Second World War the area was taken over for military training. The inhabitants left, and today Sturston is a lost, desolate place, with its buildings in ruins. The curse is almost fulfilled.

Another story of a witch's curse is that connected with the Earldom of Breadalbane. For many years visitors to the old castle at Killin, on Loch Tay, were shown the place where a witch was put to death by order of the then Earl of Breadalbane. They were told the story of how the witch cursed the family of Breadalbane, and prophesied that the earldom would not descend direct from father to son for seven generations. This came precisely true, as was noted by a letter in *The Times* on 18th May 1923, under the heading "A Witch Story".

The correspondent stated that he had heard of the curse when it had already held good for five generations; and noted that the obituary of the Earl of Breadalbane, which *The Times* had just published, completed the seventh generation, the title passing to a distant cousin.

How can we account for these things? Is there some power in the unseen which hears the words of the wronged? Or do people at the point of death sometimes discover in themselves a faculty of prophecy, and foresee the doom of their oppressors?

These possibilities might account for the above curses, but hardly for the awesome history of the Hope Diamond, a jewel which has been followed through the years by a trail of disaster too long to detail here, and which seems beyond any claim of coincidence. The stone first appeared in Europe in the time of King Louis XIV of France. It was brought to the French Court by a man called Tavernier, who had stolen it from a statue in a temple in Mandalay. The diamond is a wonderful violet-blue colour, and its present weight, after being recut, is 44¼ carats. It reposes today in the Smithsonian Institution, Washington, D.C.—where perhaps the atmosphere of science, and the fact that no one is actually wearing it or trying to make money from it, may keep in abeyance whatever strange and horrifying power has given it such an accursed history. However, the only way in which the curse of the Hope Diamond could finally be laid, might well be to return it to the temple from which it was stolen.

Lastly, here is a story of a curse that *might* have been induced auto-suggestion—but it worked just the same. In April 1795 a naval officer, Captain Anthony Molloy of H.M.S. *Caesar,* was found guilty by court-martial of a charge which amounted to cowardice in the face of the enemy, in connection with his conduct at the battle of 1st June 1794. The court, however, found that Molloy's conduct was so uncharacteristic of him that they did not impose the death-sentence he might have suffered, but merely ordered him to be dismissed from his ship.

Robert Chambers, in his *Book of Days,* tells us:

> A very curious story is told to account for this example of 'the fears of the brave'. It is said that Molloy had behaved dishonourably to a young lady to whom he was betrothed. The friends of the lady wished to bring an action of breach of promise against the inconstant captain, but she declined doing so, saying that God would punish him. Some time afterwards, they accidentally met in a public room at Bath. She steadily confronted him, while he, drawing back, mumbled some incoherent apology. The lady said, "Captain Molloy, you are a bad man. I wish you the greatest curse that can befall a British officer. When the day of battle comes, may your false heart fail you!" His subsequent conduct and irremediable disgrace formed the fulfilment of her wish.

FERTILITY, WORSHIP OF

It is not easy for present-day people, living in our glossy civilised world of supermarkets and packaged food, to realise what fertility really meant to our ancestors in past centuries.

For one thing, their expectation of life was shorter than ours, and infant mortality was much higher. They needed a big birth-rate to keep any nation or tribe strong. Also, if their crops failed, they could not easily buy food to make up for it; hunger stared them in the face.

Earlier still, before man learned to grow crops, he was dependent upon the herds of game which he hunted for meat. If they became fewer, his life became proportionately harder.

Consequently, when people in ancient times performed rituals for fertility, they were not doing this for a pastime. They were in the greatest earnest.

The principle of fertility is, after all, a very deep, fundamental and mysterious thing. It is Life itself, bursting out in myriad forms, from the earth and the waters, never standing still, ever renewing itself; eternal, yet ever changing.

Even so, the sex-drive behind human fertility is something deep and fundamental, one of the primeval forces. And, although it was the principle of Life itself that the ancients were seeking to come into harmony with, their means of doing so was usually through their own sexuality; sex made into a ritual. 'As above, so below'. As they performed the acts which stimulated life, so the powers of universal fertility would be aroused and move.

As it was the country folk who lived closest to the earth, they were more immediately involved in fertility rites than the town dwellers. Consequently, it was the rustic pagans, the *pagani* or country-folk, who clung to these old ways after the townspeople had turned to more sophisticated, intellectual creeds. Because people believed in these old rites, crude and shocking though the more refined classes found them, they were loath to give them up.

Hence Christianity, although it was the official religion of Europe, was for a long period only a veneer over deep layers of old paganism, much of which went back to the very dawn of time. In Hindu and Buddhist countries, the same situation existed, and still does, to a considerable extent. The intellectual and the refined town dweller have their creeds and practices; the peasant has his primitive magic, based on beliefs of unknown antiquity.

In Western Europe the Wise Ones, or witches, kept to the old ways; and often had more public opinion behind them in the countryside than the Christian priest could command. An instance of this occurred in Dorset, in comparatively recent times. On the side of Trendle Hill, the great hill-figure of the Cerne Giant stands, fierce and with erect phallus. A certain clergyman who objected to the Giant's frank sexuality, wanted to have ploughed up that part of the chalk-cut figure which he considered indecent. But the people of the countryside around were so much opposed to this being done, that they made him desist. "If you do that," they said, "our crops will fail."

In times past, this figure was 'scoured', or cleaned and renewed, every seven years. This occasion was accompanied by a folk-festival on the hill, at which sexual intercourse was freely indulged in. The local clergy, however, did succeed in suppressing this rite. The Giant of Cerne now belongs to the National Trust; so the old periodic scouring, which has kept this and the rest of Britain's unique hill-figures in being, is no longer necessary.

People kept up old fertility rites, not only because they frankly enjoyed them, but because they really believed these rites to work. These rituals served to keep people in touch with the forces of Life, which were also the forces of Luck. Many old lucky charms are of a frankly sexual nature. Small figures of the phallus have been worn as lucky charms since the days of Ancient Egypt. Sometimes these little phalli are fancifully decorated with wings and bells. (*See* PHALLIC WORSHIP.)

The maypole, which used to stand permanently in some of our towns and villages, is a phallic symbol; which is why the Puritans destroyed so many of the old maypoles. However, a very fine and tall maypole, one of the highest left in England, stands to this day in the significantly-named village of Paganhill, near Stroud, Gloucestershire.

Another relic of ancient sexual rites in Britain is the group of stones called the Men-an-Tol, in Cornwall. One of these stones is carefully cut away in the centre, so that it has a circular hole bored through it. On either side of it are upright stones of phallic shape. These stones represent the old Powers of Life and date from prehistoric times. For unknown centuries, they have been believed to be magical stones; and sick people have been passed through the holed stone of the Men-an-Tol in the hope of curing themselves.

The idea behind this type of ritual is that contact with the forces of life brings renewed vitality. From this mysterious *élan vital* flows the feeling of ecstatic joy that surges through so many religious and magical dances; notably the naked dance of witches at their Sabbats and Esbats.

Witchcraft is concerned with the forces of fertility, through among other things its practices of moon worship (though it is not the material moon which is worshipped, but the feminine power of Nature behind it). The moon is intimately connected with fertility, both on the earth and of human beings. On woman's monthly cycle of menstruation and ovulation her fertility depends; while that of man depends upon his sperm, which astrologically is ruled by the moon. Its appearance is reminiscent of lunar whiteness and opalescence, of moonstones and crystals. Both sperm and menstrual blood have always been believed to be potent magical substances, for this reason. (*See* MOON WORSHIP.)

Sun worship, too, is essentially the worship of Life. Without the light of the sun, no crops would ripen; and all things on earth would wither and die. Without moisture, however, to temper the sun's heat, nothing could grow in the parched land. The sun is the father of fire; the moon is the mother of water. Without these two principles, there would be no life as we know it manifested on earth. The link between the two is air; while earth is the sphere of their manifestation.

Life, therefore, to the ancients who philosophised from Nature, and all the fertility thereof, depends upon the universal interplay of positive and negative forces, counterbalancing and complementary to each other. Positive and negative; fire and water; sun and moon; man and woman; god and goddess; light and darkness; day and night; Lucifer and Diana; Pan and Hecate.

This, then, is the belief behind the sex-rites of ancient fertility cults. These rites were not only sympathetic magic, to arouse the life-giving forces of Nature. They were in their purest form the *hieros gamos,* or sacred marriage, which was the universal arcanum of Life itself—the *rebis* or 'double thing' of the alchemists.

When present-day witches perform such rites, if they are true followers of the old traditions, they do so in this spirit, and not merely for the sake of the 'sex orgies' so beloved by certain sections of the sensationalist press. It does not seem to occur to the writers of these sensational reports, that if all witches wanted was 'sex orgies', they would have no need to invent a witch cult in order to indulge in them. In our present-day 'permissive society', sex is blazoned forth everywhere, usually in some more or less commercialised form. Cheapened and degraded, sex in the form of promiscuity is so prevalent that people whose minds contain any other ideas on the subject are made to feel out-of-date, 'not with it', 'square' and so on.

And yet, how few people, in the midst of all this frantic search for satisfaction, ever seem to find it; and how many, beneath their surface gaiety, are loveless, insecure, neurotic and miserable? Perhaps the old idea of the sacredness of sex was not so foolish after all? To degrade sex is to degrade life itself.

Contrary to many misrepresentations, witches do not believe in promiscuity, any more than they believe in prudishness; because they do not think that either extreme is a natural way of living for human beings.

But, the sceptic may say, what place have the rites of an ancient fertility cult in the modern world at all? Do we still need to perform these old rituals in order to make the crops grow? And as for increasing the population, isn't the world grossly over-populated already?

The answer is that all things, including living religions, evolve; and the Craft of the Wise is a living religion. Over the years, we have begun to see a new concept of the idea of fertility; one that is not only material, but also of the mind and the soul.

The creative forces are not only creative in the physical sense; they can also beget and give birth to art, music, poetry and literature. We speak of people's minds being 'fertile' or 'barren'. We talk of 'cultivating' ideas as well as fields; of new 'conceptions' of a better way of living. There is a spiritual as well as a material fertility; and human life is a desert without it. These are the aims towards which sincere and intelligent present-day pagans, witches, and Nature-worshippers are tending.

The spirit of the old rites, therefore, continues; but in a higher form. The concern is not so much with literal fertility as with vitality, and with finding one's harmony with Nature. In this way, people seek for a philosophy of life which bestows peace of mind, as well as physical satisfaction.

Of course, initiation as a witch cannot automatically bestow anything on anyone. Witchcraft is the Craft of the Wise; and no one can be *made* wise. They can only *become* wise. All that initiation into any of the mysteries can or ever could do, is to open the gate; whether or not the individual progresses further is up to him. This, too, is something the modern world seems to find hard to understand.

Witchcraft is, and always has been, a fertility cult. As such, it is life-affirming, instead of life-repressing. Its followers throughout the ages have not been intellectuals, but people who were often unlettered, and who were concerned with the fundamentals of birth, life and death. Magic does not work through the intellect; it works through the instincts and emotions, the fundamental things that man was born with. Sex is one of the most fundamental and instinctive things of all; consequently it is one of the most potently magical things, when rightly understood.

FIRE MAGIC

The natural flame of candlelight has been the perpetual accompaniment of magical ceremonies. Both the witch and the ceremonial magician have preferred its soft glow to that of artificial illumination. Because night or twilight are more conducive to psychic results than the bright glare of day, illumination is needed. Midnight is often called the 'witching hour', from an instinctive perception of its influence upon human minds. Witches and magicians' candles burn at midnight.

In the glow of candlelight, an ordinary everyday room can take on quite a different appearance from that which it normally possesses. People's faces look different, too. The commonplace is transformed by the alchemy of fire.

Because one of the most important secrets of magic is to provide the atmosphere in which the unusual can happen, this lore of candlelight and fire-flames has acquired importance. However simple a ritual may be, a witch will always have fire in some form upon the altar; either a lighted candle, a burning joss-stick, or both.

Today, when different coloured candles are easily obtainable, their colours are chosen for their magical significance. Red is a favourite colour for the candles used in witchcraft rites, because it is the colour of life. If black candles are used, it is usually in a rite meant to summon spirits of the departed.

Sometimes, however, witches prefer to make their own candles. They use for this purpose beeswax with which a small quantity of aromatic herbs has been mingled. The figure of a pentagram, the sign of magic, is cut on the candle.

Sometimes the candle flame is used as a means of communicating with spirits. The leader of the rite will ask any spirit entity that may be present, if they will make their presence known by causing the candle flame to flicker. It is surprising how often this will happen, apparently without any physical cause.

In fact, candle flames will often do odd things, in the course of a magical ritual. Witches believe that a natural, naked flame gives off power, whether it be that of a candle or a bonfire. Outdoors, the bonfire takes the place of the candle flames of the indoor ritual.

If candles are used outdoors, as they sometimes are to mark the four cardinal points of the magic circle, then they have to be enclosed in lanterns. Otherwise, the wind would soon gutter them away.

The old story goes that when a candle flame burns blue it is a sign that a spirit is present. Strange as it may sound, this could have a foundation in fact. When I have been taking part in witchcraft rites, I have seen on a number of occasions a kind of blueish light building up over the candle on the altar. This could be something akin to the "orgone energy" described by Wilhelm Reich, the colour of which is blue. It is in fact, in my opinion, the power which is being raised by the ritual, of which spirit entities can make use in order to manifest.

The glow of a candle makes an effective point of concentration. Some people use it as an aid to clairvoyance, and profess to see pictures building up around the flame. Too bright a flame, however, will dazzle the eyes; so the seer concentrates upon the blue part of the flame, at the base, and watches for a softly shining aura to form around the light, which is the prelude to psychic sight. People also concentrate in this way upon a wish or a prayer.

Those of a philosophical turn of thought may reflect that the candle is an image of humanity. The wax corresponds to the body, the wick to the mind, and the flame to the spirit.

Outdoors, the bonfire is a frequent accompaniment to witches' rites: In this case, a witch will stand with his or her back to the wind, so that the flames will be blown away from them, and the spell will be sent outwards upon the wind and the flame. Sometimes a circle of thirteen stones is collected, and placed round the fire.

Dancing around the ritual bonfire is a time-honoured way of raising power. When the witches could venture to build a bonfire big enough, its warmth would encourage them to throw off their clothes and dance naked, in a wild and exhilarating round of joy and abandon. The magnetic emanations of power flow more freely from unclothed bodies; hence the popularity of ritual nudity down through the ages, as an adjunct to religious and magical rites. (*See* NUDITY, RITUAL.)

This is not always possible, however, even with the biggest of bonfires; and in general, in the present day, witches' bonfires have to be kept discreetly small. The countryside today is more thickly populated, and hence there are more people about to notice a fire at night, than there were in former times. Even so, some witch-fires still get lighted.

FLAGELLATION, ITS USE IN FOLK RITES

It is evident from a number of old records that flagellation entered into the rites of witchcraft, partly as a means of discipline and partly as a religious or magical act.

For instance, in August 1678, according to Law's *Memorialls* (quoted by Montague Summers in his *Geography of Witchcraft*, Kegan Paul, London, 1927), "the devil had a great meeting of witches in Loudian", that is Lothian in Scotland. This was probably the Lammas Sabbat. Prominent among the witch-leaders was a former Protestant minister, one Gideon Penman, who was later accused of taking part in this gathering. It was said that he "was in the rear in all their dances, and beat up all those that were slow".

This kind of dancing is known among primitive people from Morocco to South America, with a whip or some other means of scourging being used to urge on the dancers. Its object is to stimulate and excite the participants, and to keep them in the direction and rhythm of the dance.

Mild flagellation was also widely believed in in ancient times as driving away evil influences and arousing the forces of life. At the old Horn Fair, which used to be held at Charlton in Kent, part of the traditional ceremonies consisted of whipping women with what William Hone in *The Year Book* (William Tegg and Co., London, 1848) describes as "furze", though it is more likely to have been green broom (*Planta genista*). This old fair, which was connected with the worship of the Horned God, was such an occasion for licence and frolic that it gave rise to the proverb, "All is fair at Horn Fair." It was eventually banned, for this reason.

On the Continent, fresh green branches, called 'rods of life', were used in old-time folk festivals for ritual beating, sometimes on Holy Innocents' Day and sometimes at Easter. These rods were used by one sex upon the other, and they were believed to give renewed health and fertility to those who submitted to the rite.

Ritual flagellation goes back to the days of Ancient Egypt, and probably beyond. Herodotus states that at the annual festival held at Busiris in honour of the Goddess Isis, while the sacrifice was being performed, ritual flagellation was practised by the whole assembly, amounting to several thousands of both men and women. He adds that he is not allowed to mention the reason why these beatings were performed. That is, they were part of the Mysteries, into which Herodotus had been initiated.

When the house called 'The Villa of the Mysteries' was discovered in the ruins of Pompeii in 1910, its remarkable and beautiful fresco paintings gave the world an actual picture of initiation into one of the Mystery cults of olden time. It is thought to depict an initiation into the Mysteries of Dionysus. Part of the initiation scene shows the neophyte, a girl being scourged upon her naked flesh by the initiator, who is depicted as a winged goddess, Telete, the Daughter of Dionysus. In this instance, flagellation appears as an ordeal which the neophyte had to pass, and also perhaps as a means of purification before a person was admitted to the Mysteries.

This villa was probably a secret meeting place of initiates, after the Dionysiac Mysteries had been banned by the Roman Senate.

However, the Lupercalia Festival of Ancient Rome, which also involved ritual flagellation, was not only tolerated, but members of the nobility willingly took part in it. This is mentioned in Shakespeare's *Julius Caesar,* when Caesar's wife takes part in the Lupercalia, in order to be cured of her barrenness and be able to have a child.

The festival of the Lupercalia was performed in honour of the god Pan. It took place in February, and this month actually derives its name from the Latin *februa,* meaning 'purification'. A curious old book gives a lively description of this time-honoured rite:

> Virgil speaks of the dancing *Salii* and naked *Luperci,* and the commentators explain that these last were men who, upon particular solemnities, used to strip themselves stark naked, and who ran about the streets, carrying straps of goat's leather in their hands, with which they struck such women as they met in their way. Nor did those women run away; on the contrary, they willingly presented the palms of their hands to them in order to receive the strokes, imagining that these blows, whether applied to their hands or to other parts of their body, had the power of rendering them fruitful or procuring them an easy delivery.
>
> The *Luperci* were in early times formed into two bands, named after the most distinguished families in Rome, *Quintiliani* and *Fabiani;* and to these was afterwards added a third band, named *Juliani,* from Julius Caesar. Marc Anthony did not scruple to run as one of the *Luperci,* having once harangued the people in that condition. This feast was established in the time of Augustus, but afterwards restored and continued to the time of Anastasius. The festival was celebrated so late as the year 496, long after the establishment of Christianity. Members of noble families ran for a long time among the *Luperci,* and a great improvement was moreover made in the ceremony. The ladies, no longer contented with being slapped on the palms of their hands as formerly, began to strip themselves also, in order to give a fuller scope to the *Lupercus,* and to allow him to display the vigour and agility of his arm. It is wickedly said that the ladies became in time completely fascinated with this kind of 'diversion', and that the ceremony being brought to a degree of perfection was so well relished by all parties, that it existed long after many of the other rites of paganism were abolished; and when Pope Gelasius at length put an end to it, he met with so much opposition that he was obliged to write an apology.

(*Flagellation and the Flagellants: A History of the Rod in all Countries from the Earliest Period to the Present time,* by "the Rev. Wm. M. Cooper, B.A." (James Glass Bertram), London, 1868).

It is remarkable that this ritual should have continued publicly, so long after the official establishment of Christianity. There is evidence that rituals like this took place privately for a much longer period. A miniature from a fifteenth-century manuscript, for instance, shows an indoor gathering of thirteen people, some of whom are eating and drinking, some performing a round dance, while three of them, almost naked, are vigorously plying the birch upon themselves and each other. On one side is the figure of a scandalised Bishop, who has intruded upon this secret gathering. He bears a scroll in one hand, with a Latin inscription upon it, which translates: "They sacrifice to demons, and not to God".

This miniature has usually been taken to depict the practices of the medieval sect called Flagellants; but it could represent something quite different, and not a Christian gathering at all. The ceremony is taking place in front of two pillars, reminiscent of Masonic symbolism; and on top of each pillar is a small nude statue. The facts that those taking part are a coven of thirteen; that the flagellation is evidently accompanied, not by lugubrious repentance for sin, but by feasting and dancing; and that no Christian symbols are shown, but instead two pagan statues, are surely significant, especially when taken in conjunction with the Bishop's condemnation of "sacrificing to demons". To the medieval Church, all pagan gods and spirits were demons. What this fifteenth-century miniature really depicts is a secret gathering of pagans.

Rumours and allegations have been frequent, that present-day witches make use of ritual flagellation in their ceremonies. The truth is that some covens do make use of this, and others do not. Those which do, however, have the warrant of a good deal of antiquity behind them; the truth of which has hitherto been obscured by the difficulties encountered by anthropologists and students of comparative religion, in the frank discussion of this subject. The reason for this seems to be that, while strict moralists have no objection, indeed are all in favour, of flagellation being used for penance and punishment, to inflict pain and suffering; nevertheless, the idea of this very ancient folk-rite being used in a magical way, not to inflict pain but as part of a fertility ritual, for some reason upsets them very much.

In later years, when the witch cult was being more severely persecuted and forbidden, flagellation was used as a means of discipline. Harsh as this may sound, the security of the coven members was literally a matter of life and death. Any breaches of coven law had to be punished, sometimes severely. Traitors were killed; and people whose carelessness or vacillation endangered the lives of their companions received a sharp and painful reminder of where their loyalty lay.

It is recorded that at Arras, France, in 1460, a wealthy man called Jean Tacquet, whose loyalty to the coven he belonged to had become doubtful, was beaten by the "Devil" with a bull's pizzle. This weapon was actually the dried penis of a bull, which formed a severe instrument of flagellation. It was dried in a way which made it very strong and flexible, being stretched and drawn out to the length of an ordinary cane, and capable of administering a terrible castigation. In later times, the bull's pizzle came to be used for severe forms of flagellation inflicted upon criminals; it was still being used upon *women* prisoners in Germany in the early nineteenth century! It is such a curious weapon, however, that its origin may well have been a ritual one, used in the witch cult to punish those who were untrue to the Horned God, to whom it was sacred.

Isobel Gowdie, the young Scottish witch who made such a remarkably full confession of what happened in the coven she belonged to, in 1662, complained of the harshness with which the "Devil" behaved. "We would be beaten if we were absent any time, or neglected anything that would be appointed to be done . . . He would be beating and scourging us all up and down with cords and other sharp scourges, like naked ghosts; and we would still be crying, 'Pity! pity! Mercy! mercy our Lord!' But he would have neither pity nor mercy."

Such power, in the hands of a cruel and sadistic man, could be fearfully abused. One wonders whether this was the reason why Isobel Gowdie gave herself up to the authorities, and confessed her witchcraft, knowing as she must have done that the result would be her own execution. For some reason, her life had become intolerable, and she wanted to die. Though, of course, the alternative explanation of her conduct is that she was a voluntary human sacrifice. This beautiful, red-haired girl is one of the many enigmas of witchcraft's dark history.

FLYING OINTMENTS

One of the traditional capabilities of the legendary witch is the capacity to fly, upon a staff, a broomstick, the back of a demon goat or some similar fantastic means of transport. There were not even wanting eye-witnesses, in past centuries, who claimed to have seen such diabolical flights of witches, riding the air on moonlight nights.

Very early on, however, it was realised by serious writers that the truth behind the stories of 'flying witches' lay in mysterious potions and trance-inducing ointments they used.

Francis Bacon wrote: "The ointment that Witches use, is reported to be made of the fat of children digged out of their graves; of the juices of Smallage, Wolfe-Bane, and Cinque-Foil, mingled with the meal of fine wheat; but I suppose the soporiferous medicines are likest to do it, which are Hen-bane, Hemlock, Mandrake, Moon-shade, or rather Night-shade, Tobacco, Opium, Saffron, Poplar-leaves, etc."

In *The Book of the Sacred Magic of Abramelin the Mage*, written by Abraham the Jew for his son Lamech and dated 1458 (translated by S. L. MacGregor Mathers, the De Laurence Company Inc., Chicago, 1948), there is a noteworthy description of Abraham's experience with a young witch of Linz in Austria. Abraham had travelled extensively in search of magic, until he eventually met the Mage Abramelin, whose teachings he describes in the book; but before he encountered this adept he had had varied experiences with a number of other exponents of the magical arts, of whom this woman was one.

She gave him an unguent, with which he rubbed the principal pulses of his feet and hands, and the witch herself did likewise. Then it seemed to Abraham that he was flying in the air, and that he arrived in the place where he had wished to be, but which he had not indicated to the woman in any way.

Unfortunately, he does not tell us what the unguent was made of; nor will he describe what he saw, save that it was "admirable". He seemed to be in the trance or out-of-the-body state for some time; and when he awoke, he had pain in the head and a feeling of melancholy. The witch then recounted to him what she had seen on her own 'flight'; but it was quite different from Abraham's experience.

He was, he says, much astonished; because he felt as if he had been "really and corporeally" in the place he saw in his vision. He wished to make further experiments with the properties of this unguent; so on another occasion he asked the woman if she would go and seek news of a friend of his, at a place he named, while he remained beside her and watched.

She agreed, and proceeded to anoint herself with the unguent; whereat Abraham watched expectantly to see if she would actually fly away. Instead, she fell to the ground and lay there for three hours, as if she were dead. Abraham began to fear that she was really dead; but eventually she regained consciousness and told him what she had seen. However, her account, according to Abraham, did not correspond with what he knew of his friend; so he concluded that it was simply a fantastic dream, induced by the magical unguent. She confessed to Abraham that this unguent had been given to her by "the Devil"; and Abraham, who was a very pious man, would work no further with her.

It is curious to note how present-day users of drugs, such as L.S.D., speak of their experiences as 'taking a trip', 'getting high' and so on; expressions which are reminiscent of the idea of witches' 'flights' while under the influence of hallucinogens.

One of the earliest writers to make a detailed and reasoned study of this matter of witches' unguents was Giovanni Battista Porta, a Neapolitan, the author of *Magia Naturalis* or *Natural Magic*. This book was first called *De Miraculis Rerum Naturalium* and appeared at Antwerp in 1560. It had a section entitled *Lamiarum Unguenta,* or "Witches' Unguents"; but this was omitted from a later edition, which had been expurgated by a Dominican monk. However, the book made a big impression in its time, and was translated into French and English. Various editions exist, and one of these came into the hands of Reginald Scot, who was influenced by it in the writing of his *Discoverie of Witchcraft* (1584).

This sceptical, free-thinking book ridiculed the standard charges brought against witches, and so annoyed the witch-hunting King James I that he ordered it to be publicly burnt by the common hangman. Scot exposed the nonsense of witches being able to fly literally through the air, and revealed Porta's recipes for the witches' unguent, or witches' salve, as it was sometimes called.

Porta wrote in Latin, the common language of learned men of that time; and herewith (according to Montague Summers), is the actual Latin of his recipes:

> "*Puerorum pinguedinem ahaeno vase decoquendo ex aqua capiunt, inspissando quod ex elixatione ultimum, novissimumque subsidet, inde condunt, continuoque inserviunt usui: cum hac immiscent eleoselinum, aconitum, frondes populneas, et fuliginem.*
>
> "*Vel aliter sic: Sium, acorum vulgare, pentaphyllon, vespertilionis sanguinem, solanum somniferum, et oleum.*"

Montague Summers in his book, *The Werewolf* (Kegan Paul, London, 1933), has a very interesting chapter on witch ointments; to which he attributes the phenomena, or alleged phenomena, of lycanthropy, as well as the traditional flying. He tells us that Jean Wier, in his *De Lamiis, Of Witches,* quotes Porta's recipes; and these are evidently the ones discussed in the appendix to Margaret Murray's *Witch Cult in Western Europe.*

Summers also gives us the recipe for a witch unguent quoted by Jerome Cardan in his *De Subtilitate,* and also discussed in the appendix mentioned above:

> *"Constat ut creditur puerorum pinguedine e sepulchris eruta, succisque apii, acontique tum pentaphylli siligineque."* (Sic).

Now, it is evident that much depends upon the accurate translation of these Latin texts; and the writer would venture to query some of the translations which have been made of them.

Reginald Scot, in his *Discoverie of Witchcraft* (1584), renders Porta's recipes thus:

> The receipt is as followeth:
> The fat of young children, and seeth it with water in a brazen vessel, reserving the thickest of that which remaineth boiled in the bottom, which they lay up and keep, until occasion serveth to use it. They put hereunto *Eleoselinum, Aconitum, Frondes populeas,* and Soot.
> Another receipt to the same purpose:
> *Sium, acarum vulgare, pentaphyllon,* the blood of a flittermouse, *solanum somniferum,* and *oleum.* They stamp all these together, and then they rub all parts of their bodies exceedingly, till they look red, and be very hot, so as the pores may be opened, and their flesh soluble and loose. They join herewith either fat, or oil instead thereof, that the force of the ointment may the rather pierce inwardly, and so be more effectual. By this means (saith he) in a moonlight night they seem to be carried in the air, to feasting, singing, dancing, kissing, culling and other acts of venery, with such youths as they love and desire most.

"Aconitum" is aconite, otherwise called wolf's bane; *"frondes populeas"* are poplar leaves; *"acarum vulgare"* is probably sweet flag (*Acorus calamus*), an aromatic herb; *"pentaphyllon"* is cinquefoil; *"oleum"* is oil. "Flittermouse" is an old name for a bat. These are the ingredients whose meanings we can be reasonably certain about; but the rest present something of a problem.

The matter is further complicated by the fact that, in the reprint of Reginald Scot's book which appeared in 1886, published by Elliot Stock, a section of "explanatory notes" translates *Eleoselinum* as "mountain parsley". (*Selinum* is a Latin form of the Greek *selinon,* parsley.) It also gives *Sium* as "yellow watercress", and *Acarum vulgare* as "our *Asarum europaeum*", which is not sweet flag at all, but another plant called asarabacca.

The young leaves and buds of the poplar were long used by old-time apothecaries to make an ointment called *unguentum populeum,* which had soothing properties for inflammation and wounds. *"Solanum somniferum"* could mean several of the *Solanaceae;* henbane, thornapple, belladonna or black nightshade (all of which, incidentally, are very poisonous plants, and so also is aconite).

Montague Summers translates *"eleoselinum"* as hemlock (also extremely poisonous), and *"Solanum somniferum"* as deadly nightshade, which is the same thing as belladonna.

Of course, the "fat of young children" is simply a touch of the horrific. The most popular foundation for ointments as made by apothecaries was hog's lard; often with the addition of a little benzoin to make it keep better.

With regard to the second recipe, this consists, according to Montague Summers, of *sium* or cowbane; *acorum vulgare* or sweet flag; *pentaphyllon* or cinquefoil; *vespertilionis sanguis* or bat's blood; *solanum somniferum* or deadly nightshade; and *oleum* which is oil.

Another doubtful word here is *"sium".* If it does mean cowbane, or water hemlock, then this again is an extremely poisonous plant. But does it?

It may be useful to append Jean Wier's version of these recipes:

"1). *Du persil, de l'eau de l'Aconite, des feuilles de Peuple, et de la suye."* (These are the ingredients of the first Porta recipe, which had to be mixed with "the fat of young children". Professor A. J. Clark seems to have missed the point of this in his appendix to Margaret Murray's book mentioned above, and describes it as "a watery solution." The equivalent of *"eleoselinum"* here is *"persil",* which means parsley.)

"2). *De la Berle, de l'Acorum vulgaire, de la Quintefeuille, du sang de Chauve-souris, de la Morelle endormante, et de l'huyle."* (This is the second Porta recipe. *"La Morelle endormante"* certainly looks like a description of deadly nightshade, which has one large, cherry-like fruit. *"Berle"* means smallage, water-parsley or wild celery (*Apium graveolens*). This is not cowbane; and its occurrence here leads me to suspect that the first recipe has a misplaced comma that has proved remarkably misleading. I think its real reading is *"Du persil de l'eau, de l'Aconite",* etc., which is somewhat different from "parsley and water of aconite". Smallage is a plant growing in ditches and marshy places; it is acrid, and when bruised has a curious smell. It is one of the 'herbs of the spirit' used by sorcerers in their fumigations.)

"3). *De graisse d'enfant, de suc d'Ache, d'Aconite, de Quinte-feuille, de Morelle, et de suye.*" (This is the Cardan recipe, with the addition of *"Morelle"*, probably deadly nightshade. Summers translates it as the fat of children whose bodies have been stolen from their graves, mixed with henbane, aconite, cinquefoil and fine wheaten flour. But *"suc d'Ache"* is the juice of smallage, not henbane; and the "fine wheaten flour" may well be simply a misreading of *siligo*, wheat, for *fuligo*, soot.)

Comparing these different versions one with another, we may hope to come to some conclusions as to what the ingredients of the witches' salve really were. We can only hope that further investigations will be made by those having the necessary medical and pharmaceutical qualifications to carry them out safely.

I would very strongly caution anyone else from doing so, as most of the substances involved are dangerous and could be fatal. I refer, of course, to the active principles, the herbs mentioned above; the bat's blood, soot, and children's fat are merely fantastic ingredients, which could even have been inserted into these recipes as a blind.

Some very interesting and indeed daring research, into the secrets of the witches' salve, has been done by Dr. Erich-Will Peuckert, of the University of Gottingen, Germany. Using the recipes given by Porta as a base, Dr Peuckert made up an unguent containing thorn-apple (*Datura stramonium*), henbane (*Hyoscyamus niger*), and deadly nightshade (*Atropa belladonna*). Wild celery (*Apium graveolens*) and parsley were also included; and the basis for the salve was hog's lard.

Dr Peuckert wished for confirmation of his results, if any; so he obtained the co-operation of a friend of his, a solicitor who knew nothing about witchcraft or the supposed effects of the witches' salve, or *Unguentum Sabbati* as it is sometimes called.

On the night of the experiment, Dr Peuckert and his friend retired to a private room, and applied the unguent to their bodies according to Porta's directions. They fell into a deep sleep which lasted for twenty hours, and they ultimately awoke with very similar symptoms to those described in the account of Abraham the Jew, given above; symptoms resembling those of a bad hangover.

However, Dr Peuckert and his colleague forced themselves, in the interests of science, to write down an immediate account of what they had each experienced, before discussing it or comparing notes. The result was fantastic beyond the doctor's expectations.

Not only had each man had wild dreams of all the legendary phantasmagoria of the Sabbat; but the dream-experiences of each had been virtually the same. So strange, weird and erotic were the visions that Dr Peuckert has been understandably reticent in publishing details. He dreamed of flying through the air, of landing on a mountain-top, and of wild orgiastic rites and the appearance of monsters and demons.

The account of his colleague in the experiment tallied with his own in so many particulars, that Dr Peuckert suggests this to be, in fact, the narcotic action of the salve, which automatically induces this kind of vision. Alternatively, it has been suggested that the salve acts by stirring up some particular racial memory, lying deeply buried in the unconscious mind. But memory of what?

It would seem, following the latter theory, that something from the collective unconscious is involved; a field in which the work of Carl Gustav Jung may be relevantly studied, some of his discoveries being in their way quite as strange and thought-provoking as this.

While again emphasising strongly the folly of amateur meddling with these dangerous substances, I feel that this account would be incomplete without the details of another recipe. They are given here, however, solely for the information of qualified researchers. This recipe is one which I am told has been used by a present-day witch in England; but I have no information as to what results it produced. It consists of aconite, poppy juice, foxglove, poplar leaves, and cinquefoil, in a base of beeswax, lanoline and almond oil.

It is from the eldritch stories of such visionary Sabbats as those induced by the *Unguentum Sabbati,* that Mussorgsky derived the inspiration for his music entitled *Night on Bald Mountain.* Berlioz, too, attempted to describe a witches' Sabbat in music, in his *Symphonie Fantastique.* The descriptions of the Sabbat in art, by painters and engravers, are innumerable; but they are almost always that of the Sabbat of narcotic-induced fantasy.

FOSSILS USED AS CHARMS

It has always been a practice of witches to use in their craft things which were in some way striking or mysterious. In this way, they impressed the mind strongly with what they were trying to do.

Fossils were long considered very mysterious objects, appearing as they did to be some product of Nature changed to stone. For instance, the coiled fossils called ammonites were sometimes known as snake stones. They were believed to be a coiled snake turned to stone. In fact, they are the remains of a kind of giant, snail-like shell-fish. But even when we know what fossils are, it is strange to hold in one's hand what was once a living thing, millions of years ago.

A fossil credited with great magical properties is the shepherd's crown, a kind of fossilised sea urchin. These are often almost a perfect heart-shape, with a five-pointed pattern on the top. A closely similar variety, but more high and rounded, is called fairy loaves.

These fossilised sea urchins have been found as grave goods in Neolithic burials; and they may be the magical 'glane-stone' of the Druids, as they certainly resemble the description given of this object by ancient writers. Their magical connection is thus of great antiquity.

Sussex cottagers used to put shepherds' crowns on their window-sills, to protect the house from lightning, witchcraft and the Evil Eye. If a farm worker found one when he was digging or ploughing, he would pick it up, spit on it, and throw it over his left shoulder. This was done to avert bad luck.

I remember my mother telling me how her mother used to have some large shepherds' crowns on the mantelpiece at home. They were a prized possession, and my grandmother used to polish them regularly with black boot-polish! Why this was done is not clear; perhaps there was some idea behind it that magical objects should be given some regular service and attention, though it may have been simply part of the Victorian mania for polishing things. Their presence over the fire-place, of course, was to protect the chimney, a possible way of entrance for evil influences. Naughty children used to be threatened that 'something bad would come down the chimney after them'.

Another fossil that was used as a protective amulet for the home is the witch stone. This name is also sometimes applied to a flint with a hole in it; but the real Sussex witch stone is a small fossil in the perfect form of a bead—round, white, faintly glittering and with a hole through its middle. These fossils are also found in Yorkshire and other places. They are actually a fossil sponge, the product of warm seas millions of years ago. Their correct name is *Porosphaera globularis*. People wore these round their necks for luck, or hung them up in their homes by a piece of brightly-coloured ribbon or thread.

The long, pointed fossils called belemnites are somewhat phallic in shape, and hence doubly magical, as anything that is a life symbol is also a luck-bringer. They are sometimes known as 'thunder stones' or 'thunder bolts'; perhaps from a confusion with meteorites. They are actually the fossilised internal shell of a cephalopod, some pre-historic ancestor of our squids and cuttle-fish.

I have heard of fossil of this kind being used as a charm to strengthen cattle. It was used with two perfectly round pebbles, to symbolise testicles. The three things had to be dipped into water which was given to the cattle to drink.

Two substances long regarded as magical, jet and amber, are ac-tually fossils, though not always recognised as such. Amber is fos-silised resin and jet is fossilised wood. This is the reason why amber shows electrical properties on being rubbed. Real jet will do the same, and hence used to be known as 'black amber'; though much of what is sold today as jet is not jet at all but fine black glass. Amber and jet are two of the most time-honoured bringers of luck, being often found as necklaces in prehistoric graves. Because of their elec-trical properties, they were regarded as having life in them; which in a sense they have, being semi-precious stones which originated as living things.

Jet was anciently worn as a protection against witchcraft, and to relieve melancholy and depression, and prevent nightmares. It was sacred to Cybele, the Great Mother.

Amber was also worn as a protection against witchcraft and sor-cery, and was regarded as a safeguard for health and preventer of infection. This is the reason for its popularity as the mouth-piece of pipes and cigar or cigarette holders.

FOUR POWERS OF THE MAGUS
The Four Powers of the Magus are the attributes traditionally neces-sary for the successful practice of magic. They are: to know, to dare, to will and to be silent. These powers are often called by their Latin names: *noscere, audere, velle* and *tacere*.

A little reflection upon this traditional teaching about magic will show the reasoning behind it. None of the powers is sufficient alone in itself; the four powers must be present, balancing each other. Mere knowledge is not enough, without the will or the courage to put it into practice. Nor are will and daring of any avail without the knowledge to back them up. Audacity will not get far, without the will behind it to endure to the end. Will-power must in its turn summon the courage to take the first step. All these are in vain, unless the magician has the discretion to be silent and keep his own counsel. No babblers will ever attain to real magical power.

In fact, it has been said that the fourth power, to be silent, is the most important of all, and the most difficult to attain. Silence is a potency in itself; the silence of the great, timeless desert beneath the stars; the silence of the snow-capped mountains on the roof of the world; the silence within the vaults of the Pyramids. These are the silences of secret treasures, laid up for the initiate. No chatterers or boasters will find them.

People who blab their plans and ideas to everyone disperse their own forces. Occult operations in particular should not be talked about, or they will never come to fruition.

This is the reason why today, even though persecution by Church or State has generally ceased, all serious occult societies, including the Craft of the Wise, keep their innermost teachings and practices secret. It is not, as sensational writers suppose, because orgies of devil worship are going on; but because this is the mystical and magical tradition. Freemasonry observes it also, and defines itself as being, not a secret society, but a society with secrets.

The tradition goes back to the days of the ancient Mystery Cults, when a simple exoteric religion was taught to the general populace; while an esoteric teaching was to be found by those who wished to seek further and had the capacity to understand it. The Master Jesus evidently followed the same principle, when he told his disciples not to cast their pearls before swine or the swine would turn again and rend them.

There is a correspondence between the Four Powers of the Magus and the Four Elements. *Noscere,* to know, corresponds to air. *Audere,* to dare, corresponds to water. *Velle,* to will, corresponds to fire. *Tacere,* to be silent, corresponds to earth.

Air is the element of Mercury, the ruler of knowledge. Water brings with it the idea of launching boldly upon the waves of uncharted seas. Fire reminds us of the flame of will. Earth conveys the silent strength of rocks and mountains. When all these four are gathered together, there appears the fifth element, spirit; and its correspondence is the fifth power; *ire,* to go, the power of progression through the universe, the power of evolution.

Because the Sphinx is a representation of the Four Elements, these powers are also sometimes called the Four Powers of the Sphinx.

G

GARDNER, GERALD BROSSEAU

Whenever the subject of modern witchcraft is discussed, the name of 'G.B.G.' as he is familiarly known among members of the Craft, is sure to be mentioned sooner or later. It is mainly due to the work of Gerald Brosseau Gardner that the present-day world-wide revival of interest in witchcraft as a pagan religion has taken place.

He was of Scottish descent, though born at Blundellsands, near Liverpool, on 13th June, 1884. Amateurs of numerology will be interested in the fact that the day of his birth is the witches' thirteen, and the digits of the whole date add to four, the number attributed to Uranus, the planet of the rebel, the explorer of new and forbidden paths, the person who is different. His birth sign, Gemini, is the sign of the globe-trotter, ever restless and ever youthful in mind, whatever his age may be. I knew Gerald Gardner well in the later years of his life; and he had something in him of the eternal child, which could be very endearing, though sometimes hard to keep up with.

There has been more than one witch in the past with the surname of Gardner; and Gerald believed himself to be the descendant of Grissell Gairdner, who was burned as a witch at Newburgh in 1610. All his life he had been interested in occult matters, an interest which was stimulated by his long residence in the East, where he worked as a tea and rubber planter and as a Customs officer in Malaya, until his retirement in 1936. He had made a substantial fortune from his ventures in rubber, and was able to indulge his taste for travel and for archaeological research.

While still out East, he had made a name for himself by his pioneering research into Malaya's early civilisations. He had also written *Keris and other Malay Weapons* (Singapore, 1936), the first authoritative book upon the history and folklore of the Malay *kris*, full of curious lore which he gathered as a result of first-hand research among the native Malayan people, for whom he had a great sympathy and respect. This book brought him academic recognition, and the friendship of many eminent people in the fields of archaeology, anthropology and folklore.

On his retirement from his duties in Malaya, he and his wife settled in England, and ultimately made their home in the New Forest area of Hampshire. The Second World War was imminent; and on its outbreak G.B.G., anxious to do all he could to help defend his country, became very active in Civil Defence. But this, in his mind, was not enough. He wrote a letter to the *Daily Telegraph,* the contents of which actually found their way to Germany, and annoyed the Nazis very much. It also aroused much controversy here.

G.B.G. pointed out in this letter, that "By Magna Carta every free-born Englishman is entitled to have arms to defend himself and his household." He suggested that members of the civilian population should be armed and trained, in the event of invasion, to help defend Britain against the Nazis. The *Frankfurter Zeitung* was furious, and ranted in a front-page article against the man who had made this 'medieval' suggestion, saying that it was "an infringement of international law". However, shortly after this the famous Home Guard, first known as the Local Defence Volunteers, was formed. Whether G.B.G.'s 'Magna Carta letter' was really the impetus which started it, we shall probably never know; but it certainly stirred up matters at the time.

This was the period in his life at which G.B.G. first contacted the witch cult in Britain. Some of his neighbours in the New Forest area were members of an occult fraternity which called itself the Fellowship of Crotona and claimed to be Rosicrucian. G.B.G. was under no illusions as to the likelihood of its claims, or the somewhat flamboyant personality of its leader, one 'Brother Aurelius'. However, the fellowship had built a pleasant community theatre, which called itself 'The First Rosicrucian Theatre in England'; and in those dark days of war almost any distraction was welcome. G.B.G. helped them to put on amateur plays with an occult or spiritual theme.

Also, he liked Mrs. Besant-Scott, the daughter of Annie Besant and now an old lady, who had been persuaded to start the Fellowship of Crotona with 'Brother Aurelius'. He felt her to be genuine and sincere, and was interested in her other activities in Co-Masonry, a Masonic movement started by Annie Besant to enable women to participate in the Masonic tradition. (This Order is affiliated to the

Grand Orient of France, and consequently not recognised by the English Grand Lodge.)

G.B.G. realised that some of his friends who were Co-Masons were also members of something else, which was nothing to do with Co-Masonry or the supposed 'Rosicrucians'. They shared some secret among themselves, which was something on a different level to the highly coloured claims of 'Brother Aurelius'. He wondered, indeed, why intelligent and well-read people such as they evidently were, bothered with such an association. Eventually, he found out.

They confided in him that as Co-Masons, they had followed Mrs. Besant-Scott when she joined forces with the Fellowship of Crotona and moved to its New Forest settlement. They soon found themselves cold-shouldered by 'Brother Aurelius' and his devotees; but they also discovered something else, which made them willing to stay, in spite of everything. They contacted some New Forest people who were the last remains of an old-time witch coven. This was their secret, hidden behind the *facade* of the Fellowship of Crotona; the rest of whose members knew nothing about it.

The identity of the lady who was the leader of this coven, and in whose house in the New Forest G.B.G. was initiated as a witch, is known to me. So also is the place in the New Forest where outdoor meetings were held. However, for me to enlarge upon these points would be a breach of confidence.

At the time, at the beginning of the Second World War, witchcraft in this country was still illegal. The last of the Witchcraft Acts in Britain was not repealed until 1951. Consequently, G.B.G.'s delight, wonder and excitement at his discovery that the old Craft of the Wise still lived had to be tempered with extreme caution.

He wanted to tell the world of what he had found, because it seemed to him to be not only a discovery which in the realm of folklore was of the greatest interest; but also a happy pagan faith in which many people, unconventional like himself, could find the satisfaction they could never obtain from more orthodox creeds. However, his witch friends, and the elders of the coven, were adamant. "Don't publish anything," they said. As one of them put it, "Witchcraft doesn't pay for broken windows." They feared that, although the times of burning and hanging were past, publicity would only set the forces of persecution against them again, in other forms.

It was not until ten years later, after the old high priestess was dead, that G.B.G. revealed his knowledge about the Craft of the

Wise, and then only in the form of an historical novel. This book, *High Magic's Aid,* was published by Michael Houghton, London, 1949; and, as well as being a good story, it contained a wealth of information about what magic and witchcraft really were and how they worked.

Then, in 1951, witches in Britain obtained their legal freedom. The last Witchcraft Act was repealed, thanks mainly to the efforts of Spiritualists, who had campaigned against this old Act of Parliament being used to persecute mediums, whether the latter were genuine or not. It was replaced by the Fraudulent Mediums Act, which legally recognises genuine mediumship and psychic powers, and prosecutes only in the case of deliberate fraud committed for gain.

G.B.G. decided that the time had now arrived for members of the Craft of the Wise to come out into the open and speak out to the world about their rituals and beliefs. He accordingly proceeded to do so, by means of his writings, broadcasts, press interviews, and by his Museum of Magic and Witchcraft at Castletown, Isle of Man. Whether or not he was right in this decision is still a matter of controversy among present-day witches, and seems likely to continue to be so.

There is no doubt that G.B.G.'s action was a complete break with the witch tradition of silence and secrecy. I have reason to think that it was also contrary to the wishes of his associates. Today, many persons inside the witch cult regard G.B.G. as having done far more harm than good by his publicising of witchcraft. Furthermore, they do not agree that G.B.G.'s version of the Craft is an authoritative one; a point to which I will return later.

Such critics point to the undignified publicity in which some representatives of modern witchcraft seem to revel. They say that such antics are not only contrary to witch tradition, but serve no other purpose than the gratification of a few childish egos, and the alienation of intelligent people; and they add that this sort of thing was started by the deliberate break with the good old ways that Gerald Gardner made.

Frankly, this is a viewpoint with which the present writer feels considerable sympathy. In fact, I expressed my feelings on this matter to G.B.G. himself, very forcibly, during his lifetime—as a result of which, he and I were not on speaking terms for some while!

Looking back, however, I can see why G.B.G. acted as he did. His devotion to the Craft and the Old Gods was utterly and transparently sincere. The craft of the Wise had become his life; and he feared that it was in danger of dying out. With regard to his particular coven, in which he had been initiated, he could see that it was mostly composed of elderly people. After the big Lammas Rite in the New Forest in 1940, when they had raised the Cone of Power against Hitler's threatened invasion of Britain, no less than five of these elderly members died, one after another. It was as if the ritual, which had been repeated four times, had taken the last of their life force. Then later on, the old high priestess died; who was to carry on, when all were gone?

Gerald Gardner decided that somehow the Craft must send out a call to the younger people; people who were witches at heart, and who perhaps had been members of the Craft in previous lives, of which dim and shadowy recollections dwelt in their inner minds. On this point, of course, he was right. I have been told that one of the reasons why the authorities were willing to repeal the Witchcraft Act, was that they thought witchcraft was dead! (Once the repeal became law, they were rapidly undeceived.)

However, some will argue that the method he used was unwise. It would have been better and more fitting, they say, to have proceeded by purely occult methods; because the Craft has its own guardians, the Mighty Ones who have been great witches in the past, and who now dwell on the Inner Planes. They would not have let it die. It cannot be denied, however, that the world is changing and evolving, and the Craft cannot be static. It, too, must evolve, if it wishes to remain a living thing.

Leaving this continuing controversy, I will return to the issue mentioned previously; namely, the correctness or otherwise of Gerald Gardner's version of witchcraft.

A tradition that is passed down from one person to another, over a long period of time, is almost certain to be influenced by those of its transmitters who were themselves strong personalities. Gerald Gardner was certainly this. He was a character; a man of originality and fearless individualism. Therefore, the covens which he founded bear the imprint of his personality.

For instance, G.B.G. had a deep-rooted belief in the value of going naked when circumstances favoured it. He was a pioneer naturist, who supported the naturist movement before it became accepted, in the days when the very mention of nudity was regarded as shocking, scandalous, immoral, etc, etc. G.B.G. believed that communal nakedness, sunshine and fresh air, were things which were natural and beneficial, both physically and psychologically; and he said so fearlessly, and practised what he preached. Even when one could not be naked outdoors, he believed that nudity, for both sexes, could be beneficial, because it was natural. It made for healthy-mindedness, and lack of hypocrisy, and enabled people to be really themselves, relaxed and genuinely human, without tensions or class distinctions.

With these beliefs G.B.G. naturally approved of the very old religious and magical idea of ritual nudity, which he found in the witch cult. However, many witches of other covens than those founded by G.B.G. regard his insistence upon ritual nudity as an essential for the practice of witchcraft, to be an exaggeration. They point out the unsuitability of the English climate generally for this practice, however much the witches of Italy may have had ritual nudity commended to them in the Witches' Gospel, *Aradia*. Italy and Britain are two very different places. Although we know from Pliny's *Natural History* (6 vols, Bohn's Classical Library, London 1855-7), that the women of Ancient Britain performed religious rites in the nude, we are not told that they invariably did so.

Hence, witches of other traditions regard this aspect of G.B.G.'s version of witchcraft as being more a reflection of his own ideas than a real landmark of the Craft—a phrase which brings us to the consideration of the extent to which G.B.G.'s version of the rites was influenced by the fact that he and his friends who introduced him to witchcraft were Co-Masons.

There is a good deal in the witch rituals transmitted by G.B.G. which is reminiscent of Masonic phraseology. There are references, for instance, to "the working tools", the "Charge" given to the new initiate, who must be "properly prepared", and so on. The Craft consists of Three Degrees. It would be out of place for me to go into more detail. However, on the other hand there are references from old sources, which state that witchcraft consisted of three degrees of initiation; and G.B.G. in his writings has referred to the resemblances between some features of Masonic initiation, and some features of witch initiation. He has stated his belief that there has been in the past some definite connection between these two traditions—a belief which he bases upon these resemblances.

Gerald Gardner got to know Aleister Crowley when the latter was living at Hastings, a year before Crowley died. He was taken to see Crowley by a friend, and visited him on a number of occasions thereafter, until Crowley's death in 1947. Crowley took a liking to G.B.G., as a fellow-student of magic, and made him an honorary member of Crowley's magical order, the Ordo Templi Orientis. G.B.G. admired Aleister Crowley as a poet, and was fond of using quotations from Crowley's works in his rites.

When I pointed out to him that I thought this inappropriate for the rites of witchcraft, as it was too modern, he gave me to understand that the rituals he had received were in fact fragmentary. There were many gaps in them; and to link them together into a coherent whole, and make them workable, he had supplied words which seemed to him to convey the right atmosphere, to strike the right chords in one's mind. He felt, he said, that some of Crowley's work did this.

From my own study of these rites and traditions, I believe that this old coven which Gerald Gardner joined has fragments of ancient rituals; but fragments only. These were in the hands of the few elderly members that were left. Gerald Gardner, believing passionately that the old Craft of the Wise must not be allowed to die, gathered up these fragments and, with the assistance of his own knowledge of magic, which was considerable, and the result of many years' study all over the world, pieced them together, and added material of his own, in order to make them workable. In doing so, he of necessity put the imprint of his own personality and ideas upon them.

Another criticism made by covens of different origins is that G.B.G. knew only fragments of traditional lore possessed by a few people. He never pretended otherwise; but some of his followers have misguidedly presented him as being the oracle of all knowledge with regard to witchcraft.

Gerald Gardner did definitely possess certain magical powers of his own. I have taken part with him in witchcraft rites and can testify to this. However, he made no pretence to supernormal powers; nor did he ever claim to be anything more than a member of a coven. The titles of 'Britain's Chief Witch' and so on were conferred on him by the popular Press. He himself used no such titles, nor did he desire them. Also, he was flatly against the exploitation of the occult for money; and his outspokenness upon this point made him many enemies.

He himself, however, was a man utterly without malice. In fact, his greatest faults were his blind generosity and lack of discrimination.

He would literally have shared his last crust with his worst enemy. He could be at once lovable and exasperating.

The book for which he is best known is *Witchcraft Today,* which was published by Riders of London in 1954, and has been several times reprinted, including paperback editions. In the foreword he says that his acquaintances in the witch cult had told him to let people know that they were not perverts, nor did they practise harmful rites. I think myself that this was the argument he used, in order to get the witches to agree to his writing anything 'from the inside'; namely, to defend the Old Religion from all the highly-coloured slanders of perversion, Black Magic, devil worship, blood sacrifices and so on, that have been and still are launched against it. There is still a good deal of hate-propaganda poured out against witches; but at least Gerald Gardner showed that there is another side to the argument, and that witches are people, too.

In May, 1960, Gerald Gardner had the honour of an invitation to a garden party at Buckingham Palace—possibly the first time a witch has ever been asked to attend such a function. Although, of course, he was not asked because he was a witch, he felt that this invitation was proof that in Britain today a person can openly profess his allegiance to the Old Religion without arousing intolerance except among the hysterical, the bigoted, or the ignorant.

The end of G.B.G.'s colourful earthly life came in February 1964. He died at sea, of heart failure, while on one of the globe-trotting journeys he loved. A biography of him was published during his lifetime, entitled *Gerald Gardner: Witch,* by J. L. Bracelin (The Octagon Press, London, 1960).

GARTERS AS WITCHES' SIGNS

As far back as 1892, a French writer, Jules Lemoine, in *La Tradition,* noted the importance of the garter as a sign of rank among witches. He wrote: *"Les mauvaises gens forment une confrerie qui est dirigée par une sorcière. Celle-ci a la jarretière comme marque de sa dignité".* ("The bad people [witches] form a brotherhood, which is directed by a female witch. This woman wears a *garter* as a mark of her dignity.")

Margaret Murray quotes this passage in her *Witch-Cult in Western Europe* (Oxford University Press, 1921): and in her later book *The God of the Witches* (Faber, London, 1952), she advances the remarkable theory that the foundation of Britain's premier order of chivalry, the Order of the Garter, had its origin in the Old Religion of witchcraft. She believed the Plantagenet king, Edward III, the founder of the Order of the Garter, to have been certainly a sympathiser with witchcraft, if not an actual member of the cult.

We tend today to look upon a garter as a piece of feminine frippery, connected in the mind with can-can dancers and Edwardian belles. But of course the garters of long ago were not frilly things made of elastic. They were long laces or strings, which were bound round the leg and tied; and they were used by men as well as by women.

Margaret Murray has suggested that the significance of the garter in witchcraft is the real explanation of the old story of how the Order of the Garter came to be founded. The story goes that when King Edward III was dancing with a lady of his court, either the Fair Maid of Kent or the Countess of Salisbury, her garter fell to the floor. The lady was embarrassed; but the King gallantly picked up the garter, saying *"Honi soit qui mal y pense"* ("Shame to him who thinks ill of it"), and tied the garter upon his own leg. This incident gave him the idea to found the Order of the Garter, with twelve knights for the King, and twelve for his son, the Black Prince, making two thirteens, or twenty-six knights in all.

The number of thirteen was given further significance by the King's regalia as Chief of the Order. His mantle was ornamented with the figures of 168 garters, which, with the actual garter worn on his leg, made 169, or thirteen times thirteen.

The above incident of court life seems a very trivial one for this noble Order to have been founded upon, unless it had some inner significance. But if the garter that the lady dropped was a witch-garter, then the whole episode assumes quite a different aspect. Both the lady's confusion and the King's gesture are seen to have a much deeper meaning than in a mere pretty story of courtly gallantry. She stood revealed as a leading witch; and he publicly showed his willingness to protect the Old Religion and its followers.

Further evidence of the importance of the garter as a witches' sign may be seen in a rare old wood-engraving which is found as a frontispiece, in some copies only, of a sixteenth-century book about witches, *Dialogues Touchant le Pouvoir des Sorcières et la Punition qu'elles Méritent* (*Dialogues about the Power of Witches and of the Punishment They Deserve*) by Thomas Erastus (Geneva, 1579).

This picture shows the interior of a witch's cottage, set in some remote place among woods and hills. Four witches are in the act of departing on their fabled broomstick-flight to the Sabbat. Two of them have already flown up the wide cottage chimney; while a third, before she departs, is binding one leg with a garter. A fourth witch, broomstick in hand, awaits her turn; and outside, unknown to them, a man spies upon their proceedings through the keyhole.

The artist evidently accepted the story about witches flying on broomsticks; but he mingled with his fantasy a detail of fact, namely the garter. Artists who drew pictures of witches in the old days often did this, because they were depicting the popular notions about witches, which were a mixture of actual knowledge and fantasy.

GREEN MAN, THE

One of the most frequently recurring and most beautiful motifs of medieval art, is that of the Green Man. This figure represents a human face surrounded by foliage, which it seems to be peering through. Often the leafy branches are shown coming from the figure's mouth, as if he were in a sense breathing them forth. Some of the oldest representations of the Green Man show him as horned.

He represents the spirit of the trees, and the green growing things of earth; the god of the woodlands. Hence he is distinctly a pagan divinity. Yet he frequently appears among the carved decoration of our oldest churches and cathedrals, especially upon such things as roof bosses and the little seats called misericords.

As an old name for inns, too, 'The Green Man' makes his appearance; though here he is usually explained as representing either an old-time apothecary who gathered green herbs, or else as a forester dressed in Lincoln green.

In folk plays and customs, we find the Green Man in the guise of 'Green Jack' or 'Green George'. This part was enacted by a man who appeared among the May Day revellers, covered in a sort of framework of leafy garlands, so that his face peered through the leaves, like the figure in the old church carvings. At Castleton in Derbyshire, where the ceremony is kept up to this day, he rides on horseback and is called the Garland King.

The Green Man as a woodland god, is a relic of the old pagan rites and beliefs; and his popularity as a motif of church decoration proves that for a long time in Britain, pagan and Christian concepts existed side by side. When used in decoration, the Green Man is sometimes referred to as the foliate mask; and the foliage which surrounds him is most frequently oak, the old sacred tree of Britain. So

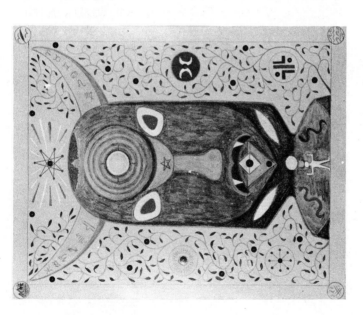

(*above left*) ATHO, the Horned God of Witchcraft, as shown in a painting by the author. (*above right*) BAPHOMET, the god of the Knights Templars.

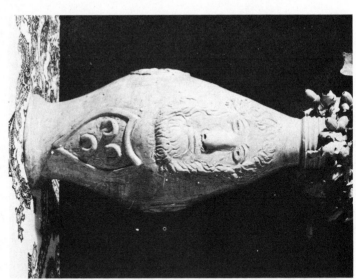

(*above left*) BELLARMINE JUGS. One example. (*above right*)
BROCKEN, THE. An old engraving. "The Spectre of the Brocken".

(*right*) CATS AS WITCHES' FAMILIARS. "A Male Witch and his Familiar", a print after the seventeenth-century picture attributed to Jordaens. (*below*) CIMA-RUTA. This Italian witch amulet, representing a sprig of rue, is surrounded here by other amulets from the author's collection.

Chat malin et Sou dangereux MOMUS. *De me Souffrir Vivre loin d'eux:*
Sont bien ensemble tous les deux ; Il Saut pour cherir leur presence,
Mais je les prie avec instance Avoir aussi le Cerveau Creux.
a Londres chez Vint.

DEVIL. (*above left*) Two woodcuts illustrating conceptions of the Devil. (*above right*) An old engraving of the Wild Hunt riding the night wind at the full moon.

ESBAT. The Witches' Frolic, from an engraving by the nineteenth-century artist, George Cruikshank.

EVIL EYE. Witch amulets against the Evil Eye: *mano in fica* and *mano cornuta*

FLAGELLATION. "They sacrifice to the Devil, and not to God" are the words on this miniature in a fifteenth-century French manuscript of St. Augustine's *Civitas Dei*.

(*above*) FOSSILS. Some examples from the author's collection. (*left*) GARDNER, GERALD. "Witch on a broomstick", a plaque made by Gerald Gardner.

INCUBI AND SUCCUBI. A drawing from a book by the nineteenth-century French occultist, Jules Bois.

LOVE CHARMS. A young witch performs a love spell in "The Charm of Love" by the Master of Niederheim, an unknown Flemish artist of the fifteenth century.

MANDRAKE. Strangely-shaped roots, reproduced from old prints which declared them to be genuine.

NUDITY, RITUAL. Albrecht Durer's engraving of four witches.

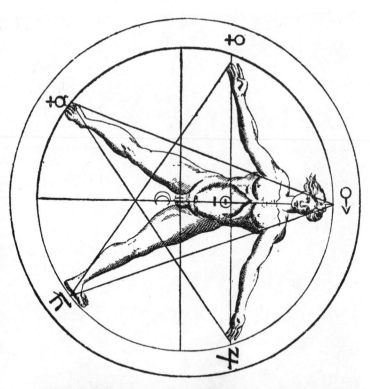

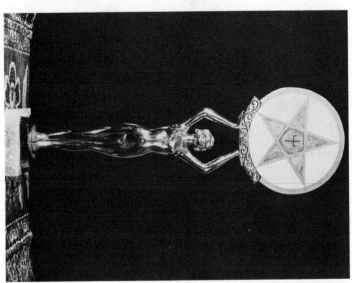

PENTAGRAM, THE. (*above left*) Man the microcosm, the pentagram of Cornelius Agrippa. (*above right*) The pentagram from a modern witch's altar.

(above) PERSECUTION OF
WITCHES. Woodcut showing
the 'swimming' of witches from
the pamphlet, "Witches Apprehended, Examined and Executed"
published in London in 1613
(reproduced by courtesy of the
Bodleian Library, Oxford). (right)
SABBAT, THE. A fifteenth-
century French miniature showing
witches meeting (reproduced by
courtesy of the Bodleian Library,
Oxford).

Dieu tout puissant acateur du
monde vniuersel fist et crea
tous les celestiens espritz bon
et vertueuv seur sonnât ses
baulx dons de nature et de grace · Car

SABBAT, THE. The seventeenth-century idea of a witches' Sabbat from *Tableau de L'Inconstance des Mauvais Anges* by Pierre De Lancre.

(*right*) TREES AND WITCHCRAFT. The World Tree, Yggdrasill. (*below*) WITCHCRAFT. Some tools of witchcraft, set out as if upon a witch's altar.

ZODIAC, THE. The Leo the
Lion figure from the Glastonbury
Zodiac.

he may be the spirit that Reginald Scot in his *Discoverie of Witch-craft* (1584) tells us about, "the man in the oke", who was among the fearsome company of unearthly beings that his mother's maid used to terrify him with, when he was a boy.

I have been told, by a present-day witch in Britain who claimed to have traditional knowledge, that an old name for people who were secretly devoted to pagan lore was 'Green Jack's Children'. So far, I have been unable to obtain any confirmation of this; but there is no doubt that the colour green is still regarded as somewhat uncanny, even in the present day. Some people think it unlucky, and this seems to arise from the idea that it is the fairies' colour, and they resent outsiders wearing it. It is a witches' colour, as is its complement, scarlet; both, in a sense, being colours of life, the green of vegetable and the scarlet of animal life.

GYPSIES AND WITCHCRAFT

Ki shan i Romani,
Adoi san' i chov'hani,

So runs the old gypsy proverb, meaning "Wherever the Romanies go, there witches may be found." The first President of the Gypsy-Lore Society, Charles Godfrey Leland, regarded gypsies as the great carriers and disseminators of magic and witchcraft, wherever they travelled.

Certainly, one reason given for the persecution of gypsies in the past has been that they provided a rallying-point for disaffected and shiftless persons of all kinds, among whom witches were counted. There is a certain amount of truth in this, in that the gypsies attracted to their way of life a good many people who were at odds with so-ciety. In fact, they still do; and there are probably more travelling people in Britain today than there are real Romanies.

The Romanies came originally from the East, probably from India; but as they journeyed by way of Egypt, or claimed to have done so, they were called Egyptians, of which 'gypsy' is a worn-down version, a name given to them by the *gorgios,* or non-gypsies. They, however, held themselves proudly in their rags, and called themselves 'Lords of Little Egypt', their name for gypsydom in general.

Their great profession has always been fortune-telling, either by the lines of the hand, *dukkerin' drey the vast* as they call it, or by means of the cards. On the Continent the Tarot cards have come to be so much associated with gypsy fortune tellers, that these cards are sometimes called 'the Tarot of the Bohemians', meaning the gypsies. However, the real origin of these mysterious cards of fortune remains a mystery. (*See* TAROT CARDS.)

It is remarkable that the Romany word for God is Devel or Duvel, which derives from the Sanskrit Deva, meaning 'a shining one'. No wonder, then, if the gypsies felt some kinship with the European witches, who were like themselves hounded for being different, for not conforming, and for being alleged devil worshippers.

The Romanies, too, believe in the Great Mother, Amari De, or De Develeski, the personification of Nature; thinly disguised today as Sara-Kali, the Black Madonna, or alleged gypsy-saint Sara, whose little statue can still sometimes be found, dark-faced and bedizened, in the smart motor-drawn caravans of well-to-do modern gypsy families.

The real old-time gypsies of England would never willingly allow their dead to be buried in Christian consecrated ground, or have anything to do with the religion of the *gorgios*. Nor would the gypsies of the European continent; though they did have a reverence for the Virgin Mary, whom they prayed to as a goddess. The famous Spanish Madonna, La Macarena of Seville, in all her goddess-like beauty and magnificence, is regarded as the special Madonna of the gypsies.

People like this, pagans at heart with strong traits of goddess worship, and with an inborn aptitude for all things of magic, sorcery and the occult, were natural sympathisers with the pagan witches, their companions in misfortune and outlawry. They share, too, another characteristic with them, namely a belief in reincarnation, which Charles Godfrey Leland noted among the witches of Italy, and George Borrow has witnessed to among the gypsies he knew. (*See* REINCARNATION.)

In his introduction to *The Zincali: an Account of the Gypsies of Spain* (John Murray, London, 1841), Borrow tells us:

> Throughout my life the gypsy race has always had a peculiar interest for me. Indeed I can remember no period when the mere mention of the name of Gypsy did not awaken within me feelings hard to be described. I cannot account for this—I merely state a fact.
>
> Some of the Gypsies, to whom I have stated this circumstance, have accounted for it on the supposition that the soul which at present animates my body has at some former period tenanted that of one of their people; for many among them are believers in metempsychosis, and, like the fol-

lowers of Bouddha, imagine that their souls, by passing through an infinite number of bodies, attain at length sufficient purity to be admitted
to a state of perfect rest and quietude, which is the only idea of heaven
they can form.

Among the gypsies themselves the *chovihani* and the *drabarni,*
the witch and the herb woman, are held in honour. The profession
of tribal *chovihani* is handed down from mother to daughter; even
as among non-gypsy witches, with whom the respect for heredity
is strong. The whole truth about gypsy religion and gypsy witchcraft
has not yet been fully investigated; though some ceremonies and
customs have been recorded, which illustrate their beliefs. Many of
these are strikingly similar to those of the witch cult among non-
gypsies.

For instance, there is the custom of praying to the new moon,
which among some of the wildest and most primitive gypsy tribes
is performed naked. On the night when the new moon first appears
in the sky, they will take off their clothes to her, bow their heads,
and pray that she will bring them good fortune, health and money
during the coming month.

There is also a considerable resemblance between the outdoor
Sabbats and Esbats of the witches, held at a crossroads or in a wood,
and the nocturnal gatherings of gypsies, as Jean-Paul Clébert has
noted in his book *The Gypsies* (Vista Books, London, 1963). The
open fire with its bubbling cauldron, the music and dancing, must
have looked very reminiscent of witches' meetings to a suspicious
passer-by. In fact, the small cauldrons called gypsy pots are much
sought after today by witches, as being more convenient to use than
the big cooking-pot variety; and both kinds, alas, are becoming collectors' pieces, expensive and hard to find.

There is a definite belief among some present-day witches that
when the persecution against witches grew fiercer in England, in the
sixteenth and seventeenth centuries, many witches fled from their
homes and took to the roads, becoming *mumpers,* or travelling folk
who followed the gypsy way of life though they were not themselves
of gypsy blood. Because of the beliefs they held in common a certain
amount of interchange of ideas took place between witches and gypsies, and they tended to protect each other against the mutual enemy,
that settled Christian society which tormented, dispossessed and
hanged them both in the name of the God of Love.

Throughout history, witchcraft seems to have been the religion of the dispossessed and the outlawed: the down-trodden serfs of medieval Europe, whose misery and resentment are described in *Aradia;* the people who fled before the conquering sword of Islam; the gypsies who prayed to the moon, and to the spirits of stream and woodland, the Nivashi and the Puvushi; and earlier, the dark aboriginal people of these islands, who were here before the Celts, and the priests and priestesses of pagan mysteries, whose temples were closed and whose rites forbidden by the Early Christian Church.

Because witchcraft is old, its origins are complex; and yet its real essence is simple—devotion to Nature, the Great Mother, and to looking into Nature to find magic. The intellectuals and the sophisticated scoff at it, and yet fear while they scoff; because they recognise, consciously or otherwise, that witchcraft is linked to the primitive, to the depths within themselves that they do not wish to look into, or even acknowledge the existence of.

H

HALLOWEEN

> Hey, hey, for Halloween!
> Then the witches shall be seen,
> Some in black, and some in green,
> Hey, hey, for Halloween!
> Horse and hattock, horse and go,
> Horse and pellatis, ho! ho!

These are the words of an old folk-song referring to the festival of Halloween, on 31st October. This is the one of the four Great Sabbats of the witches that everyone has heard about. It is traditionally a weird and ghostly season, when spirits of all kinds walk abroad, as if released for one night of the year to hold communication with mortals.

In America the celebration of Halloween, by both children and adults, is more popular than it is in Britain. The children dress up in fancy costumes and masks, and go round knocking on people's doors and calling "Trick or treat?" If the 'treat' is not forthcoming, in the shape of sweets, apples or pocket-money, then the house gets the 'trick' by having the maskers play some prank upon its occupants.

Adults, too, often dress up for Halloween parties in America, to dance by the flickering light of candles in pumpkin lanterns, and scare each other with spooky frolics.

To witches, however, Halloween is a serious occasion, however merrily celebrated. It is the old Celtic Eve of Samhain (pronounced something like 'sowen'). Samhain means 'Summer's End', when the winter half of the year begins on 1st November. This night and all the first week of November once blazed with ritual bonfires. This is the real origin of our Bonfire Night on 5th November, which is much older than Guy Fawkes and his abortive Gunpowder Plot.

On the blazing fires, the Celts symbolically burned all the frustrations and anxieties of the preceding year. Such rituals in pre-Christian times were organised by the Druids, the Celtic priest-philosophers. (*See* DRUIDS.)

With the coming of Christianity, the Church tried to Christianise the old festival by making 1st November All Saints Day, or All Hallows as the old term was. Thus Samhain Eve became All Hallows Eve, or Halloween. But the attempts to discourage the pagan celebrations were so unavailing that the festival was eventually banned from the Church calendar.

It was not until 1928 that the Church of England formally restored All Hallows to its calendar, on the assumption that the old pagan associations of Halloween were at last really dead and forgotten; a supposition that was certainly premature.

The many kinds of divination associated with Halloween have been immortalised by Robert Burns in his poem of that name. These are mostly directed to discovering the person one is fated to marry, and hence were usually practised by young people. Nuts and apples were the popular fare for these family fireside celebrations; in the north of England Halloween is sometimes called Nutcrack Night, for this reason.

The witches' magical gatherings on Halloween were (and are) taken more seriously than the fun and mischief of popular folklore. To them, Halloween is the festival of the dead. This is not as grim as it sounds. Death, to the pagan Celt, was the door which opened on to another life. The idea that those who have gone before still retain an interest in the living, and are willing to aid them, has for centuries been part of the witches' creed. The Church has given a kind of back-handed recognition of this fact, by the way in which Spiritualism has often been denounced by clergymen as witchcraft.

It was believed that not only the souls of the dead, but also spirits and goblins of all kinds, were abroad on Halloween. The witches took advantage of this belief as a cover for their meetings; and one of the ways in which they did this was by using the pumpkin and turnip lanterns that have come to be a part of Halloween decorations.

The big orange-yellow pumpkins, that ripen around this time of year, were plentiful in cottage gardens. It was easy to hollow them out, cut a grinning face on them, and then put a candle inside to shine through. Slung from a pole, they would look at a distance in the dark like a procession of goblins. In a similar way, hollowed-out turnips would provide smaller pixy faces. They served the double purpose of a lantern to light the way through woodlands and across fields, and an effective scaring device to frighten off anyone who might get too curious.

The black cloaks and hoods worn by the witches would be invisible in the dark. The goblin lanterns would be all that could be seen, and the effect of a cluster of them bobbing along through the misty autumn night must have been hair-raising indeed to anyone not in on the secret.

HAUNTINGS CONNECTED WITH WITCHCRAFT

The late Elliott O'Donnell, who was responsible for many volumes of ghostly tales, recorded a number of hauntings attributed to witchcraft in one way or another. The most frequent cause of such weird happenings was believed to be the lingering presence of the witch's familiar spirits.

This, it seems, was particularly likely to occur if the witch had met a violent death. O'Donnell himself was a witness to one such apparition, that of a large black bird which haunted a crossroads somewhere in the north of England.

Apparently the bird had been the pet of an old woman who lived in a cottage nearby, and was reputed to practise witchcraft. One night a mob had dragged her from her bed and subjected her to the notorious swimming test in a pond. In the course of the proceedings she died, and her friendless corpse had been buried at the crossroads. The bird, at first in material and then in phantom form, had haunted the spot ever afterwards. Its most frequent spectral appearances were in March and September, the months of the equinoxes—periods well known to occultists as being times of psychic stress.

O'Donnell also recorded several phantom cats, reputed to have been witches' familiars. People may sneer at the possibility of the spirit of an animal surviving death; but why should it not? An animal that has been closely associated with humans develops as an individual. It has a personality, as any pet-lover can testify. It is no longer merely part of a group-soul.

Animals which do not develop as individuals may simply return to their own group-soul at death; but what of those who *are* distinct personalities? A witch's familiar in particular would be likely to survive because it would be a creature selected for its intelligence, and closely attached to its owner.

However, another haunting recorded by O'Donnell scarcely seems to come into this category. It is simply one of those inexplicable and rather horrible things that one finds on the borderlands of occult lore. The story was told to him by a man in Ireland, whose parents once took an old house in which strange things occurred. On several occasions, the family had seen the apparition of a horde of mice, apparently dragging some large, shapeless object across the floor. The noise they made could be heard, but they were evidently phantom mice, because when pursued they and their mysterious burden simply disappeared. No dog or cat would stay in the house, and the family eventually left before their lease had ended.

Upon enquiry, it was discovered that a previous occupant of the house had been a woman reputed to be a witch, whose craft was of a dark and sinister kind.

Another haunting, which was described to Elliott O'Donnell's mother by a Worcestershire farmer, concerned a strange spectral figure, something like an animal yet not an animal. It may have been an elemental spirit. Its abode was an old elm-tree by the side of a road, and it was locally believed to be the familiar of an old woman called Nancy Bell, a witch who had lived nearby many years ago.

The farmer declared that he had seen it one moonlight night, as it crossed the road and disappeared into the tree. He said it was something like a rabbit, but much larger, and with a strangely-shaped head. Elementals of certain other frightening types are often described as appearing in misshapen, semi-animal forms such as this.

Any place where magical rites have been performed is likely to have curious things occurring there, if the power that has built up there is not dispersed. The magic need not necessarily be black magic, either. The performance of magical ritual creates an atmosphere which attracts spirits and elementals. This is why experienced occultists never abandon a place of working without ceremonially clearing it first. Sometimes, however, circumstances prevent this being done, and odd phenomena often ensue.

A haunting directly connected with a famous witchcraft case in Scotland, was that which afflicted a grim old house at the Bow Head, Edinburgh. This house was once the residence of Major Thomas Weir and his sister Jean, who were both executed for witchcraft in 1670. Robert Chambers, in his *Traditions of Edinburgh* (Chambers, London and Edinburgh, 1896), tells how the house and its neighbourhood were believed to be haunted by the unquiet spirits of Weir and his sister: "His apparition was frequently seen at night, flitting, like a black and silent shadow about the street. His house, though known to be deserted by everything human, was sometimes observed at midnight to be full of lights, and heard to emit strange sounds as of dancing, howling, and, what is strangest of all, spinning."

One of the accusations against Jean Weir at her trial was that her prowess in using a spinning-wheel had been aided by witchcraft. Presumably, this sound was thought to be the witch-woman still plying her ghostly wheel. Sometimes, too, there were sounds and apparitions of galloping horses, which the fear-stricken inhabitants of Edinburgh believed to be caused by the spirits riding abroad at night.

No one would venture to live in the house, until one bold sceptic, an ex-soldier named William Patullo, obtained the tenancy of it at a very low rent. But on the first—and only—night he spent in the old house, Patullo's scepticism was turned to terror. Robert Chambers continues the story:

> On the very first night after Patullo and his spouse had taken up their abode in the house, as the worthy couple were lying awake in their bed, not unconscious of a certain degree of fear—a dim uncertain light proceeding from the gathered embers of their fire, and all being silent around them—they suddenly saw a form like that of a calf, which came forward to the bed, and, setting its fore-feet upon the stock, looked steadfastly at the unfortunate pair. When it had contemplated them thus for a few minutes, to their great relief it at length took itself away, and slowly retiring, gradually vanished from their sight. As might be expected, they deserted the house next morning; and for another half-century no other attempt was made to embank this part of the world of light from the aggressions of the world of darkness.

(*See also* WITCH OF SCRAPFAGGOT GREEN and TREES AND WITCHCRAFT.)

HECATE

Hecate is the Ancient Greek goddess of witchcraft. She is represented on a Roman engraved gem of the classical period as enthroned in triple form, with three heads and three pairs of arms, which hold daggers, whips and torches. Coiled at her feet are two huge serpents. Engraved gems of this kind were carried as amulets, especially by people interested in the occult sciences.

Hecate is a very ancient goddess, considered to be older than the Olympian gods and goddesses of classical myth. She was venerated by Zeus himself, who never denied her time-honoured power of granting or withholding from mortals whatever their hearts desired.

For this reason, Hecate was a goddess much invoked by magicians and witches. Her power was threefold: in heaven, upon earth and in the underworld of ghosts and spirits. One of her symbols was a key, indicating her ability to lock up or release spirits and phantoms of all kinds. Euripides, the Greek poet, called her "Queen of the phantom-world".

Her statue stood at the cross-roads, or where three ways met; and here those who wished to invoke her foregathered by night. In later years, witches assembled at the cross-roads to celebrate their rites.

Although her rulership extended over heaven, earth and the underworld, Hecate came to be particularly associated with the moon, and with the other moon goddesses, Diana, Artemis and Selene, with whom she was identified. Her triplicity mirrored the moon's three phases, waxing, full and waning.

She was depicted as being accompanied by howling dogs, probably because of the way dogs have of baying at the moon, though dogs are also said to howl when a ghost is nigh, even though no spectre is seen; and they react strongly to haunted places.

The Gnostic philosophers, who foregathered in the Egyptian city of Alexandria, revered a collection of ancient fragments of poetry called the Chaldean Oracles. Some of these have come down to us, written in Greek; and in them Hecate appears as the Great Mother, or the life of the universe. Nature is her garment or mantle: "And from her back, on either side the Goddess, boundless Nature hangs."

The name of Hecate may not be a Greek word; some authorities doubt this, and in general there is much uncertainty about its derivation. Some have suggested that it means 'the Far-off One', or 'The One who Stands Aloof'. There is a resemblance between the name Hecate and the Ancient Egyptian *hekau,* meaning 'magic'. Two of Hecate's ancient titles are Aphrattos, the 'Nameless One', and Pandeina, the 'All-Terrible'.

Robert Graves, however, in his *Greek Myths* (Penguin Books, London, 1957 and Baltimore, Maryland, 1955), gives the name of Hecate as meaning 'one hundred', and connects it with the Great Year of one hundred lunar months, during which in very ancient days the Sacred King was permitted to reign. At the end of it he was sacrificed, so that his blood might enrich the land and renew the prosperity of his people. This institution of the divine king who was sacrificed was very widespread in the ancient world, and goes back a long way into human history. It is intimately connected with the matriarchal order of primitive times, when the Great Goddess of Nature, the Magna Mater, was pre-eminent.

Shakespeare in *Macbeth* represents his three witches as worshippers of Hecate; not as invokers of the Devil or Satan, although the latter was what witches had for centuries been accused of being. A number of Shakespeare's contemporaries also introduced 'Dame Hecate' into their plays and poems, as the goddess of the witches.

In Thomas Middleton's play *The Witch,* his principal character takes the name of Hecate, naming herself as a witch after the goddess of witchcraft.

If, therefore, we wished to choose a name which was probably used by people in Shakespeare's day and afterwards, to invoke the goddess of the witches, 'Hecate' would be a natural choice. The Greek pronunciation of this name is *Hek*-a-tee; but this became Anglicised into *Hek*-at.

The sigil used by magicians to invoke Hecate is a crescent moon with the two points upwards, and a third point in the middle between them.

HERBS USED BY WITCHES

The folklore of flowers, plants and trees is a vast subject, which would need a book to itself to expound fully. The old word used for the knowledge of the secret properties of herbs is 'Wortcunning'; and this has always been a particular study of witches.

Herbal lore has two aspects. The first one treats of the actual medicinal properties of herbs; the second is concerned with their occult, hidden, magical properties. Witches used both sides of this knowledge in their craft.

We may note that the word 'pharmacy' is derived from the Ancient Greek *pharmakeia,* and this word meant not only the compounding of medicinal drugs, but also the making of magical potions and philtres. The Greek goddess who was the patroness of witchcraft was Hecate, the triple moon goddess, and there are many classical allusions to her, and to Medea and Circe, the famous witches of Greek legend. (*See* HECATE.) The second Idyll of Theocritus, called the *Pharmaceutria,* deals not with innocent medicines, but, in the words of Montague Summers, "gives a vividly realistic and impassioned picture of Greek sorcery". (*The Geography of Witchcraft,* Kegan Paul, London, 1927.)

The witch and her bubbling cauldron, therefore, demonstrably go back to pre-Christian times; though the contents of the cauldron might be either beneficent or baleful. Herbs were studied in Ancient Egypt also; and before Hecate was Isis, the Egyptian Lady of the Moon and Mistress of Magic. The famous Ebers Papyrus, which was found buried with a mummy in the Theban Necropolis, contains a great many herbal recipes; and the simples it prescribes include a number of herbal substances still used by herbalists and witches today. Among them are onions, pomegranates, poppies, gentian, squills, elderberries, mint, aloes, myrrh and colchicum.

Of the 400 simples (i.e. single herbs) used by the great Greek doctor, Hippocrates, half that number are still in use today. But the authorities from whom European witches and magicians derived most of their knowledge were the first-century Greek physician Dioscorides, who compiled the earliest herbal in existence, which continued to be used for 1,600 years; and the *Natural History* of Pliny, which is packed with curious lore, and from which Cornelius Agrippa in the sixteenth century borrowed much of the material on "Natural Magick" in his *Occult Philosophy* (Cologne, 1533; English translation published in London in 1651).

In such centres as Toledo in Spain, where European and Islamic culture mingled, medicine was studied as well as magic, alchemy and astrology; and so the knowledge of Eastern drugs such as hashish, derived from the hemp plant, was added to the learning handed down from the old classical writers. The knowledge of these things gradually spread, and filtered its way down to the village witch, mingled with traditions derived from Norse, Celtic and pre-Celtic sources.

The village witch of olden time was herbalist, spell-caster, interpreter of dreams, healer, midwife and psychologist, all rolled into one. In the days when present-day medical science, let alone the National Health Service, was unknown, she was practically the only resource of poor people in remote parts of the country. In fact, in those times when surgery was in its infancy, and blistering and bleeding were the order of the day among orthodox medical men, the village witch, with her simple herbal brews and her practical psychology, probably killed fewer people than the doctors.

Not all witches lived in obscurity, however. There was a famous lady called Trotula, of Salerno in Italy, who became known all over

Europe for her remedies and recipes. Her name is the origin of the expression 'Dame Trot' or 'Old Trot', applied to a witch.

The time when magical and medicinal herbs were gathered was ruled by astrology (*See* ASTROLOGY), and particularly by the phases of the moon. The waxing moon was the time for constructive magic: and the waning moon was for destructive magic and banishing; but herbs were generally supposed to attain their maximum virtue for good if gathered at the full moon. On the other hand, herbs used for dark purposes would be gathered in the dark of the moon; and Shakespeare's witches in *Macbeth* used "root of hemlock digged i' the dark".

Herbs which have a narcotic or soporific effect have been specially associated with witchcraft, because of their use in compounding the Witches' Salve. (*See* FLYING OINTMENTS.) Apart from these, a number of herbs have been given popular names which show their association with witches.

For instance, the great mullein (*Verbascum thapsus*), which grows in hedgerows with a tall downy spike of yellow flowers, was called Hag-taper. The Old English word *haegtesse* means 'witch'; so Hag-taper means 'the witch's candle'. Foxgloves are sometimes called witches' bells; and periwinkle (*Vinca minor*) is known as sorcerers' violet.

This pretty blue flower is the *Provinsa* of Albertus Magnus, the reputed author of the magical book called *Le Grand Albert* (many editions; that printed in Paris in 1885 and edited by Marius Descrepe is considered probably most authentic). He calls it the most powerful flower for producing love. Another beautiful flower with the same reputation is the wild orchid, called satyrion. The plant received this name because its root resembles a pair of testicles; hence probably its magical repute. There are a number of wild orchids growing in Britain which have a root of this kind.

The romantically-named enchanter's nightshade (*Circaea lutetiana*) is another plant with an aura of magic, which grows in English woods. It is not actually one of the nightshades at all, but a pretty, delicate-looking spike of white or pinkish flowers. Other attractive-looking plants with a magical reputation are Solomon's Seal, a cottage garden flower, and the little mauve-flowered vervain, which is often found growing among ancient ruins.

On the side of magical protection, there is the splendid golden-yellow St. John's wort (*Hypericum perforatum*), which used to be called *Fuga demonum,* because it banished evil spirits. The rowan tree, or mountain ash, with its handsome red berries, performs the same good office, and dissolves evil spells. It was the great Gaelic charm against all bewitchment. An old Scottish greeting was, "Peace be here and rowan tree."

The list of the magical properties attributed to flowers, trees and roots could be extended almost indefinitely. An important department of herbal lore was the making of 'suffumigations' or magical incenses, which would attract spirits and cause them to appear. (*See* INCENSE, MAGICAL USES OF.)

Centuries of mystic lore have accumulated around the plant called the mandrake. However, the true mandrake does not grow wild in Britain; so the plant used by witches for similar purposes, that is, the making of magical figures in the shape of a little man or woman, are the roots of the black or white briony. (*See* MANDRAKE.)

Believing as they do in the magic of numbers, witches like to use either three, seven or nine herbs in compounding a charm or a spell. These numbers have from time immemorial been considered to have potent occult properties.

Mugwort (*Artemisia vulgaris*) was called by the old-time herbalists *Mater Herbarum*, 'the Mother of Herbs', because of its pre-eminent qualities. It was particularly associated with the goddess Diana, and the pictures in old herbals show her holding a spray of it. Its leaves are silver underneath, and it is generally regarded as ruled by the moon, though Culpeper ascribes it to Venus. An infusion of tea made of mugwort is believed to aid in the development of clairvoyance. The young leaves are used, sweetened with a little honey; but of course the herb has to be gathered at full moon to be most effective.

As a witches' herb, mugwort often appears in magical recipes. For instance, the magic mirror was sometimes anointed with its juice, and the herb was mingled with the burning incense when the mirror was used. (*See* SCRYING.)

HILLS ASSOCIATED WITH WITCHCRAFT

Perhaps the most famous British hill to figure in stories of witches is Pendle Hill, in Lancashire. Today, cheerful village shops cash in on its witchcraft associations by selling souvenir models of witches on broomsticks, to tourists in its vicinity. But in times past the shadow of Pendle Hill, and the wild doings that were said to take place upon and around it, lay dark across the countryside, and people spoke of it in whispers. The gypsies in George Borrow's day called Lancashire Chohawniskytem, 'Witch-country'.

Pendle Hill itself is almost a mountain; a dark, almost treeless bulk, flat on top, and giving a wide view over the countryside to the far-off waves of the Irish Sea. The name of Pendle became known all over England, when in 1613 appeared a book by Thomas Potts entitled *The Wonderful Discovery of Witches in the County of Lancaster*. This was a detailed account of the events of the previous year, 1612, when twenty people from the Pendle area stood trial as witches. Ten of them ended their lives on the gallows, and another, an old woman called Demdike, said to be a leading witch, died in jail before the trial started.

The Lancashire witches were accused of holding their meetings in Pendle Forest, close by the shadow of the great hill; but it is evident that Pendle Hill itself is a place with an unwritten history of ancient sanctity, dating from prehistoric times. Like Chanctonbury Ring, another witches' meeting place on a hill, Pendle has a tradition of gatherings at the beginning of May, to see the sun rise from its height. An old festival called Nick o' Thung's Charity, which used to be held for this purpose, was revived in 1854; and on the first Sunday in May hundreds of working people from the countryside round used to gather on the slopes of Pendle Hill. They brought food with them, and cooked it in the open on camp-fires, just as the common people had done at the Great Sabbats in times past. This popular celebration was evidently connected with the old May Eve and May Day festivals.

It is not so well known about Pendle Hill, that upon its summit George Fox, the founder of the Quaker movement, saw a vision and had a mystical experience which inspired him in his religious mission. This happened in 1652, at a time when the persecution of witches was still very active in Britain. Fox was lucky not to have been accused as a witch, in view of the place where his vision occurred. He tells us that he climbed Pendle Hill because he was "moved of the Lord" to do so. One may wonder whether something numinous, some psychic atmosphere, lingers upon the hill of Pendle, from days of long ago when it was a sacred height.

The connections between Chanctonbury Ring in Sussex and the practice of witchcraft have already been noted. (*See* CHANCTONBURY RING.) The notorious Brocken in Germany and Glastonbury Tor with its mystic associations have also been described elsewhere. (*See* BROCKEN, THE, and AVALON, THE ANCIENT BRITISH PARADISE.)

Another hill with witchcraft associations is Bredon Hill, near Tewkesbury in Gloucestershire. On its summit are the remains of a prehistoric camp, and an ancient stone called the Bambury Stone. Harold T. Wilkins, who writes of Bredon Hill in his book *Mysteries Solved and Unsolved* (Odhams, London, 1960), suggests that this stone derives its name from *Ambroisie petrie*, 'anointed stone'. It seems possible to me that another origin of the name is derived from the Latin *ambire*, 'to go round', meaning 'the stone that is danced around'. Both derivations relate to the fact that this stone, as Wilkins notes, was a focus for witchcraft ceremonies in centuries past.

Bredon Hill earns its place in Harold Wilkins' book, because in May 1939 it was the scene of the mysterious death of a man called Harry Dean, an event still surrounded with uncertainty and dark questioning. He was found dead in a deserted quarry, apparently strangled; in a place which itself seems to have been adapted at some time for ritual use, because it is described as having a level floor, and four boulders roughly marking the cardinal points, north, south, east and west. It was beside the boulder on the south side that Dean's body was found. The coroner's verdict was "Accidental Death"; a verdict which seems questionable, to say the least.

Bredon Hill marks an angle of a triangle, formed in the Cotswold area and which can be drawn on the map; the other two angles being occupied by Meon Hill, the scene of another mysterious death associated with witchcraft, and Seven Wells, the witches' meeting-place referred to in Hugh Ross Williamson's historical novel about Cotswold witchcraft, *The Silver Bowl*. The death of Charles Walton upon Meon Hill in February 1945 was definitely murder, still unsolved. (*See* COTSWOLDS, WITCHCRAFT IN THE.) Another triangle can be drawn between Seven Wells, Meon Hill and the Rollright Stones, another traditional haunt of witches.

Upon the heights of the Shropshire hills is the strange natural rock formation called the Stiperstones. Among these rocks is a throne-like elevation known as The Devil's Chair. Upon this natural throne the Devil was supposed to sit, when he presided over the meetings of the Shropshire witches. The story goes that if anyone else ventures to sit in the Devil's Chair, a storm will arise soon afterwards.

Ditchling Beacon, the highest point of the Sussex Downs, seems very innocuous in the summer season, occupied only by picnic-munching tourists admiring the view. In the winter, however, when these hills are lonely and deserted, it is a different story. Then the

Wild Hunt, locally known as the Witch Hounds, goes yelling and raging across Ditchling Beacon upon windy nights; a rush of phantom hounds and horsemen, whose cries and hoofbeats pass by upon the wind, though nothing is seen.

Stray whispers of witch-gatherings upon lonely heights cling to The Wrekin, in Shropshire, close to where the old Roman road of Watling Street passes on the way to the ruins of Uriconium, an important town of ancient days. From here, perhaps, in the times of the Roman occupation, followers of pagan mystery cults went up to The Wrekin to celebrate their rites.

Britain has quite a few places called Herne Hill or some variant of this. These are usually explained as being named after *hern,* the old English name for a heron. But did herons really nest on all these hills? Or is this name, like that of Herne the Hunter, the horned phantom of Windsor Forest, derived from a name of the old Horned God?

Some gatherings were held also in times past upon Snaefell, in the Isle of Man; but, apart from calling them 'disgraceful scenes' and so on, local historians are very vague as to what they were.

As long ago as the days when the Old Testament was written, moralists have been denouncing 'disgraceful scenes' upon pagan high places. The Maenads and Bacchantes of Ancient Greece held their wild revels upon the hills. Yet upon high places also, men have experienced religious visions which changed their lives. The gods of many pantheons were believed to dwell upon mountain-tops. Perhaps it is the very inaccessibility of the height itself, the effort needed to climb it, which invests it with the sense of other worlds beyond the everyday.

There is a sense, too, of eternity upon heights seldom trodden by the feet of men; as evidenced in the popular saying, "As old as the hills". There, indeed, "the Old Gods guard their round", and the veil between the seen and unseen may grow thin. Pagan temples were frequently built upon hilltops; and the memory of these old gatherings and rites is often behind the association of a particular hill-top with witchcraft. This is certainly so in the case of Chanctonbury Ring and of the Brocken, as already noted; and another instance of the same thing is the Puy-de-Dome in France, which was once the site of a pagan sanctuary, and in later years became the traditional scene of witch rites.

HOLED STONES

Sir Wallis Budge, in his authoritative book *Amulets and Superstitions* (Oxford University Press, 1930), states that the first man who ever found a stone with a hole in it and thought to thread it on a string and hang it round his neck, had the credit of introducing the wearing of amulets into the world.

This is what happened back in the beginnings of history. Today, holiday-makers on a seaside beach amuse themselves by looking for holed stones; and if they find an attractive one, they may well keep it 'for luck'.

The first holy stone very probably was actually a 'holey' stone; that is, a stone with a hole in it. The reason for its magical powers is the same as that for another very ancient amulet, the cowrie shell; namely, that it is a female emblem, representing the portal of birth. Hence it is a life symbol and a luck bringer.

Holed stones are also known as hag stones, because they are a protection against the spells of witches. An old antiquarian, Grose, tells us that "a Stone with a Hole in it, hung at the Bed's head, will prevent the Night Mare; it is therefore called a Hag Stone, from that disorder which is occasioned by a Hag or Witch sitting on the Stomach of the party afflicted. It also prevents Witches riding Horses: for which purpose it is often tied to a Stable Key." (Quoted in *Observations on Popular Antiquities,* John Brand and Sir Henry Ellis, Chatto and Windus, London, 1877).

If a holed stone repelled black witchcraft, on the other hand white witchcraft valued it as a lucky find. Some people believed that by looking through a holed stone one could see the fairies; that is, if the time and place and other conditions were right.

In *Aradia,* the witches' gospel of Italy, we are told that "to find a stone with a hole in it is a special sign of the favour of Diana". The finder should pick it up, and thank the spirit that led him to encounter it.

This belief, like that in the protection and luck of the horseshoe, is another instance of things that are sacred to the witches' goddess being amulets against the darker uses of witchcraft. It will be noted how the affliction of nightmares and evil dreams was anciently ascribed to witches. It was, of course, the spirit of the hag or witch that came and oppressed people by night; or, as present-day occultists would say, the projection of their astral body.

HOPKINS, MATTHEW

The name of Matthew Hopkins is the most ill-famed in the story of English witchcraft. Although his career as self-appointed 'Witch-Finder General' lasted only for about two years, from 1644 to 1646, he was responsible for more executions than are recorded of any other person.

What made Hopkins particularly odious is that his witch-hunting was conducted for money, and his victims were the old, the poor and the most feeble and defenceless members of the community. In one instance, using his pretended commission from Parliament, he actually directed the citizens of Stowmarket, in Suffolk, to levy a special rate in order to pay the expenses of himself and his assistants. The sum of £28.0s.3d. (worth a good deal more in those days than it would be today) is recorded as having been extorted from the people of Stowmarket in this way.

The disordered state of the country, in consequence of the Civil War then in progress between the Royalists and the supporters of Cromwell, gave Hopkins and other rogues like him their chance to impose upon the disturbed minds of the people. The place, too, where Hopkins carried out his campaign, namely Essex and East Anglia, is an area of Britain where belief in witchcraft has always been strong and still lingers to this day.

Matthew Hopkins was the son of a Puritan minister, James Hopkins of Wenham in Suffolk. In his earlier years he had been a lawyer, and practised at Ipswich and later at Manningtree; without, however, making any particular figure in the world, until he found his real career in witch hunting.

He commenced his rise to fame while living at Manningtree, Essex. Here, as he tells us in his book *The Discovery of Witches* (London, 1647), "In March, 1644, he had some seven or eight of that horrible sect of Witches living in the Towne where he lived, a Towne in Essex called Manningtree, with diverse other adjacent Witches of other towns, who every six weeks in the night (being always on the Friday night) had their meeting close to his house, and had their several solemn sacrifices there offered to the Devil, one of whom this Discoverer heard speaking to her imps and bid them go to another Witch, who was thereupon apprehended."

Hopkins seems to imply that he daringly acted as eavesdropper upon one of these meetings. At any rate, a poor old one-legged woman called Elizabeth Clarke, whose mother had been hanged as a witch, was arrested at Hopkins' instigation. After being searched for witches' marks, and kept from sleep for three nights, upon the fourth night she started to 'confess' what was required of her and to name others as her accomplices. Hopkins avers that five familiar spirits, upon being named and called by her, then came one after another into the room, "there being ten of us in the room", after which these apparitions vanished.

By the time Hopkins and his friends had finished their investigation no less than thirty-two people from various parts of Essex had been arrested and remanded to the county sessions at Chelmsford. Hopkins' career as Witch-Finder General was fairly launched. So also were the careers of his assistants, John Stearne, Mary Phillipps, Edward Parsley and Frances Mills, all of whom swore that they had witnessed the appearance of the familiar spirits aforesaid. After this, of course, the assistants became indispensable as Hopkins' 'company', which was later extended to six.

As a result of this first essay in witch-hunting by Hopkins, nineteen people were hanged and four died in prison. As a lawyer, Hopkins knew that torture in England was illegal; but his evil ingenuity had found various means of extracting 'confessions' by cruelty and browbeating, which did not legally rank as torture.

These methods included firstly, the pain and humiliation of being stripped and searched for witches' marks; then, of being made to sit upon a stool or table, cross-legged, and bound in this posture with cords, sometimes for as much as twenty-four hours, without food or sleep. Alternatively, the accused were kept walking without respite, up and down the room, until their feet were blistered; and this treatment is recorded as having been kept up for more than three days in some instances, until the victims broke down and 'confessed'. Hopkins piously protested that he never called anyone a witch, "only after her trial by search and their own confession".

Another favourite method of trial used by Hopkins, and one which provided an edifying public spectacle, was the 'swimming' or 'fleeting' of witches; that is, putting them into water to see if they would float. This idea had in fact been current for many years, and was based upon the belief that, as the witches had rejected the water of baptism, even so the element of water would reject them, and they would float thereon in an unnatural manner. It had been given more importance by being recommended by King James I in his book *Daemonologie* (Edinburgh, 1597), as a test of witchcraft guilt.

The method of applying the test, however, as used by Hopkins, was not merely to throw the person into some pond or stream. Hopkins was more careful and detailed than that. The accused had to be bound in a special manner, with their arms crossed, and their thumbs tied to their big toes. Then a rope was tied around their waist, and held by a man on either side. This was ostensibly to prevent the accused from drowning, if they started to sink; but it is obvious that whether or not the person sank would depend very much on the men who handled the rope.

Hopkins did not, however, originate this technique. It is depicted on the title-page of a pamphlet *Witches Apprehended, Examined and Executed* (London, 1613), in an old woodcut which shows the swimming of a woman called Mary Sutton in 1612. She is not only tied in this manner, but is also wearing a voluminous shift of underclothing which would help to keep her afloat for a few moments at any rate.

If a certain relic which I have seen in the Museum of Magic and Witchcraft at Castletown, Isle of Man, is authentic, then it is evidence of another money-making racket worked by Hopkins and his company. This relic consists of an example of a preventive charm supposed to have been sold by Hopkins, to protect people's households from witchcraft.

The charm consists of a wooden box, lined with cloth and with a pane of glass on the top so that the contents can be seen. Inside is a bizarre collection of odds and ends, among which is the finger bone of a child. The idea was that the purchaser kept the box in his house, to prevent the spells of witches from harming him and his family. Of course, no one *had* to buy these boxes, when they were offered to them; but if anyone refused, they would come under suspicion of favouring witchcraft.

This practice of selling witch boxes was carried on by other members of the witch-hunting fraternity. I have seen another such box, in the collection of a friend of mine in London, which was sold by a 'cunning man' a couple of centuries or so ago, to protect people from witches. It is very similar to the one in the museum at Castletown, containing bits of long-dried and faded herbs, rowan-wood and so on. It has a similar glass front, also. One can picture some superstitious countryman, many years ago, sitting in his cottage on a dark winter's night, listening to the wind howling outside, and looking for reassurance towards the shelf or chimney-piece, where the glass-fronted witch box stood, with its weird contents. No wonder there were so many fearful tales told, of the evils and dangers of witchcraft; there were so many people making money out of them!

Matthew Hopkins' successful beginning in Essex set the pattern which he followed throughout East Anglia. How many people's deaths he procured in all, or how much money he and his followers amassed in the process, will probably never be known precisely. These were troubled times; and the records are incomplete or have been lost. Hopkins visited Norfolk, Suffolk, Cambridgeshire, Huntingdonshire, Northamptonshire and Bedfordshire, as well as Essex. From such records as we do possess, we may guess that the final total of executions ran into several hundreds.

Eventually, however, the tide began to turn against Hopkins. Not all magistrates were as cruel and credulous as those of Manningtree in those days. In 1645 a special "Commission of Oyer and Terminer", formed to deal with witchcraft trials, told Hopkins to stop his practice of swimming witches; but they did not stop his other brutal proceedings, and one wonders just how much authenticity there was in Hopkins' claim that he had a Commission from Parliament, on the strength of which he called himself the Witch-Finder General. This has been generally regarded as being a fabrication. Yet it was on the strength of this pretended commission that Hopkins required the authorities of the towns he 'visited' to pay him and his company handsomely, for their professional services. Did no magistrate ever ask to see proof of this commission? Or is the truth of the matter that Hopkins did in fact possess some sort of official status; but when the scandal of his cruelty, brutality and fraud was exposed, the authorities found it prudent to disown him?

Samuel Butler, in his satire *Hudibras,* twitted the Parliamentarians with the Hopkins scandal:

> Hath not this present Parliament
>   A Lieger to the Devil sent,
> Fully impowered to treat about
>   Finding revolted Witches out?
> And has he not within a year
>   Hanged threescore of them in one Shire?
> Some only for not being drowned,
>   And some for sitting above ground
> Whole days and nights upon their Breeches,
>   And feeling pain, were hanged for Witches.

And some for putting knavish Tricks
    Upon green Geese or Turkey Chicks;
Or Pigs that suddenly deceast
    Of griefs unnatural, as he guesst;
Who after proved himself a Witch,
    And made a rod for his own Breech.

The last two lines of Butler's verse refer to a tradition that Hopkins was eventually publicly discredited by a group of people, disgusted at his cruelties, who seized him and submitted him to his own test of "swimming"—and he floated! According to another version, Hopkins was drowned on this occasion. Bishop Hutchinson, in his *Historical Essay Concerning Witchcraft* (London, 1718), accepted this tradition as factual: "That clear'd the Country of him; and it was a great deal of Pity that they did not think of the Experiment sooner." But again, this is one of those matters we shall probably never know the precise truth about.

What is a matter of certain record, however, is the courage of an old country parson, John Gaule, the Vicar of Great Staughton, Huntingdonshire, who took a stand against the Witch-Finder General which played a big part in restoring sanity in East Anglia. John Gaule preached outspokenly against Hopkins, who was proposing to visit his part of the country. Hopkins retaliated with a blustering letter, full of veiled threats, addressed to one of Gaule's parishioners. But he prudently avoided visiting Great Staughton.

John Gaule, who meanwhile had been collecting evidence about Hopkins' proceedings, then published a book, *Select Cases of Conscience Touching Witches and Witchcraft* (London, 1646). It was well-written and convincing, and public opinion was aroused against the abuses it exposed.

The Witch-Finder General was forced on the defensive; and in 1647 Hopkins' book *The Discovery of Witchcraft* appeared in an attempt to counteract the accusations brought against him. But by this time Hopkins was a spent force. He had retired to the town where he started his career, Manningtree in Essex; and in 1647 he died in the nearby village of Mistley. The Church Registers record his burial, on the 12th August 1647. He did not live long to enjoy his ill-gotten gains, whatever was the actual cause of his death.

His associate John Stearne wrote that Hopkins died "after a long sickness of a Consumption . . . without any trouble of conscience for what he had done, as was falsely reported of him."

Hopkins was not the only villain to ply the trade of witch-finder in England. In 1649 or 1650 a Scottish witch-finder was invited by the magistrates to Newcastle, to search men and women for the Devil's mark. His fees were twenty shillings for every witch discovered, and his expenses for his journey to and from Scotland, where pricking suspected witches to find the Devil's mark had now become a regular profession. His trip to Newcastle proved lucrative; as a result of it fourteen women and one man were hanged.

However, this rogue too met his downfall. He was eventually indicted for his activities, and himself sentenced to be hanged. "And upon the Gallows he confessed he had been the death of above two hundred and twenty women in England and Scotland, for the gain of twenty shillings a piece, and beseeched forgiveness. And was executed."

So says Ralph Gardiner, in his book *England's Grievance Discovered in Relation to the Coal Trade* (London, 1655). This book is illustrated by a significant and terrible picture. It shows four women hanging from a mass gallows, while three more below wait their turn to die. The executioner, standing on a ladder, is in the act of adjusting the rope round one woman's neck. Mounted sergeants and foot-soldiers look on, while a bellman shouts a proclamation; and in the corner of the picture, a well-dressed man, the witch-finder, is holding out his hand and having money counted into it.

HORNED GOD, THE

The greatest temple ever raised by man, that of Karnak in Ancient Egypt, was built in honour of a horned god, Ammon-Ra, who bore the curling horns of the ram.

The attribute of horns as a symbol of power was wide-spread throughout the ancient world. Many Egyptian gods and goddesses were depicted with horned head-dresses. In Ancient Crete, to set up a pair of horns was the sign of a sacred place. The Old Testament speaks of "the horns of the altar"; and there was a legend that Moses, after he had talked with God upon Mount Sinai, came down from the mountain horned. Michelangelo's famous statue of Moses bears witness to this belief, as it depicts him with small horns upon his forehead.

Alexander the Great was known as 'The Two-Horned'. Greek warriors wore horns upon their helmets, as in later years did the Vikings, the Celts and the Teutonic races. The horned helmet, as the insignia of a powerful warrior, survived into the Middle Ages. There are many pictures of armoured knights wearing such helmets. The idea is found even in the Far East. The Samurai, or armoured warriors of old Japan, wore helmets with horns.

African witch-doctors, too, often wear a horned head-dress as part of their ceremonial attire; while on the other side of the world, the Red Indian medicine man wears a horned helmet as the emblem of his power.

The oldest known representations of a male deity, the pictures from the painted caves of the Stone Age, show him as a horned, ithyphallic figure. (*See* CAVE ART, RELIGIOUS AND MAGICAL.) The connection between this most primeval of gods, and the sophisticated, wide-ruling deities of Ancient Egypt, is far-stretched, but quite clearly traceable. It stretched again to the Great God Pan of the mountains and forests of Greece, the god of fertility and vitality; and to Cernunnos, 'The Horned One', worshipped in Celtic Europe and in Ancient Britain. Many statues of Cernunnos have been discovered in Britain; and a temple to him stood upon the site of the Church of Notre Dame in Paris.

Still more tenuous, the link stretches to the Horned God worshipped at the witches' Sabbats, and denounced by the Christian Church as the Devil; "Auld Hornie, Satan, Nick or Clootie", as Robert Burns called him. However, we do not find horns referred to in the Bible as a symbol of evil, but of sacredness and protection. *"He is my shield, and the horn of my salvation"* (2 Samuel, XXII, 3). *"My buckler, and the horn of my salvation"* (Psalm XVIII, 2). *"And hath raised up a horn of salvation for us"* (Luke, I, 69). There are many Biblical texts containing such expressions as "The horns of the righteous shall be exalted", "Mine horn is exalted in the Lord", and so on. The idea of horns as a sign of wickedness is a comparatively modern one.

On the Continent of Europe, horns were, and still are, an extremely popular amulet against the Evil Eye; so much so, that in Italy the word *corno* has come to mean almost any kind of lucky charm. (*See* EVIL EYE.) The same belief, less marked perhaps but still existing, can be found in Britain. A pair of horns hung up in the house as a decoration is still believed to be lucky, by some country folk.

The idea that there is something magical about horns derives from a very distant past, the time before man discovered agriculture. When our remote ancestors, the primitive hunters, roamed the land in search of the herds of wild game on which they depended for food, they must have admired the mighty stag, or the splendid bison, with his imposing horns, his beauty, his power, his strength and virility. He was the incarnation of maleness, the sire of the herds. They painted his likeness upon the walls of their caves; and their priest-magicians wore his horns and his skin in their magical rites.

Some of this hunting magic may have been of a very practical kind. It has been conjectured that one of the ways in which men of the Old Stone Age hunted was to have a clever and daring member of the tribe to act as a decoy. This man would dress himself in the horns and skin of the hunted animal, and lure a number of animals into a trap; for instance, towards some steep place, over which they could be stampeded, and then despatched with bows and arrows, if they were not killed by the fall. This is in fact a possible form of hunting for people armed only with primitive weapons and their own cunning; but all depends upon the nerve and sagacity of the man who acts the part of the decoy 'beast'. He would certainly have been the magician of the tribe.

This magician who was *en rapport* with the great beasts, is one very probable origin of the concept of the Horned God, but the Horned God himself is more than that. He is the masculine, active side of Nature, as the Moon Goddess represents the feminine side, in the witches' theology. The Horned God is the opener of the Gates of Life and Death; because that which is born through the Gate of Life must return through the Gate of Death, when the time comes to leave this world again.

Hence the Horned God is the power of returning vitality in the spring; but he is also the Old God of the Underworld, that Dis from whom, according to Caesar, the Gauls claimed to be descended. Every year we see re-enacted the Fall of Lucifer, the Light-Bearer, when the sun, the source of vitality for this planet, attains the height of his power at midsummer, and then falls from that height to hide himself in the realms below. Osiris, the Egyptian sun god, was also ruler over the realms of the dead; and his consort Isis, the moon goddess, was mistress of magic. The heart of paganism is a philosophy based upon Nature, and veiled in symbol and myth.

One wonders how much the Ancient Britons and Gauls knew of astrology; because the particular attribute of Cernunnos in Celtic art is the serpent with a ram's head. Now, the ram's head is the emblem of Aries, the sign of the spring equinox; while the serpent is one of the emblems of Scorpio, which astrologers call the natural ruler of the House of Death, and which is the sun sign at the time of Halloween, the Celtic festival of the dead. Both Aries and Scorpio are ruled by Mars, the planet which is so much the emblem of male virility that its symbol is used by naturalists for that purpose, to indicate the masculine gender.

The Horned God, then, is the phallic god, the personification of the masculine side of Nature. When man discovered agriculture, and started to till the land and keep flocks and herds, the potency of the bull, the ram, and the goat became important to him also, and these animals played their part in the cult of the Horned God.

Kings and priests wore the horned helmet, crown, or head-dress, in its various forms, all over the ancient world. In Egypt actual bulls and rams were kept as sacred beasts and regarded as dwelling-places for the spirit of the god; even as the god Shiva has his sacred bull in the temples of India today. Extraordinary scenes were enacted in the temple of the ram god Mendes, when women regarded it as a religious rite to couple ceremonially with the sacred ram. The historian Herodotus witnessed this fantastic ritual.

Stories like this, and the many representations in Egyptian art of worshippers, especially women, adoring a sacred horned animal which stands upon an altar, remind us of the shocked descriptions, many years later, of what is supposed to have happened at the witches' Sabbats; when a horned beast, or a man in the guise of one, was adored in similar fashion.

The gods of paganism are not remote. Their living symbols can be found close at hand in the world of Nature. But this does not preclude the god who is immanent being also transcendent, beyond the veil of manifested Nature.

Pagan and primitive mankind, however, liked to be able to contact, literally, the likeness of their god. He was there for them in the beast upon the altar; or at any rate, the principle of him was there. Even, probably, as the principle of the goddess, the Great Feminine, was present among her priestesses, dancing girls and temple prostitutes of ancient times.

This idea of contact with the living representative of the Horned God was probably the origin of the bull-leaping cult of Ancient Crete, a dangerous sport in which both youths and girls participated, and of which wonderfully graceful representations are found in Cretan art.

Later still, we have the bull fight as the continuation of the same idea; not, however, as it is put on today, a bloody and sadistic spectacle but as its name of *corrida de toros* describes it, 'a running of bulls'. In some of the old towns and villages of Southern France and Spain, the original dangerous and exciting 'running of bulls' can still be seen, when the young bulls are released to career through the narrow streets of the town, while the young men vie with each other to see who can play the most hair-raising pranks with them, coming within inches of the horns, and often having to save themselves by leaping over fences or shinning up lamp-posts.

But how did this magical image of a Horned God come to be especially the god of the witches? Of all the ancient gods whose cults were displaced by that of Christianity, why is it specifically this god who survived in the secret covens?

The Horned God of witchcraft, has, of course, absorbed many of the characteristics of other popular pagan gods. For instance, the figure of Herne the Hunter, specifically associated with witchcraft in Windsor Forest, has taken on some of the attributes of Woden, and of Gwynn ap Nudd, both of whom were leaders of the phantom Wild Hunt.

The horned and hoofed 'Devil' of the witches' coven has a strong resemblance to the Greek god Pan, worshipped with orgiastic rites by the witches of Thessaly. He also has obvious links with the Celtic Cernunnos, especially as the Ruler of the Underworld or Otherworld, beyond the veil of mortal life. Cernunnos, incidentally, ruled beer and ale in Celtic Europe; even as in Greece the horned Dionysus presided over wine. In the days when every good housewife was proud of her home-brewed ale, and tea and coffee were unknown, it was Cernunnos who was the spirit of the working man's tipple, as downed by thirsty harvesters in the summer fields, or sipped cheerfully by the winter's log fire.

It was the grass-roots antiquity of the old Horned God that made him survive, when more sophisticated god-forms were forgotten. He was from the morning of the world, deep down in man's mind, among the primeval things. The impression of him has lasted longer because it is deeper. He is the oldest god man has; even as the White Lady of the Moon, the Great Mother, is the oldest goddess.

The Christian Church might denounce him as 'The Devil' as much as it liked; and obviously many of the things he represents are antipathetic to the medieval Church's version of Christianity;

strong drink, merry-making, and ithyphallic vigour, for instance. His cult could be driven underground; but it could not be extirpated, because both he and his female counterpart, the moon goddess of the witches, represent forces vitally present in Nature, and in human nature.

Christian morality, however, did manage to twist the significance of horns into the sign of a cuckold. There has been a great deal of speculation among antiquaries as to why this significance should be. The reason is that Christian moralists regarded pagan women as whores, because of their free-living, emancipated ways; and regarded pagan deities with their orgiastic rites as the promoters of fornication. Hence, men who were pagans were cuckolds, because of the shamelessness of their women; or so the Church taught people to believe.

The Horned God was degraded into the Devil; and the Horns of Honour were made into a badge of shame. The moves of propaganda were known in the old days, even as they are today; but even so, this denigration of ancient symbols has never been entirely successful.

HORSES AND WITCHCRAFT

In the days before the coming of the motor-car, when nearly all transport depended upon the horse, the importance of horses to man was such that they were certain to come within the sphere of magic.

The horse is notoriously a highly sensitive animal, and will seem to react to presences invisible to humans. Hence witches were often accused of bewitching horses, and making them stand still and refuse to move or refuse to pass a certain place.

Witches were also believed to borrow horses at night, and take them on wild rides through the darkness, returning them by daybreak with tangled manes and their hides lathered with sweat. The expression 'hag-ridden', used of someone strangely oppressed, derives from this belief.

Naturally, there were charms used by farmers and carters, to prevent their horses from being molested by witches. One of the most popular was to hang up a holed stone in the stables; and such stones came to be called hag stones, for this reason. Sometimes, such a stone was tied to the key of the stables also. (*See* HOLED STONES.)

The handsome ornaments called horse brasses were originally not only for decoration. They were amulets to protect the horse from bewitchment and from the Evil Eye. Their shining would reflect the baleful glance away from the animal; and the pattern of the horse brass itself often contained some fortunate and magical figure. Such, for instance, were the sun, the crescent moon, a sprig of oak leaves with acorns, or a single acorn, a star, a trefoil, a heart, and so on. Horse brasses display an amazing and delightful variety of subjects and designs, which make them today much sought after by collectors; but their original purpose was to ward off evil magic. The purely decorative, commemorative or heraldic designs came later.

Closely allied to witchcraft, in the popular mind at any rate, were the secret fraternities among horsemen, such as the Society of the Horseman's Word. These fraternities had jealously guarded secrets of how to tame and govern horses by means which certainly appeared to be magical; and they had regular ceremonies of initiation, by means of which new members were admitted.

If the description given to me of how men used to be initiated into the Society of the Horseman's Word is correct, then there is an evident relationship between this society and the beliefs of the witches. This fraternity flourished particularly in Scotland; and I was told that when a horseman was felt to have earned the privilege of being admitted, which was by no means easily come by, he was taken one night, blindfolded, to some lonely spot. This would probably be some old, half-ruined bothy, or a remote barn or stable, where other members would be assembled.

I was not given a full description of what ensued, save that everything was done with the utmost seriousness, to instil suitable awe and terror into the novice. The climax of the ceremony consisted of requiring him to take a solemn oath of secrecy, and to seal this he was told, being still blindfolded, to "tak' a grip o' the Old Chiel's hand".

The novice held out his hand; and into it was thrust the end of a kind of ceremonial staff, which consisted of an actual cloven hoof of some animal, dried and preserved. The effect of such an experience, in a strange, dimly-lit place by night, must have been well-remembered, even after the man had attained sufficient status in the guild to know how it was worked.

The ceremony ended, I was told, with the newly-admitted member paying for drinks for the whole company, and being told some of the secrets which the society preserved.

These secrets were far from being mere mumbo-jumbo. On the contrary, they consisted of a very thorough and practical knowledge of herbs and other substances which would enable a man to influence horses, if he knew how to use this knowledge. The men sometimes committed these matters to paper; but if they did, something essential, either an ingredient or some trick of using the recipe, had to be left out, and communicated only by word of mouth; so that no outsider could profit by it even if it fell into his hands.

These recipes were mainly of two kinds: substances which were 'drawing' and substances which were 'jading'. The former attracted and pleased horses; the latter repelled and alarmed them. In the light of this knowledge, one can understand the many tales of witches who were able apparently to bewitch horses belonging to someone who had offended them, and cause them to stop still until released from the spell, or else to become wild and unmanageable. Like most other beliefs about witches, this story has a basis of fact, if one seeks deep enough to find it.

A good deal of very valuable research about the secret fraternities among old-time horsemen, especially in East Anglia, has been done by George Ewart Evans; and much interesting information on this subject may be found in Mr Evans' book, *The Pattern Under the Plough* (Faber and Faber, London, 1966).

The Society of the Horseman's Word took its name from the story that its members were taught a secret word, which when whispered into a horse's ear, would give the whisperer immediate command over the animal. Popular legend embroidered this tale by saying that in return for this mysterious power over horses, the horseman sold his soul to the Devil.

Such horse-whisperers, as they were called, undoubtedly existed. Probably the most famous one was an Irishman called Sullivan, who flourished around the beginning of the nineteenth century. He became well known as a result of taming a fine but very intractable racehorse belonging to Colonel Westenra, afterwards Lord Rosmore. Sullivan asked to be shut in alone with the animal and this was done. After about a quarter of an hour, he called for those outside to come into the stable. When they entered, they found the erstwhile savage horse lying down quite happily, and letting Sullivan sit beside him. Both horse and man, however, seemed very tired, and Sullivan had to be revived with brandy; but the cure of the horse was lasting. Sullivan would never reveal how he accomplished his taming of horses, declaring that in fact the best horse-whisperers could not explain the source of their power, it was an innate gift. Similar mysterious powers over horses are believed in and practised among the gypsies of Europe, and in North and South America.

One of the most popular of lucky charms continues to be the horseshoe. In many places in Britain, actual horseshoes can still be seen, nailed up over doorways. It is said that a horseshoe found accidentally upon the road is the luckiest one, and that it should always be hung with the ends of the shoe upwards, or 'the luck will run out'. In this position, it is an upward-pointing crescent, and hence a symbol of the moon, from which it derives its magic. Some old representations of the moon goddesses Diana and Hecate show them as having the heads of mares.

According to old John Aubrey in his *Miscellanies,* "it is a thing very common to nail horseshoes on the thresholds of doors; which is to hinder the power of witches that enter the house". Whether or not Lord Nelson believed in witches is not known; but the great admiral had a horseshoe nailed to the mast of his ship *Victory*.

It may seem strange that a symbol associated with the witch goddess of the moon should be regarded as a protection against witchcraft. Perhaps, however, the display of the horseshoe derives from a kind of propitiation of the moon goddess, and thus a protection against the powers of her darker aspect.

The only exception to the rule of hanging the horseshoe with its ends pointing upwards is made in the case of the blacksmith. Smiths have always been regarded as natural magicians; and the smith hangs his lucky horseshoe with the points downwards, 'to pour out the luck upon the forge'. The three horseshoes which are displayed upon the coat of arms of the Worshipful Company of Farriers (founded in 1356) are shown in this position.

HYPNOSIS, WITCHCRAFT AND

There is no doubt that, under many different names, hypnosis has been known from very early times and practised as a secret technique of magic.

Given a knowledge of hypnosis, and of post-hypnotic suggestion, many strange tales of alleged bewitchments begin to make sense. There are the stories, for instance, of witches who relieved women from the pains of childbirth by casting the pains upon a dog or a cat. The woman was hypnotised, and then told that this had been done. She felt better, and the dog or cat was none the worse.

In some cases, however, the witch went a step further, and cast the pains upon the woman's husband. Suggestion skilfully applied can be a very powerful thing! If the husband saw that his wife's pain was relieved he would assume that the spell was working, and start to suffer accordingly; which was not a bad idea in the case of a man who forced upon his wife one pregnancy after another.

Suggestion has played a very big part in the practice of witches and magicians of all kinds, the world over. For this reason, the village 'wise woman', white witch, or 'cunning man' would take care to have a show of occult lore to meet the eye of the visitor to their cottage. There would, for instance, be jars of dried herbs on shelves; a few strange objects, such as preserved snakes or mummified bats, on display; perhaps a human skull or two; and some impressive-looking tome such as Culpeper's *Herbal* or Lilly's *Astrology* (whether the witch could read it or not). The rustic visitor would be suitably overawed; especially if the witch proceeded to tell them some simple facts about themselves, which they would assume had been gained by clairvoyance.

The 'cunning man' or 'wise woman' might even know enough about their affairs, unknown to them, to make a shrewd guess at what they had come for. This would really amaze their minds; and from then on the visitor would be as putty in the spell-binder's hands. Actually, the thing is not so difficult, especially in a small village where gossip is one of the few recreations. The famous voodoo priestess, Marie Laveau of New Orleans, employed a regular corps of intelligence agents, recruited among the house servants of leading families, to glean information with which to startle her fashionable clients.

Of course, suggestion can be used, like any other power, for bad ends or for good. Actually, the village witch, with her knowledge of herbal medicines, her experience in midwifery (there was an old saying, "The better the midwife, the better the witch") and her use of hypnosis and practical psychology, as we call them today, probably did far more good than harm. The famous medieval doctor, Paracelsus, who has been called the father of modern surgery, admitted that he had gained a good deal of knowledge from witches.

It is recorded that in 1570 the Vicar of St. Dunstan's, near Canterbury, complained to the authorities about an imprisoned witch in Canterbury who was being treated far too leniently. Apparently, the keeper of the jail there had publicly remarked that "the witch did more good by her physic than Mr. Pundall and Mr. Wood being preachers of God's word"; and the preachers were much offended.

One of the means witches used to induce hypnosis was to get their patient to gaze steadily at the bright blade of a sword or a knife. A compendium of the laws of England, made in the thirteenth century, condemns the practice of "enchantment, as those who send people to sleep". The actual methods of doing this were kept as a great magical secret; and it was not until the early years of the nineteenth century that medical hypnosis began to be seriously studied by doctors, in the teeth of fierce opposition from those who regarded it as black magic.

One of the pioneers of medical hypnosis was Dr. James Braid, who was actually the first person to use the word 'hypnotism', in 1843; and he re-discovered one of the methods witches had been using for centuries; namely, that of getting his patient to gaze steadily at a bright object. Here in his own words, is Dr. Braid's method:

> Take any bright object (I generally use my lancet case) between the thumb and fore and middle fingers of the left hand; hold it from about eight to fifteen inches from the eyes, at such a position above the forehead as may be necessary to produce the greatest possible strain upon the eyes and the eyelids, and enable the patient to maintain a steady, fixed stare at the object. The patient must be made to understand that he must keep the eyes steadily fixed on the object. It will be observed that, owing to the consensual adjustment of the eyes, the pupils will be at first contracted, they will shortly begin to dilate, and after they have done so to a considerable extent, and have assumed a very wary position, if the fore and middle fingers of the right hand, extended and a little separated, are carried from the object towards the eyes, most likely the eyelid will close involuntarily, with a vibratory motion. If this is not the case, or the patient allows the *eyeballs to move*, desire him to begin again, giving him to understand that he is to allow the eyelids to close when the fingers are again carried to the eyes, but that the eyeballs *must* be kept fixed on the same position, and the mind riveted to the *one idea* of the object held above the eyes.

Another means used by witches to induce hypnosis in this way, as well as the knife or sword-blade, was the bright shiny ball known as a witch ball. These are often seen today hanging up in antique shops. They vary in size and colour, from the massive ones suspended by a chain, to others which are quite small, no larger than the Christmas tree decorations which they probably originated. (*See* WITCH BALLS.)

Witches, however, put these balls to definite magical uses, one of which was the induction of hypnosis as stated above. The shining ball was hung from the ceiling, or some convenient suspension, and the subject was told to sit in a chair, relax, and look upwards at it. In a candlelit cottage, with the light carefully arranged and a scent of herbs and incense in the air, this was an effective method of inducing trance.

A few years ago the *Brighton Evening Argus* featured a story about a local dentist, who was using hypnosis in his practice and finding it very helpful. His method of inducing the hypnotic state in his patients was the very thing the witches used to use—a shiny silver witch ball, hung from the ceiling of his surgery! The newspaper story gave no indication that the dentist realised this; but he was, in fact, using the witch ball in the traditional way.

Truly, "there is nothing new except what has been forgotten".

Many old writers go into long arguments about whether or not witches could turn people into animals. Given a knowledge of hypnosis, a powerful practitioner could certainly have made a person *believe* that he had been turned into an animal. Some of the old time stage mesmerists regularly did this sort of thing as part of their entertainment; and if they could do it, a witch could also, especially in the days when almost everyone implicitly believed that such transformations were possible. The stage mesmerist's subject would have realised afterwards that he had been the victim of an illusion; but the person whom the witch spellbound generally knew nothing of such powers other than as witchcraft.

However, long before the days of Friedrich Anton Mesmer (1733-1815), who is generally regarded as the originator of mesmerism (the old term for hypnosis), some intelligent men had realised that this supposed diabolical power of witchcraft was simply a fact in nature.

Van Helmont, for instance, called it 'magnetism', and stated that it was active everywhere and had nothing new but the name; "it is a paradox only to those who ridicule everything, and who attribute to the power of Satan whatever they are unable to explain". Like Mesmer, the early students of this subject regarded the effects as being produced by a kind of invisible fluid, which passed from one person to another, and which they compared to the force emanating from a magnet; hence the word 'magnetism' being used in this context. Most modern hypnotists discount this idea; but many occultists consider it to contain some truth.

I

IMAGES USED IN MAGIC

From the earliest times, the idea that by means of an image or like-ness, the person or animal that image represented could be influenced, has been one of the fundamentals of magical belief.

An Egyptian papyrus tells us of a palace conspiracy against the Pharaoh Rameses III, which called in the dubious aid of black magic in this way. One of the conspirators, an official named Hui, man-aged to steal a book of magic spells from the royal library. With the aid of this manuscript, he made wax images, with the intention of destroying the Pharaoh by their means. However, the plot was dis-covered, the conspirators punished, and Hui committed suicide.

It is notable that this powerful book of magic was in the royal li-brary. Perhaps the plot failed because the Pharaoh was a better ma-gician than his attackers; in which case their efforts would have rebounded on their own heads.

This story from Ancient Egypt is only one of many conspiracies in high places which have involved black magic, and the use of the image or puppet, made in a person's likeness, and pierced with pins or thorns to bring about their death.

In the reign of the first Queen Elizabeth, the Court was once greatly excited and alarmed by the news that a wax image of the Queen had been found lying in Lincoln's In Fields. Black magic was obviously intended, because the image had a great pin struck through its breast. In those days, most people believed implicitly in the power of such things to cause sickness and even death.

Messengers were sent to summon the famous occultist, Dr. John Dee, to advise the Queen on what should be done. He went to Hamp-ton Court, and met the Queen there in her garden by the river. The Earl of Leicester and the Lords of the Privy Council were in attend-ance also; and the fact that the latter had been sent for shows how seriously the affair was taken.

Dr. Dee reassured the Queen, and told her that the image "in no way menaced Her Majesty's well-being", which, says the record, "pleased Elizabeth well". We are not told what was done with the evil puppet; probably Dee took possession of it, and took steps of his own to neutralise its baleful power. (*See* DEE, DR JOHN.)

In humbler circles, too, the image, made of wax or clay, played its secret part in spells. It is, like the burning of incense, the drawing of magical circles, and the practice of divination, part of the general heritage shared by witches and magicians all over the world.

A very frank description of this spell was given by one of the Lancashire witches, Mother Demdike, when she was examined in 1612. She confessed as follows: "The speediest way to take a man's life away by witchcraft is to make a picture of clay, like unto the shape of the person whom they mean to kill, and dry it thoroughly. And when you would have them to be ill in any one place more than another, then take a thorn or pin and prick it in that part of the picture you would so have to be ill. And when you would have any part of the body to consume away, then take that part of the picture and burn it. And so thereupon by that means the body shall die".

Sometimes the waxen image was melted, bit by bit, at a slow fire, to cause the person it was intended for to waste away. Sometimes, if the image was made of clay, it would have pins stuck into it, and then be placed in a running stream, so that it would slowly but surely be worn away by the water, and the person with it. This clay image was known in Scotland as a *corp chreadh,* and specimens of these can be found in some of our museums.

In the English countryside, the old word for these images was 'mommets'. In France, they were sometimes called a *volt,* or a *dagyde.* The first word comes from the Latin *vultus* or *voltus,* an image or likeness. The practice of *envoutement,* or psychic attack, usually by means of a *volt,* was widely believed in, and still is. Many French books on occultism discuss it.

Cottage and castle alike feared the spell of the pierced image; and when anger and a sense of wrong burned in someone's breast, then the peasant and the noble, even the highest in the land, might be tempted in their turn to resort to it.

There is an extraordinary passage in *The Diary of a Lady in Waiting,* by Lady Charlotte Bury (4 Vols, London, 1838-9; a later edition by John Lane, London, 1908), referring to that unhappy woman, Princess Caroline, the estranged wife of the Prince Regent. When her husband became George IV on his father's death, she was given the title but never the position of queen. Apparently she disliked her royal husband as heartily as he detested her. Lady Charlotte tells us:

> After dinner, her Royal Highness made a wax figure as usual and gave it an amiable addition of large horns; then took three pins out of her garment and stuck them through and through, and put the figure to roast and melt at the fire. If it was not too melancholy to have to do with this, I could have died of laughing. Lady—says the Princess indulges in this amusement whenever there are no strangers at table; and she thinks her Royal Highness really has a superstitious belief that destroying this effigy of her husband will bring to pass the destruction of his royal person.

The age of materialism and scepticism had dawned in Princess Caroline's day; and well for her that it had. Ladies-in-waiting of earlier centuries would not have felt in the least like laughing. They would have been terrified of the headsman's block, or burning at the stake for high treason—the punishment inflicted for witchcraft directed against the Sovereign.

And can we be quite sure that the fat and self-indulgent 'Prinny' did *not* feel, at least, a few extra twinges of gout, as a result of his wife's concentrated malice?

The facts of telepathy are accepted by many psychic researchers today, who would nevertheless sneer at witchcraft. Yet the image of wax or clay is simply a means of concentrating the power of the witch's thought. For this reason, it is made as like the hated person as possible, in order to suggest their actual presence. So that it should have no connection with anyone else but the person it is intended for, the image should be made of virgin wax, usually beeswax; that is, wax that has never been used for any other purpose. Some old-time witches used to keep bees, in order to have a supply of wax without having to buy it, and so arouse suspicion.

When clay is the material used, the operator digs it himself—in the waning of the moon if the spell is to be directed against someone.

Not all spells with images, however, are intended for baleful purposes. Sometimes a love spell is attempted by this means; and I have seen an image successfully used by a present-day witch, for the purpose of healing someone of rheumatic pains. Of course, images of this kind would be the subject of very different ritual from that used in witchcraft of a darker shade. But the force behind the rite is the same; the power of the witch's concentrated thought.

In September 1963 a considerable local sensation was caused when

two images, one of a man, the other of a woman, were found nailed
to the door of the old ruined castle at Castle Rising, in Norfolk. Between the sinister little figures was a sheep's heart, pierced with thirteen thorns. On the ground, in front of the door, was a circle and an
X-shaped cross; a sign used among witches as a conventionalised
figure of a skull and cross bones. The symbols were drawn in soot.
The rite was carried out at the time of the waning moon.

People in the village denied any knowledge of the matter, and
assured journalists that "it must have been done by outsiders". They
admitted however, that they had heard of witchcraft being practised
in surrounding districts.

The mystery remains unsolved, and eventually the interest evoked
by it died down. But it flared up again four months later, when another
strange discovery was made in a ruined church at Bawsey, 4 miles
away. Two young lads found another sheep's heart pierced with
thorns, nailed to one of the walls. There was also a circle of soot,
with a stump of burned-down black candle within it; but there were
no figures.

The father of one of the boys told the police: but no clue to the
identity of the person who used the old church ruins for this dark
rite, was ever discovered. Less than a month later, traces of a third
ritual in the area were found. This time, there was an even greater
sensation; because the place where they were discovered was actually
on the royal estate at nearby Sandringham.

In the ivy-covered ruin of Babingley Church, were found yet another thorn-pierced heart nailed to a wall, another black circle of
soot, another burnt-down black candle, and this time a little effigy of
a woman, with a sharp thorn stuck in its breast. A young boy found
the objects while exploring the ruin, and returned home to tell his
father. When the father went to see for himself, he was overcome
with a paralysing sensation of terror. He drove to a police station,
where he arrived in a state of near collapse. It took him two days to
recover from the experience.

Again the police investigated, but without any success, except to
conclude that all three rituals were carried out by the same person. In
this they were probably right. Three is a potent magical number; and
someone in the area was evidently very determined to get results.

It is a long way from the remote Norfolk countryside to the cities
of New York, Chicago or Los Angeles, with their highly sophisticated
living—or is it? In the same year that the images were discovered

nailed to the door at Castle Rising, an advertisement appeared in American magazines for a "Psychotherapy Kit". It read: "This will definitely release stress and relax nerves as well as escape tension. A hex doll with four pins plus directions for use. Clever gag gift for husband, wife, boss, mother-in-law." Other similar advertisements have described their wares as "Voodoo Dolls"; and one jokingly invited its readers to "Voodoo it yourself".

Many mail order businesses in America sell these, and other magical supplies. In order to keep within the law, such goods are described as being merely a joke or a curio; what uses the buyers put them to is up to them.

INCENSE, MAGICAL USES OF

One of the oldest religious and magical rites is the burning of incense. The Ancient Egyptians used it extensively, and recipes for incense, composed of aromatic gums and other scented substances from nature, are found in their papyri.

Incense and perfume seem originally to have been one and the same, because the word 'perfume' comes from the Latin *profumum*, 'by means of smoke'. That is, the scented smoke which arose from ancient altars was a means of carrying prayers and invocations, and also a sacrifice pleasing to the unseen powers.

Incense has a third very important use also; namely, its potent effect upon the human mind. Scents of all kinds have a swift and subtle influence upon the emotions. Their appeal is not only to the conscious mind, but to the deeper levels below the threshold of consciousness. Here their impact can be evocative, even disturbingly so. None knew this better than the old-time exponents of magic; much of which today would be called practical psychology.

The atmosphere created by incense and candle-light, can transform an ordinary room into a cave of mystery, a shrine wherein strange powers can manifest. If you wish to work magic, then you must create an atmosphere, both mental and physical, in which magic can work.

Some curious little round vessels, made of thick pottery, with perforations all round them, have been recovered from barrows on Salisbury Plain near Stonehenge. Archaeologists think these may have been meant for the purpose of burning incense, and have named them incense cups. If this is correct (and it is hard to see what else they could have been used for), then the burning of incense has been practised in Britain since very ancient times.

Incense as we have it today is of two kinds, and both are extensively used by occultists and witches. The first kind is that which will burn by itself when lighted, such as joss sticks and incense cones. The second variety is that which requires some already burning substance, usually hot charcoal, upon which it is sprinkled.

The latter kind of incense is generally much stronger, and gives off a bigger volume of smoke; but the former kind is easier to handle. The popularity of incense has increased a good deal in recent years, and many varieties of joss sticks and incense cones are now imported from the East. The best way to burn joss sticks or cones is the way in which the Eastern people do it; namely, to get a metal bowl, or one of thick pottery, fill it three parts full of fine sand, and stick the joss sticks or cones upright in the sand. The cones will obviously rest easily upon the sand; while the joss sticks, if stuck in far enough to be held firmly upright, will burn well and safely, look pleasing, and the ash will fall back upon the sand without making a mess.

For the stronger kind of incense, which is burned on charcoal, one can make do with a bowl of sand if one has no thurible or incenseburner; but it is better and safer to procure a proper incense-burner, or censer as it is sometimes called.

The charcoal can be bought in boxes of little square blocks, from a shop which sells church furnishings; and this kind of shop also generally sells the best type of incense, namely that made of aromatic gums. It may sound somewhat strange that witches should patronise this kind of shop; but I can assure the reader that they do, simply because they seek for incense of the best quality and most beautiful perfume.

This kind of incense, being made from gum-resins which are crushed and blended together, looks rather like fine gravel. One will need, as well as a censer, a suitable metal spoon to sprinkle the incense. The kind of censer called a thurible, which is swung from chains, is rather difficult for the beginner to handle; and I would recommend rather an Indian or Arabic incense-burner, which has a domed, perforated lid, and a bowl which stands on legs, and preferably has a metal plate for a base. This last is useful, if one wants to cense round the magic circle; because if used for any length of time, the incense-burner will become quite hot to the touch, unless there is something to lift it by.

A small pair of tongs is useful, too, if one wants to lift the lid of the censer in order to replenish it, when the lid has become hot; and also to handle the charcoal blocks without soiling or burning one's fingers.

If the censer is a large one, it is generally a good idea to put a little sand in the bowl, for the charcoal to rest on. Then one lights the charcoal block, and puts it in the censer. The so-called self-igniting charcoal, which is mixed with a little saltpetre to make it burn more easily, is the simplest to handle. Once the charcoal, or most of it, has begun to glow, one is ready to sprinkle on the incense, and replace the lid on the censer. Then the blue spirals of scented smoke will slowly rise, and wreathe themselves about the room, twisting and twining and dissolving, with their rich perfume filling the air.

Most of the gum-resins which are the ingredients of this kind of incense are obtained from trees which grow in the tropical countries of the world. The Ancient Egyptians used to send regular expeditions into other parts of Africa, to obtain the gum-resins and rich spices they needed, for incense and for embalming. The gum called myrrh was particularly sought by them.

Other gum-resins which have been in use from ancient times are frankincense, which is another name for olibanum; galbanum; opoponax; benzoin, which in medieval days was called gum benjamin; storax; and mastic.

Fragrant woods are used also, in the blending of incense. Sandalwood is a favourite; so is aloes wood, or *lignum aloes* as it is often called in old receipes. Cedar and myrtle wood are sometimes used. The usual practice is for such woods and other vegetable ingredients to be dried and powdered, or at any rate to be reduced to small shavings.

The strongest vegetable odour in the world of scents is that obtained from the leaves of patchouli. Genuine patchouli perfume (which should not be confused with patchouli oil) is one of the most potent and evocative odours in the world. Like musk, it has a deserved reputation as an aphrodisiac. Powdered dried patchouli leaves are sometimes introduced into incense.

So also is powdered cinnamon. Incidentally, this easily-obtained spice, when a little of it is burnt on charcoal, has been found to make a good incense for aiding meditation and clairvoyance. Cardamom seeds are spicy and fragrant when burnt, also. The reader who cares to experiment may try discovering herbs and spices for himself, and blending incenses of his own, now that such things are easily obtainable in most large grocery stores, as a result of the greater interest taken today in herbs and condiments. He will find, however, that the scent released when a substance is burned is often different from that which it has in its normal state. Some other vegetable substances which yield perfume are mace, which is the inner bark of the nutmeg; orris root (obtainable from herbalists); saffron and cloves.

The chief perfumes obtained from the animal kingdom are musk, ambergris and civet. Musk comes from the musk-deer, which is hunted in the Himalayas. Ambergris is a substance ejected from the stomach of the sperm-whale; it looks like grey amber, hence its name. Civet comes from an African animal, the civet-cat. All these substances are very expensive; and, in their pure state, smell far from pleasant. They need to be handled by a skilled perfumer; but they are sometimes blended into expensive Oriental incense.

Innumerable writers have given lists of different incenses for different magical purposes—most of them contradictory. Probably the best course for the aspirant to magic is to experiment with the psychological effect of various perfumes upon himself. Then he can make his own list of perfumes, grading them according to their correspondences and astrological rulerships. He might, for instance, regard sandalwood as being 'right' for the works of Venus, frankincense for those of the sun, *lignum aloes* for those of the moon, and so on. As in most matters of magic, an ounce of practical experience is worth whole heaps of 'booklarnin'.

INCUBI AND SUCCUBI

The belief in the possibility of sexual intercourse between a spiritual being and a mortal man or woman is very old, and world-wide. In Ancient Greek mythology, the offspring of such strange loves were often demigods. With the coming of Christianity, however, the subject took on a more sombre aspect. The incubus and the succubus were alike regarded as devils.

The word 'incubus' is derived from the Latin, meaning 'that which lies upon'. The 'succubus', by similar derivation, was 'that which lies beneath'. The incubi were regarded as demons who infested women, while the succubi debauched men.

Learned doctors of the Church had much debate about the nature of incubi and succubi and of the sin involved in coupling with them. Some of them declared that the same demon, being basically sexless, because inhuman, could turn itself into an incubus to lie with a woman and a succubus to tempt a man into carnal sin. Indeed, they stated that such was a devil's ingenuity in sexual depravity, that it could receive semen from a man by acting as a succubus, usually while he slept, and then, in the form of an incubus, convey this semen into a woman and cause her to conceive a child.

Others, however, denied that the loves of the incubi and succubi could be fruitful, and averred that their sole purpose was to cause men and women to enjoy sex, to their damnation. Still other learned Churchmen believed that devils could themselves beget children, and had done so; indeed, that Antichrist would be begotten by a devil upon a witch. This theme has been revived in our own day, in the very successful book and film, *Rosemary's Baby*.

The idea of the demon-lover has appealed to many writers, one of whom, Joris-Karl Huysmans, treated it with rather more insight than most, in his brilliant and frightening book, *La-Bas*. Huysmans set out in this book to give a picture of Satanism as it was being practised in the Paris of his day, the 1890s; and much of what he writes is based on fact.

His hero, Durtal, is seduced into having an affair with a young married woman, Madame Chantelouve, who is a secret Satanist. She boasts to him of a certain strange power she possesses. If there is any man whom she desires, she has only to think fixedly of him before she goes to sleep, to be able to enjoy intercourse with him, or a form in his likeness, in her dreams. This power, she tells the horrified Durtal, was given to her by the Master Satanist, an unfrocked priest named Canon Docre. Later, she takes Durtal to a Black Mass performed by Canon Docre; but eventually, sickened by what he witnesses, he breaks away from her evil influence.

What is particularly interesting about this account of copulation with incubi, is that it precisely echoes another much older account, which it seems rather unlikely that Huysmans would have known about, because it comes from England.

In Thomas Middleton's old play *The Witch*, from which Shakespeare quotes the song "Black Spirits" used in *Macbeth*, one of the witches is made to say:

> What young man can we wish to pleasure us,
> But we enjoy him in an Incubus?

Most of Middleton's witch lore is taken from Reginald Scot's *Dis-*

coverie of Witchcraft, in which Scot describes the effects of the Witches' Salve, as given by Giovanni Battista Porta: "By this means (saith he) in a moonlight night they seem to be carried in the air, to feasting, singing, dancing, kissing, culling, and other acts of venery, with such youths as they love and desire most." (*See* FLYING OINT-MENTS.)

There is no mention of the Witches' Salve in *La-Bas* (by Joris-Karl Huysmans, Paris, 1891); however, the possibility of such experiences through sheer autosuggestion seems by no means too difficult to imagine. With regard to sexual experiences while under the influence of hallucinatory drugs, there are certain Mexican witches who make use of an unguent called toloachi. They say that women who use this 'have no need of men'. Its composition is secret; but a main ingredient is *Datura Tatula,* a plant which is a relative of the thorn-apple.

This particular kind of hallucination, or dream-experience, seems to me to be the real basis of all the stories about incubi and succubi, without needing any recourse to demons and devils.

It may surprise readers to know that the phenomena of incubi and succubi still take place today. This is nevertheless a fact. A friend of mine, an occultist, gave me a personal account of his experience with a case of this kind.

He had been asked by a married couple to help them get rid of an unpleasant and frightening haunting, at the lonely farmhouse where they lived. Precise details cannot be given, for obvious reasons. Suffice it to say that he went to visit them, and tried sincerely to help. The phenomena had been occurring intermittently for some time, and the husband had called in various mediums and psychics, without success. The young and attractive wife seemed to be the focus of the phenomena; and my friend came to the conclusion than an earth-bound spirit was obsessing her.

On one occasion this spirit, that of a man, truculent and abusive, purported to take possession of the woman and speak through her. He gave some particulars of his earthly life, and defied my friend's efforts to banish him.

Indeed, my friend could make no progress in the case, because he could not in practice get the woman to co-operate in anything he wanted her to do or to avoid doing. Outwardly willing, she would always find some excuse for not carrying out his instructions.

Eventually, in the absence of her husband, he tackled her about her attitude to the case. She admitted that she was not trying to get rid of the obsessing entity; because, she said, he came to her as a lover, and gave her such sexual pleasure and thrills as she had never experienced from a man.

My friend was so shocked and disgusted at the details of the woman's confession that he abandoned the case forthwith. He said nothing to the husband, except that he could do no more and was leaving. When he told me the details of this case, he was evidently moved by genuine horror, and said that he believed the shock of what he had seen and heard had affected his health. He was in fact far from well for some time afterwards.

Such a story, of course, raises many questions, both occult and psychological. Psychic researchers have encountered similar phenomena, sometimes with the added horror of alleged vampirism.

The theme of sexual intercourse with the Devil, or with a demon lover, often occurs in the confessions extorted from witches, and read during the witch trials of olden times. A great many such 'confessions', of course, were simply forced from the accused by torture, and in many cases people were tortured into confessing what their accusers required. One confession, however, which was made voluntarily, is that by the young Scottish witch, Isobel Gowdie, who gave herself up and was hanged. Her motives in doing so have never been fathomed; but her confession is very detailed, and includes a description of her sexual intercourse with the Devil. She says that he was "a meikle, blak, roch man, werie cold; and I fand his nature als cold within me as spring-well-water".

This detail, of the Devil's icy coldness, is found in the confessions of witches at many different times and places. For another instance, a witch of the Pays de Labourde, in 1616, one Sylvanie de la Plaine, confessed that the Devil's member was like that of a stallion, and "in entering it is cold like ice, jets very cold sperm, and in coming out it burns as if it were fire".

These descriptions are typical of a great many more, from all parts of Europe; and the details of the Devil's cold penis and ice-cold sperm have intrigued many modern writers. Margaret Murray believed they could be explained by the Devil being a man in ritual disguise, wearing a horned mask, a costume of skins which covered his whole body, and an artificial phallus. (*See* PHALLIC WORSHIP.)

This explanation does in fact cover the details of many stories of copulation with the Devil. The 'Devil' of the coven was a man playing the part of the Horned God. Intercourse with him was a religious rite; this is why the artificial phallus was used. The Great God Pan was always potent; he was not subject to human weaknesses. The *frisson* which a woman would have experienced when the cold phallus entered her, was enough to produce the illusion of ice-cold sperm.

In many of the earlier accounts of sexual relations between incubi and succubi and human beings, emphasis is placed on the intense pleasure derived from such embraces. After about 1470, however, the accounts (all of course compiled and published by the witch-hunters) begin to change their attitude, and horrifying and disgusting stories are told, of how intercourse with the Devil was repulsive and agonising. As in the case of descriptions of the witches' Sabbat, the authorities realised that it must not be made to sound attractive. Accused witches were therefore, under torture, required to assent to every farrago of sexual repulsiveness that the prurient imaginations of sadistic and repressed celibates could devise.

The authors of the *Malleus Maleficarum* are notably interested in the details of witches' sexual relations with devils. This book, first published *circa* 1486, was the official handbook for many years of the persecution of witches. Its priestly authors give a less unpleasant description of copulation between women and incubi than many, and one which shows the possibly auto-suggestive nature of such intercourse. They say that in all the cases of which they have had knowledge, the devil has always appeared visibly to the witch. "But with regard to any bystanders, the witches themselves have often been seen lying on their backs in the fields or the woods, naked up to the very navel, and it has been apparent from the disposition of those limbs and members which pertain to the venereal act and orgasm, as also from the agitation of their legs and thighs, that, all invisibly to the bystanders, they have been copulating with Incubus devils; yet sometimes, howbeit this is rare, at the end of the act a very black vapour, of about the stature of a man, rises up into the air from the witch."

Given the atmosphere of the Middle Ages, when sexual enjoyment was equated with sin, and ignorance, superstition and repression ruled people's minds, such scenes are fully understandable without the intervention of any 'devils', except those which existed in the minds of the participants, both the woman and the concealed 'bystander'.

Accounts of the relations of men with succubi are less frequently met with. When they do occur, they sometimes follow the pattern of the stories of incubi. The succubus takes the form of a beautiful woman, but her vagina is ice-cold; and sometimes her lover sees her shapely legs terminating in cloven hoofs. Again, the earlier accounts of succubi present them as beautiful and passionately alluring she-devils, who appeared to priests and holy hermits in order to tempt them—an enterprise in which they were often successful. Pope Sylvester II (999-1003) is one of the Popes who is supposed to have been secretly addicted to sorcery, and legend says that he enjoyed the embraces of a succubus called Meridiana, who was his familiar spirit.

The accounts of the ice-cold body of the succubus seem to be merely imitated from those similar tales of incubi; because the majority of the stories of succubi represent them as being diabolically seductive and alluring, and even as taking the form of courtesans and prostitutes to tempt men. The Lamiae and Empusae of pagan legend were similar beings, and the origin of most of these stories seems to lie in erotic dreams, which come to men by night without their conscious volition. Mostly such dreams are pleasurable; but if feelings of guilt and the terror of sin intervene, the phantasms take on a darker tone, and the dreamer enters the realms of nightmare.

INITIATIONS

When witchcraft became an underground organisation, the Craft of the Wise, it shared a characteristic common to all secret societies. Admission to it was by initiation.

Such initiation required the newly admitted member to swear a solemn oath of loyalty. When witchcraft was punishable by torture and death, such an oath was a serious matter. Today, when witchcraft has become like Freemasonry, not a secret society but a society with secrets, the idea of initiation still remains.

Initiations into witch circles nowadays take varying forms, as they probably always did. However, the old idea that initiation must pass from the male to the female, and from the female to the male, still persists. A male witch must be initiated by a woman, and a female witch by a man. This belief may be found in other forms, in traditional folklore. For instance, the words of healing charms are often required to be passed on from a man to a woman, or from a woman to a man. Otherwise, the charm will have no potency.

There is also an old and deep-seated belief, both in Britain and in Italy, that witches cannot die until they have passed on their power to someone else. This belief in itself shows that witchcraft has been for centuries an initiatory organisation, in which a tradition was handed on from one person to another.

The exception to the rule that a person must be initiated by one of the opposite sex occurs in the case of a witch's own children. A mother may initiate her daughter, or a father his son.

In general, for their own protection, covens have made a rule that they will not accept anyone as a member under the age of 21. Witches' children are presented as babies to the Old Gods, and then not admitted to coven membership until they have reached their majority.

This rule became general in the times of persecution. Secrecy upon which people's lives depended was too great a burden for children's shoulders to bear. It is evident, from the stories of witch persecutions, that witch-hunters realised how witchcraft was handed down in families. Any blood relative of a convicted witch was suspect.

The witch-hunting friar, Francesco-Maria Guazzo, in his *Compendium Maleficarum* (Milan, 1608, 1626; English translation edited Montague Summers, London, 1929), tells us that "it is one among many sure and certain indications against those accused of witchcraft, if one of their parents were found guilty of this crime". When the infamous Matthew Hopkins started his career as Witch-Finder General, the first victim he seized upon was an old woman whose mother had been hanged as a witch.

There are a number of fragmentary accounts of old-time witch initiations, and from these a composite picture can be built up. The whole-hearted acceptance of the witch religion, and the oath of loyalty, were the main features. There was also the giving of a new name, or nick-name, by which the novice was henceforth to be known in the circle of the coven. These things were sealed by ceremonial acts, the novice was given a certain amount of instruction, and, if the initiation took place at a Sabbat, as it often did, they were permitted to join in the feast and dancing that followed.

In some cases, in the days of really fierce persecution, a candidate was also required to make a formal renunciation of the official faith of the Christian Church, and to fortify this by some ritual act, such as trampling on a cross. This was to ensure that the postulant was no hypocritical spy; because such a one would not dare to commit an act which he or she would believe to be a mortal sin. Once the postulant had formally done such an act, they had in the eyes of the Church damned themselves, and abandoned themselves to hellfire; so it was a real test of sincerity, and an effective deterrent to those who wanted to run with the hare and hunt with the hounds. Such acts are not, however, to my knowledge, required of witches today.

One of the ritual acts recorded as being part of a witch initiation is that described by Sir George Mackenzie, writing in 1699 about witchcraft in Scotland, in his book *Laws and Customs of Scotland* (Edinburgh, 1699): "The Solemnity confest by our Witches, is the putting one hand to the crown of the Head, and another to the sole of the Foot, renouncing their Baptism in that posture." Joseph Glanvill's book *Sadducismus Triumphatus* (London, 1726), had a frontispiece of pictures illustrating various stories of mysterious happenings, and one of these old woodcuts shows a witch in the act of doing this.

Her initiation is taking place out of doors, in some lonely spot between two big trees. With her are three other women, one of whom seems to be presenting her to the Devil, who appears as the conventional figure of a horned and winged demon. In practice, however, the Devil of the coven was a man dressed in black, who was sometimes called the Man in Black, for this reason. The "grand array" of the horned mask, etc, was only assumed upon special occasions.

A variant of this ritual was for the Man in Black to lay his hand upon the new witch's head, and bid her to "give over all to him that was under his hand". This, too, is recorded from Scotland, in 1661.

Information about the initiation of men into witchcraft is much less than that referring to women. However, here is an account from the record of the trial of William Barton at Edinburgh, about 1655, evidently partly in his words and partly in those of his accusers, which tells how a young woman witch took a fancy to him, and initiated him:

> One day, says he, going from my own house in Kirkliston, to the Queens Ferry, I overtook in Dalmeny Muire, a young Gentlewoman, as to appearance beautiful and comely. I drew near to her, but she shunned my company, and when I insisted, she became angry and very nyce. Said I, we are both going one way, be pleased to accept of a convoy. At last after much entreaty she grew better natured, and at length came to that Familiarity, that she suffered me to embrace her, and to do that which Christian ears ought not to hear of. At this time I parted with her very joyful. The next night, she appeared to him in that very same place, and after that which should not be named, he became sensible, that it was the Devil. Here he renounced his Baptism, and gave up himself to her service, and she called him her beloved, and gave him this new name of John Baptist, and received the Mark.

The Devil's mark was made much of by professional witch-hunters, being supposed to be an indelible mark given by the Devil in person to each witch, upon his or her initiation. However, it would surely have been very foolish of the Devil to have marked his followers in this way, and thus indicated a means by which they might always be known. From the confused descriptions given at various times and places, it seems evident that the witch-hunters knew there was some ceremony of marking, but did not know what it was. (*See* DEVIL'S MARK.)

In witchcraft ceremonies today, the new initiate is marked with oil, wine, or some pigment, such as charcoal. However, as Margaret Murray has pointed out, there is a possibility, judging by the many old accounts of a small red or blue mark being given, the infliction of which was painful but healed after a while, that this may have been a tattoo mark. Ritual tattooing is a very old practice; and some relics of it survive today, in the fact that people have themselves tattooed with various designs 'for luck'. However, when persecution became very severe, it would have been unwise to continue this form of marking.

The most up-to-date instance I have heard, of the marking of new initiates, is the practice of a certain coven in Britain today, which uses eye-shadow for this purpose; because it is available in pleasing colours, is easily washed off, and does no harm to the skin. One wonders what old-time witches would think of it!

INVOCATIONS

The words 'invocation' and 'evocation' are commonly regarded as meaning the same thing. This, however, is an error from the magical point of view. One invokes a God into the magic circle; one evokes a spirit into the magic triangle, which is drawn outside the circle. The circle is the symbol of infinity and eternity; the triangle is the symbol of manifestation.

The true secret of invocation, according to Aleister Crowley, can be summed up in four words, taken from that mysterious manuscript, *The Sacred Magic of Abramelin the Mage*. These four words are "Enflame thyself in praying". The actual words of the invocation have little importance, so long as they have this effect upon the operator.

Crowley's own "Hymn to Pan" (in *Magick in Theory and Practice*, privately printed, London, 1929) has often been used by students of magic. So have the beautiful invocations of the goddess of the moon, contained in Dion Fortune's occult novel, *The Sea Priestess* (Aquarian Press, London, 1957). These are in verse, and therefore easier to remember, poetry being a magical thing in itself. There are, however, many fine examples of invocation couched in prose. One such is the Invocation of Isis, from *The Golden Ass,* by Lucius Apuleius, which has been translated into English by William Adlington and by Robert Graves.

The object of invocation is a heightening of the consciousness of the operator. We do not so much call down a god or a goddess, as raise ourselves up, to a spiritual condition in which we are capable of working magic.

Many practising magicians find that the most potent invocations are those which are framed in the sonorous words of some ancient language. The invocations contained in magical books often involve strings of almost unintelligible 'words of power'; usually the worn-down remnants of Greek, Latin, or Hebrew titles of God. An interesting example of this is the famous Magical Papyrus, preserved in the British Museum, which was translated and edited in 1852 for the Cambridge Antiquarian Society.

This papyrus came from Alexandria, and dates from about A.D. 200. Its author may have been a priest of Isis. It gives a tremendous succession of magical words, deriving from Greek, Syriac, Hebrew, Coptic and possibly Ancient Egyptian sources. It tells the magician to recite these to the North, uttering them as an invocation, with the words: "Make all the spirits subject to me, so that every spirit of heaven and of the air, upon the earth and under the earth, on dry land and in the water, and every spell and scourge of God may be obedient to me."

Another ancient invocation is that which is preserved in a thirteenth-century play, *Le Miracle de Théophile,* written by a famous *trouvère* or troubadour called Ruteboeuf (quoted in *A Pictorial Anthology of Witchcraft, Magic and Alchemy,* by Grillot de Givry, translated by J. Courtenay Locke, University Books, New York, 1958). The *trouvères* or 'finders', were so called because they were poets who travelled the countryside of France in search of time-honoured lore and legend, which they incorporated into their works. They were often suspected of heresy and paganism.

This play by Ruteboeuf has a scene which involves 'conjuring the Devil', and it contains this extraordinary invocation, which is in no known language:

> *Bagabi laca bachabe*
> *Lamac cahi achababe*
> *Karrelyos*

Lamac lamec Bachalyas
Cabahagy sabalyos
Baryolos
Lagoz atha cabyolas
Samahac et famyolas
Harrahya.

The triumphant *"Harrahya!"* at the end is reminiscent of the cries of the witches' Sabbat. In the thirteenth century, 'conjuring the Devil' and 'invoking the Old Gods' would have been synonymous. So this may well be a genuine specimen of an invocation used at the Sabbat, discovered by a *trouvère* and perpetuated by him under the orthodox guise of being part of a miracle play.

I wished to include here a sample of a present-day witches' invocation. However, I found it difficult to do this without giving offence to friends who preferred not to have their rituals published. So I am compelled to present an invocation I wrote myself, to the goddess of the moon and witchcraft:

Our Lady of the Moon, enchantment's queen,
And of midnight the potent sorceress,
O goddess from the darkest deep of time,
Diana, Isis, Tanith, Artemis,
Your power we invoke to aid us here!
Your moon a magic mirror hangs in space,
Reflecting mystic light upon the earth,
And every month your threefold image shines.
Mistress of magic, ruler of the tides
Both seen and unseen; spinner of the threads
Of birth and death and fate; O ancient one,
Nearest to us of heaven's lights, upon
Whose shoulders nature is exalted, vast
And shadowy, to farthest realms unknown,
Your power we invoke to aid us here!

O goddess of the silver light, that shines
In magic rays through deepest woodland glade,
And over sacred and enchanted hills
At still midnight, when witches cast their spells,
When spirits walk, and strange things are abroad;
By the dark cauldron of your inspiration,
Goddess three fold, upon you thrice we call;
Your power we invoke to aid us here!

J

JANICOT

The history of witchcraft is an obscure and difficult subject, because most of the documents are written, not by witches themselves, but by the witch-hunters. The latter not only have a strong vested interest in proving witches to be either vile and malicious, or else the dupes of evil spirits, or both. They are also committed to the view that witchcraft is devil worship, and therefore any deity invoked by a witch must be Satan, either in person or under some disguise.

To find out the truth about what witches really believed and did, is therefore rather like a detective story, in that one has to look into the evidence we possess, for small but significant clues. The pioneer in this respect was Margaret Murray. Abuse has been heaped upon her work since her death, even to the extent of students being advised not to read it—a fact which in itself shows that Dr. Murray's books are worth reading.

However, her essential thesis, that behind all the horrors and fantasies of the witch persecutions, there lay the remains of an old religion, which was a hated rival of Christianity, cannot be disproved.

One of the clues which Margaret Murray noted was in the appearance of the name of the old Basque god Janicot in the account given by Pierre De Lancre of his crusade against witchcraft in the Pays de Labourde in the early seventeenth century.

De Lancre had been sent by the Parlement of Bordeaux, to investigate the alleged prevalence of witchcraft among the Basque-speaking people of the countryside called the Pays de Labourde. He found, to his horror and indignation, that the rumours were all too true. Big Sabbats were being held, at which large numbers of country people attended; and what was worse, many of the clergy, instead of denouncing witchcraft, actually belonged to the Old Religion themselves, by a sort of dual allegiance. In fact, some of them had permitted witch meetings to be held in their churches.

In spite of the hostility of the populace, De Lancre proceeded to carry out a purge of the district, with the usual concomitants of torture and burning at the stake. Later he wrote a detailed account of his experiences, entitled *Tableau de l'Inconstance des Mauvais Anges* (*A description of the Inconstancy of Evil Angels*), which was published in Paris in 1612, and was followed by two other works of a similar nature.

De Lancre found among the Basque witches a sort of rhyme, mentioning the old Basque god Janicot:

> *In nomine patrica,*
> *Aragueaco petrica*
> *Gastellaco Janicot,*
> *Equidae ipordian pot.*

He had the impression that this was used instead of Christian words when the witches made the sign of the cross; and they told him that it was translated: *"Au nom du Patrique, petrique d'Arragon, Janicot de Castille, faites-moi un baiser au derrière."* This seems to mean, "In the name of the Father, the father of Aragon, Janicot of Castile, give me a kiss on the backside"—a reference to the *Osculum infame*.

A male witch, Gentien Le Clerc, confessed that, while at a witches' Sabbat, they had poked fun at the Christian Mass, saying that the Host was *"un beau Janicot"*. This may be interpreted as meaning that Janicot to them was synonymous with God. Margaret Murray points out that in the Basque countryside still, there are legends of *Basa-Jaun,* "now degenerated into a sprite". His name means *homme de bouc,* 'goat-man', according to Dr. Murray; and it is significant that the Basque word for the witches' Sabbat is *Akhelarre,* meaning 'The Field of the Goat'. *Basa-Jaun,* or *Jaunis,* is a spirit of the woods, a satyr.

The Basque word for God is *Jaincoa,* which is believed to be the origin of our term 'By Jingo!' According to *Chambers' Dictionary,* the word 'Jingo' appears first as a conjurer's summoning call, which may be significant in this connection. There is also an old-time children's game called the Jingo-Ring, in which the players form a ring and dance round one of their company, who stands in the middle; just as the witches at their Sabbats danced round the Devil, according to the old accounts. The dance of the Sabbat has survived in attenuated form as a children's game.

What is particularly notable about the name Janicot is that it connects back to the old Roman deities Diana and her consort Dianus or Janus. Dianus was known as the King of the Wood, *Rex Nemorensis;* and the priest of Diana was named after him.

Sir James Frazer, in his famous book on ancient mythology, *The Golden Bough,* tells us of these woodland divinities. Their connection with witchcraft is shown by the fact that in Naples a witch is still known as *jana* or *janara.*

Dianus was particularly connected with the oak tree, and it was in the oak-grove of Nemi that Frazer found the figure of that mysterious priest which so intrigued him and which inspired his book, that has become a classic of its kind. So much of the religion of our pagan ancestors, Roman, Celtic and Teutonic, is bound up with the oak-tree; it is natural that it should be the representative of the mysterious king of the wood, from its wonderful longevity, its imposing beauty, and its usefulness to man. The concept of the god of the woods lingered long in medieval art, as the figure of the Green Man, depicted with oak-leaves surrounding him and growing from his mouth. (*See* GREEN MAN.)

As Janus, he was the god of doors, both literally and figuratively. His image, with two faces, was set up at doors; and Frazer thinks that the Latin *janua,* a door, is derived from his name. In the figurative sense, he opened the door of the year; the month of January is named after him. But as the consort of Diana, there would have been another door that he opened. Diana of Nemi was a goddess of fertility. Frazer tells us that on the site of her shrine "there have been found many models of the organs of generation, both male and female". The god of the woods is the male spirit of life, typified by the phallus, the opener.

But that which is born into this world by the gate of life, must in its time depart hence by the gate of death. Hence the phallic gods are also gods of death and what lies beyond. The phallic 'Devil' of the Tarot is called in certain occult titles of the cards, 'The Lord of the Gates of Matter', 'The Child of the Forces of Time'. Some figures of Janus represent him with two faces, one that of a young man, the other that of an old one.

It is a curious fact that this is what the Basque witches described the Devil's grand array as possessing, when he appeared at the Sabbats; namely, two faces, one in the usual place, and the other, evidently a mask, upon his buttocks. This was offered to his worshippers to kiss, in the *osculum infame* which the old writers about witchcraft found so shocking and shameful. A folk-memory of this practice may well linger in the popular vulgar expressions such as 'you may kiss my arse', and so on. What was originally a religious rite of genuine solemnity, became a piece of buffoonery; even as the most sacred words of consecration in the Catholic Mass, *Hoc est corpus,* were jeeringly made into the expression 'hocus-pocus'.

To kneel and kiss the mask upon the Devil's buttocks was an act of homage by his worshippers, and there are many references to it in old writings. But it should be recognised that by 'the Devil', his followers understood the human representative of their time-honoured pagan god, who was the giver of life, not a being of evil.

The reference to "Janicot of Castile" may be explained by the Devil of the Basque witches being a Spaniard. He was certainly Spanish-speaking. De Lancre describes how he learned that the Devil made marriages between the male and female witches at the Sabbat, by joining their hands and saying:

> *Esta es buena parati*
> *Esta parati lo toma.*

This is simply Spanish for "This woman is good for thee, Take this woman for thyself." De Lancre added that, before the married pairs lay with each other, the Devil coupled with the girls, and took their virginity (*"Mais avant qu'ils couchent ensemble, il s'accouple avec elles, oste la virginité des filles"*). This is in accordance with very old religious ideas, by which a maiden sacrificed her virginity to the god before she gave herself to man.

De Lancre was very interested in obtaining detailed accounts from the young witches of how they coupled with the Devil, and of what his member was like, and so on; and he does not seem to have been content until he obtained a suitably horrifying description. The truth, however, probably was that an artificial phallus was used; as it was in the worship of the phallic god Priapus, to whom brides sacrificed their virginity in ancient Rome. This is the rite which became debased into the notorious *droit de seigneur* of the Middle Ages, which the Church seems to have permitted. Was it only the pagan version of it which they objected to?

K

KYTELER, DAME ALICE

The case of Dame Alice Kyteler is of particular interest, because it was the first big witch trial to take place in Ireland. It happened in 1324, and the accused was a lady of wealth and high social position in Kilkenny.

She had been married four times, and at least two of her previous husbands had been widowers, with children by a previous marriage. Her husband at the time of her trial was Sir John le Poer. He was a sick man, suffering from some chronic illness, and a mischief-making maid-servant had hinted to him that his wife was poisoning him.

Sir John seems not to have been too ill to take forcible possession of his wife's keys, in spite of her struggles to prevent him. He opened the boxes and chests she kept in her room, and sent their contents to the Bishop of Ossory, as evidence of poisoning and witchcraft.

Her stepchildren by her previous marriages joined in the accusations against her, saying that she had killed their fathers by witchcraft, and robbed them of their inheritance (because, of course, she had inherited their fathers' estates).

What the truth of the matter was, we do not have enough evidence to be certain. Was Lady Alice a *femme fatale,* a poisoner who enriched herself by the death of three wealthy husbands and tried to encompass the death of a fourth? Or was she wrongfully accused by a spiteful maid and jealous step-children? Or was all the talk of poisoning an excuse by the Bishop of Ossory, whom the Seneschal of Kilkenny called "a vile, rustic, interloping monk", to put down the heresy of Lady Alice and her followers, who were practising pagans?

Certain it is that many of the nobility of Ireland supported Lady Alice and opposed the Bishop. Here is the account given by Holinshed in his *Chronicle of Ireland* (London, 1587):

> 1323. In the eighteenth year of King Edward II, his reign, the Lord John Darcie came into Ireland, and to be lord justice, and the King's lieutenant

there. In these days lived in the diocese of Ossorie the Lady Alice Kettle, whom the bishop asscited to purge herself of the fame of enchantment and witchcraft imposed unto her and to one Petronill and Basill her complices. She was charged to have nightly conference with a spirit call Robert Artisson, to whom she sacrificed in the highway nine red cocks and nine peacocks' eyes. Also that she swept the streets of Kilkennie between compline and twilight, raking all the filth towards the doors of her son William Outlawe, murmuring secretly with herself these words:

> 'To the house of William my son,
> Hie all the wealth of Kilkennie town'.

At the first conviction they abjured and did penance, but shortly after they were found in relapse, and then was Petronill burnt at Kilkennie, the other twain might not be heard of. She at the hour of her death accused the said William as privy to their sorceries, whom the Bishop held in durance nine weeks, forbidding his keepers to eat or to drink with him, or to speak to him more than once in the day. But at length, through the suit and instance of Arnold le Powre, then Seneschall of Kilkennie, he was delivered, and after corrupted with bribes the Seneschall to persecute the bishop; so that he thrust him into prison for three months. In rifling the closet of the lady, they found a wafer of sacramental bread, having the devil's name stamped thereon instead of Jesus Christ, and a pipe of ointment, wherewith she greased a staff, upon which she ambled and galloped through thick and thin, when and in what manner she listed. This business about these witches troubled all the state of Ireland the more, for that the lady was supported by certain of the nobility, and lastly conveyed over into England, since which time it could never be understood what became of her.

This quotation gives us some insight into the magical arts Dame Alice and her coven engaged in. The sweeping of the streets towards her son's door is a typical piece of sympathetic magic. Compline was the last religious service of the day; and it may be relevant that some old-fashioned housewives still believe it to be unlucky to use a broom after sunset. For 'unlucky', perhaps we should read 'uncanny', as such sweeping might have some purpose of witchcraft behind it.

The story of the sacrifice of "nine peacocks' eyes" most probably refers, not to the actual eyes of the birds, but to their tail-feathers, which bear eyelike markings. In spite of their beauty, peacocks' feathers have long had a sinister reputation and been associated with the Devil. Many people believe them to be unlucky, and will not have them in their houses. In Italy, peacocks' feathers are called *la penna maligna,* and are associated with witchcraft and the Evil Eye. The marking upon them is indeed wonderfully and strangely like a dark eye, contrasted by the iridescent green of the feathers. In the Near East the obscure sect of the Yezidis is said to worship the Devil under the form of Melek Taos, the Peacock Angel.

The sacrifice was carried out, says another account, at the cross-roads; and the name of the 'spirit' is given as "Robin, Son of Art". However, the account also tells us that he was Dame Alice's lover, which shows that he was no spirit, but a man. His appearance is described as being "like an Ethiop". Perhaps he blacked his face so as not to be recognised, as the Morris Dancers used to.

It is interesting that the names of the people accused with Dame Alice have survived; and, with "Robin, Son of Art", they number thirteen. The roll call of the coven is as follows:

> Dame Alice herself.
> William Outlawe, her son, a wealthy banker.
> Robert of Bristol, a cleric in Minor Orders.
> Alice, the wife of Henry Faber.
> John Galrussyn.
> Helen Galrussyn.
> Syssoh Galrussyn.
> Petronilla de Meath, Dame Alice's maid.
> Sarah, Petronilla's daughter, who was also known as Basilia
>   (this was probably her witch name).
> William Payne de Boly.
> Eva de Brounestoun.
> Annota Lange.
> Robert Artisson, the 'Devil'.

It is notable also that in the *Annales* of John Clynn (quoted in *The Geography of Witchcraft* by Montague Summers, Kegan Paul, London, 1927), these people are spoken of as being *"de secta et doctrina praedictae dominae Aliciae"*, "of the sect and doctrine of the aforesaid lady Alice". They are repeatedly accused of heresy, and of renouncing the Christian faith and refusing to come to the Christian Church; in fact it is obvious that it was the accusation of heresy, and not the alleged poisonings, that the trial was really all about. Dame Alice and her associates were quite clearly a coven of thirteen, who held a non-Christian faith.

After a good deal of controversy, in which, as we have seen, the Bishop by no means had all his own way, Dame Alice was found guilty of witchcraft, heresy and sacrificing to demons. However, she had by this time fled to England, taking with her Sarah, Petronilla's daughter; and the two were never found again.

The Bishop had, meantime, with typical religious zeal, imprisoned Petronilla, Dame Alice's maid, and had her subjected to six floggings, before he got her to confess to witchcraft. She was burned at the stake, refusing to the last to accept any Christian rites.

William Outlawe, the son, was released from prison upon agreeing publicly to recant and abjure his heresies in the Cathedral Church of St. Mary at Kilkenny, to perform a religious pilgrimage to the shrine of St. Thomas at Canterbury, and—a nice commercial touch— to roof the Cathedral with lead. As for the rest of the coven, some were burned at the stake, others whipped in the market-place and through the streets, and others were banished and declared excommunicate, which probably meant that they had already fled. The identity of Robin, the Son of Art, was never discovered.

The Bishop had troubles of his own. As we have seen, he was imprisoned in his turn by the Seneschall of Kilkenny. The Archbishop of Dublin brought a charge of heresy against him, and he took refuge in flight and appealed to the Pope for protection. In 1329 King Edward III seized his revenues, and it was not until 1347-8 that he returned from exile. He remained under a cloud until 1354, when peace seems to have been restored. He was then an old man, and he died six years later.

For human drama as well as occult interest, the case of Dame Alice Kyteler and her coven is outstanding in the history of witchcraft. We have the story of the alleged poisoning of rich husbands; and the tale of midnight orgies at lonely crossroads, where the witches are accused of using the skull of an executed criminal as a cauldron in which to boil a mixture of loathsome ingredients over a fire of oak-wood, in order to make magical powders and ointments.

We have also the curious details about the mysterious figure of "Robin, Son of Art". The Bishop insisted that Dame Alice's lover was an incubus demon, and the prosecution stated at her trial (held in her absence) that Robin or Robert had appeared not only as a man but in the shapes of a cat and of a big black dog. On one occasion, when he appeared as a dark-visaged man, he had brought with him two tall companions, one of whom carried an iron rod in his hand; probably some kind of ceremonial wand. Perhaps the two companions were visitors from some other coven.

The evidence forced from Petronilla de Meath shows that Robin,

Son of Art was no bodiless demon. As usual with celibate clerics, the Bishop was very interested in the details of the sexual relations between Dame Alice and her supposed demon lover, and Petronilla was questioned about them. She confessed that she had been present when Robin had intercourse with the Lady Alice, and after this sinful act, she herself had wiped with a handkerchief the place of wickedness upon the bed. Dame Alice, she said, had taught her the secrets of witchcraft, and she herself was a mere novice in comparison to her mistress, than whom there was not a greater witch in all the English realm.

Petronilla died bravely and unrepentant; and if Dame Alice could not save her maid, at least she rescued Petronilla's daughter, and took her on her flight to England. After these events, there was continuing drama; for some influence, probably that of Dame Alice's friends and sympathisers, effectively pursued asd ruined Bishop Ledrede of Ossory, who had brought the prosecution.

This case of 1324 is of historical importance, for several reasons. A good deal of evidence has survived in our own day, and can be found (though much of it is in Latin) in *Proceedings Against Dame Alice Kyteler,* edited by Thomas Wright for the Camden Society in 1843. Furthermore, the affair shows clearly the early stages of the struggle between the Christian Church and the Old Religion, in the days when the former was by no means so firmly entrenched as it became later, especially in the wilder and remoter countries such as Ireland. It also demonstrates the existence of the coven of thirteen; the people who recorded the names of those involved, amounting to twelve with Robert Artisson as the thirteenth, did not do so because they had been reading Margaret Murray.

The commencement of the use of torture to extract confessions, and of the blatant self-enrichment of the witch-hunters from witch trials, two features which assumed major importance in later years, are also plainly evident here.

L

LAMMAS

Lammas, 1st August, is one of the four Great Sabbats of the witches' year. It is notable as the time when, "on the morrow of Lammas" (that is, on the day after Lammas), King William Rufus was mysteriously slain in the New Forest, in the year 1100, the thirteenth year of his reign.

So well remembered is the Red King's death, that to this day people in that area sometimes visit the Rufus Stone in the New Forest on 2nd August, the anniversary of the day he was killed.

Margaret Murray and Hugh Ross Williamson, both of whom have made a close historical study of William Rufus, regard him as a sacrificial victim, a sacred king of the Old Religion. Accounts of his death vary in detail; but all agree that he was killed by an arrow, in the vicinity of an oak tree. The original tree has long perished, having been reduced to a stump by people who cut pieces from it to keep as relics. In 1745, a triangular pillar was erected on the site of the former oak tree; but this too was chipped and defaced by pilgrims to the spot, to such an extent that it had to be replaced by the present memorial.

This circumstance in itself shows the mysterious regard in which King William Rufus was held. The monkish chroniclers of his time detested him, because he was an open pagan; but he was popular with the common people, and no worse a king than others of his period.

The Feast of Lammas itself is sometimes called 'the Gule of August', from the old British word *gwyl*, meaning a feast or a holiday. The first week in August had always been the working people's holiday time, until the Government introduced 'staggered holidays'; and Lammas was the great season for fairs.

The word Lammas is usually derived from 'loaf-mass', the time when the first corn is harvested. However, it is more likely to be a shortened version of the old Celtic Lughnasadh, the Druidic festival at the beginning of August. This was dedicated to Lugh, the Celtic sun god; and it is notable that Llew, the Welsh version of this ancient god, is told of in the *Mabinogion* (translated by Lady Charlotte Guest, J. M. Dent, Everyman's Library Edition, London, 1913) as a king who was murdered and came back to life.

Lughnasadh means 'the commemoration of Lugh'. It was the day upon which the country people of Britain and Ireland held processions in honour of the dead sun god; hence, if Margaret Murray is correct, it was a singularly appropriate season for the death of Rufus as the sacred king. After the summer solstice, the sun's power begins to decline; hence the sun god dies symbolically, only to be reborn again at the winter solstice. Lammas is the time of the first signs of autumn, even as Candlemas is the celebration of the first sign of spring.

These festivals, which go back to time immemorial, are part of the deep oneness with Nature that the people of olden days experienced; even to the extent of being willing victims for sacrifice.

LAWS AGAINST WITCHCRAFT

Laws against the misuse of occult powers have existed from the earliest times and amongst all peoples. However, the distinction between white magic and black has been clearly recognised. The Roman emperors made many laws against black magic; but they themselves had personal astrologers and soothsayers whom they protected and consulted.

However, with the commencement of the Christian dispensation came the new idea that all other gods except the Christian Trinity were devils. The pagans had willingly recognised the gods of other nations as being different aspects of their own gods; but to the Christians such an idea was blasphemous. The old gods and the magical practices connected with them were alike denounced as devil worship.

Nevertheless, for a long time the officials of the Church could not get their congregations to accept this idea. We find, for instance, the complaint of the Venerable Bede about Redwald, King of the East Saxons, who died about A.D. 627. Bede indignantly records in his chronicle that King Redwald had in the same temple "an altar to sacrifice to Christ, and another small one to offer victims to devils".

The early history of the Church in England, and indeed throughout Europe, is one of constant struggle against this state of dual allegiance, at once to the new god and to the older, well-remembered divinities. In just the same way—as we can see from hints in the Old Testament, notably in the *Book of Jeremiah*—the official religion of the Hebrews, the cult of Yahweh or Jehovah, was in constant conflict with the so-called heathenism of the common people, who still wanted to worship the older divinities, such as the Moon Goddess, the Queen of Heaven, after such worship had been denounced and forbidden.

We find in the laws of the old English kings, and in the books of ecclesiastical discipline and penance, frequent mention of witchcraft and magic. These things are equated with heathenism, and priests are strongly exhorted to forbid them, and the people to abandon them. They are being so urged in the seventh century A.D.; under King Edward and King Guthrum in the tenth century, witchcraft and heathen customs are still being denounced; and in the days of King Canute the same legal and ecclesiastical bans are still being promulgated.

King Canute died in 1035; and it is evident from the wording of the law in his time that the country was still not entirely Christian, nor had witchcraft yielded to the pressure of Church and State: "We earnestly forbid every heathenism. Heathenism is, that men worship idols; that is, they worship heathen gods, and the sun or moon, fire or rivers, water-wells or stones, or forest-trees of any kind; or love witchcraft, or promote *morth-work* in any wise; or by *blot,* or *fyrht,* or perform anything pertaining to such illusions."

If these things had not been happening, there would have been no need to forbid them.

In the next century, John of Salisbury, who died in 1180, writes in his book *Policraticus* (quoted by Montague Summers in *The Geography of Witchcraft,* Kegan Paul, London, 1927) of the belief in the witch goddess Herodias, and of the witch-meetings and revels held at night in her honour. This belief had already been denounced by the Council of Ancyra, whose condemnation of the women who worshipped Diana and Herodias by night had become part of the Church's Canon Law—a decree which in later years the Church was to find very embarrassing, when it wished to foster the idea that witchcraft was the worship of Satan.

In the earlier days, however, much more sanity seems to have prevailed in the treatment of witches than was later evidenced. Neither the hysteria of persecution, nor the money-making trade of witch-hunting, had yet arisen. A witch had to be shown to have committed some definite act of evil, before he or she was condemned; though the actual penalties seem to have varied considerably, probably according to the personal viewpoint of the judges, either ecclesiastical or lay. In those days the Church had its own courts, in addition to those of the State.

Gradually, however, the persecution of witches as heretics gathered momentum. The powers of the ecclesiastical courts were increased and sharpened by the statute *De Haeretico Comburendo,* "Of the Burning of Heretics", which was passed in 1401 at the instigation of Archbishop Thomas Arundel. According to the famous English judge, Sir Matthew Hale (1609-1676), who himself played a considerable part in the history of legal proceedings against witches: "Witchcraft, *Sortilegium,* was by the ancient laws of England of ecclesiastical cognizance, and upon conviction thereof, without abjuration, punishable by death by writ *de haeretico comburendo*." (*See* BURNING AT THE STAKE.)

The Reverend Montague Summers, commenting upon this hideous statute in his *Geography of Witchcraft,* remarks airily that it was "in fact nothing more than the application in England of the general law of Christendom".

This is true; on the Continent the witch pyres had long been blazing. In England, however, the full fury of persecution was never attained, in comparison to what happened in the rest of Europe; though Scotland continued to burn witches until the eighteenth century, and scenes of horror were enacted there which were as much a shame to humanity as those which took place across the seas. Also, torture was not legal in England, but it was in Scotland, and there are records of even children being subjected to torture there, to extort confessions of witchcraft.

The doubtful distinction of the first definitely recorded case of a witch-burning belongs to France. It took place in 1275, at Toulouse, where a woman named Angèle de la Barthe was burned as a witch, upon the orders of Hugues de Baniols, the Inquisitor of Toulouse. She was alleged to have attended the Sabbat, had sexual intercourse with the Devil and murdered babies for the purpose of cannibalism.

One fact has not been sufficiently clearly grasped, with regard to the horrific crimes that witches allegedly confessed. If a witch, in Scotland or on the Continent, where burning at the stake was the standard punishment for witchcraft, agreed to confess whatever he or she was accused of, then they were accorded the mercy of being strangled by the executioner before the sentence of burning was carried out. If, however, they refused to confess after being found guilty, or having confessed, later denied their confession, then they were adjudged obdurate and unrepentant and burnt alive. When one reads the account of the tortures inflicted upon alleged witches, it is only too understandable that those who found themselves trapped in the pitiless mechanism of the witch-hunt, knowing that there was no escape, confessed to what would bring them a comparatively quick death.

Nor would any confession, however obscenely horrible, be disbelieved. Public opinion was so conditioned by a succession of psychopathic books written against witches and witchcraft, such as the infamous *Malleus Maleficarum,* and the works of Nicholas Remy, Jean Bodin, Francesco-Maria Guazzo, Martin Del Rio, Henri Boguet, to name only a few, that people had almost ceased to be able to think straight upon this subject. Moreover, those who did have doubts of the official stories about the frightful crimes and diabolical powers of witches, generally found it wiser to keep their mouths shut. Martin Del Rio is typical of many writers when he affirms that it is an indication of witchcraft if a person is willing to defend a witch, or to cast doubt upon stories about witches.

Another very significant point of law was that the estate of a convicted witch was confiscated. This, especially in Germany, opened the floodgates of horror. In Britain, Matthew Hopkins made witch-hunting a profitable business; but his activities were petty, compared to what was done in this way on the Continent. The exploitation of torture and death to gratify human greed became so appalling that a number of Churchmen took their lives in their hands to denounce it; though their voices were few. One such, for instance, was Father Cornelius Loos, who in 1592 protested that "by cruel butchery innocent lives are taken; and by a new alchemy, gold and silver are coined from human blood".

Again, in the early seventeenth century, Canon Linden of Trèves exposed the motives of the witch-hunters in his area, making the significant comment, "This movement was promoted by many in office, who looked to wealth in the ashes of the victims." In areas where this law was repealed, as it was by the Emperor Ferdinand II of Germany in the seventeenth century, the fervour of the witch-hunters soon died down.

In England after the Reformation, burning at the stake ceased to be the punishment for witchcraft, and hanging was substituted. Actual records of how many witches were executed in England are scanty, and the number can only be guessed at. The records we have, however, show that a peak period for executions was the reign of the first Queen Elizabeth.

The government of King Henry VIII had passed a statute against witchcraft, containing the death penalty for invoking or conjuring an evil spirit; a conveniently wide and severe clause. Under King Edward VI this statute was repealed. However, Queen Elizabeth I was strongly urged by a Calvinistic Bishop, John Jewel, to pass more severe laws against witches. In a sermon preached before the Queen, Jewel proclaimed: "This kind of people (I mean witches and sorcerers) within these few last years are marvellously increased within this Your Grace's realm." Accordingly, in 1563 a strongly-worded law was passed, whereby the previous statute was resurrected, and anyone who should "use, practice, or exercise any Witchcraft, Enchantment, Charm or Sorcery, whereby any person shall happen to be killed or destroyed", could be sentenced to death.

There were lesser penalties for other acts of witchcraft. If, for instance, a person was bewitched so that they were wasted, consumed or lamed, the punishment of the witch was a year's imprisonment, with four exposures in the pillory; and for a second offence, the sentence was death.

However, this Act was not enough for the learned King James I, author of *Daemonologie* (Edinburgh, 1597), in spite of the number of executions that had been carried out under it. When James I came to the throne in 1603, he at once set about making sure that witchcraft was prosecuted as a capital crime in itself, whether or not the witch could be shown to have harmed anyone.

Accordingly, in 1604 the most extensive Act against witchcraft in English law was passed. It was particularly directed against anyone who invoked evil spirits or communed in any way with familiars, which it presumed to be evil spirits. This was something new in English law, and explains the emphasis on familiars often found in English witch trials.

Although there are actually more recorded executions under Elizabeth I than there are under King James, the importance of the increased severity of the law passed in his reign, was that it made possible the fierce persecution of witches by the Puritans, in the days of the Civil War and the Commonwealth.

In general, both in England and on the Continent, the seventeenth century was about the worst time for a witch to be living in. However, it was a great darkness before the dawn. In the eighteenth century, the belief in the dangers of witchcraft, and the desire to persecute witches, began notably to decline. This was not because of any change of heart on the part of the religious authorities, but the result of the rise of rationalism, of scepticism, and a general attitude of questioning accepted beliefs, which gained momentum as the century advanced.

The clergy protested vehemently against any change in the popular attitude to witchcraft, because they regarded a belief in the supernatural as an important part of religion. John Wesley wrote in his *Journal,* in 1768 (J. M. Dent, Everyman Library Edition, London, 1906): "The giving up of witchcraft is, in effect, giving up the Bible." In 1743, certain Scottish Churchmen at Edinburgh included in their published "Confession of National and Personal Sins" the fact that the penal statutes against witches had been repealed contrary to the express law of God.

In England, an enlightened Chief Justice, Sir John Holt (1642-1710), did much to put an end to witchcraft persecution, by throwing out case after case, especially those in which hysterical or mischievous children accused people of bewitching them. (There are a horrifying number of cases of this type in the records of witchcraft trials. As an instance, one 11-year old girl, Christian Shaw of Bargarran in Scotland, caused seven people to be burned at the stake in Paisley in 1697 as a result of her accusations. The executions in Salem, Massachusetts, were the direct result also of the lies of hysterical girls, combined with the sick-minded credulity of their elders.)

In 1736, in the reign of George II, a great change was made in English law. The Act of James I was repealed, and so were the similar laws in Scotland. Witchcraft ceased to be a capital offence in Britain. What this really reflected was a fundamental change in public opinion because the law now took an entirely different attitude to witchcraft. Witchcraft was still illegal; but the law now stated that anyone *pretending* to exercise witchcraft should be punished, usually by imprisonment.

It was under this Act, and under the Vagrancy Act of 1824, that

Spiritualist mediums were harassed and prosecuted. The last big trial under the Witchcraft Act of 1736 was that of the medium Helen Duncan in 1944. This took place at the Old Bailey, and the case went on for eight days. Her offence, according to the prosecution, was that she pretended to communicate with spirits.

According to Maurice Barbanell, who wrote about this famous case in the Spiritualist journal *Two Worlds* in December 1956, the decision to prosecute was taken because of a series of seances Helen Duncan gave in Portsmouth in 1944. World War II was raging then, and among the spirits who manifested at these seances were those of seamen who said they had gone down with H.M.S. *Barham*. At that time, the news of the ship's sinking had not yet been released by the Admiralty.

Helen Duncan was sentenced to nine months' imprisonment. She appealed, but the appeal was dismissed. It was the interest created by this case that urged Spiritualists to renewed efforts to get the Witchcraft Act repealed, because under it any seance could be illegal.

In 1951 they were at length successful. The old Witchcraft Act was finally repealed, and replaced by the Fraudulent Mediums Act. This is a remarkable piece of legislation, in that it recognises the possibility of genuine mediumship and prosecutes only when deliberate fraud is committed for gain.

LELAND, CHARLES GODFREY

Charles Godfrey Leland was a remarkable, many-sided personality, to whom students of folklore and witchcraft owe a great deal. His most famous books on these subjects are *Gypsy Sorcery and Fortune-Telling,* first published in London in 1891 (University Books Inc, New York, 1962); *Etruscan-Roman Remains in Popular Tradition,* first published in London in 1892; and *Aradia, or the Gospel of the Witches,* published in London in 1899.

In addition to these, Leland was the author of over fifty books on a variety of subjects, and was probably most famous in his lifetime for the book he wrote as a joke, *Hans Breitmann's Ballads,* a series of comic verses in the idiom of old-time German-American immigrants (Trubner and Co, London, 1872).

Not only was Leland a pioneer in the systematic collection and study of folklore, legends, and old and curious languages such as Romany and Shelta (the Celtic tinkers' language which he discovered); he was also a pioneer in education and psychology, and his ideas were far in advance of his day. Moreover, his own talents as an artist and craftsman were outstanding. His illustrations to his own works have an originality, strangeness and charm which capture the true spirit of magic and fairy-tale.

Leland not only studied magic and witchcraft; he practised them. His letters and other writings are full of references to successful spells he accomplished. For instance, he once wrote to a friend, while he was in England and was staying at Brighton:

> On the steamboat to England Mrs. Leland found that a diamond worth perhaps $40 or $50 had fallen from her ring, probably while asleep in her berth. The whole stateroom was overhauled in vain. I invoked the spirit and I predicted its recovery. A few days after, here in Brighton, she found it loose at the bottom of her travelling bag. And I had another invocation to find a friend who I was confidentially assured had left Brighton. One day I invoked the spirit, and he bade me follow two girls on the other side of the way. I did so for some distance, when I met my friend, who had just returned to Brighton; I might have been here a year without doing so.

One of his most prized possessions was the Black Stone of the Voodoos. There were only five or six of these 'conjuring stones' in the whole of America. They were small black pebbles, which had originally come from Africa, and whoever succeeded in obtaining one became thereby a Master of Voodoo, and was recognised as such by the practitioners of Voodoo in America. Leland was given one, which he exhibited to the Folk-Lore Congress in London in 1891.

In 1888 Leland became the first President of the Gypsy-Lore Society. In the winter of that year, in Florence, he was initiated into the witch-lore of Italy, *La Vecchia Religione* as it was called, meaning 'The Old Religion'. He had made friends in Florence with a beautiful young witch called Maddalena. She came from the wild countryside of the Romagna Toscana; and members of her family had, from time immemorial, told fortunes, preserved ancient legends and incantations, and practised spells and enchantments. Her grandmother, her aunt and her stepmother had all been witches and had trained her from childhood in the rites and beliefs of the Old Religion.

Maddalena gave Leland a mass of legends and incantations, upon which he based his books about Italian witchcraft; and she also introduced him to other witches.

Leland states, in his *Etruscan-Roman Remains:* "There are many people in Italy, and I have met such, who, while knowing nothing about Diana as a Roman goddess, are quite familiar with her as Queen of the Witches." Leland was not, however, the first to realise that witchcraft in Italy was the survival of the old cult of the moon goddess Diana. In 1749 Girolamo Tartarotti had published a book, *A Study of the Midnight Sabbats of Witches,* in which he stated that "The identity of the Dianic cult with modern witchcraft is demonstrated and proven"; but his book had made no particular impact. The credit for first lifting the study of witchcraft out of the category of fantasies about broomstick-flying and consorting with demons, and into that of comparative religion and anthropology, belongs to Charles Godfrey Leland.

The lore of ghosts, witches and fairies surrounded Leland from boyhood. He was born in Philadelphia, Pennsylvania, on 15th August 1824; and when he was only a few days old, his old Dutch nurse carried him up to the garret of the house, and placed a Bible, a key, and a knife on the baby's breast, and lighted candles, money, and a plate of salt at his head. The object of this rite was to cause him to rise in life, to be lucky, and to become a scholar and a wizard; it certainly seems to have succeeded.

He was a descendant of John Leland, who became the Royal Antiquary in 1533, and of Charles Leland, who was Secretary of the Society of Antiquaries in the reign of Charles I. His family came to America in 1636 and settled in Massachusetts.

Charles Godfrey Leland was educated at Princeton, from which he graduated at the end of four years. He then went to Europe, where he studied at the universities of Heidelberg and Munich, and at the Sorbonne in Paris. He took part in the Paris Revolution of 1848; and later he fought in the American Civil War, on the Union side, and saw the Battle of Gettysburg.

He worked extensively as a journalist in America, and also prospected for oil; travelling in the old Wild West, and once staying with General Custer at Fort Harker. His appearance was striking; over 6 feet tall, bearded, and with handsome features and blue eyes, which his niece and biographer, Elizabeth Robins Pennell, described as "the eyes of the seer, the mystic".

Deeply devoted to his wife, Isabel, whom he married in 1856, he survived her death by less than a year. His long and active life closed at Florence in 1903.

LILITH

The moon goddess Lilith is the archetypal seductress, the personification of the dangerous feminine glamour of the moon. Like Hecate, she is a patroness of witches; but where Hecate is visualised as an old crone, Lilith is instead the enticing sorceress, the beautiful vampire, the *femme fatale*. Her loveliness is more than human; but her beauty has one strange blemish. Her feet are great claws, like those of a giant bird of prey.

She is depicted in this way on a terra-cotta relief from Sumer, dating from about 2,000 B.C. The same figure of humanity's dreams recurred in medieval France, where she was known as *La Reine Pedauque,* the queen with a bird's foot, a mysterious figure of legend who flew by night at the head of a crowd of phantoms, something like the Wild Hunt.

The Jewish legends about Lilith say that she was the first wife of Adam, before Eve was given to him. Lilith, however, came to Adam as he lay asleep, and coupled with him in his dreams. By this means, she became the mother of all the uncanny beings who share this planet invisibly with mortals, and are known as the fairy races or the *djinn.*

The Jews regarded her as a queen of evil spirits, and made amulets to protect themselves against her. She is a personification of the erotic dreams which trouble men; the suppressed desire for forbidden delights.

Charles Godfrey Leland, in his *Etruscan-Roman Remains* (London, 1892), identifies Lilith with Herodias, or Aradia. He notes that in the old Slavonian spells and charms, Lilith is mentioned, and that she is said to have twelve daughters, who are the twelve kinds of fever. This is another instance of the witches' thirteen.

LOVE CHARMS

The idea of the love charm seems to be one that never dies, because the human race wants so much to believe in it. From the tragic legend of Tristan and Isolde, through the concoctions of medieval witches, to the slyly-worded advertisements of today, the love charm, potion or philtre still keeps its place in our folklore. Doctors have repeatedly assured us that the effects of so-called love potions and aphrodisiacs are mainly, if not entirely, psychological; but it seems to make no difference.

In America, practitioners of what is called in the U.S.A. voodoo, but which has gathered to itself many of the practices of European witchcraft, sell "lucky roots" and various brands of scented oils and powders, which are bought as love charms. Perhaps the most famous of these, and one particularly favoured by men to aid them in their love enterprises, is John the Conqueror Root. This is a dried root with a prong or spike growing out of it, an obvious piece of phallic symbolism. It is carried in a little bag, of chamois leather or red cloth, as a lucky piece.

What this root actually is has been kept a big secret by those who sell it; but I am told that it is the root of the marsh St. John's wort (*Hypericum elodes*). If this is correct, then the belief in it goes back many centuries, because the St. John's wort, of which there are a number of varieties, has a time-honoured reputation as a magical plant. It gets its name from being one of the plants traditionally gathered for magical purposes on Midsummer Eve, or the Eve of St. John the Baptist, the night of 23rd-24th June.

Young men whose fancy turns to thoughts of love may be glad to know that marsh St. John's wort grows in Britain and Europe also. However, it is more often women who have resorted to love charms throughout the ages. The sweet-scented verbena has a reputation of attracting love to its user; so have the scents of musk and patchouli. The fragrant orris root, sometimes called 'love root', was used by our grandmothers to scent their best underclothes.

The number of foods, drinks, perfumes, herbs and so on, that have at one time or another been believed to be love charms or aphrodisiacs, is absolutely legion. When tomatoes were first introduced into this country, they were regarded with much suspicion, and were known as love apples. Potatoes, too, when they arrived here in the first Queen Elizabeth's time, were believed to be stimulating in matters of love; which is why Shakespeare in his *Troilus and Cressida* speaks of "the devil luxury, with his fat rump and potato-finger".

Fish as an article of food has an even more ancient reputation as an aphrodisiac, probably because Venus herself was said to have been born from the sea. Hence, perhaps, the British fondness for fish and chips is not quite so innocent as it seems.

There is, of course, a difference between a real love charm, which is something with a magical influence, and an aphrodisiac. The latter, named after the Greek goddess of love, Aphrodite, is simply something which stimulates sexual ardour. In practice, however, the two have become much confused; and most so-called love potions or philtres are really just aphrodisiacs.

A liqueur wine with a piece of ginseng root in it is imported from the Far East, and widely sold in London today, to those who believe in it as a love potion of this sort. It retails at over £3 a bottle, but still finds eager purchasers. In fact, the ginseng root is a Chinese counterpart of the mandrake, being in form like a tiny human figure, and said to utter "a low musical cry" when taken from the earth. Its legend is less sinister and more benign than that of the mandrake; but nevertheless, the real basis of the belief in the virtues of the ginseng elixir is a magical one. The lore of the mandrake deserves an article to itself. (*See* MANDRAKE.)

Many love charms of the olden time consisted of the most disgusting and revolting ingredients, such as the genital parts of animals or birds, especially those renowned for their sexual activity. Also, the products of the human body, such as semen, menstrual blood and even excrement, were used. In fact, some devotees of sorcery seem to have had the idea that the more repulsive their magic was, the more likely it was to work.

One turns with relief from such nastiness, to the rather charming picture in the Leipzig Museum, which shows a beautiful young witch preparing a love charm. This painting dates from about the middle of the fifteenth century; and although the artist is unknown, we may be certain from the details he shows that his acquaintance with witchcraft was remarkably close.

For one thing, the witch in the picture, instead of being a horrible old hag, is a young and attractive girl. Instead of being depicted in some fantastic setting, such as a dark and gloomy cave with demons and bats flying around, this witch is working in an ordinary room in a house, where most witches really did (and do) work. She is naked, with loose flowing hair, and her feet are shod with sandals; the age-old custom of ritual nudity in order to work magic. The room has a convenient fireplace, so she need not be cold.

Scattered about the floor are sprigs of herbs and flowers; and beside the witch is a little table, serving as an altar. On this is an open casket, with something inside it which looks like a heart, which has probably been cut out of red cloth or modelled in wax. On this heart-symbol the witch is pouring some drops of magical oil or essence. Couched at her feet is her familiar; not some weird creature of fantasy, but a normal little animal, a dog.

Evidently her spell is working; for just opening the door of the room, with a trance-like expression on his face, is the young man she has been trying to draw to her. Probably some of his hair, or something similar, to make a magical link between him and the witch, has been incorporated in the symbolic heart.

Two other notable details of this picture may be mentioned. On the wall, the artist has shown a typical witch mirror hanging; a small, round mirror in a frame, such as witches use for spells and clairvoyance (I have two examples of these in my own collection). Lastly, apparently floating about the room are curious ribbons of light, which seem to be an attempt to depict the power the young witch is raising. This scene could have been taking place today—and somewhere, something like it probably was, because the desire for love is one of the strongest human emotions, in any age.

There are many old country magics, which might have been commended to village girls by the local witch when they came to her cottage for a confidential talk. She might, for instance, tell them about the rather indelicate, though time-honoured charm called 'cocklebread'. This was described in the seventeenth century by John Aubrey, who called it "a relique of Naturall Magick, an unlawful Philtrum". Briefly, it consisted of a small loaf, the dough for which had been kneaded in a very peculiar way. The girl who made it had to lift up her skirts and press the dough with the intimate parts of her bare body. (The name 'cockle-bread' comes from the fact that 'cockles' is an old vulgar term for the *labia minora*.) Then the dough so treated was baked into a loaf, and given to the man she wanted. If she could persuade him to eat it, of course without telling him what it was, he was as good as hers.

An old book on fortune-telling gives this version of another traditional spell:

> Let any unmarried woman take the bladebone of a shoulder of lamb, and borrowing a penknife (without saying for what purpose), she must, on going to bed, stick the knife once through the bone every night for nine nights in succession—in different places—repeating every night while so doing, these words:
>
> > 'Tis not the bone I mean to stick,
> > But my lover's heart I mean to prick;
> > Wishing him neither rest nor sleep,
> > Till he comes to me to speak.

Accordingly at the end of nine days, or shortly after, he will come and ask for something to put to a wound, inflicted during the time you were charming him.

This account, however, has omitted what was considered an essential detail, namely that the girl should whisper the man's name when she stuck in the knife, instead of just saying "my lover". Also, she must do this regularly for nine successive nights; to forget one night would break the spell. In other words, will-power and concentration were needed, and when such spells as this worked, it was by the power of thought.

Some old love charms were forms of divination, to see one's future lover in a dream. One of these was worked with the aid of the wild flower called yarrow (*Achillea millefolium*). The girl had to pluck a handful of yarrow flowers, sew them into a little bag of flannel, and put the bag beneath her pillow at night, repeating these words:

> Thou pretty herb of Venus' tree,
> Thy true name it is yarrow;
> Now who my bosom friend may be
> Pray tell thou me tomorrow.

One version of this charm advised that the yarrow should be plucked when the new moon was in the sky; and another said that the flowers had to be growing on a young man's grave. If a man worked the spell, he had to take the yarrow from a young woman's grave.

Folklore preserves so many of these spells for seeing the lover in a dream, that one wonders if, by the power of suggestion, someone who performed such a ceremony *in complete faith* might really have a meaningful dream. This is a question for the student of the psychology of dreams to resolve.

The above are only a few typical examples of the innumerable spells, charms and philtres connected with love and desire. Egyptian papyri contain recipes for love potions; and human nature has not really changed much, if at all, since the days of the Pyramids.

M

MAGIC

Many people, and perhaps especially educated people, have an entirely wrong conception of what magic is. They think of it as something which miraculously violates the laws of Nature. Therefore, they say, it is absurd and impossible. But magic does not work like this at all.

Aleister Crowley defined magic as: "The Science and Art of causing Change to occur in conformity with Will".

S. L. MacGregor Mathers, who was one of the founders of that famous magical order, The Golden Dawn, gave his definition of magic as: "The Science of the Control of the Secret Forces of Nature."

It will be seen that both these definitions differ radically from the popular idea of magic. These definitions apply as much to witches' magic as they do to other forms of magic.

A third definition of magic is found in the famous grimoire called *The Lemegeton, or Lesser Key of King Solomon,* which states: "Magic is the Highest, most Absolute, and most Divine Knowledge of Natural Philosophy, advanced in its works and wonderful operations by a right understanding of the inward and occult virtue of things; so that true Agents being applied to proper Patients, strange and admirable effects will thereby be produced. Whence magicians are profound and diligent searchers into Nature; they, because of their skill, know how to anticipate an effect, the which to the vulgar shall seem to be a miracle."

Again, there is no suggestion that magic acts by anything other than the forces of Nature, being understood and used by one whose knowledge penetrates to the hidden side of Nature, and to the workings of those powers commonly called occult.

Magic is generally regarded as being of two kinds, designated as white or black; though much confusion reigns as to how these categories may be defined.

I remember once discussing this matter with a lawyer in connection with a certain case into which allegations about various occult matters entered. He had not had much contact with such things before; and after considering a good deal of information about magical practices and practitioners, he said to me, "Well, I've come to one conclusion—black magic can be defined as what the other fellow does!"

In the world of present-day occultism, this remark certainly very often applies. However, it should not be assumed that the distinction between black and white magic has no validity. If people misuse occult powers, sooner or later they will pay the penalty; no matter how high-sounding their pretensions may be. Black magic is the wrongful use of occult powers; and it is generally coupled with the use of repulsive means, such as blood sacrifice, to attain one's ends.

The word 'magic' is from the Greek *Magikē technē,* meaning the art of the Magi, or priests of Ancient Persia, from whence the Greeks believed magic to have originated. (However, the magic arts were being practised in Ancient Egypt, long before the days of the Persian Magi.)

It seems that the Magi belonged to the oldest stock of Persia, rather than to the orthodox followers of the religion of Zoroaster, some of whom regarded the doctrines of the Magi with suspicion, as being heretical. They seem to have borne some resemblance to the Druids, as they are said to have worn white robes and favoured a simple mode of life and a vegetarian diet. They worshipped no idols, choosing rather as their symbol the Divine and Sacred Fire, which burned in their sanctuaries and was never allowed to go out.

They were also Magi in Chaldea and Babylon; and, again like the Druids, they studied astronomy. In Chapter 39 of the *Book of Jeremiah,* we find one "Nergal-sharezer, Rab-Mag" as one of the princes who attended upon the King of Babylon when he captured Jerusalem. The words "Rab-Mag" are a title and mean 'Great Magus'.

The town of Hamadan, in Persia (nowadays called Iran), was known to the Greeks in ancient times as 'Ecbatana of the Magi'. The Three Wise Men of the East, who brought gifts to the infant Jesus, are generally regarded as having been of the Magi. This mysterious caste of initiated priest-magicians, who have given their name to the magic art itself, is one of the enigmas of history.

But how does one become a magician? What is the secret that separates a magician from the rest of mankind? According to many of the old magical texts, a person has to be born a magician; though his powers can be developed by study and practice. One of the first requisites, of course, is psychic sensitivity; but this must be coupled with strength of character and self-control. One sees in the accounts of the rites of the primitive tribes, how many of these ceremonies are evidently designed to discover and develop these qualities. The methods may be crude; but they work.

In our own society, such rituals are paralleled by those of occult groups, more or less secret, which confer degrees of initiation. The most famous one of these in modern times is the Order of the Golden Dawn, which was formed in London in 1887 from sources which claimed descent from the even more famous Rosicrucians of the Middle Ages. A number of well-known people belonged to this order, which included W. B. Yeats, Wynn Westcott, Allen Bennett, Arthur Machen, Florence Farr, Brodie Innes, Algernon Blackwood, A. E. Waite, MacGregor Mathers and his wife (who was a sister of Henri Bergson the philosopher) and Aleister Crowley.

The rites and teachings of the Order of the Golden Dawn, which have been published in our own day by Dr. Francis Israel Regardie (*The Golden Dawn,* Two vols., Hazel Hills Corporation, Wisconsin, 1969), are of a most elaborate and elevated character; yet their basic principles are simple, and rest upon the same age-old philosophy from Nature which has characterised genuine magical thinking throughout the ages.

One sees this process at work, both in the ceremonial magic of our own and previous times, and in the practices of witchcraft. The rites of the ceremonial magician may be much more complicated than those of the witch; but the principles involved are very similar, if not identical.

Witchcraft, however, is the Old Religion of the common people. So the witch uses in her magical arts the things of everyday life, un-like the elaborate armoury of the ceremonial magician. Such things, for instance, as the broomstick, the knotted cord, the cauldron, and the black-hilted knife, which were simply the household articles of any woman's home; together with the herbs which she grew in her cottage garden, or culled from the woods and hedgerows. Her pentacle was of wax or wood, instead of the metal, or even gold or silver, of the wealthy occultist; and the waxen or wooden pentacles had the advantage that they could be quickly destroyed in the kitchen fire at any alarm of danger.

In the present-day ceremonies of Freemasonry, we can see a reflection of this process, whereby the simple tools of an ancient and highly skilled craft are taken and made to symbolise the highest concepts and ideals. The Operative Mason of the medieval craftsmen's guild has become the Speculative Mason of the Lodge. And, like the witch, he has been abused and vilified by those who just cannot believe, or do not want to believe, that there is no sinister 'devil worship' or mystery of iniquity in his brotherhood.

What, however, is the true object of magic? Is it to foretell the future, to gain power over others, to make talismans to work one's will for various ends, to communicate with spirits, and so on?

No; to the true magician, these things are incidentals. They can be done; but to pursue them *as ends in themselves* is to fall into the trap of black magic. They should be regarded rather as means to an end. By developing their powers, the magician and witch develop themselves. They aid their own evolution, their growth as a human being; and in so far as they truly do this, they aid the evolution of the human race.

The human race, after all, consists of individuals; and evolution, like charity, begins at home. Before people set out to reform the world, they need to take a good look at their own defects. Magic, if they take up the study of it seriously, will force them to do this. Perhaps the most famous injunction of the old temples of the Mysteries was "Know thyself".

MANDRAKE

So many strange legends have gathered about the mandrake root that people often doubt whether such a plant actually exists. It is, however, a genuine inhabitant of the vegetable kingdom; specimens of very curious mandrake roots may sometimes be seen in museums.

The true mandrake, *Atropa mandragora,* belongs to the *Solanaceae,* that order of plants which has contributed so much to witchcraft and sorcery. Among the *Solanaceae* also are the henbane, the deadly nightshade and the thornapple, all plants of sinister reputation.

The mandrake was believed by sorcerers of the Middle Ages to be a kind of half-way creature between the vegetable and the human kind. Its leaves shone by night with a baleful glow. Its flowers and fruits gave forth a narcotic, stupefying scent. Its root was in the shape of a tiny human figure, an homunculus, alive with a weird and devilish life of its own—ready to become the familiar of the daring mortal who could possess himself of it.

This enterprise, however, was fraught with peril; because the mandrake, on being torn from the earth, gave forth such a fearful and deadly cry that he who heard it would either go mad or fall dead upon the spot.

Accordingly, the sorcerer who wished to possess himself of a mandrake had to follow a curious ritual. Having found the plant, which usually grew at the foot of a gibbet, upon which the remains of an executed criminal hung, the operator had to go there at sunset.

By the light of the dying sun's last rays, he must draw three circles round the mandrake with his magical sword; but he must first have taken the precaution of stopping his ears with wax, so that he could not hear the mandrake's cry; and he must be sure that the wind was not blowing in his face, or he would be overcome by the narcotic odour of the plant.

He would have brought with him a hungry dog, and some tempting meat, with which the dog could be enticed. He was also to be armed with an ivory staff, wherewith he was to loosen the earth carefully around the mandrake root. Then he had to tie the unfortunate dog securely to the root, retire to a distance, and show the dog the food. The dog would leap at the meat, and thus pull the mandrake from the earth; and the dog, it was believed, would die on the spot.

As an extra precaution, the operator was advised to blow loudly upon a horn, as soon as he saw the plant begin to lift from the earth, to drown its hideous scream as much as possible.

Then the sorcerer, having taken up the fearful plant, and wrapped it in a white linen cloth, could hurry away with his prize through the shadows of the gathering darkness.

Fantastic as it may sound, some of these old beliefs about the mandrake are based upon fact. The plant does have a large, fleshy root, which bears a rough resemblance to the human form. It does have a strange scent, which some find pleasant and some much the reverse; and it certainly has narcotic properties. In fact, the mandrake is probably man's oldest anaesthetic.

In the very early days of surgery, it was used to put patients into a deep drugged sleep, during which operations could be performed on them. The root was steeped or boiled in wine, and a little of this given to the patient to drink; but primitive surgeons had to be careful with the dose, as too much would cause a sleep from which there was no waking. Sometimes the mandrake was combined with other narcotics, and used to impregnate a sponge, which could be applied to the patient's nostrils until he fell asleep; thus probably giving a lighter state of somnolence than when taken internally.

Perhaps strangest of all, the belief that the mandrake shines at night has a basis of fact. For some reason, its leaves are attractive to glow-worms, and it is these little creatures, whose greenish luminescence is quite remarkable, that make it glow in the darkness. Anyone who did not know this could certainly be startled by the plant's appearance after dark, and think the old legends about its devilish powers might be true. It is from this circumstance that the mandrake gets its name of 'the Devil's candle'.

Even the story about the mandrake screaming as it is pulled from the earth could have at least a grain of truth in it, from which the legend has grown. Plants with large fleshy roots usually grow in damp places; and when pulled slowly from the earth, they are quite likely to make a squeaking sound. The timid mandrake-seeker would have waited for no more than the first squeak!

Of course, all the horrific details of the mandrake legend were kept alive by those who had mandrakes for sale. People paid high prices for a good, life-like mandrake, and valued it highly as a talisman. It was believed to bring luck to its owner in all departments of life, but especially in matters of love and fertility. This latter belief was general throughout the ancient world, as the story in the Bible about Rachel, Leah and the mandrakes shows; and it has persisted right down to the present day. Whole mandrakes are sometimes offered for sale, imported into Britain, at high prices; and some occult herbalists sell pieces of mandrake root for people to carry as lucky charms.

To possess a mandrake which housed a familiar spirit, was one of the practices of witches in old-time Europe. In 1603 a woman was hanged as a witch at Romorantin near Orleans, for the alleged crime of keeping a familiar spirit in the form of a mandrake. She was the wife of a Moor, and had probably obtained the root from the Middle East, where the drying and shaping of mandrake roots was carried on almost as a profession by some specialists in the art.

When Joan of Arc was tried as a witch, one of the accusations brought against her was that she had a mandrake, which she carried in her bosom as a familiar; but she denied this. In 1630, three women were executed in Hamburg, accused of witchcraft and possessing mandrakes.

One of the ways in which the mandrake familiar was used, was for the witch to put it under her pillow at night, so that the spirit of the mandrake might instruct her in dreams. The mandrake had various other names by which it was known: 'the earth-mannikin', 'the little gallows-man' (alluding to its being found beneath the gibbet), or the 'alraun'. This word seems originally to have meant a witch, and eventually changed its implication to mean a witch's familiar. It was especially used in Germany, where the 'alraun' was a prized possession, handed down very secretly as a family heirloom. It had to be kept in a box, wrapped up in silk, and bathed four times a year, probably in wine or brandy. The liquid which had served to bathe it would have magical virtues, and might be sprinkled round the house to bring good luck, using a sprinkler of fragrant herbs.

The true mandrake, *Atropa mandragora,* is not indigenous to Britain, but grows in the warmer countries around the Mediterranean Sea and in the Near East. However, the wonders and virtues of the mandrake are extolled in old English herbals dating from the eleventh century, so it may have been imported. In the time of Henry VIII, roots purporting to be mandrakes were being sold in boxes for magical purposes.

Francis Bacon alludes in his works to witchcraft and the mandrake: "Some plants there are, but rare, that have a mossie or downie root and likewise that have a number of threads like beards as mandrakes, whereof witches and impostours make an ugly image, giving it the form of a face at the top of the root, and these strings to make a beard down to the foot."

Poor country witches in Britain, who could not afford or obtain the true mandrake root, made use of the roots of white and black briony, two hedgerow plants which have very big fleshy roots. Hence these plants have come to be called English mandrake. (In the United States, a medicinal plant called *Podophyllum peltatum* is known as American mandrake; but it is quite a different plant from any of the above.)

The early herbalists, Gerarde, Parkinson and Turner, denounced the lifelike mandrake mannikins as being a counterfeit, produced by art rather than Nature, to get money out of credulous people. An old book called *A Thousand Notable Things* (by Thomas Lupton; first published London, 1579, many subsequent editions) tells in quaint language how it was done:

> Take the great double root of briony newly taken out of the ground, and with a fine sharp kinfe, frame the shape of a man or woman (the woman-drake of our rustics), with his stones and cods and other members thereto, and when it is clean done, prick all these places with a sharp steel, as the head, the eyebrows, the chin and privities, and put into the said holes the seeds of millet or any other that brings forth small roots that do resemble hairs (which leek seed will do very well, or else barley). After this, put it into the ground and let it be covered with earth until it hath gotten upon it a certain little skin, and then thou shalt see a monstrous idol and hairy, which will become the parts if it be workmanlike or cunningly made or figured.

To assume, however, that the only reason for "witches and impostours" to do this was to impose upon the credulous, would be incorrect. Some people sold these things at a profit, certainly; but witches made a mandrake to house a familiar spirit, giving an elemental an effigy in which it might take up its dwelling, if the work was performed with proper ceremony. The virtue of using a root for this purpose, was that the root had life in it, and this living essence would help towards the ends required.

The right time to dig up the briony root was on the night of the full moon. Then the necessary shaping, etc., was done, and the root reburied until the next full moon, by which time the skin would have grown over it again, so that it looked natural. The straggling threads of 'hair' were trimmed, and the root was carefully and slowly dried; usually over a fire upon which the magical herb vervain was burned, to bathe the mandrake in its smoke. Some, however, dried the mandrake in a bath of hot sand, the *Balneum Arenae* of the alchemists; and this operation bore some resemblance to the legendary making of a *homunculus,* or artificial man. Indeed it may have been the origin of the legend.

Once the mandrake was dried, it was wrapped in a white silk cloth, and kept in a box. Sometimes the mandrake was dressed in a little red cloak, embroidered with magical figures; red being the colour of life. Then, on some propitious night, such as that of one of the Great Sabbats, the mandrake would be formally consecrated, and a helpful spirit invited to take up its abode in the figure, and ensoul it.

This may account for some of the old stories of the Devil giving

familiar spirits to witches. What he really gave them was either a
small living creature, which would sometimes be possessed by a spirit,
or else something like the mandrake, which a spirit could ensoul.

MANSON, CHARLES

When dawn broke over Los Angeles, California, on 9th August
1969, it revealed a scene of macabre horror. In a luxurious Hollywood mansion five people, the film star Sharon Tate and four house
guests, had died in what seemed to be a ritual murder, carried out
in the dark of the moon. It was apparently quite motiveless, and the
victims had been shot and stabbed repeatedly, with a degree of ferocity
that caused even veteran police officers to blench.

The strangest feature of the case was the way in which the bodies
of Sharon Tate and her friend Jay Sebring, an internationally famous
hair stylist, had been posed in death. Looped around Miss Tate's neck
was a nylon rope. The rope had been slung over a ceiling beam, and
the other end of it tied around Sebring's neck, while his head had
been muffled in a hood. Yet neither of them had died from hanging.

Two days later, another very similar discovery again shook an
already terrified city. Two more wealthy people, Mr and Mrs La
Bianca, were found dead in their Los Angeles home. They had been
tied up and stabbed repeatedly, and Mr La Bianca's head was hooded
in a white pillowcase.

On account of their bizarre nature, and the social eminence of
the people involved in them, the killings received world-wide publicity. The term 'ritual murder' was used from the start to describe
them, and possible connections with the occult were probed. It was
recalled that Miss Tate's husband, Roman Polanski, had been the
producer of the sensational film about Satanism, *Rosemary's Baby*.
It was rumoured that this film had angered some secret groups because of the matters it dealt with, and that Mr Polanski had received
threats. He himself had escaped the massacre by sheer luck; he had
been filming in London when it occurred.

It seemed that some element of impersonal hatred was involved;
at the scene of each crime, references to 'pigs' had been daubed in
letters of blood. By another strange twist of fate, Sharon Tate was
eight months pregnant when she died, and the name of the woman
victim in the second killings was Rosemary.

Sharon and her husband were admittedly interested in the occult;
and she had made her film debut in a picture called *13*, a story about

a girl with the powers of a witch. She also made a picture called *Evil Eye*.

California is well known as a centre for occult groups and orders of all kinds, some of them internationally respected, others strange and fantastic in the extreme. As police pursued their enquiries, many cultists were interviewed, but without significant results.

Eventually, however, a girl hippie, while detained in prison on another charge, boasted to her cell-mates that she had been one of the killers at the Sharon Tate mansion. The authorities were told; and as a result a communal group of hippies, who had been living on deserted ranches in the vicinity of Los Angeles, was closely investigated, and six of them, four girls and two men, were charged with the murders. Police stated that they believed this hippie clan to be responsible for a number of other unexplained killings as well, and to have planned more.

So the world came to hear the name of Charles Manson, leader of the hippie 'family' which called itself Satan's Slaves. His lean, bearded face, with hypnotic eyes, stared disturbingly from every newspaper. The disquieting facts that black magic and ritual murder were poisonously alive in the modern world could no longer be ignored.

Two of his girl followers, Susan Atkins and Linda Kasabian, gave chilling descriptions of how the murders took place. Both said that the killings were done under Manson's hypnotic influence; he gave the orders to kill, and his followers carried them out. Susan Atkins later tried to retract her testimony, and say that Manson knew nothing about the murders; but it was too late and the court had heard too much for this to be accepted. Linda Kasabian, who took no part in the actual killings, was granted immunity from prosecution in return for her evidence. Manson's lieutenant, Charles 'Tex' Watson, suffered a mental breakdown while in custody, and was detained in a hospital. The other two girls accused were Patricia Krenwinkel and Leslie Van Houten.

The motive for the murders was twofold. Firstly, to express hatred for what Manson called 'the piggy world', that is, the world of established wealth and convention, the world of non-hippies; secondly, to strike terror into that world, and so precipitate what Manson believed was the coming revolution, when the white Establishment and the black militants would fight each other to extinction, and only hippies would be left. He thought that the killings would be blamed upon negro militants.

It seems incredible that a man should have been able to make others follow him blindly in such a scheme. But Manson and his devotees lived in a world of their own, out in the California desert; a world distorted by drugs, especially LSD. His followers regarded him as a man with divine powers. They recounted in court how they had seen him work miracles, such as charming snakes, healing sick animals and birds, and making old people become young again. Even after he was arrested, groups of his followers sat outside the court house day after day, confident that he would be triumphantly released. When Los Angeles was shaken by an earthquake while the trial was proceeding, some of them took it for a sign. Where they thought the 'sign' came from, however, is not clear; because Manson regarded himself as being a combination of both Christ and Satan. Where he derived this belief from is not known, but the idea that God was manifest in three aspects, those of Lucifer, Jehovah and Satan (all three of whom should be worshipped) had already been put forward, and Manson may have come across it.

Manson was born on 11th November 1934, an illegitimate child in poor circumstances. At the time of the murders he was in his thirty-fifth year; and twenty-two of those years had been spent in various prisons, on a variety of charges none of which involved violence.

Manson's birth-sign is Scorpio, one of the most complex signs in the whole Zodiac. It is the fixed sign of water; the still water which runs deep. Ruled by Mars, it is a sign associated with sex, death, and the unseen worlds. Its natives have a magnetic personality, and a strange ability to bend others to their will. They often have remarkable psychic gifts, and are naturally drawn towards occultism and mysticism. They have a powerful sexual drive, and strong emotions.

The complexity of Scorpio is shown by the fact that it has three different symbols: the Scorpion, the Serpent and the Eagle. Its natives can soar to the heights and also plumb the depths. The serpent is an emblem of occult wisdom; the eagle soars above all other birds, and signifies sublimation; the scorpion personifies lust and cruelty, and is a creature of the sun-scorched desert, as Manson was.

Manson boasted that he lived like a king among his hippie followers and at one time had fifteen girls to wait on him and minister to his every wish. On moonlight nights, he presided over rites of orgiastic sex. The eye-witness descriptions given of these show that he did indeed have some knowledge of magical sex rituals. He was described as standing in the centre of a circle of men and girls. When he signalled the rite to commence, the girls would surround him, kissing his feet and treating him as an incarnate god. Meanwhile, the men sat back in meditation, while the drugs they were using took effect. When Manson judged the time was right, all joined in communal sexual acts, passing round the circle from one partner to another until they were too exhausted to continue. These practices were supposed to raise magical power, and produce dreams and visions.

Manson seems to have pictured himself as being something like the Devil of a medieval witches' coven—regarded as an incarnate god, having power of life and death over his devotees, rewarding his female followers with his sexual favours or punishing them with beatings, and having a male officer who carried out his orders.

According to Linda Kasabian's testimony, the men of Manson's clan called themselves witches, and "Charlie called all the girls witches". He told them to make "witchy things" to hang in the trees, marking the way to their camp site—signs made of weeds, stones and branches, held together with wire. According to the same witness, before the party of killers set off for Sharon Tate's house, all of them dressed eerily in black, Manson told them to "leave a sign—something witchy". He himself did not accompany them, but awaited their return, confident that his orders would be obeyed.

However, there is no evidence that Manson was a witch in anything except his own fantasy. He seems to have gathered his followers together originally in the Haight-Ashbury area of San Francisco, birthplace of the hippie dream, and travelled with them through California on a dilapidated school bus. He may have derived some mystic ideas from his name: Manson, the Son of Man.

The trial of Manson and the others accused lasted nine months, and cost an estimated one million dollars. The only one of them to express any regret for the killings was Linda Kasabian. The rest made it plain that they regarded the trial as a mockery, and treated it accordingly. This led to bizarre court-room scenes, reminiscent of the behaviour of the supposedly bewitched girls at Salem in the seventeenth century.

The three girls, Susan Atkins, Patricia Krenwinkel and Leslie Van Houten, acted throughout as if Manson had them under a spell. Whatever he did, they copied. When he laughed, they laughed; when he got angry, they got angry; when he appeared in the courtroom with a shaven head, they shaved their heads also. Manson made his appearance like this, sacrificing his long hair and beard, after he had been found guilty. Through his lawyer, he said, "I did it because I'm the Devil, and the Devil always has a bald head." Together with Manson, Susan Atkins, Patricia Krenwinkel and Leslie Van Houten were found guilty, and all four were sentenced to death in the gas chamber.

Manson claimed that he took the people whom society had cast aside as human garbage, and gave them love, forming them into his 'family'. But his mind had been twisted by twenty-two years in American jails. The 'love' had an opposite side—hatred for the 'straight' people, the 'piggies'; and he infected his followers with his own ruthless hate.

Maybe if society had more compassion for its human garbage, if it could have found something better to do with the young Charles Manson than to lock him up in one jail after another, then the hideous events of August 1969 in Los Angeles might never have happened.

MOON WORSHIP

"If I beheld the sun when it shined, or the moon walking in brightness;

"And my heart hath been secretly enticed, or my mouth hath kissed my hand:

"This also were an iniquity to be punished by the judge: for I should have denied the God that is above."

These words from the Book of Job, believed to be the oldest book in the Bible, testify to the antiquity of moon worship. Moreover, they bear witness to the enticement of the moon and to the writer's fear of arousing the jealous wrath of Yahweh by carrying out the old rite of saluting her.

As the most conspicuous luminary of the night, and the nearest heavenly body to our earth, the moon has hung like a shining magic mirror, reflecting man's dreams. From the Stone Age to the age of space travel, she has bewitched and allured mankind.

The moon has always been primarily regarded as feminine, although there are many moon gods as well as moon goddesses. Psychology has confirmed this; the moon in man's dream-life is a symbol of feminine influence, and especially of the mother. The moon gods, of whom our old storybook 'Man in the Moon' is a last vestige, represented the positive powers of the moon, when she is waxing or increasing in light.

The moon's relation to human fertility, in that she revolves around the Earth in about twenty-eight days, the time of a woman's menstrual cycle, was noted by our distant ancestors; and this was another reason for regarding the moon as feminine. However, she also rules the fluid secretions of the body, in astrological parlance; and these include the seminal fluid, white and pearl-like. So semen and menstrual blood, the signs and essentials of human fertility, are alike ruled by the moon.

She also rules the tides, which are highest at new moon and full moon. To old-time fishing communities this was very important. But even more important is the age-old belief in the influence of the moon upon the tides of psychic energy and those of human affairs.

Today, there is a difference of opinion about this. Some authorities aver that the old belief in the phases of the moon influencing human behaviour is all nonsense. Others declare with equal assurance that this supposed influence is a fact, and they say that anyone brought into contact with human nature in all its strange vagaries, can vouch for this. Policemen all over the world, they say, recognise full moon as the time when unusual things are likely to happen; not merely the ordinary sorts of crime, but bizarre acts, especially those with a sexual bias. Many slayers of women have, by the press at any rate, been dubbed "moon-murderers."

The light of the full moon, and especially the midsummer moon, has for so long been believed to have an unsettling effect upon the mind, that it has given us the word 'lunatic' for the mentally disturbed. Again, some people agree with this belief, saying that crises of mental illness coincide with the full moon; while others scoff at it as an old wives' tale. However, the writer can testify to having known a successful businessman, otherwise quite normal, whose speech was affected at the time of the full moon. His way of stumbling over words at this time of the month was so well known to his family that they used to call it "the moons."

Old almanacks, on which country people put great dependence, used to give whole lists of things to do and not to do, with regard to planting crops, cutting timber, and so on, according to the different phases of the moon. In general, the rule was to use the increase of the moon for those matters which you wished to increase, and the waning of the moon for clearing away things you wanted to get rid of.

The waning of the moon, too, was a time of sinister magic, as the waxing of the moon was of beneficent magic. This is why 'wanion' is an old word for a curse, because it was put on in the waning of the moon.

All these things are part of the antique lore of moon worship and moon magic. As the old rhyme has it:

> Pray to the Moon when she is round.
> Luck with you will then abound.
> What you seek for shall be found,
> On the sea or solid ground.

One of the traditional Bardic Triads, said to be handed down from the Druids, tells us: "Three embellishing names of the Moon: The Sun of the Night, the Light of the Beautiful, and the Lamp of the Fairies."

The rays of the moon are indeed "The Light of the Beautiful"; whether they are stealing through the branches of some woodland scene, or silvering the roofs of a city, or making a pathway of light across the waves of the sea. Things tend to look quite different by moonlight; and it has called to lovers through the ages, since before the Pyramids were built. The moon goddess was the love goddess, and also the lady of enchantment and mystery, in all the lands and cities that flourished when the world was young. Beautiful women of Ancient Egypt hailed her as Queen Isis. The moon rays were the arrows of white Artemis, shot through the murmuring trees in the forests of Greece. The wild and joyous festivals of Ishtar were held in her honour. She was Diana of the oak groves of Nemi; and Lucius Apuleius in his magical vision beheld her rising at midnight from the enchanted ocean.

To the occult philosophers of the Middle Ages, the moon was alchemical silver, as the sun was alchemical gold. Those who would work magic of any kind, observed the moon; and particularly witches, skilled in the works of both the waxing and the waning moon. From the thirteen lunar months of the year, their revered and dreaded number of thirteen was taken.

Today, for the first time in history, man has fulfilled one of his oldest dreams. He has journeyed to the moon and set foot upon the lunar surface. Some people—I think rather devoid of imagination—have cried out that this has robbed the moon of her ancient splendour; that her glamour and magic are dissipated. Nothing, in my opinion, could be further from the truth. The flight to the moon, the quest of the White Goddess, has been one of man's greatest adventures, and one of the most magical.

It had no common reason to it; any more than did the ascent of Everest or Columbus's crazy voyage across the Atlantic, with his sailors in constant fear lest they fall over the edge of the world—the voyage that discovered a New World by mistake. Of course, the money could more reasonably have been spent on social services or famine relief; but man is sometimes led by feelings much deeper than those of the reasoning mind. The urge of an ancestral magic lured his ship to that truly unearthly realm; that shining mirror that hangs in space; that crescent-argent upon the shield of night.

The first samples of moon-rock to be examined proved to be coated and fused with a glass-like substance, presumed to be volcanic in origin. So the moon's surface is indeed mirror-like and reflecting, even as the old occultists claimed its function to be, namely, that of gathering and reflecting the rays of the sun and the stars and planets on to the earth, but infused with the peculiar magnetism of the moon's own influence.

No intelligent pagan was ever silly enough to think that the moon he saw in the sky was a goddess. On the contrary, the planets and the luminaries were named after the gods, and not vice versa. It was the great powers of Nature, personified as gods and goddesses, whose influences manifested through the heavenly bodies. This, at any rate, was and is the initiates' conception of astrology.

The same power that ruled the sun, ruled fire. The power that ruled the moon, ruled water. The sun was basically masculine; the moon basically feminine. All of manifested Nature was force incarnating in form; and so that men might come closer to these forces, which are *not* blind, but of intelligence beyond that of humanity, they built images for the 'powers that be' to ensoul, and bestowed upon them the names of gods and goddesses. "For by Names and Images are all Powers awakened and re-awakened," as one great rubric of the Western tradition of the Mysteries tells us.

A great part of genuine witchcraft is moon magic, derived from the age-old lore of moon worship. In spite of the large number of books that have been written about witchcraft in modern times, in response to renewed public interest in the subject, very little has been said about this aspect of it.

One of the very few people who have ever written with an inside knowledge of witchcraft is Charles Godfrey Leland; and he tells us a good deal about moon magic in his books. Another writer who evidences unusual knowledge on this subject is the late Dion Fortune. While not dealing specifically with witchcraft, two of her occult novels, *The Sea Priestess* and *Moon Magic* (both re-issued in recent years by the Aquarian Press), contain much curious lunar lore.

From being a widely popular religion which spread all over the Roman Empire, the cults of such moon goddesses as Isis and Diana eventually sank into forced obscurity, with the take-over by Christianity. Contrary to general belief, the pagan religious Mysteries did *not* die out. They were forcibly suppressed; but in a clandestine and underground form they continued to live, because of their emotional appeal, especially to women. One form they eventually took was that of the Old Religion, the cult of witchcraft.

MOTHER SHIPTON

It is not always realised that the famous prophetess, Mother Shipton, was a witch. At her birthplace, Knaresborough in Yorkshire, there is no doubt of it. She is depicted there on an inn sign, which is more than 200 years old, and painted on copper. The picture shows her as the traditional wise old woman, with a black cat by her side, and in her hand a broomstick with a curious forked top to the handle. Behind her is Knaresborough's famous Petrifying Well, near which she was born, in the year 1488.

Her mother's name was Agatha Sontheil, a poor girl who was left an orphan at the age of 15, and was reduced to begging in order to live. The story goes that Agatha one day met in a wood a handsome, well-dressed young man. She asked him for alms, which he gave her; and he persuaded her to meet him again in the wood the next day. Their acquaintance ripened into a love affair, and Agatha found herself pregnant.

When she told her lover of her predicament, he revealed to her that he was the Devil. He told her that if she would be faithful to him, he would give her supernormal powers, including the ability to raise storms and tempests, and to foretell the future.

Agatha travelled about the countryside with her mysterious lover, sometimes being away for several days at a time. The local busybodies became very curious, especially when they saw that the poor beggar girl now seemed to have a sufficiency of money. So on her return, on one occasion, a number of them came to her house to question her.

Angry at their impertinence, Agatha showed her new-found powers by invoking the wind. A violent storm of wind sprang up, and blew the inquisitive neighbours back to their own homes.

Of course, the talk about this and similar incidents soon reached the ears of the authorities, and Agatha was brought before the local magistrates on a charge of witchcraft. However, she was by some means acquitted.

She may have been spared because she was pregnant, as soon afterwards her child was born. It was a girl, and the mother named it Ursula. This baby was the future Mother Shipton. It was a strange, misshapen infant, ugly and deformed, but strong and healthy.

Not long afterwards, Agatha Sontheil died—"in peace, in the shelter of a convent", says the legend. One wonders what really happened to her, and how voluntary the "shelter" was. The baby was given to the parish nurse to bring up; but the little girl turned out be such a handful that the old dame could not cope with her. So she was sent to a school.

Here Ursula began to display the unusual powers that might have been expected from her ancestry. When her fellow pupils teased her about her deformities, something invisible pulled their hair, beat them and knocked them to the ground. Ursula was sent away from the school, and never went to another, although she had been a bright pupil and surprised her teachers by her ability.

Not much is known of her early life; but at the age of 24 she married a man called Toby Shipton. She soon made a reputation for herself as a seer, and many people came to consult her. As Mother Shipton, she became widely known; and although she was generally regarded as a witch, she seems to have been held in so much esteem in Yorkshire that the authorities never molested her.

She foretold her own death some time before it happened; and in 1561, the year in which she had said her time would come to depart from this world, she took leave of her friends, lay down on her bed and died peacefully.

A memorial stone was erected to her memory near Clifton, about a mile from York. It bore this inscription:

> Here lies she who never ly'd,
> Whose skill so often has been try'd,
> Her prophecies shall still survive,
> And ever keep her name alive.

This has certainly proved true; because a good deal of prophecy in doggerel verse, ascribed at any rate to Mother Shipton, has long been extant. Of course, as usual in these matters, the problem is to know just how much is genuine, and how much was forged by other people after her death. If we were to accept the authenticity of all the verses that are credited to her, then Mother Shipton predicted practically the entire course of English history, from her time to the present day. However, some are admitted forgeries, and a good deal of her supposed writings sound nothing like the idiom of her time, 1488-1561.

Mother Shipton became famous in her own day by predicting the fall of Cardinal Wolsey, who died in 1530. She called him 'the Mitred Peacock' because of his pride. This was also a play upon words because of the splendour of the peacock's train and the 'train' of Cardinal Wolsey, a showy retinue of some 800 followers.

This prophecy is quoted in an old book, *The Life, Prophecies and Death of the Famous Mother Shipton,* which is said to have been first printed in 1687 and reprinted 'verbatim' in 1862. It reads as follows: "Now shall the Mitred Peacock first begin to plume, whose Train shall make a great show in the World for a time, but shall afterwards vanish away, and his Honour come to nothing, which shall take its ends at Kingston."

The old book continues: "The Cardinal being told of this prophecy, would never pass through the town of Kingston, though lying directly in the road from his own house to the Court; but afterwards being arrested for high treason by the Earl of Northumberland and Sir Anthony Kingstone, the Lieutenant of the Tower, sent unto him, his very name (remembering the prophecy) struck such a terror to his heart that he soon after expired."

The story about Mother Shipton being the Devil's daughter becomes understandable when we remember that 'the Devil' was the title given to the male leader of a witches' coven.

MURRAY, MARGARET ALICE

One of the world's most famous and original writers on witchcraft, Margaret Alice Murray, was born in Calcutta on 13th July 1863. She lived to be over 100 years old and published a lively autobiography, *My First Hundred Years* (William Kimber, London, 1963)—a remarkable literary feat in itself.

I only met Margaret Murray once; but I remember her as a very little old lady, bright-eyed and alert, and with a mischievous sense of humour.

She claims in her autobiography that her life had no adventures. However, she disguised herself as a visiting artist when she went to the Cotswolds to investigate the mysterious 'witchcraft murder' at Meon Hill. (*See* COTSWOLDS, WITCHCRAFT IN THE.) She braved a storm of adverse criticism when her first book about witchcraft, *The Witch Cult in Western Europe,* was published in 1921. She studied anthropology in the early days, when this was considered a subject 'not quite nice' for ladies to take up. She was a pioneer Suffragette. She worked on archaeological excavations in Egypt; and on one occasion there, she underwent a magical ceremony to preserve her from rabies, after being bitten by a dog that might have been mad. One wonders what Miss Murray *would* have counted as adventures!

Margaret Murray was a shrewd and critical scholar, and by no means credulous. Her main career was in Egyptology, and her interest in witchcraft was really a side-line; though, curiously enough, it is for the latter that she became best known.

She was not, however, as popularly supposed, the first person to advance the idea that witchcraft is the Old Religion, or to call it "the Dianic cult". Both these ideas had been advanced previously by Charles Godfrey Leland. (*See* LELAND, CHARLES GODFREY.)

In her autobiography, Miss Murray tells us rather frustratingly little about her researches into witchcraft, except to reveal that the idea of witchcraft being really a secret religion was suggested to her by another person. She started to investigate for herself, working from the contemporary records of witches and witchcraft; and when she realised that the so-called 'Devil' who appeared at the witches' Sabbats was actually a man in a ritual disguise, she tells us that she was "startled, almost alarmed" by the way in which the recorded details she had been reading fell into place and made sense.

Later, in 1933, she published a second book on witchcraft, *The God of the Witches.* The book was almost ignored when it first appeared; but after the Second World War, when interest in witchcraft had re-awakened, it was republished and became a best seller. Miss Murray followed it in 1954, with her third and perhaps most controversial book on this subject, *The Divine King in England* (Faber and Faber, London).

In this book, she advanced the idea that many early English sovereigns had died by ritual murder; and that the concepts of royalty and kingship were inextricably bound up with the human sacrifice of the Sacred King, demanded by primitive religion.

Although sceptical of the highly-coloured stories of occult happenings connected with Egyptian relics, Margaret Murray was interested in the phenomena of telepathy and apparitions. She advanced a theory that ghosts were really a kind of photographic image, somehow recorded upon the atmosphere of a place, and becoming visible under certain circumstances.

In her autobiography, she also records her firm faith in the human soul and its survival of bodily death, and her belief in reincarnation.

During her long career, Margaret Alice Murray received many academic honours. She was Assistant Professor of Egyptology at University College, London, from 1924 to her retirement in 1935; and from 1953 to 1955 she was President of the Folk-Lore Society. She never married, though her photographs show her to have been most attractive in her youth, and still very good-looking at the age of 50. She was undoubtedly one of the most remarkable women of her generation.

N

NORTH DOOR, THE

The really old churches of Britain, and indeed throughout Europe, often contain remarkable relics of the pre-Christian pagan faith. Figures occur in their decoration which point to a long transitional period between paganism and Christianity; a period in which the two were intermingled, and much dual allegiance must have existed.

One such figure, already noted, is that of the Green Man, a form of the old god of the woodlands. (*See* GREEN MAN.) Another is the Sheila-na-Gig, found more often in Ireland, but upon some English churches also. It is a very frank representation of woman's sexuality, and probably originated as some old goddess of fertility, a primitive *Magna Mater*. Still another is the charming little figure known as the Lincoln Imp, whose cross-legged posture is very reminiscent of old Gaulish statues of the Celtic horned god, Cernunnos.

The place to look for anything of a pagan nature in an old church or cathedral, is upon the north side. This is because of a strange belief, which connects the north with the Devil.

Why this should be so, is rather shrouded in mystery; but it seems to be yet another instance of the god of the old religion becoming the devil of the new. The north to the pagans was the place of power, the mysterious hub upon which the great wheel of the heavens turns. We may remember how one of the passages in the Great Pyramid in Egypt has been found to be orientated to the star Alpha Draconis, which is not the North Star in these present days, but was once, many centuries ago. The constellation of Draco, the Dragon, which coils about the Pole of the heavens, may have seemed to Christians a representation of the Devil; though to the Celts, as to Eastern people, a dragon was a guardian of wisdom and the Mysteries. Witness the proud Red Dragon which still stands upon the banner of Wales.

Old churchyards showed but few interments upon the north side; and those generally of persons who had only grudgingly been given

Christian burial, such as unbaptised children or suicides. Commenting upon this prejudice against the north side of the church, the Reverend George S. Tyack, in his *Lore and Legend of the English Church* (William Andrews, London, 1899), says: "The north was of old mystically supposed to typify the Devil, and a usage prevailed in some places of opening a door on that side of the church at the administration of Holy Baptism, for the exit of the exorcised demon."

For this reason, the north door of old churches was known as 'the Devil's door'. It is remarkable how often in old churches these days, this door will be found to have been bricked up. Enquiry can seldom elicit any reason for this having been done, or at any rate any convincing reason. Yet traces of such north doors, filled in with masonry, exist in innumerable old churches.

A story which does explain this peculiar fact, says that in olden days, when attendance at church was more or less compulsory, people who secretly adhered to the Old Religion, in other words those who were witches, made a point of coming into the church by the north door, and taking their seats near it.

They dared not absent themselves from the Christian church, especially in a small village where everyone knew everyone else. In fact, at one time attendance at church was actually compulsory by law, and those who failed to attend could be punished. So the pagans adopted this method of secretly distinguishing themselves from the rest of the congregation, by using the Devil's door. Curious graffiti, embodying pagan magical symbols, can sometimes be found around the north door, or upon the northern side, of old churches. These are usually described in the guide-book as "masons' marks"; but a little study of this subject will enable an enquirer to distinguish a real mason's mark from a mark which has quite a different origin.

Eventually, however, the church authorities realised that this custom was being secretly observed by the obstinately pagan element within their congregations. They decided to frustrate it by blocking up the Devil's door in many instances; and traces of their precautions in this respect may still be seen.

NUDITY, RITUAL

The fact that some present-day witches believe in the old idea of ritual nudity, is one of the things that sensation-mongers have pounced on with delight. Every so often we are regaled by a certain section of the Sunday press with vivid descriptions of "nude orgies of devil-worship" and so on, that are supposed to be happening in

Britain today. However, the older covens, which avoid publicity like the plague, in general make no great insistence upon ritual nudity, though they see nothing in it to make a fuss about. For some rites, on a really warm summer night, or indoors by a fire, it is pleasant to be naked. For others, outdoors in the darkness on Halloween, or at midnight of the full moon in some lonely wood, it is reasonable to be warmly clad.

The idea of nudity as part of a magical or religious rite is found throughout the ancient world. In the famous paintings in the Villa of the Mysteries at Pompeii, the young girl who is being initiated starts off clothed and veiled; but at the end of the initiation ceremony she is shown dancing naked, in a state of religious ecstasy. She has cast off all worldly cares, all class distinctions; she is one with Nature and with the vitality of the universe. It was this freedom and beauty which constituted religious ecstasy to the pagan.

It appears from the Old Testament, particularly I Samuel, Chapter 19, verse 24, that the ancient prophets or seers of Israel did their prophesying in a state of ritual nudity. In this, they were like the Gymnosophists, or Naked Wise Men of ancient India. (Greek *gymnos,* naked, *sophos,* wise.) Perhaps for this reason, the idea came down to the Greeks and Romans that ritual nudity was favourable for the performance of magical rites. What had started as a religious custom, ended as a magical one.

Charles Godfrey Leland, in his *Gypsy Sorcery* (reprinted by University Books, Inc., New York, 1962), has noted the frequent appearances of ritual nudity in witch spells, and in magical folklore generally. He remarks on the likeness between the wild naked dances of the old-time Sabbats, as described by Pierre de Lancre, and the festivals of gypsies; and he reminds us that the Romanys come from the East, from whence so much erotic dancing by women in honour of the gods derives. Witches and gypsies have long been closely akin.

Maimonides tells us that the young women of Ancient Persia used to dance at dawn in honour of the sun, naked and singing to music; and we have the account given by Pliny in his *Natural History,* of how the women of Ancient Britain also performed religious rites in the nude. Pliny regarded Persia of the Magi as being the home of magic; but he says that its rituals were so well performed in Ancient Britain, that we might have taught magic to Persia, instead of the other way about. The custom of ritual nudity was certainly common to both.

Relics of the old belief in the magical power of nakedness may sometimes be found in folklore. For instance, there is an old idea that a woman can be cured of barrenness by walking about naked in her vegetable garden on Midsummer Eve, a date which, it will be remembered, is that of one of the witches' Sabbats.

Thomas Wright, in his essay which accompanies Payne Knight's *Discourse on the Worship of Priapus* (London, privately printed, 1865), has an interesting passage relevant to this matter.

> We remember that, we believe in one of the earlier editions of Mother Bunch, maidens who wished to know if their lovers were constant or not were directed to go out exactly at midnight on St. John's Eve, to strip themselves entirely naked, and in that condition to proceed to a plant or shrub, the name of which was given, and round it they were to form a circle and dance, repeating at the same time certain words which they had been taught by their instructress. Having completed this ceremony, they were to gather leaves of the plant round which they had danced, which they were to carry home and place under their pillows, and what they wished to know would be revealed to them in their dreams. We have seen in some of the medieval treatises on the virtue of plants directions for gathering some plants of especial importance in which it was required that this should be performed by young girls in a similar state of complete nakedness.

In *Aradia, or the Gospel of the Witches,* the followers of Diana are commanded to be naked in their rites, in sign that they are truly free. For this reason, many present-day witch covens insist on performing their rites in the nude. However, there is a big difference between the climates of Italy or the Near East, and the climate of the British Isles, as other witches point out. To demand ritual nudity at all times for witch ceremonies in Britain today is simply not practical.

Also, many of the older witches feel that all the publicity about nude witch dances has attracted quite the wrong sort of interest in what is, or ought to be, the Craft of the Wise. People come to it who are just looking for a bit of sexual excitement, without any serious commitment or belief. Too much emphasis, they feel, has been put on this feature of the Old Religion. They think that, along with the other old practice of ritual flagellation, ritual nudity is something that could well fade into the past, without any detriment to the witch cult, but rather the reverse.

Which, of course, leaves us with a question: is the public's reaction to the idea of witches dancing naked, a criticism of witches—or a criticism of the popular mentality, after nearly 2,000 years of 'Christian civilisation'?

The real spirit of witchcraft has nothing in common with the banal sexual fantasies of thriller writers and the yellow press. Nor is it anything like the over-intellectualised occultism of both East and West, that takes to itself much importance today, and requires many long words to express itself.

The real secrets cannot be expressed in words. They are much more matters of feeling and intuition, than they are of the intellect. The joy and exhilaration of dancing naked is one way of drawing close to them.

However, present-day 'exposers' of witchcraft are not the first to be excited by the idea of naked witches. A number of artists in times past have delighted to represent witches as voluptuous young women, naked and shameless. A notable artist of this *genre* was Hans Baldung Grun; and it was a picture of his that gave Albrecht Durer the idea for Durer's famous engraving, *The Four Witches*.

This wonderful work of art, dated 1497, shows four buxom women stripping for a witch rite. The point of the picture, not always realised, is this: the women have removed all their clothes except their head-dresses, and these head-dresses, all different, show the various classes of society from which they come.

There is the great lady, with an elaborate coif of delicate material upon her head. There is the courtesan, with loose flowing hair, bound only with a garland of leaves. There is the respectable burgess's wife, with a plain, rather severe head-dress, which covers all her hair closely and modestly. Lastly, there is the peasant woman, with merely the end of a scarf or shawl over her head. The artist is saying that all these are sisters in witchcraft, and that witches come from all classes of society. When they are naked, they meet as equals, and social distinctions are forgotten.

NUMBERS, THEIR OCCULT SIGNIFICANCE

A great deal of magical lore, some of which pertains to witchcraft, is concerned with numbers, and their occult properties and associations.

The witches' number *par excellence* is thirteen. Its significance goes back far beyond recorded history; so the accusation that witches used the number thirteen to mock Christ and his twelve disciples is untrue. Indeed, it is very possible that the reason Jesus chose twelve disciples was that he knew the mystical significance of twelve plus one. (*See* COVEN.)

The number seven also has great importance in lore and legend. Traditionally, the seventh son of a seventh son, or the seventh daughter of a seventh daughter, is a born witch. In some of the rural parts of Italy, seven months' children are believed to grow up with similar powers.

The original sacred seven are the seven heavenly bodies, which the ancients called the Seven Sacred Planets, though two of them, the sun and the moon, are strictly speaking not planets but luminaries. The order of the Seven Planets is usually written thus: Saturn, Jupiter, Mars, Sun, Venus, Mercury, Moon. In astrological belief, all things on earth are ruled in some way by these seven powers.

Our seven days of the week derive from this very old concept. The sun rules Sunday, the moon Monday, Mars Tuesday, Mercury Wednesday, Jupiter Thursday, Venus Friday and Saturn Saturday.

The Old Testament is full of allusions to the number seven. In later times, the Christian Church formulated its Seven Sacraments, its Seven Deadly Sins, and so on. The pagan world has its Seven Wonders, and also the Seven Sages of Greece and the Seven Rishis of India. The world-wide and time-honoured sacredness of this number is proved by innumerable mystic groupings and uses of seven.

Another reason for the potency of seven is the most important and well-known constellation of our northern skies, the Plough, which consists of seven bright stars, and acts as a pointer to the Pole Star of the North. In Celtic myth, the North was the place of secret and dangerous powers. Spirits rode the Northern Lights, and dead heroes dwelt at the back of the north wind.

It is easy to understand, therefore, how the age-old magic of the number seven wove itself into witchcraft; as did the equally sacred and potent number three. There is a pre-Christian belief in the potency of odd numbers, which is remarked on by the Roman poet Virgil: *Numero Deus impare gaudet,* "God delights in odd numbers". Shakespeare repeated this belief in *The Merry Wives of Windsor:* "Good luck lies in odd numbers . . . they say, there is divinity in odd numbers, either in nativity, chance, or death."

The occult philosophers regarded man as a triad: *spiritus, anima,* and *corpus,* or spirit, soul and body; though this triad by sub-division was extended into seven principles. In Nature, we have the father, the mother and the child. Also, the three kingdoms, animal, vegetable and mineral. The alchemists recognised three principles in their art, salt, sulphur and mercury, which are closely paralleled by the Indian concepts of *sattwas, rajas* and *tamas.*

Three represents the mean between two extremes, and this is the way in which most of the ancient philosophers used it in their symbolic systems. The Druids expressed their lore in triads; and their symbol was the *Tribann,* or Three Rays of Light. Qabalistic symbolism reveals this ancient idea as the Three Pillars: the Pillar of Mercy, the Pillar of Severity and the Middle Pillar of Mildness, which harmonises the other two; and Masonic ritual retains it under the form of three columns.

No wonder we constantly find the injunction in witchcraft, that the words of charms are to be repeated three times; or that concoctions of magical herbs should be of three, seven or nine different kinds, compounded together.

There is an old belief that certain years in people's lives are years of destiny, called climacteric years. These are the 7th and the 9th, and their multiples by the odd numbers: 3, 5, 7 and 9. Thus the climacteric years of human life are 7, 9, 21, 27, 35, 45, 49, 63 and 81. Our custom of regarding a person as 'coming of age' at 21 is a relic of this belief; it is the *third* climacteric year.

The mystic symbolism of numbers is an important part of practical magic. Magic squares, that is, numbers so arranged in a square that they add in all directions to the same figure, are powerful talismans, used in many ways in magical rituals. The simplest magic square, or Kamea, is that of the first nine digits, arranged thus:

4	9	2
3	5	7
8	1	6

Whichever way these figures are added, including diagonally, their sum will always be 15.

Many more complicated magic squares than this have been evolved. Strange as it may seem, mathematics is yet another human activity which long ago was linked with magic; and numerology, or divination of numbers, is still popular today. People believe in their 'lucky number'; and conversely, refuse to live in a house numbered thirteen. Indeed, the fear of the number thirteen is prevalent enough for some local authorities to have discreetly removed it from the numbering of houses; while hotel keepers banish it from the doors of their rooms. Some people carry their avoidance of thirteen to such lengths that psychologists have invented a name for their reaction: trisked-ekaphobia, a morbid fear of the number thirteen.

When we recollect that thirteen is the number of lunar months in a year, we can see how both this and the number seven are associated with moon magic. This may be the real secret of their magical reputation; as the waxing and waning of the moon are man's oldest astrological observations.

The old common-law month was twenty-eight days, during which the moon displayed all her phases, and went round the compass of the zodiac. The number twenty-eight is not only four times seven, but also the sum of numbers from one to seven. Each period of seven days in the lunar month was associated with a different phase of the moon, and with a different state of the tides of the sea. There are thirteen lunar months to the solar year, with one day left over, which is why the expression 'a year and a day' occurs so often in old Celtic myths.

The number three also associates with moon magic, because of the moon's three appearances: waxing, full and waning; and again, this is possibly the oldest reason for its importance.

An old magical co-relation of numbers and astrology is as follows: Sun, 1 and 4; Moon, 2 and 7; Jupiter, 3; Mercury, 5; Venus, 6; Saturn, 8; and Mars, 9. Another magical relationship of numbers, based on the Qabalah, is: Saturn, 3; Jupiter, 4; Mars, 5; Sun, 6; Venus, 7; Mercury, 8; Moon, 9. These systems are not contradictory, though they might appear so; because they are used in different ways in magical practice.

O

OLD ONE, THE

'The Old 'Un' is a dialect term frequently used to indicate the Devil. It is a significant pointer to the fact that 'The Devil' is really a pre-Christian god, who has been degraded to devildom because his characteristics did not fit in with the new puritanical conception of deity.

Yet the Old Religion, with its roots in Nature, still lived on in the hearts and minds of the people. The way of referring to the Devil as 'The Old 'Un' is an instance of this, and so is another term for the same mysterious personage, 'Old Harry'.

This comes from the Saxon *hearh,* a hill-top sanctuary where the pagan gods were worshipped. It survives in Mount Harry, a height of the Sussex Downs, and the Old Harry Rocks on the South Coast, which were supposed to have been put there by the Devil. 'Old Harry' is the Old One who was worshipped on the hills.

Christina Hole, in her book *English Folklore* (Batsford, London, 1940), notes the fact that the word 'providence' is sometimes used by old-fashioned country folk to mean, not the Christian idea of providence, but the Devil, or the ancient powers of paganism. She quotes a farmer's wife who defended some old pagan good-luck rite in connection with the harvest, by saying that it didn't do to forget "Owd Providence", and perhaps it was best to keep in with both parties!

This little story is very revealing, in its insight into the thoughts and feelings of old-time country people, who lived close to Nature and had an unlettered wisdom of their own.

Another term for the Devil is 'Old Hornie', an obvious reference to his famous attribute of horns; while 'Old Splitfoot' or 'Clootie' refer to his cloven hoofs, the characteristics of the Great God Pan.

A dialect term for the Devil, almost forgotten now, is 'Old Poker'. It is similar in origin to the words Puck or 'pooke', and is a relic of the Old English *puca* and Welsh *pwca,* meaning an uncanny being or spirit. Another dialect term is 'Old Scratch', from the Old Norse *skratte*, a goblin or monster.

Perhaps the best-known reference to the Devil beginning with 'Old' is 'Old Nick'. This takes us directly back to pagan times, because Nik was a name for Woden, the Old English version of Odin, the All-Father, the Master Magician. Like the Devil in later years, Woden was believed sometimes to amuse himself by taking on human form and wandering about among mankind. Any mysterious stranger might be he, especially if he had an uncanny air about him, and seemed to possess knowledge beyond the ordinary.

Woden's followers were the Wild Women, the Waelcyrges, whom the more northern nations called Valkyries. The Old English Wael- cyrges, however, were more akin to witches than the warrior women whom Richard Wagner has depicted in his operas. They fly by night with Woden in the Wild Hunt, when the winter wind blows high and clouds scud across the moon. Indeed, the word Waelcyrge in old manuscripts has sometimes been translated as 'witch'.

It is not difficult to see how Nik and his Waelcyrges contributed to the idea of Old Nick and his witches.

In places where a Christian church was built upon a site of heathen worship, Nik was sometimes transformed and Christianised into St. Nicholas. For instance, Abbots Bromley, in Staffordshire, where the famous Horn Dance is performed every September, has its very old parish church of St. Nicholas. In this church the horns and other properties of the dance are stored when not in use; and at one time the dance was performed in the church porch. The dance is generally agreed to be a survival from very ancient times, and to have a pre- Christian origin.

Again, the oldest church in Brighton, Sussex, is that of St. Nicholas. It is built on a hill, where, according to local tradition, there once stood a pagan stone circle. Churches dedicated to St. Nicholas will nearly always be found to rest upon very old foundations.

There is also more relationship between 'jolly old St. Nicholas' and the pagan Saxon festival of Yule, than there is with the Christian version that we call Christmas. The merry, scarlet-clad old fellow, who drives a team of reindeer from the North Pole, has much more in common with some old god of fertility and revelry than he has with a sainted Christian bishop.

P

PALMISTRY

The art of palmistry is more truly described by its old name of cheiromancy, or divination by the hand; because this term includes all the varied lore connected with the human hand throughout the ages, instead of merely referring to the study of the lines on the palm.

How old palmistry is no one really knows. It may have originated in ancient India. The Greeks certainly studied it, and Aristotle in particular is believed to have taken much interest in it. The story goes that when travelling in Egypt Aristotle discovered a manuscript treatise on the art and science of hand-reading, which he sent to Alexander the Great, commending it as "a study worthy of the attention of an elevated and enquiring mind".

This treatise was translated into Latin by one Hispanus, and what purported to be the book discovered by Aristotle was printed at Ulme in 1490, under the title *Chyromantia Aristotelis cum Figuris*. An even earlier book, *Die Kunst Ciromantia* (The Art of Cheiromancy), by Johann Hartlieb, was printed at Augsberg in 1475. Medieval practitioners of this art claimed that it was sanctioned by Holy Writ, quoting a text from the book of Job, Chapter 37, verse 7: "He sealeth up the hand of every man; that all men may know His work." The original Hebrew of this passage reads "In the hand He will seal", or "sealeth every man"; and the defenders of palmistry argued that this meant God had placed signs in men's hands, which the wise could read and interpret.

Some churchmen agreed with this and some did not. The palmists were perhaps on safer ground when they associated palmistry with astrology, and with the doctrine of man as the microcosm or little world, in which all the correspondences of the heavens could be symbolically traced. The sun, moon and planets, together with the signs of the zodiac, were all assigned their places and governorship upon the human hand. A fragment of medieval Latin verse told the story:

> Est pollex Veneris; sed Juppiter indice gaudet,
> Saturnus medium; Sol medicumque tenet,
> Hinc Stilbon minimum; ferientem candida Luna
> Possidet; in cavea Mars sua castra tenet.

The translation reads: "The thumb is of Venus; but Jupiter delights in the index finger, and Saturn in the middle finger, and the Sun holds the third finger (*medicus*). Mercury is here at the smallest finger, and the chaste Moon occupies the percussion [i.e. the outside of the hand, opposite to the thumb]; in the hollow of the hand Mars holds his camp."

The four fingers each have three divisions, or phalanges, making twelve in all, a natural correspondence with the twelve signs of the zodiac. Thus one can in a sense clasp the whole of the starry heavens in one's hand.

A good hand-reader had no need to cast an elaborate horoscope for his client. The horoscope was there upon the hand, formed and imprinted by nature, only requiring skill and intuition to read it. Hence practitioners from the poorer classes, like witches and gypsies, who had no expensive astronomical instruments or books for the casting of horoscopes, cultivated palmistry. "To know the secrets of the hand" is one of the powers of witchcraft mentioned in *Aradia*. (*See* ARADIA.)

The magical number seven figures largely in palmistry. There are seven chief lines upon the palm of the hand: the line of life, the line of heart, the line of head, the line of Saturn or fortune, the line of the Sun or brilliancy, the hepatica or line of health, and the girdle of Venus. There are also seven mounts upon the palm, named after the sun, moon and planets. Moreover, the famous French palmist, D'Arpentigny, who wrote in the early part of the nineteenth century, distinguished seven types of hand: the elementary hand, the spatulate or active hand, the conical or artistic hand, the square or useful hand, the knotty or philosophic hand, the pointed or psychic hand, and the mixed hand, which is a combination of several types. The terms 'spatulate', 'conical', 'square' and 'pointed' refer to the four different types of finger-tips; and they have a certain affinity with the four elements and the types of temperament they govern.

As might be expected, the four elements and the quintessence, or spirit, are also included in the general symbolism of the hand. Water belongs to the first finger, earth to the second, fire to the third, and air to the little finger; while the thumb, which to a palmist indicates the will-power of the subject, is the place of spirit.

In order to arrive at a truthful estimate of a person's character, and therefore of their prospects, both hands must be examined and compared. The left hand will show the inherited tendencies of the subject, and the right will manifest what use the subject has made of those tendencies, and how they have been developed or modified by life. If the subject happens to be left-handed, however, the reverse will apply, as it is the active hand which shows the life of the person.

Space does not permit a detailed instruction on hand-reading here. However, many good books are today available on the subject, including those by the famous palmist Louis Hamon, who practised under the pseudonym of 'Cheiro'. Cheiro's work may be considered by some today to be out of date; but we owe him a considerable debt, because by his successful reading of the hands of many famous people he helped to make palmistry socially acceptable, whereas it had for many years been illegal in Britain.

Under the so-called Rogues and Vagabonds Act of 1824, in the reign of George IV, it was laid down that "every person pretending or professing to tell fortunes, or using any subtle craft, means or device, by palmistry or otherwise, to deceive and impose on any of His Majesty's subjects" could be sentenced to three months' hard labour. This act was sometimes held to apply to witchcraft, as well as palmistry.

PAN

Pan, the goat-footed god, is the Greek version of the Horned God, who has been worshipped under various guises since the beginning of time. In Greek, *Pan* means 'All, everything'; and the various representations of Pan show him as the positive Life Force of the world.

The spotted fawn-skin over his shoulders represents the starry heavens. His body, part-animal and part-human, is living Nature as a whole. His shaggy hair is the primeval forest. His strong hoofs are the enduring rocks. His horns are rays of power and light.

The seven-reeded Pan-pipe upon which he plays, is the emblem of the septenary nature of things, and the rulership of the seven heavenly bodies. Its melody is the secret song of Life, underlying all other sound. He is beautiful, and yet able to inspire panic terror, even as the varying moods of Nature can be.

Although worshipped by the Greeks, he was never really counted among the later and more civilised gods of Olympus. His home in Greece was Arcadia, where the people were regarded as being the most primitive among the Greeks. They were farmers and hunters; and Pan was the patron god of these pursuits, away from the life of the cities. He was the lover of the nymphs of the forest, and of the Maenads, the Wild Women who took part in the Orgies of Dionysus. Dionysus himself, the horned child, was something like a younger version of Pan.

Pan was the only one among the gods to whom the virginal Artemis ever yielded. Artemis, the moon goddess, was worshipped by the Romans as Diana; and they also revered Pan, whom they called Faunus or Silvanus. Like Diana, his cult spread with the extension of the Roman Empire and mingled with that of native divinities.

There are different versions of Pan's origin among the Greek mythographers, as there are different derivations of his name. Some regard the latter as being derived from *paein*, 'to pasture'; but, considering the primitive nature of this God, and his pantheistic attributes, there seems no need to seek any other derivation than *to Pan*, 'the All'. One myth of his origin says that he was the son of Hermes. This is meaningful, when we remember that the original *herm* was a sacred stone, a phallic menhir around which dances and fertility rites were held. Pan was then the spirit of the stone, the masculine power of life which it symbolised.

He was the power which the occult philosophers called *Natura naturans,* as the feminine side of Nature was called *Natura naturata.*

When the old pagan faith was superseded by Christianity, a legend grew up that 'Great Pan was dead'. The sound of a great, sad voice crying this was said to have been heard over the Mediterranean Sea. But in fact, the worship of Pan and the other divinities of Nature had only disappeared for a time, and gone underground, to reappear as the witch cult all over Europe.

Pan was noted among the gods of Greece, for summoning his worshippers naked to his rites. Later, the witches who honoured the Horned God delighted in nude dances, a direct derivation from the customs of antiquity.

Two of the titles by which Pan was known to his worshippers were Pamphage, Pangenetor, 'All-Devourer, All-Begetter', that is the forces of growth in Nature, and the forces of destruction. Nothing in Nature stands still. All is constantly changing, being born, flowering, dying and coming again to birth. The same idea is seen in the Hindu concept of the god Shiva, who is both begetter and destroyer. By the *Lila* or love-play of Shiva and his consort Shakti, all the phenomena of the manifested world are brought into being. But Shiva is also the Lord of Yoga, the means by which men can find their way beyond the world of appearances, and discover the numinous reality. Even so, the concept of Pan was really something more profound than the jolly, sensual god of primitive life that he is usually taken to be.

However, he was primarily a god of kindly merriment, worshipped with music and dancing. Dancing and play are a basic activity of all life. Children are natural dancers, and so are animals. Forest creatures leap and gambol in the woodland. The mating dances of birds, the amazing springtime antics of hares, even the constant circling of a swarm of gnats on a summer evening, all are part of the same instinctive impulse. The earth, the moon and all the planets join in a great circling dance about the sun. The island universes of the nebulae seem to be circling about a centre. The merry circle dance of the witches was a deeply instinctive response to the living Nature with which they sought kinship.

The medieval Church had ceased to be able to comprehend a religion which sought to worship the gods by dancing and merriment. The idea was growing among Churchmen that anything enjoyable must be sinful. We are still suffering from this strange aberration of human thought today; although humanity is beginning at last to emerge from the Dark Ages—much to the indignation of those who rage against what they call the 'permissive society'.

It was this dark view of human life, the regarding of pleasure as sinful, which in turn darkened the survivals of paganism in Europe. The merry goat-footed god became 'the Devil', and the witches who worshipped him were forced into secret association, an underground movement beset by fear and suspicion, and with the torture-chamber, the gallows or the stake constantly in the background.

We tend to think of medieval times as being colourful, picturesque, and rather gay, with rosy-cheeked peasants dancing round the maypole, and so on. In practice, they were days of fear, suffering and oppression; and much of the colour and gaiety of olden days, like the art and learning of the Renaissance, was either the survival or the revival of paganism. If we look at the beautiful figures of Pan which have survived from Greek and Roman Art, and contrast them with the twisted, leering, horned demons of medieval times, we can see this change of vision and attitude mirrored in the artforms, which are the visual expression of men's souls.

PENTAGRAM, THE

The pentagram, or five-pointed star, is a favourite symbol of witches and magicians. It has been so widely used throughout the centuries that the word 'pentacle', also originally meaning a five-pointed star, has come to designate any disc or plate of metal or wood, engraved with magical symbols, and used in magical rites.

The origin of the magical five-pointed star is lost in the mists of time. Early examples occur in the relics of Babylon. The Christians regarded it as representing the Five Wounds of Christ, and hence it is sometimes found in church architecture. There is a very beautiful form of a pentagram in one of the windows of Exeter Cathedral.

This sign also occurs among the emblems of Freemasonry. Some regard it as being the Seal of Solomon; though this designation is more often given to the six-pointed star, formed by two interlaced triangles, which is the sign of the Jewish faith. However, the pentagram is certainly a Qabalistic sign, known to those occult fraternities which claim to derive from the Rosicrucians.

The followers of Pythagoras called the pentagram the *pentalpha,* regarding it as being formed of five letter A's. In medieval Europe it was known as 'The Druid's Foot', or 'Wizard's Foot'; and sometimes as 'The Goblins' Cross'. In the old romance of *Sir Gawaine and the Green Knight,* it is the device which Gawaine bears on his shield.

It also occurs in the old song 'Green Grow the Rushes-O'. This curious old chant of questions and responses contains hints of hidden meanings; and one of its lines is "Five is the symbol at your door" meaning the pentagram, which was inscribed on doors and windows to keep out evil.

Some old Celtic coins show the figure of a pentagram upon them. Something very like the five-pointed star occurs naturally upon some fossils, and these objects have always been prized by witches for this reason, as being highly magical. One kind of fossil with a five-pointed figure upon it is the so-called shepherd's crown, a fossil sea-urchin. (*See* FOSSILS USED AS CHARMS.) But an even more potent magical object than this is the true star stone, a fossil which occurs in the perfect shape of a five-pointed star. It is actually part of the fossilised stem of a *Crinoid* or sea lily.

The reason why the pentagram is regarded as the symbol of magic is because its five points represent the Four Elements of Life, plus Spirit, the Unseen, the Beyond, the source of occult power. For this reason, the pentagram should be drawn with one point upwards, the point of Spirit presiding over the other four. It is Mind ruling over the World of Matter.

The other way up, the pentagram is often regarded as a more sinister symbol. According to Madame Blavatsky, in her *Secret Doctrine* (Theosophical Publishing Co., London, 1888), the reversed pentagram is the symbol of Kali Yuga, the Dark Age in which we live, an age of materialism, sensuality and violence. Other occultists have regarded the reversed pentagram as the face of the Goat of Mendes, with the two upward points representing the goat's horns. In this sense, it is the face of the Horned God. It has sometimes been called a symbol of black magic; but what it really represents is the light of the Spirit hidden in Matter.

The pentagram with one point upwards is used by occultists to control elementals, because of its inner meaning. Worn as a lamen upon the breast, it is a protection in magical rites, against hostile or undesirable influences.

It is sometimes called the Star of the Microcosm, because it has the shape of a human being with arms and legs outstretched. The old occult philosophers regarded man as a microcosm, or little world in himself, containing in potentiality all that was in the cosmos without him. The pentagram also represents the five senses of man, the gateways by which impressions of the outer world reach him.

Yet another name for the pentagram is the Endless Knot, because it can be drawn without lifting the pen from the paper, though it requires concentration and care to draw a symmetrical figure in this way; qualities which were necessary for the successful making of a magical sign.

PERSECUTION OF WITCHES

The law making witchcraft a capital offence in England was repealed in 1735. For some years previously, enlightened judges had been thwarting any attempt to have wretched old creatures hanged as witches, in spite of popular outcry against them. The more educated people of the nation had become sickened at the superstition and

imposture connected with trials for witchcraft. The pendulum had
swung completely the other way, so that many now completely disbelieved in witchcraft at all.

This attitude, however, was by no means shared by the less educated classes. They still vehemently believed in witchcraft, both black
and white, and moreover believed that witches who worked harm
should die, or at any rate suffer severely. So when the law of the land
was relaxed, lynch law sometimes took over.

The self-styled 'wise woman' or 'cunning man' often played a very
sinister part in these proceedings. At that time (as now) there were
many clever and greedy impostors, who made a good living out of
public credulity. One of their specialities was pointing out dangerous
witches, with profit to themselves, and sometimes a tragic and fatal
result to some unfortunate old man or woman whom they picked on.

A sensational case of this kind occurred at Tring, in Hertfordshire, in 1751, when a poor old couple, John and Ruth Osborne,
were attacked by a mob, and Ruth Osborne died as a result.

They may well not have been witches at all; but a man called Butterfield had got it into his head that they were, on account of some
ill-health and misfortune he had encountered, after quarrelling with
Mrs Osborne.

He accordingly sent as far as Northamptonshire, for a renowned
wise woman to come and help him. She confirmed that he was bewitched, but her services proved both expensive and without result,
so far as improvement in Butterfield's affairs was concerned. However, curiosity and excitement had by now been aroused in the neigh-
bouring countryside; and someone caused the public criers of three
adjoining towns, Hemel Hempstead, Leighton Buzzard, and Winslow,
to make this announcement: "This is to give notice, that on Monday
next, a man and woman are to be publicly ducked at Tring, in this
county, for their wicked crimes".

When the parish overseer of Tring learned that the Osbornes were
the people referred to, he lodged them for their own safety in the
workhouse. They were again moved from there to the vestry of the
parish church, late on the Sunday night.

On the Monday morning, a mob, estimated at over 5,000 persons,
many of them on horseback, assailed the workhouse, demanding the
Osbornes. When the workhouse master told them the couple were
not there, the mob rushed in and searched the building. Baulked of
their victims they then turned on the wretched workhouse master, and

threatened him with death if he did not reveal where the Osbornes were.

Having discovered by this means that the supposed witches were hidden in the church, the mob broke open the church doors, seized John and Ruth Osborne, and dragged them to a pond at Long Marston.

Here they were both stripped naked and wrapped each in a sheet. Their thumbs and great toes were tied together, and a cord was put round each one's body, precisely as witches had been 'swum' in Matthew Hopkins' time. Each suspect was then separately thrown into the pond. When Ruth Osborne seemed to float somewhat, a man named Thomas Colley pushed her down with a stick. This treatment was three times repeated in each case, and one account says that the prisoners were then laid naked on the shore, where they were kicked and beaten until Ruth Osborne was dead and her husband nearly so. Thomas Colley then "went among the spectators and collected money for the pains he had taken in showing them sport"; so the account of his subsequent trial tells us.

Neither the local clergy nor the magistrates had raised a finger to save the Osbornes. However, a riot of such proportions, and its fatal consequence, could not be hidden; and many people were indignant and horrified. A coroner's inquest was held upon the death of Ruth Osborne; and twelve of the principal gentlemen of Hertfordshire were summoned to form the jury, because at an inquest held in a similar case a short time before, at Frome in Somersetshire, the jury had refused to bring in an obviously justified verdict of murder.

The result was that Thomas Colley was in due course tried for the murder of Ruth Osborne at the County Assizes. John Osborne had recovered, but did not appear to give evidence. Nevertheless Colley was found guilty, and sentenced to be hanged. On the scaffold, a solemn declaration of Colley's faith relating to witchcraft was read for him by the minister of Tring. A strong military escort accompanied him to the scaffold, on account of the public sympathy for him, and a good deal of grumbling among the people "that it was a hard case to hang a man for destroying an old wicked woman that had done so much mischief by her witchcraft."

This was the most notorious case of mob violence against alleged witches in England; but by no means the only one. There are many recorded instances of people attacking those they accused as witches, and trying to 'swim' them or 'draw blood upon them'. The latter is another very old belief, that if you can strike a witch so as to draw blood, they lose their power over you. It has been responsible for a number of deaths, notably those of Nanny Morgan in Shropshire in 1857, and Ann Turner in Warwickshire in 1875.

Both these women were killed by men who believed themselves bewitched by them. Nanny Morgan, who lived at Westwood Common, near Wenlock, belonged to a witch family. The old country saying was applied to her kinsfolk, "that they could see further through a barn door than most". The method of her death dated back to Anglo-Saxon times, when it was called *pricca,* meaning staking down the suspected witch with a sharp weapon, so that the blood flowed. Nanny Morgan was found in her cottage, pinned down with an eel spear through her throat.

That she did actually practise witchcraft was proved by the fact that a number of letters were found in her cottage, some from people of eminent local position, asking for her services. There was also a box of gold sovereigns, which she had apparently accumulated by the practice of occult arts. Witches today believe that it is wrong to practise witchcraft for money, and that it ultimately brings retribution upon the person who does so.

The young man who killed her had been a lodger in her house. He had wanted to leave, but was too afraid of her to break away. In the end he committed this desperate act.

Ann Turner was killed in the village of Long Compton, near the Rollright Stones; a village which, like Canewdon in Essex, has a strong local tradition of witchcraft. A young man, who believed she had bewitched him, attacked her with a hayfork. He may only have meant to draw blood upon her; but she was an elderly woman, and she died of her injuries.

A contemporary account has come down to us, of a similar case in Wiveliscombe, Somerset, in 1823, which fortunately did not end in murder, but came very near to doing so. This case is notable, for the way in which it illustrates the part that a 'cunning man' often played in these matters. This supposed protector against black witchcraft was one Old Baker, known as the Somerset Wizard.

Three women named Bryant, a mother and her two daughters, had consulted him because one of the girls was thought to be bewitched. He, of course, confirmed that this was so, and sold the mother some pills and potions for the girl to take, and also a mysterious packet of herbs. The actual prescription, in Old Baker's illiterate hand, read as follows: "The paper of arbs [herbs] is to be burnt, a small bit at a time, on a few coals, with a little hay and rosemary, and while it is burning, read the two first verses of the 68th Salm, and say the Lord's Prayer after".

After Old Baker's instructions had been carried out, the daughter had no further fits of supposed possession. But one thing remained to do; blood must be drawn upon the witch, to break her spell for ever. Mrs. Bryant told a neighbour "that old Mrs. Burges was the witch, and that she was going to get blood from her."

In the meantime, old Mrs. Burges had heard what she was being accused of, and went to Mrs. Bryant's house to confront her and deny the charge. Fortunately for her, she took a woman friend with her, whose exertions saved her life. The three Bryant women fell upon the old lady, and two of them held her down, while the third, the allegedly bewitched daughter, attacked her. They cried out for a knife, but none being handy, they used the nearest weapon, a large nail, with which they lacerated her arms.

The woman who had accompanied Mrs. Burges cried "Murder!" A mob soon assembled round the door of the house; but they did nothing to stop the 'blooding', saying that the old woman was a witch. By the time her friend had dragged her away from her attackers, Mrs. Burges had sustained fifteen or sixteen wounds, and was bleeding severely. She was taken to a surgeon, who dressed her injuries; and as a result of the affray, the Bryants found themselves summoned before a judge at Taunton Assizes.

Here the whole story came out, including the part played in it by Old Baker; of whom the judge observed, "I wish we had the fellow here. Tell him, if he does not leave off his conjuring, he will be caught, and charmed in a manner he will not like."

All three of the accused were found guilty, and sentenced to four months' imprisonment.

The belief in drawing blood on a witch was still lively in Devonshire 100 years later. In 1924 a Devonshire farmer was prosecuted for assaulting a woman neighbour, whom he accused of afflicting him by witchcraft. He had scratched her on the arm with a pin, and threatened to shoot her. The man insisted in court that the woman had ill-wished him and bewitched his pig. This was why he had tried to draw blood on her. He wanted the police to raid the woman's house and take possession of a crystal ball, which he said she used in her spells. Nothing the magistrates said would make him change his belief; and he was sentenced to one month's imprisonment.

It might be supposed that the flourishing technological society of modern Germany, after two World Wars, would have changed to such an extent that the days of witch persecutions would be quite forgotten. Nothing could be further from the truth. In the 1950s German newspapers carried frequent reports of the activities of 'witch-exorcists'—activities which sometimes ended in the death of the person they accused of being a witch.

In 1951 Johann Kruse founded in Hamburg The Archives for the Investigation of Witchery in Modern Times. In the same year Herr Kruse published a startling book, entitled *Witches among Us? Witchery and Magical Beliefs in Our Times* (West Germany, 1951). This book revealed facts about the continuing belief in witchcraft in Germany, which amazed his contemporaries.

The West German newspaper in 1952 reported no less than sixty-five cases involving witchcraft. Many of them were so horrible that it seems incredible they were printed in the columns of a modern newspaper, and not in some centuries-old black-lettered book.

For instance, there was the case of a young woman who was admitted to hospital at Haltern, three weeks after her wedding. She was dying; but before she expired she was able to tell how she came by her injuries. It appeared that just after her marriage an outbreak of some cattle disease had occurred on the farm of her husband's parents. A woman from Gelsenkirchen, who was a so-called soothsayer, had declared that the new bride was a witch, and responsible for the disease among the cattle. At the soothsayer's instigation, the family had imprisoned the poor girl in a dark room, where she was slowly done to death by starvation and beatings.

These self-styled 'soothsayers' or 'witch-exorcists', although professing to practise "white magic", in fact recommended the most revolting cruelties against both humans and animals, in their war against witchcraft. The idea very often was (one hopes that the past tense is appropriate, though this is doubtful), that if they could not torture the witch, the ill-treatment of an animal would somehow be conveyed to her.

Thus, a remedy for headaches supposedly caused by witchcraft was to tear a live black cat in two and lay the bloody remains upon the patient's head, where they must stay for three hours. The remedy for hens who were allegedly bewitched by the Evil Eye was to burn two hens alive in an oven. This was actually done, on the advice of a 'witch-exorcist', and reported in a German newspaper in May 1952.

Another practice recommended by the 'de-witchers' was the profanation of graves. Bones gathered from churchyards were sought for as a protection against bewitchment; and a prescription against fever (probably thought to be witch-induced) was: "Take human bones from three different graveyards, reduce them to charcoal, and give them, pounded to a powder, to the patient with brandy."

Other 'de-witching remedies' consisted of asafoetida—which is an evil-smelling gum-resin popularly known as 'Devil's dung'—horse dung and urine; and even human urine, which one 'witch-exorcist's' patients were induced to *drink*—at three marks a bottle!

Sometimes, among all this welter of filth and horror, there appeared a glimpse of a real memory of the ancient witchcraft. In the province of Hamburg, for instance, a peasant who believed his house was bewitched got his family to strip themselves naked every night, and sweep the floors with brooms, to drive the evil influence away. Knowingly or not, he was in fact carrying out an old witch rite, of being in a state of ritual nudity, and symbolically sweeping away evil, one of the things that a witch's broomstick is actually used for.

The authorities in Germany took notice of Herr Kruse's revelations, and in subsequent years several of these modern witch-finders were brought to trial and punished for their crimes and their defamation of innocent people. A book often mentioned in the course of these trials is the so-called *Sixth and Seventh Books of Moses, or Moses' Magical Art of Spirits,* which was a favourite of the 'witch-exorcists'. As a result, the sale of this book was banned in Germany. However, I have a copy in my own magical collection. (English translations have appeared in U.S.A., often clandestinely, without date or publisher's name). What it purports to be is the secret Words of Power which Moses used, and the signs and symbols which accompany them, which give the operator power over evil spirits. It is not a book of witchcraft, but derives from the darker side of ceremonial magic.

History shows us that the witch-finder expresses the loftiest motives; but at the same time his hand is always held out to receive money.

PHALLIC WORSHIP
It is only in comparatively modern times that the real nature of much

ancient religious symbolism has been able to be publicly discussed. The idea that people used the attributes of sexuality to represent something holy, was so shocking—to the eighteenth and nineteenth centuries in particular—that books which treated this subject, in however scholarly a manner, were sold from under the counter.

Nevertheless, it seems a very natural thing that the means of the transmission of life should represent, in the deeps of man's mind, the unknown and divine source of that life.

This has been recognised in the East since time immemorial, and the Sacred *Lingam*, or phallus of Shiva, has been worshipped in India as the emblem of the Life Force, without any embarrassment or idea of 'obscenity'. Until, that is, the civilised white man arrived, and usually either sniggered or was horrified, according to his temperament.

In years long past (and in some places not so long past), however, Western Europe also revered the cult of the phallus and its female counterpart, the *cteis* or *yoni*. Indeed, it was the phallic element in the Old Religion of witchcraft, which the Christian Church found particularly abominable.

Old pictures and woodcuts of the Devil, either presiding over a dance of witches, or going about the countryside looking for mischief, nearly always represent him with huge sexual organs prominently displayed. It is notable also, how the interrogators of witches, usually clerics, were always very interested in getting a detailed description of the Devil's sexual organs, from the person they were putting to the question. Nor would they be satisfied without an intimate account of what sexual relations the Devil had with his followers.

Most of this was the excited and prurient curiosity of enforced celibates; but perhaps not all of it. The more learned churchmen, who had read the classical authors' accounts of pagan worship, may well have realised that the artificial phallus had a definite religious significance. They were looking for survivals of the old pagan fertility cults; and they well knew that witchcraft was a continuation of these cults.

The jumping dance that witches performed, with a broomstick between their legs, was an obviously phallic rite. It was done to make the crops grow taller; and it had the same idea behind it as that which caused the Greeks and Romans to place in their gardens a statue of Priapus, the phallus god, with an enormous genital member, as magic to make the garden grow.

The phallus was also a luck-bringer, and an averter of the Evil Eye. In the latter role it was sometimes called the *fascinum,* because it was supposed to exercise the power of fascinating the sight, and drawing all glances to it; which was not a bad piece of practical psychology. People cannot help being interested in sex. Even prudery is only an inverted form of being fascinated by sexual matters.

Many little amulets or charms in the form of phalli have been found. They were made to hang around the neck usually; though some are in the form of brooches. Two specimens, which I have in my own collection of magical objects, illustrate the antiquity and widespread nature of the phallic cult. One is from Ancient Egypt, and is made of green faience. It is the form of a little man with an enormous genital member; and this amulet is made to hang around the neck.

The other was obtained a few years ago in Italy. Also to hang around the neck as a lucky charm, it is a good replica of an old Etruscan original, a winged phallus. I was told that these definitely pagan amulets, while not on public sale, are nevertheless quite easily obtained, and very popular. Their power to bring good fortune and avert the Evil Eye is still very definitely believed in.

In Ancient Rome the consecrated effigy of a phallus was regarded as bestowing sanctification and fertility, in certain circumstances. Thus a Roman bride sacrificed her virginity upon the life-sized phallus of a statue of the god Mutinus. Also, in the ancient world, and particularly in Egypt, statues of the gods of fertility were often made with a removable phallus, which was used separately in rituals designed to invoke the powers of fertility.

We are reminded of these ancient rites of a simpler age, when we read the many stories of the 'Devil' who presided over the witches' Sabbat having intercourse, or simulating intercourse, with the many women present, by means of an artificial phallus, which was part of his 'grand array', along with the horned mask and costume of animals' skins.

This rite was not done simply for sexual gratification; and the inquisitors who examined suspected witches knew it was not. The reason for its performance goes back a very long way into ancient history.

Of course, the published accounts of it were deliberately made as repulsive and horrifying as possible; because the Sabbat had to be represented in the Church's propaganda in such a way that people would not wish to go to it. However, the very repulsiveness of these accounts defeats its own ends; because if the witches' Sabbat was really as vile, agonising, filthy and generally repellent as the Church propagandists alleged, why on earth would anyone attend it, when they might be safe and warm in their beds? Yet we are informed that many people, particularly women, did.

It is amusing to note, as Rossell Hope Robbins has pointed out in his *Encyclopedia of Witchcraft and Demonology* (Crown Publishers Inc., New York, 1959), that most of the earlier accounts of the Sabbat declare that it included a sexual orgy of the most voluptuous and satisfying kind. Women, it was said, enjoyed sexual relations with the Devil *"maxima cum voluptate"*. Then, in the latter part of the fifteenth century, someone in the Church's propaganda department seems to have realised that this was not the sort of public image of the Sabbat that helped the Church's cause. So from that time on, the published stories of the Sabbat change. Intercourse with the Devil is said to be painful and horrible and only submitted to by force and with reluctance.

One feature in common, that nearly all the accounts possessed, was the statement that the Devil's penis was unnaturally cold. It was this that caused Margaret Murray to speculate, in her writings about the witch cult, that an artificial phallus was used in many cases.

Montague Summers, in his *History of Witchcraft and Demonology* (Kegan Paul, London, 1926, reprinted 1969), agrees with Margaret Murray's findings in this respect; though of course he goes on to hint that there were darker mysteries still, of demonic materialisation. However, he tells us significantly that the use of artificial phalli was well known to 'demonologists', and regarded by the Catholic Church as a grave sin. It is frequently mentioned in old Penitentials.

Representations of the phallus may be seen in the curious round towers attached to certain Sussex churches, notably the one at Piddinghoe. These are reminiscent of the round towers of Ireland, which antiquaries have long considered to be phallic monuments. There are some seventy or eighty of these towers to be found in Ireland, and no one knows who built them, or what their purpose was, though their phallic shape is self-evident. Some of them are over 100 feet in height. All are of great antiquity; so old, in fact, that some are supposed to be sunk beneath the surface of Lough Neagh, becoming visible beneath the waters when the weather is calm. Some famous sites of round towers are those at Glendalough, Ardmore, and upon the Rock of Cashel.

The beauty and mystery of these strange old monuments is another link with that basic worship of life which lies at the root of all ancient faiths.

Other instances of phallic symbolism are the tall, solitary standing stones called menhirs. A number of these ancient sacred stones may still be seen in Britain. For instance, at Borobridge in Yorkshire is a huge phallic monolith called The Devil's Arrow. In the same county at Rudston, one of the finest phallic menhirs still surviving may be seen standing next to a Christian church. The place-name of Rudston comes from the old Norse *hrodr-steinn*, 'the famous stone'. As the stone is much older than the church, the latter must have been deliberately built there, as a confrontation between the old faith and the new.

(*See also* FERTILITY, WORSHIP OF.)

Q

QUINTESSENCE

The occult philosophers of the most ancient times have handed down to us the idea of the Four Elements of Life, namely earth, air, fire and water. But above and beyond these, the elements of the visible world, they assigned a fifth, which they called the Quintessence, Aether or Spirit.

In this book there has inevitably been a frequent mention of the word 'power'. The power of magic, the power which is raised by the practices of witchcraft, and so on. But what is this power, so vaguely referred to? Is it merely suggestion, or a form of hypnotism? Or does it have a basis and origin in some unknown kind of energy?

These are questions not easily answered, for several reasons. However, consideration of the old idea of the Fifth Element, or Quintessence, is not irrelevant to such enquiry.

It is at least curious to note the universality of this belief. The people of the Ancient East share it equally with European alchemists and magicians of the Middle Ages. The Eastern yogis and fakirs, however, have their own words for what we call the Elements. They name them the Tattvas, the five manifestations of universal energy. The Hindu terms are as follows: Prithivi, symbolised by a yellow square, the equivalent of earth; Apas, whose symbol is a white crescent, meaning water; Tejas, a red triangle, fire; Vayu, a blue circle, air; Akasha, a black oval, Spirit or Aether.

And in the old Welsh Druidic traditions found in *Barddas*, we may note the following: "Earth, water, firmament, fire and *nyu;* and the *nyu* is God, and life, and intellect. From the first four are all death and mortality; and from the fifth are all life and animation, all power, knowledge and motion."

It is remarkable, too, how this ancient idea of an unseen universal energy has demanded re-examination in our own day, in view of the completely new concept (new to us, at any rate), which modern atomic physics has given us of the universe. We have become quite accustomed to the idea that matter and energy are interchangeable terms; yet this is the very idea that the old occult philosophers advanced, and that nineteenth-century materialism laughed to scorn.

In our own day, however, we have seen, not only an entirely new concept of matter and energy, but the serious study of such phenomena as those of what used to be called 'dowsing' or 'water-witching' and is now grandly termed radiesthesia.

This has led to a general consideration of what we may term 'borderline energies'. It seems very possible that in this mysterious region some, at any rate, of the real secrets of magical power may be found. (The pioneer work of Mr. T. C. Lethbridge, and the series of books he has published, detailing his investigations, deserve particular notice in this connection.)

Many scholars in the past have already studied these matters; but great confusion has been caused by the fact that nearly all of them, according to their own idiosyncrasies, have bestowed their own particular title upon what is fundamentally the same thing.

Mesmer, for instance, had his theory of 'animal magnetism', which he called: "A most fine, subtle fluid, which penetrates everything, and is capable of receiving and communicating all kinds of motions and impressions". He was, however, merely repeating in different terms the teachings of Paracelsus (1493-1534).

Paracelsus believed that the human body resembled a magnet, and that its 'magnetism' was directable by the will. He, too, advanced the idea of a 'universal fluid'—a concept which scientists of the Age of Reason regarded with ridicule. An invisible 'fluid', that could interpenetrate solid objects—what nonsense! Today, with our knowledge of radio waves and other kinds of radiation, it does not seem such nonsense after all.

The founders of the Spiritualist movement based many of their ideas on this concept of a 'borderline energy', something between the physical and the astral worlds, and partaking somewhat of the characteristics of both. They believed it to be the agent for the manifestations, at least those of a physical nature, which took place at their seances.

On the other side of the world, the Kahunas, or native magicians, of the Pacific Islands, had always believed in this force as the vehicle for their wonder-working. They called it Mana, and this word has come into general use by the students of comparative religion.

Lord Lytton, in his strange imaginative novel, *The Coming Race* (London, 1871), called this force Vril. He refers in his book to the factual researches by Baron Von Reichenbach, into a mysterious force which the Baron called Od or Odyle.

Other occultists have called this force 'Universal Life Energy', or 'The Great Magical Agent'. In Mary Anne Attwood's remarkable book, *A Suggestive Enquiry into the Hermetic Mystery* (first published in London in 1850), she suggests that this "Quintessence of the Philosophers" is the thing which the alchemists really meant by "Mercury", and not any material mercury or quicksilver.

It can at least be theorised that this Quintessence is the real subject of the mysterious inscription said to have been found upon the Emerald Tablet of Hermes. This tablet was so called because according to legend it was an inscribed plate of pure emerald, held in the hands of the corpse of the great Adept, Hermes Trismegistus. It is said to have been found in a cave-sepulchre near Hebron. Some versions of the legend say that the discoverer was Sara, the wife of Abraham; others that it was Alexander the Great or Apollonius of Tyana. Very early Arabic versions of the mysterious inscriptions have been found; and Latin versions circulated among occult students in medieval Europe.

The translation reads as follows:

> True without lie, certain and most true: that which is below is like unto that which is above, and that which is above is like unto that which is below, in order to carry out the miracles of the One Thing [*ad perpetranda miracula Rei Unius*].
>
> And as all things were from One, by one contemplation, so all things were born from that One Thing, by adaptation. [*Et sicut omnes res fuerunt ab Uno meditatione unius, sic omnes res natae fuerunt ab hac una re, adaptatione.*]
>
> Its father is the Sun, its mother is the Moon; the Wind has borne it in its womb; its nurse is the Earth.
>
> The father of all the forms [*telesmi*] of the world is here.
>
> Its power is complete [*integra*] if it is turned to the Earth.
>
> Thou shalt separate the Earth from the Fire, the subtle from the gross, gently, with much ingenuity.
>
> It rises from Earth to Heaven, and returns again to the Earth; and receives power from above and from below.
>
> Thus thou shalt possess the glory of the whole world; and all darkness will flee from you.

Here is the potent power of all strength; which overcomes all subtle things, and penetrates all solid things.

Thus was the world created.

Hence will be miraculous adaptations, of which the mode is here.

Therefore I am called Hermes, the Thrice Great; having three parts of the philosophy of the whole world.

That which I have said about the Operation of the Sun is fulfilled. [*Completum est quod dixi de Operatione Solis.*]

This inscription is supposed to contain the most profound magical secrets, for those who can understand its cryptic message.

It certainly accords with what many occultists believe about the universal life energy, the immediate source of which for our solar system is thought to be the sun. Our sun sends out a great field of force, which the planets, having no light of their own, each reflect, and by so doing impart to it their own influences. The moon, although comparatively very small, reflects a great amount of force upon our earth, because of her nearness. Human beings absorb vital energy, which the Hindus call Prana, by breathing, and its great storehouse in the human body is said to be the solar plexus.

A great deal could be written about this aspect of occultism, and the relations of this Quintessence and its modifications to some, at any rate, of the real powers of witchcraft, as indeed of magic generally. However, considerations of space forbid me here to do more than indicate a possible line of study.

I must, nevertheless, remark on the work of Wilhelm Reich, and his discovery of what he calls orgone. The famous psychologist has written extensively about the properties of this subtle energy, which he says can be demonstrated in living organisms, in the atmosphere, the earth and in the radiation of the sun.

He claims it to be a universal cosmic energy, which can be measured and made visible. Its colour is blue-violet; and Reich considers the blue of the sky, and the blue haze seen at a distance in sunny weather, to be manifestations of orgone energy. The earth, he says, is surrounded by a field of orgone energy, which moves round it with a pulsating motion, from west to east. According to Reich, all substances contain orgone, as it penetrates everything; but only living substances radiate it.

R

REINCARNATION

Some years ago, in the 1950s, Mr Geoffrey Gorer made an enquiry into the current religious beliefs of the English people. Its results were printed in *The Observer;* and Mr Gorer wrote that the most surprising thing he had discovered was the prevalence of the belief in reincarnation. Thinking that this idea belonged exclusively to the creeds of the East, he was at a loss to account for its widespread acceptance in modern England.

The work of occultists such as Madame Blavatsky, and popular romantic stories like Ivor Novello's *Perchance to Dream,* made the belief that we live more lives than one known among the public generally. However, this is far from giving such an idea widespread and serious acceptance; unless it was not in reality an alien idea to the soul of the British race at all.

In fact, reincarnation is a very old idea indeed; and it is part of the Old Religion of Western Europe, as well as of the faiths of India and Asia. Charles Godfrey Leland has testified to its survival among the secrets of *La Vecchia Religione* in Italy; and Leland's own beautiful poem, "One Thousand Years Ago", is evidence of his own belief in this doctrine. The last verse of it runs:

> Thou and I but yesterday
> Met in fashion's show.
> Love, did you remember me,
> Love of long ago?
> Yes: we kept the fond oath sworn
> One thousand years ago.

So general was the acceptance of reincarnation throughout the civilised world at the beginning of the Christian era, that the Early Christian Church had many eminent members who subscribed to the belief. Only slowly did it fall into disfavour, and become replaced by the doctrines of death, judgement, heaven and hell, final and fixed for eternity; of vicarious atonement instead of working out one's own destiny; or of the dead sleeping in their graves until the Last Judgement.

All of these latter doctrines were frightening and depressing, but they were very good for keeping people in order, and submissive to the rule of the Church. Also, however monstrously wicked a medieval nobleman, for instance, might have been, he had only to make a good death-bed repentance and die fortified by the rites of Holy Church, and all was well. He had no need to fear the destiny he had made for himself catching up with him in subsequent lives on earth, as the pagan philosophers had taught. It was the Pope who held the keys of heaven and hell, and delegated his power to the bishops and priests. The old powers of Fate, Destiny or Nemesis were just accursed heathen notions.

As for the serf, it was God who had appointed his servitude to his feudal lord; and his chief virtue was to know his place and submit. There was only one life, in which some were appointed lords and barons, and others artisans and serfs. The one blood was noble, the other base. To contemplate the possibility of more than one life, meant that things might get dangerously mixed up, to the subversion of the social order.

Subversion is what the witch cult was constantly being accused of by its ecclesiastical critics. In other words, there were doctrines being secretly taught and disseminated among the common people, which were not orthodox doctrines. Ideas were being kept alive, against which the Church had pronounced its anathema.

The old Druidical teachings, for instance, very definitely contained the idea of reincarnation. So did the Qabalistic teachings, secretly studied by the Rosicrucians. The Gnostics and Neo-Platonists retained much of the philosophy of the ancient world. This philosophy had as one of its most respected masters Pythagoras, who taught reincarnation and claimed to remember his past lives.

In Dryden's version of the Roman poet Ovid, Pythagoras speaks as follows:

> Death has no power th' immortal soul to slay,
> That, when its present body turns to clay,
> Seeks a fresh home; and with unlessened might
> Inspires another frame with life and light.
> So I myself (well I the past recall),

When the fierce Greeks begirt Troy's holy wall,
Was brave Euphorbus: and in conflict drear
Poured forth my blood beneath Atrides' spear.
The shield this arm did bear I lately saw
In Juno's shrine, a trophy of that war.

Virgil, in the Sixth Book of his *Aeneid,* also expounds the doctrine of reincarnation, and describes how the souls in the Otherworld gathered to drink the waters of Lethe, which made them forget the memories of the past, before being reborn in new bodies upon earth.

Apollonius of Tyana, the famous philosopher and Adept of the first century A.D., also believed in reincarnation, and said he could remember a previous life in which he was a ship's pilot.

Thus it can be amply shown that reincarnation is not an idea confined to the religions of the East. Herodotus, who was an initiate of the Egyptian Mysteries, claimed that the Ancient Egyptians were the first to teach immortality of the soul, and its evolution through a cycle of many lives; and that the Greeks later adopted this opinion as if it were their own.

The old versions of reincarnation sometimes also involved the transmigration of souls, or metempsychosis. The latter teaches that the soul may be reborn in the body of an animal or even a plant or tree; whereas present-day believers in reincarnation generally hold that, while the soul may *ascend* to the human level through other life-forms, once that level has been reached there is no going back. Evolution continues by means of other human lives; until this earth's level is transcended, and the soul is confined in flesh no more. Between earthly lives, the soul dwells upon the planes of the Unseen, at such a level, high or low, as its attainment is fitted for.

The Eastern doctrine of Karma has been much misunderstood in the West. It does not mean 'reward and punishment'; at least not in the way that many people think. It says nothing about our limited earthly ideas of reward and punishment at all. The Sanscrit word *karma* simply means 'action'. This carries the implication that every action must produce its appropriate reaction, sooner or later; and if this process is not worked out in one life, then it will be worked out in succeeding lives.

We cannot dogmatise about the deep things of human destiny, from our limited viewpoint. This is why the pagan religions conceived of Karma in the form of Fate, Destiny, or Wyrd, being dispensed to mortals by the triple goddess. The Greeks had their idea

of the Three Fates, who were also called the Moirai. The Romans
called them the Parcae. Romano-Celtic Britain had the Three
Mothers, the Matres. To the Old Norse peoples who were our northern ancestors, the three goddesses of Fate were the Nornir; and the
Old English concept of them was 'The Weird Sisters', combined
eventually into one goddess, Wyrd, meaning 'Destiny'. There is still
an old expression, 'to dree one's weird', meaning to fulfil one's
destiny.

The triple goddess of Fate was associated with the phases of the
moon, probably because the moon is man's oldest meter-out of time.
As they revered the moon goddess, so the ideas of reincarnation
and destiny naturally commended themselves to witches. Also, they
provided an alternative idea of life after death, and the destiny of
the soul, to that of the Christian Church; an idea, moreover, which
was much older, and part of the racial mythology of Western Europe.

Caesar, in his brief references to the Druids, tells us: "As one
of their leading dogmas, they inculcate this: that souls are not annihilated but pass after death from one body to another, and they
hold that by this teaching men are much encouraged to valour,
through disregarding the fear of death."

Diodorus Siculus says of the Druids: "Among them the doctrine
of Pythagoras prevails, according to which the souls of men are im-
mortal, and after a fixed term recommence to live, taking upon themselves a new body."

In some ancient Gaelic stories, we find the idea of reincarnation
appearing. For instance, the men of Ulster urged their hero
Cuchulainn to marry, because they believed that "his rebirth would
be of himself"; that is, he would be reborn as one of his own descendants. They wanted the soul of this great warrior to remain with
their tribe.

Also, another great warrior, Finn MacCoul, was said to have been
reborn after 200 years, as an Ulster king called Mongan. This king
was an historical personage, who died about A.D. 625.

The story is well-known, of the inscription which was found upon
the tomb of King Arthur, *"Hic jacet Arthurus, Rex quondam, Rexque
futurus";* meaning, "Here lies Arthur, the once and future King."

However, it has generally been argued by commentators upon our
Celtic past, that the Celts did not believe in reincarnation, or trans-
migration of souls, in quite the same way that the peoples of the
East do. The Celtic genius cast its own glamour over all things that it

touched, hiding its beliefs in legends and tales. The atmosphere of haunted twilight, and the peat-fire flame, that comes with Celtic things, is very different from that of the Orient or of Ancient Greece or Alexandria. But this does not mean that the arcane traditions of the British race are in any way belittled, rather the reverse, by being of their own nature. The diamond of Truth is a jewel with many facets, flashing now one colour and now another; but the jewel does not change.

Commentators have also frequently stated that the idea of Karma is peculiar to the Far East. However, it can be found, either implied or openly revealed, in Western beliefs as well.

For instance, Plotinus, who was born in Egypt in 205 or 206 A.D., tells us in his works: "The gods bestow on each the destiny which appertains to him, and which harmonises with his antecedents in his successive existences. Every one who is not aware of this is grossly ignorant of divine matters."

RITUAL MURDER

In recent years, the western world has been appalled by the slaying of the beautiful film star, Sharon Tate, and the other victims of ritual killings in California. (*See* MANSON, CHARLES.) Ritual murder has been all too much in the news. One of man's most primitive and truly savage rites has been shown, in the grimmest manner, to have survived into our own day.

Hideous as these stories are, they are by no means the only evidence of ritual murder in connection with black magic, to be found in modern times. There are still sorcerers who believe that 'the blood is the life', and that the life-force of a sacrificed victim can give their dark rituals the power to succeed.

It is idle to pretend that black magic does not exist. There are many power-hungry people in the twilight regions of the occult, who seek merely the most direct means to get what they want. Sometimes they put forward the old argument that the end justifies the means, forgetting that the means also conditions the end.

In more primitive days, the sacrifice of living things was a regular part of religious ritual of all kinds. Blood sacrifice on a considerable scale is enjoined in the Old Testament upon the worshippers of Jehovah. On one occasion, in the case of Jephthah's daughter, it is quite clear that a human sacrifice was demanded and given.

The sacrifice of the Divine King was distinguished by the fact that in this case the victim was a voluntary one. He knew what accepting the office of king meant. In the eyes of his subjects also, his death would not have been murder at all; simply the following of ancient and sacred custom.

Some Egyptologists now believe that the earlier Pharaohs of Egypt died sacrificial deaths, probably by the bite of the sacred serpent. This sheds a new light on the way in which Cleopatra, the last heiress of the Pharaohs, died. By accepting the fatal bite of the asp, she met death in the traditional manner of her proud ancestors.

The cult of the Thugs in India, who worshipped the goddess Kali, regarded ritual murder as a sacred religious duty. This cult survived until the early nineteenth century, and accounted in its day for the killing of literally thousands of people. Its organisation was complex and thorough, and the slaying of the victim was carried out according to a strictly prescribed ritual. He was swiftly and expertly strangled by a scarf, in which a silver coin, dedicated to Kali, had been knotted.

In many primitive societies ritual murder was closely associated with ritual cannibalism. Garry Hogg, in his book *Cannibalism and Human Sacrifice* (Robert Hale, London, 1958), points out that the motive for cannibalism, while sometimes sheer hunger for tasty flesh-meat, was more often a magical one. It was based upon the belief that by eating the body, or some part of it, or drinking the blood of a sacrificial victim, one could acquire that victim's 'soul-substance' or life-force.

An example of this was found in England, when archaeologists investigated a long barrow near the great earth-work called Maiden Castle, in Dorset. It was evidently a burial-place of some importance, as it extended for nearly a third of a mile. The skeleton of a man was found buried within it; and from the condition of the bones, the archaeologists formed the conclusion that ritual cannibalism was involved. The man had been killed and eaten. He was probably a sacrificial victim; perhaps a Sacred King.

Such ceremonies belong to our primitive past. When ritual killing takes place in our own days, its aspect is truly dark and terrible, and belongs to the realm of black magic. Yet take place it does, as many of the police forces of the world could amply verify.

In 1963, a well-attested story of human sacrifice for black magic came from Spain. On 21st May of that year, a 10-year-old-girl called Maria Diaz, of Figueras, disappeared. She was never seen again; but a piece of her dress was found, in strange and suspicious circumstances, upon the Holy Mountain of San Salvador. This mountain is crowned by an old, roofed-over sanctuary or altar-place, built in former days by monks. In the small hours of the morning after Maria disappeared, a shepherd heard strange sounds coming through the darkness, from the summit of San Salvador above him. He listened in fear to shrill wailings, a kind of chanting, and wild cries. The next day, he climbed up to the old altar-place, to see what had been happening. He found various symbols drawn upon the dry earth of the floor. The embers of a fire were still smouldering. A smell of incense hung in the air. There were the burnt-down remains of black candles. And there was a piece of charred cloth, with a faded pattern of pink check. Maria's mother later identified this as being from her daughter's dress. Police enquiries unearthed the fact that Maria had been last seen getting into a large car, driven by two men in bright-coloured summer shirts. The authorities believed it to be a case of black magic, and probably ritual murder.

One of California's Satanist cults has found a nastily ingenious way to hold a 'human sacrifice' and yet keep within the law. Their Satanic chapel is the basement of an old building, where a 6-foot-tall crucifix hangs upside down over an altar made of oak, and adorned with weird carvings. Skulls are used as chalices, and the scene is dimly lit by flickering candles. But the naked girl victim who lies upon the altar is actually a realistic, life-size plastic doll.

The doll is hollow, and inside is a plastic bag filled with fake 'blood' and 'entrails'. In the course of the ritual, the self-styled priest of Satan gashes the figure open with a knife, and the 'blood' flows freely, to the accompaniment of wild yells from his congregation, many of whom are young girls. Magic signs are drawn upon the girls' bodies in 'blood', and the ritual ends with a sexual orgy.

One may dismiss this sort of thing as merely childish mumbo-jumbo; but what ideas might it suggest to a person of precariously-balanced mind, who attended a ritual like this?

When the bodies of Dr Victor Ohta and his family were found in Santa Cruz, California, in October 1970, the Santa Cruz authorities had no doubt that they were dealing with yet another ritual killing. Five people died in this massacre; and at the scene of the crime police found a note which read as follows:

Today World War Three will begin as brought to you by the people of the Free Universe. From this day forward anyone and/or company of persons who misuses the natural environment or destroys same will suffer the penalty of death by the people of the Free Universe.

I and my comrades from this day forth will fight until death or freedom against anything or anyone who does not support natural life on this planet. Materialism must die or mankind will.

The note was signed "Knight of Wands", "Knight of Cups", "Knight of Swords", and "Knight of Pentacles". There was much speculation as to what these strange signatures meant. They are, of course, the four knights or horsemen of the Tarot pack. (*See* TAROT.) My own theory is that in this context they were meant to symbolise the Four Horsemen of the Apocalypse, the embodiments of Plague, Warfare, Famine and Death.

Another grisly idea from the distant past has appeared in the horrific series of murders in San Francisco, perpetrated by a killer who calls himself Zodiac. Evidently influenced by the occult, this man sent messages to the police claiming that when he died he would be reborn in paradise, and all those whom he had killed would be his slaves. This is reminiscent of the beliefs behind ancient sacrifices carried out at the tombs of kings, when their slaves and concubines were sent to accompany them in the next world.

The combination of a smattering of occultism and the use of hallucinogenic drugs, without any deep knowledge of either, can undoubtedly produce a kind of uprush from the abyss of the collective unconscious, with highly dangerous results. This, it seems to me, is a possible explanation of the events in California which have shocked the world.

Another form of ritual murder was the foundation sacrifice; that is, a sacrificial victim killed when the foundations of a building were laid. The blood of the victim was offered to the gods, and his soul was believed to become a guardian ghost, keeping watch over the building.

In 1966 archaeologists excavated the remains of a Roman fort at Reculver, on the coast of Kent. Beneath the foundations of the building no less than eleven skeletons of infants, young babies between two and eight weeks old, were discovered.

The archaeologist who made this discovery, Mr B. J. Phelp, gave his opinion that three of these infants were definitely foundation sacrifices, laid down sometime during the third century A.D.

A strange sidelight on this grim discovery was afforded by a local ghost story. There was a tradition that the ghostly crying of a child could be heard by night on the shore, where the fort once stood. People avoided the place after dark. This is one of many instances, where an old ghost story has been found by archaeologists to have some sort of basis in fact.

Today, the ceremony of laying a foundation stone is still carried out; and apart from the speechmaking by the mayor or some distinguished visitor, there still remains an echo of the older rites. Very often coins, or some objects of interest or value, are laid beneath the stone. This is the modern form of the foundation sacrifice.

A remarkable thing is that the custom of foundation sacrifice, and even of a human victim, did not by any means cease with the coming of Christianity. Quite a number of old churches have yielded proof of this, when their foundations were for some reason dug up. Many strange details on this subject can be found in *Builders' Rites and Ceremonies: the Folk Lore of Masonry,* by G. W. Speth (privately printed for the Quatuor Coronati Lodge, London, 1931).

A notable example was Holsworthy Church in Devonshire. When some restoration work was being done here in 1885, a skeleton was found beneath one of the walls. The evidence indicated that it was that of someone who had been hurriedly buried alive, undoubtedly a foundation sacrifice.

Sometimes animal bones have been discovered, concealed in old churches and other buildings. We may deduce from this that as time passed, animals were substituted for human victims; and later still the bones of animals were supposed to be sufficient, perhaps with the original purpose half forgotten.

When the roof of St. George's Chapel, Windsor, was repaired in the nineteenth century, some bones of animals were found concealed there. A similar discovery was made when Old Blackfriars Bridge, over the River Thames in London, was pulled down in 1867. The foundations of one of the arches were found to have been laid upon a quantity of bones, some of which were human.

This custom of foundation sacrifice prevailed all over Europe and also in Eastern countries. Nor is it entirely forgotten in the present day. It was reported in 1969 that a bizarre rumour was frightening people of Mexico City. A new underground railway was under construction; and fantastic stories were being circulated, that children and adults were being kidnapped and buried under the foundations of the subway, in order to make it safe against earthquakes and subsidences. Official denials of the 'human sacrifice' story were made; but some superstitious Mexicans remained unconvinced.

ROYALTY, ITS CONNECTIONS WITH WITCHCRAFT

The name of King William Rufus has often been linked with witchcraft. 'Rufus' means 'red', which, as the colour of life, is sacred to the Old Religion. Rufus was the Red King. The grandson of Robert the Devil, he was openly pagan, and disliked by the Christian monks who compiled the chronicles of history. Hence his notoriety as a 'bad king', though in fact he was no worse a king than most of his contemporaries.

His death in the New Forest "on the morrow of Lammas", one of the Great Sabbats of the Old Religion, is still one of Britain's historical mysteries. (*See* LAMMAS.)

Less well-known is the tradition that the Plantagenet kings favoured the Old Religion, and some of them actively, though secretly, followed it. The name Plantagenet is derived from *Planta genista*, the old name for the broom plant, which was their badge. Another old name for the green broom is hag-weed, meaning 'witch-weed', because it made the brooms that witches were popularly supposed to fly upon.

Evelyn Eaton's remarkable historical novel *The King is a Witch* (Cassell, London, 1965) is based upon the connection of the Plantagenets and especially Edward III, with witchcraft.

The foundation of the Order of the Garter by Edward III certainly seems to have been connected with the Old Religion. (*See* GARTERS AS WITCHES' SIGNS.) His son, associated with him in the Order, was always known as the Black Prince. No really adequate reason for this title has ever been given; except that it was supposedly because he wore black armour. It could, however, have had quite another significance. The male leader of a coven was sometimes known as "The Man in Black".

The lady whom the Black Prince married was called 'The Fair Maid of Kent'; and again, the female leader of a coven was sometimes known as 'The Maiden'. All these things, taken singly, could be mere coincidence. Added together, they make a significant picture.

Their son, who became the tragic Richard II, adopted a badge, the White Hart, which is an emblem directly connected with the Old Religion. As the white roebuck hidden in the thicket, it appears in bardic myths, sometimes as a symbol of the human soul, sometimes representing the secret of the Mysteries, and sometimes standing for the sacrificed Divine King himself.

The idea of the Divine King, who has to die at the end of an appointed term, in order that his blood may bring prosperity and fertility to the land, goes back to the remotest antiquity. The whole mystique of royalty and kingship is involved in it. So is the feeling of the sacredness of the king's person, the belief in the Divine Rights of Kings, and so on.

Margaret Murray, in her book *The Divine King in England,* argues that Britain's earlier kings were in fact ritually killed. Sometimes, she says, another victim was offered in their place, so that the king might live for a further term of years; but eventually he had to make the supreme sacrifice, because that was the real purpose and secret of kingship.

A suggestion of witchcraft in connection with the Plantagenet dynasty appears again in the time of King Edward IV. The story began in a place which to this day has a reputation for hauntings and uncanny happenings, namely Whittlewood Forest in Northamptonshire. Here Edward IV first met the beautiful Elizabeth Woodville, under a tree which was long after known as the Queen's Oak.

She was a widow, whose husband had fought on what proved to be the wrong side in the Wars of the Roses. On his death in battle, his estates had been forfeited. Elizabeth pleaded with the king to restore them, for the sake of her orphaned children. The king, enchanted by the fair lady he had met under the oak tree, did far more. He fell headlong in love with her, and they were secretly married, early on May Day morning, in the nearby town of Grafton.

The circumstances of this romantic meeting in the fairy-haunted forest, and the secret marriage on the morrow of one of the witches' Sabbats, no doubt suggested to many people a connection with the Old Religion. Moreover, Elizabeth's mother, Jacquetta, Duchess of Bedford, was later accused, during a troubled period of rebellion, of practising witchcraft; though at the time the affair came to nothing.

It was not forgotten, however. When King Edward IV died in 1483, by the terms of the king's will his brother Richard was named as Protector of the Realm and guardian of the young prince who was heir to the throne. But before the boy could be crowned Parliament proclaimed the late king's children illegitimate, saying that his marriage with Elizabeth Woodville was unlawful.

One of the grounds for this declaration was that the marriage "was made of great presumption, without the knowing and assent of the lords of this land, and also by sorcery and witchcraft, committed by the said Elizabeth and her mother Jacquetta Duchess of Bedford, as the common opinion of the people, and the public voice and fame is through all this land".

It has often been presumed by historians that because the accusation of witchcraft against Elizabeth Woodville was instrumental in placing Richard III on the throne, it was therefore without any foundation. However, the circumstances of her marriage to King Edward IV were certainly unusual, and it seems possible that it was a marriage according to the Old Religion rather than a Christian one. No adequate reason was ever given for Henry VII's action in depriving the widowed Elizabeth Woodville of all her possessions, and shutting her up in a nunnery for the rest of her life—even though he had married her daughter by Edward IV.

Richard III, who was defeated and killed at the Battle of Bosworth in 1485, was the last of the Plantagenets. His famous banner of the White Boar is another example of a device connected with the Old Religion. The boar's curving tusks, resembling the crescent moon, are still valued as amulets and luck-bringers; and white pigs were sacred to the Druidic moon goddess Cerridwen. Some historians now believe that Richard was by no means as villainous as the Tudors made him out to be. There is even a society which exists for the purpose of clearing the name of Richard III.

With the arrival of the Tudor dynasty, many changes took place in England. One by one, any possible claimants to the throne that remained of the older stock were ruthlessly eliminated. But the sovereigns of England continued to be crowned, with Christian ceremony, upon the pagan Stone of Destiny that forms the basis of the Coronation Chair in Westminster Abbey. King Edward I brought this mysterious stone from Scotland in 1297; and it was sanctified by a legend that it was the stone upon which Jacob had rested his head at Bethel. However, the Saxon kings were also crowned upon a sacred stone, which is still preserved at Kingston-on-Thames. According to ancient Celtic legend, the Lia Fail, or Stone of Destiny, is one of the four treasures of the Tuatha De Danaan, the people of the goddess Dana, and its origin is certainly pagan. (*See* TAROT CARDS.)

One of the ancestors of our present Queen, Janet Douglas, Lady Glamis, was burned as a witch. Her execution took place in 1537 on the Castle Hill at Edinburgh. She was accused of having plotted

to take away the life of King James V of Scotland, by poison and
witchcraft. Her beauty and her noble birth made the case long remembered. By some accounts, she was entirely innocent of the charge,
and the motive behind the accusations against her was political
intrigue.

Others, however, have claimed that Janet Douglas was indeed a
witch, and that some part at any rate of the famous haunting of
Glamis Castle is attributable to her. A spirit that was her familiar,
the legend says, continues to trouble the castle, and so does the
phantom of the lady herself.

In the fifteenth and sixteenth centuries accusations of witchcraft
in high places were numerous. They were often made against someone the ruling monarch wanted to get rid of; because a charge of
witchcraft was a very difficult thing to disprove. Frequently, too,
people in high positions did employ witches, astrologers and other
practitioners of occult arts, for their own purposes. If anything went
wrong and awkward revelations became public, it was usually the
low-born witch who was hanged or burned at the stake, while their
aristocratic employer escaped the severest punishment.

King James I, in whose reign the most severe law against witchcraft was passed, had good reason to fear witches. Some years earlier,
in Scotland, a number of witches had conspired against him, in the
hope of putting their own Grand Master, Francis, Earl of Bothwell,
on the throne. Bothwell had a claim to the Scottish throne if James
died without an heir. However, their plot was discovered, and many
of them were burned at the stake, having confessed that they had
made an image of the king "so that another might rule in his place,
and the government might go to the Devil".

Bothwell himself was imprisoned in Edinburgh Castle. But before
he could be brought to trial, his friends organised his escape. For
some time the king lived in terror of Bothwell. But when a son was
born to James and his queen, Bothwell realised that his chances were
slender, and decided to leave the country. He settled in Naples, probably because it was near Benevento, the witch centre of Italy; and
he continued to be known there as a practitioner of magic.

King James had, very naturally, taken a close personal interest
in the examination of the North Berwick witches who had been Bothwell's followers. One leading witch, Agnes Sampson, he questioned
himself, and she told him such strange things, says a contemporary
account, "that his Majesty said they [the witches] were all extreme

liars". Stung by this remark, Agnes Sampson had proceeded to prove her powers to him. "Taking his Majesty a little aside, she declared unto him the very words which passed between the King's Majesty and his Queen at Upslo in Norway, the first night of their marriage, with their answer each to other. Whereat the King's Majesty wondered greatly, and swore by the living God, that he believed that all the Devils in hell could not have discovered the same: acknowledging her words to be most true, and therefore gave the more credit to the rest which is before declared".

James I virtually declared war on witches; and under the Puritan Commonwealth they had an even worse time. But the restoration of Charles II must have seemed to them as if the old connection between royalty and the Craft of the Wise had returned. The incident of the fugitive king being saved by hiding in the oak-tree at Boscobel is often depicted in contemporary designs. The way in which the king's face looks through the foliage very much resembles the old picture of the Green Man, the pagan god of the woods. (*See* GREEN MAN.)

The belief that the sovereign's touch could cure diseases is certainly connected with the sacredness of the royal blood, and this again goes back to the ideas of the Old Religion. The last British monarch to carry out public ceremonies of touching the sick was Queen Anne. The chief, though not the only disease supposed to be healed by the royal touch, was scrofula, which was called 'the king's evil' for this reason.

S

SABBAT

There are eight Sabbats in the witches' year, four Greater Sabbats and four Lesser Sabbats.

The four Greater Sabbats are Candlemas (2nd February), May Eve (30th April), Lammas (1st August), and Halloween (31st October). These occasions correspond to the four great yearly feasts celebrated by the Druids and by our Celtic ancestors. The Druidic names for them were Imbolc or Oimelc (Candlemas), Beltane (May Eve), Lughnassadh (Lammas) and Samhein (Halloween). May Eve was also known as Walpurgis Night.

The Lesser Sabbats were the two solstices at midsummer and midwinter, and the two equinoxes in spring and autumn. These may vary by a day or two each year, as they depend upon the sun's apparent entry into the zodiacal signs of Capricorn (winter solstice), Cancer (summer solstice), Aries (spring equinox) and Libra (autumn equinox). These occasions also were celebrated as festivals by the Druids.

Some modern witches believe that a certain psychic impulse, or magical current or tide, commences at the equinox or solstice, reaches its peak at the following Greater Sabbat, and then declines until the next station of the sun, when a new magical tide commences, and so on. Thus, for instance, the tide which is set in motion, coursing invisibly through all Nature at the spring equinox, reaches its peak on May Eve, and then slowly ebbs until the summer solstice, when a new impulse commences; and so on.

Witches celebrated (and continue to celebrate) these old ritual occasions with dancing and enjoyment, drinking the health of the Old Gods, and generally holding high revel. In the olden times, they lit big bonfires outdoors in some lonely place, and several covens might gather together on the Sabbat night.

Sometimes they met in houses belonging to some member of the cult. It is notable that one of the most detailed descriptions we have of such a meeting in a house comes from Sweden, where the cold climate would have made such shelter particularly welcome. In 1670 some Swedish witches confessed that their meeting place, which they called Blockula, was situated in a large meadow; it had a gate before it, painted in various colours.

"In a huge large Room of this House, they said, there stood a very long table, at which the Witches did sit down; And that hard by this Room was another Chamber in which there were very lovely and delicate Beds." (*Sadducismus Triumphatus,* London, 1681). In other words, this was someone's well-appointed country house, as seen through the eyes of poor peasants. In more southern latitudes, the accounts of the Sabbat by confessing witches more often describe outdoor meetings, though with a good blazing bonfire to provide light and heat, and to cook food.

The word 'Sabbat' has caused much speculation as to its origin. Some think it is simply the witches' 'Sabbath night', as opposed to the Christian day of rest. However, the latter is more properly Sunday. The Jewish Sabbath is Saturday, the seventh day that was kept holy. It takes its name from *Shabbathai,* Saturn, the planet which rules the seventh day. Sunday is the first day of the week; so to call it the Sabbath, though often done, is not really correct.

However, the word, 'Sabbat' has associations which are older than Christianity; and there is no reason whatever to connect the festival of the witches with the Jewish Sabbath.

Sabadius or Sabazius was a title of the orgiastic god Dionysus, the god of ecstasy, who was worshipped with wild dances and revelry. The celebrants of his Mysteries raised the cry of *Sabai!* or *Evoi Sabai!*

This seems the most likely derivation of the word 'Sabbat'. We find, centuries later, accounts of the witches' dancing, in which this word is used as a cry: *"Har, har, Hou, Hou, danse ici, danse la, joue ici, jou la, Sabbat, Sabbat!"* ("Har, har, Hou, Hou, dance here, dance there, play here, play there, Sabbat, Sabbat!")

This old chant is given by the French demonologist, Bodin; and Margaret Murray in her book *The God of the Witches* (Faber, London, 1952), has pointed out how in Bodin's version he substituted '*diable*' for the word 'Hou'. The version which was used by the witches of Guernsey, in the Channel Islands, is identical with Bodin's, save for containing this old Celtic word Hou, which is a name of the god who appears in British myth as Hu Gadarn, Hu the Mighty. This shows how anti-witch writers substituted devils for any mention of the witches' gods, because they wanted to prove witches guilty of devil worship. Some present-day journalists still make use of the same technique.

Other old names for the Sabbat are the Basque Akhelarre, the French Lanne de Bouc, and the Spanish Prado del Cabron, all of which mean the same thing, 'The Field of the Goat'. Another Spanish name for the Sabbat is La Treguenda.

A curious detail in many old accounts of the witches' Sabbat, is the statement that there was never any salt at their feasts. This would have made the meal very savourless and uninviting, if it were true. Priestly commentators explained it by saying that salt was the symbol of salvation, and therefore witches hated it; but I think there is quite another explanation.

What was missing from the food table at the Sabbat was not the salt, but the salt-cellar, or salt-vat as it used to be called. The reason for this was, that the placing of this object upon the table was a mark of social distinctions: and at the Sabbat there were no social distinctions. All members of the witch cult were brothers and sisters.

Chambers' *Book of Days* has some relevant observations on this subject: "One of the customs of great houses, in former times, was to place a large ornamental *salt-vat* (commonly but erroneously called salt-foot) upon the table, about the centre, to mark the part below which it was proper for tenants and dependents to sit."

The account states further: "This practice of old days, so invidiously distinguishing one part of a company from another, appears to have been in use throughout both England and Scotland, and to have extended at least to France. It would be an error to suppose that the distinction was little regarded on either hand, or was always taken good-humouredly on the part of the inferior persons. There is full evidence in old plays, and other early productions of the press, that both parties were fully sensible of what sitting below the salt inferred."

Chambers quotes an old English ballad, as containing a pointed allusion to this humiliating practice:

> Thou art a carle of mean degree,
> The salt it doth stand between me and thee.

This quotation shows further how the word 'salt' could mean salt-cellar. It was only in this sense that the salt was banished from the witches' feast.

Some writers have stated that there are no real accounts of the Sabbat being held in Britain, and that it only appears in the stories of Continental authors, who were dedicated witch-hunters and demonologists. This statement, however, is against quite a reasonable amount of evidence.

It is true that the stories of Sabbats in England are less detailed than the accounts from Scotland, or from the Continent. One reason is, obviously, that in England witches were not subjected to torture (legally, at any rate) in order to make them confess; whereas in Scotland and elsewhere in Europe, torture was applied mercilessly. However, it does not necessarily follow that English witches did not meet in covens, or attend Sabbats, the same as witches in other places did.

The descriptions of Sabbats held in Somerset, as given by Joseph Glanvil in the seventeenth century, are fairly detailed. He tells us of two covens, one at Wincanton and the other at Brewham. Both consisted of thirteen people, whose names are preserved in legal records. They met by night, either in each others' cottages or in the open air. Two named meeting-places are "the Common near Trister Gate" and "a place called Hussey's-Knap" in Brewham Forest.

At these meetings, according to one of their number, a witch called Elisabeth Style, "They have usually Wine or good Beer, Cakes, Meat or the like." This meal was set out on a white tablecloth, and the leader, the Man in Black, presided over the feast. After the meal, the witches danced to the music of a pipe or a cittern (an old-fashioned stringed instrument, played with a plectrum).

The chief also instructed them in magic, showing them how to make and use wax images. He gave them a greenish-coloured ointment, with which they anointed themselves on the forehead and wrists. This seems to have been a 'flying ointment,' made from narcotic herbs.

Glanvil gives an interesting detail: "At their parting they say *A Boy! Merry meet, merry part.*" This is almost certainly a worn-down version of an old pagan cry: 'Evohe!' It would have become on the lips of English witches something like 'Ah Voy!' And the plain Somerset magistrates, who took down the evidence in 1664, wrote it down as 'A Boy!'

It is notable that traditions of Sabbat rites linger in Somerset to this day. This fact has been recorded by Ruth Tongue, in her remarkable first-hand collection of ancient lore, entitled *Somerset Folklore* (The Folk-lore Society, London, 1965). She records how she was told that, up to within the last 100 years or less, Beltane rites took place at certain time-honoured spots, on May Eve and Midsummer Eve.

There is also a clear enough story of how the Lancashire witches met in 1612 at Malking Tower, held a feast of stolen mutton and discussed their future plans. This meeting was on a Good Friday, seemingly about the middle of April. This is not a usual date for a Sabbat; but the coven was in trouble. Some of its members had been arrested; so perhaps the May Eve meeting was brought forward to deal with the emergency. The fact that they met regularly like this, is indicated by their making an arrangement that the similar meeting next year was to be held at the house of another member of the coven.

In 1673 a servant girl named Anne Armstrong gave a long and detailed account of Sabbats she claimed to have witnessed in the Northumberland area. Her story was that the witches had tried to lure her into joining them, but that she had resisted, and eventually escaped. However, she added so many fantastic things, such as having been turned into a horse and ridden by a witch, that it is hard to know when, if ever, fantasy ends and fact begins. She may have been drugged or hypnotised.

Anne Armstrong stated that on one occasion five covens, of thirteen persons each, met together for a feast. The Grand Master of the district presided over these meetings, sitting at the head of the table, and she describes him as "their protector, which they called their god". The food was good and plentiful, but provided by magic.

The magistrates made some enquiry into Anne Armstrong's allegations; but the people whom she named as witches denied everything, and very little seems to have come of it. It seems curious, however, that an illiterate servant girl should have had such a detailed knowledge of the alleged organisation of witches if there was no substance in her story at all.

What really did (and does) happen at a witches' Sabbat?

If the Sabbat is held outdoors, there will certainly be a fire burning. Also, the statement by many old-time writers, about witches liking to hold their Sabbat at a place where there is some natural source of water, is true. The reason is that water is one of the Four Elements of Life, the others being fire, air and earth. So with the ritual bonfire and perhaps a lake or a running stream nearby, the witches have all the sacred Four Elements, being already surrounded by air and standing upon earth.

Upon a solemn occasion, the leader of the coven will use a consecrated magical sword to draw the circle. However, in the old days covens did not always have a sword, because a sword was an indication of rank, and only a nobleman would normally possess one. So the magical knife, or Athame, tended to take the place of the magical sword.

There will certainly be dancing; the old hand-in-hand round dance probably to begin with, eventually warming up into swifter and wilder measures as the spirit of the Sabbat begins to take over the participants. There will be either music or chanting, according to the individual talents of the coven members for providing it.

It is remarkable how in the present day, time has turned full circle. The old formal ballroom dancing has today been largely superseded by individual free movement to rhythm, precisely like the dances of the witches' Sabbats. Even rhythmic chanting has come back into popular favour; for example, 'Hara Krishna', which is in fact a magical mantram, a form of chanted words or sounds to raise magical power —something witches have been doing for centuries.

There will be food and drink, with a libation of wine to the Old Gods of Nature. If there is any specific magical work to be performed the matter will be discussed and explained if there are people present who are not fully cognisant of it. Then all will be asked to concentrate upon the object of the working, forming a kind of battery of wills, in order to bring it to pass. The power of thought is a potent force; especially in the excited, worked-up atmosphere of the magical circle. However, sometimes the Sabbat will not concern itself with a specific magical working, but be held simply for the enjoyment of communion with the Old Gods and to further the power of the Craft.

When the Sabbat has to be held indoors, the ritual is modified accordingly. Then there is usually a small altar in the centre of the circle. This altar must have fire and water upon it, in some form; and witches of the older traditions sometimes include a skull and crossed bones, or a representation of them. This is a symbol of death and resurrection, and therefore of immortality. It is sometimes called 'Old Simon'.

There is a very curious old Christian belief that so long as a skull and two leg bones of a man remained, that was enough to secure him a place in the general resurrection at the Last Day. This belief may well have originated from the real symbolism of the skull and crossed bones emblem. The Masonic fraternities also make use of the skull and crossed bones, in their ceremonies; which are descended, if not actually derived, from the ancient Mystery cults.

Outsiders might consider this emblem somewhat awesome and grim, especially when viewed by the flickering light of candles. However, the proceedings at most Sabbats I have attended were cheerful and spontaneous. They afford some of my most enjoyable memories.

It has been alleged that nothing was ever heard of witches' Sabbats surviving into the present day, until Gerald Gardner published his now famous book *Witchcraft Today* (Riders, London, 1954). Nevertheless, anyone who makes a close study of witchcraft will find that this is not so; though very little information found its way into public print before the last Witchcraft Act was repealed in 1951.

One very intriguing story that did get printed, appeared in a weekly periodical called *Illustrated Police News,* under the dateline of 28th April, 1939. This was admittedly a sensational publication, as was evidenced by the story's headline: "Satan Cult's Sex Orgies in Rural England". However, shorn of the blood-and-thunder embellishments of sensational journalism, the story was substantially this: that a reporter had heard about the forthcoming celebration of May Eve, or Walpurgis Night, planned to take place in a number of districts in England that year.

His informant, who had been given a pledge that her name should not be revealed, was a 22-year-old woman, an artist by profession. "A complicated series of introductions" had allegedly led the reporter to this contact.

She informed him that the Sabbat would be held at a lonely place, somewhere in Sussex. She gave no precise details, except that it was among thick trees, near a stream, and a mile from the main road.

The man who would be in charge of the ceremony she described as being about 30 years old, and well known in the West End of London and in Bloomsbury. She believed him to be a Finn by birth. He would be assisted by an older woman. The artist herself was a comparative newcomer to the cult, having only been a member for six months (which explains how she came to be gullible enough to reveal so much to a reporter).

It is, of course, difficult to know how much of the lurid detail of the expected 'orgy' of feasting, drinking and dancing in the nude, followed by sexual intercourse by all who desired it, was actually given by this young woman, and how much was supplied by the reporter. The account reads to me as if it has been 'worked-up' from a very little given information, with the reporter's imagination filling up the rest.

The meeting itself is erroneously termed a "coven" instead of a Sabbat; and the cult is referred to throughout as "Satanism". I would therefore dismiss the whole account, were it not for certain points of detail which cause me to think, as stated above, that this particular reporter had got a genuine contact, extracted a little real information and worked it up into a sensational story—as reporters have been known to do, before and since.

One remarkable statement made in the article was that the worshippers were hoping for an actual manifestation of the Horned God to appear. At the climax of the ceremony, when the leader uttered an invocation, a great shadowy form, they hoped, would take shape gradually above the altar.

It was added that there were whispers of other meetings, beside the one in Sussex, which would be held in Wiltshire, Buckinghamshire and Yorkshire. The number of people who would be celebrating the rites of this Walpurgis Night in England was described as "hundreds".

Later in that fatal year of 1939 the Second World War turned the attention of the British press to other things. They had no shortage of headline stories; and witchcraft was temporarily forgotten. Little was heard of the subject again until 1949, when there were press reports of a Sabbat held at the Rollright Stones in the Cotswolds. (*See* COTSWOLDS, WITCHCRAFT IN THE.) It was not until 1951 that the Witchcraft Museum at Castletown, Isle of Man, was opened, with the attendant publicity about present-day witches and their meetings.

SCRYING

Scrying is an old word for the practice of crystal-gazing or using some similar means to obtain clairvoyance. It is akin to the word 'descry', which originally meant to reveal, as well as to discover by seeing. Scrying is a more general term than crystal-gazing, because it embraces all forms of developing clairvoyance by gazing at or into some object.

The object used in scrying is called a speculum; and throughout the ages a great many different objects have been used for this purpose. The transparent crystal globe, with the use of which most people are familiar, is only one of a great variety of such specula.

The practice of scrying is common to magicians of all ages and countries. Like magic in general, it is as old as man himself; and it is still as popular with contemporary witches as it was long ago.

However, witches seldom possessed a crystal ball, for two reasons. Firstly, a genuine crystal ball is a valuable and expensive object. Most so-called 'crystals' are actually simply glass. The very latest development in this field is that of transparent globes of acrylic plastic. These are nevertheless described as 'crystal balls' in the advertisements for them in American magazines. Real rock crystal is a semi-precious stone; a ball made from it is heavy, and icy cold. It takes an expert to distinguish the real thing from imitations. Hence, valuable crystals, usually round but sometimes egg-shaped or pear-shaped, became precious heirlooms handed down for generations, and beyond the pocket of the poorer witch.

Secondly, such a possession was not only expensive and valuable; it was dangerous. To have such a thing found in one's house, immediately convicted the owner of magical practices. In the days when witchcraft was a hanging matter, witches found it wise to improvise their speculum out of things which could be found innocently in any cottage; a rule which they followed with many of their other tools as well.

Consequently, a black bowl filled with water is quite popular. So also are the old-fashioned glass globes used by fishermen as floats for their nets. These often come in beautiful dark green or blue glass, and make fine specula. Witches in sea-coast towns particularly liked these, because they could always be passed off as an innocent fishing-float, something which could be lying about in any cottage near the sea. Today, antique dealers sometimes sell these old fishing-floats as 'witch balls'. These they are not, although witches did use them. The real 'witch ball' is either brightly shining and reflecting, or else a kaleidoscopic medley of colours, as in the examples made of Nailsea glass. (*See* WITCH BALLS.)

The famous Irish witch, Biddy Early, used a blue glass bottle as a speculum. So did other witches, such bottles being usually filled with water. A ball of black glass would be particularly prized, some thinking it superior even to a genuine crystal ball. Others considered that the best speculum was a ball of pale greenish-coloured beryl. The natural beryl crystal comes in bluish and greenish shades, as well as the completely transparent kind.

Dr. Dee, the famous occultist of the first Queen Elizabeth's time, had two specula. (*See* DEE, DR. JOHN.) One was a crystal globe, which he called a "shew-stone"; and the other was his famous magic mirror. This was described in *Notes and Queries* (*1863*) as follows: "This magic speculum of Dr. Dee is composed of a flat black stone of very close texture, with a highly polished surface, half an inch in thickness, and seven inches and a quarter in diameter; of a circular form, except at the top, where there is a hole for suspension." When not in use, it was kept in a leather case.

Precisely what kind of stone this mirror was made of is uncertain. It is usually described as 'polished cannel-coal', which is a very fine kind of coal; but there are other descriptions of it as being of jet, or of obsidian. (The latter is a kind of volcanic glass.) A magic mirror of a similar kind (that is, with a shining black surface, instead of a brightly reflecting one), can be made by a witch, simply by obtaining a round, concave piece of glass and painting the back of it with some good black enamel or similar substance. Many witches prefer to make their own magic mirror, and consecrate it themselves.

A piece of round glass of suitable shape can sometimes be got from an old round picture-frame. Such glasses are set convexly in the frame, and just need to be taken out and turned over, when of course they will be concave (i.e., slightly bowl-shaped or hollowed). Alternatively, a small mirror of this kind can be made by obtaining the glass from an old clock-face of suitable shape; though naturally it is best if you can get a piece of suitably shaped new glass, which has never been put to any other use.

The mirror should be made in the increase of the moon, and given three coats of black upon the back of it; that is, upon the convex or upward-curving side. Let each coat dry thoroughly before applying the next. Then the mirror needs to be framed, according to the worker's own ingenuity. My own magic mirror is let into a box, which has a lid that can be closed. This is useful, because no speculum should be exposed to bright light, especially direct sunlight, as this can completely upset its sensitivity. Moonlight, however, is good for it, and has the effect of charging it with power.

Consequently, witches choose the full moon as the right time to consecrate a magic mirror, or any other speculum they may use. When not in use, such a speculum should be kept in a special case or box, or at least wrapped up in a black silk or velvet cloth.

The instructions for using a speculum, a crystal ball or a magic mirror, are to sit in a dim light, preferably by candlelight. The light should be behind the scryer. Some like a point or points of light to be reflected in the speculum, others do not. Clairvoyance by this or any other means is an individual affair, subject to certain broad and general rules.

There is no need to gaze in a strained, unwinking manner at the speculum. Simply relax, and look intently but naturally. A little burning incense, or a joss-stick, usually helps. The art of scrying needs concentration and practice; but eventually, if you have the faculty, the speculum will seem to mist over. Then something will be seen, dim and shadowy at first; and with perseverance the pictures will become brighter and clearer.

The things seen are sometimes actual, and sometimes symbolic. One has to learn to interpret symbols, as in any other form of clairvoyance. An important point is that clairvoyance can be sometimes objective and sometimes subjective. That is, sometimes the scene actually appears before you in the speculum, and sometimes it presents itself as a vivid picture within your mind. What really matters is, not how the picture appears, but how accurate and meaningful it is. Sometimes you get a blending of both. That is, you see something in the speculum, and at the same time you get an impression in your mind as to what it means.

I have been personally interested in scrying as part of witch rites, for some years. Two experiences of mine may be of interest, and serve to illustrate what has been said above.

In the first of these, I was using my black concave magic mirror. I was sitting within the magic circle, and enquiring about the outcome of a letter I had just sent to someone, a fellow witch with whom I had lost contact for some time. I saw quite objectively in the mirror the symbol of an X-shaped cross. The thought immediately came into my mind that my letter had crossed with a letter from the other person. Then I reasoned that this was too fantastic, and it must mean something else. However, I could get no other symbol or impression. Sure enough, on the mat the next morning was a letter from the person I had written to; our letters had crossed.

On another occasion, also within the magic circle, I was using a fishing-float, a hollow ball of dark green glass, as a speculum. This was mounted on a little wooden stand. I saw the visionary picture of a rather desolate valley, dotted here and there with strangely-shaped boulders. I received the mental impression that this was an actual place, and that in the past it had been the scene of pagan rites of some kind.

Shortly after this, I went on a visit to Cornwall, where I had never been before. Passing in a train through a wooded valley, I realised that this was the very place I had seen in my vision. I noted the name of it, and from subsequent enquiry I was able to confirm that it was believed to have been a place where what were described as "Druidic rites" were performed in the distant past.

Another method of scrying is that used by Italian witches as described by Charles Godfrey Leland in his *Legends of Florence* (David Nutt, London, 1896). He says:

> I once asked a witch in Florence if such a being as a spirit of the water or one of the bridges and streams existed; and she replied: "Yes, there is a spirit of the water as there is of fire, and everything else. They are rarely seen, but you can make them appear. How? Oh, easily enough, but you must remember that they are capricious, and appear in many delusive forms. And this is the way to see them. You must go at twilight and look over a bridge, or it will do if it be in the day-time in the woods at a smooth stream or a dark pool—*che sia un poco oscuro*—and pronounce the incantation, and throw a handful or a few drops of its water into the water itself. And then you must look long and patiently, always thinking of it for several days, when, *poco a poco,* you will see dim shapes passing by in the water, at first one or two, then more and more, and if you remain quiet they will come in great numbers, and show you what you want to know. But if you tell anyone what you have seen, they will never appear again, and it will be well for you should nothing worse happen."

STONES AND STONE CIRCLES

Because of their association with the rites of paganism, standing stones and stone circles became natural meeting places for witches.

Probably the best-known place in this connection is the locality of the Rollright Stones, in the Cotswolds. (*See* COTSWOLDS, WITCHCRAFT IN THE.) The legend of these stones associates them with a witch.

The story goes that they were once a king and his army, who had invaded the country with the intention of usurping the kingdom of England. When he got as far as Rollright, he met a witch. He asked her to prophesy if he would be king of England. She replied that he

must take seven strides to the top of the rising ground that looks over
Long Compton, and if he could then see the village, he would be
king.

> If Long Compton thou shalt see,
> King of England thou shalt be.

This looked easy, so he strode out confident of success; but when
he had taken the seventh step, he found that the green mound of a
long barrow hid the village from his view.

The witch cried triumphantly:

> Sink down man, and rise up stone!
> King of England thou shalt be none.

Immediately the invading king was turned into the standing stone
called the King Stone. His followers became the stone circle, sometimes called the King's Men; while some of his knights, who had
hung back to plot among themselves, became the further group of
stones called the Whispering Knights.

This story was firmly believed in by the country people of olden
time. Furthermore, it was said that at midnight the Rollright Stones
might become men again. They would join hands and dance; and
anyone who saw this would either die or go mad.

This latter part of the legend must have been very useful in keeping people away from the stones after dark. One wonders whether
the witches themselves aided the spread of this belief. We know that
smugglers used to spread gruesome ghost stories about some place
they did not want outsiders to come near, because they were using it
for their own purposes. Witches could have done the same thing.

The belief that old standing stones and stone circles have an uncanny life of their own after dark, is widespread throughout Britain.
People who live near the great stones of Avebury do not mind them
at all in daylight; but many will not go near them at night.

There are innumerable stories about stones being really people,
who have been turned to stone. Very often, especially in Cornwall,
this is said to have been a punishment for some impiety, such as
dancing or playing games on a Sunday. Originally, however, standing
stones may have been regarded as the effigies of the dead, who were
buried underneath. In Ireland and some parts of Scotland, standing
stones used to have the rather sinister name in Gaelic of *fear brea-
gach,* that is 'false men' or 'counterfeit men'.

There are also a great many stories about stones and stone circles being a favourite haunt of the fairies. Sometimes country folk would surreptitiously leave offerings to the fairies there, to gain good luck or to avert ill luck. A frequent form which such offerings took was a libation of milk poured over the stone. Here 'the fairies' may be the lingering folk-memory of pagan divinities. Sometimes a cup-like depression is found in such a stone, which has been hollowed out artificially, for the purpose of receiving offerings.

The early kings of England issued a number of edicts forbidding pagan rites at stones, along with various other observances which they classed as witchcraft. As late as the time of King Canute, at the beginning of the eleventh century A.D., such laws were proclaimed. (*See* LAWS AGAINST WITCHCRAFT.)

Another group of standing stones associated with witches' meetings is the Hoar Stones in Pendle Forest. Here the Lancashire witches used to foregather in the seventeenth century. The Bambury Stone on Bredon Hill also marks a traditional meeting-place of witches. The witches of Aberdeen in 1596 admitted to dancing round "ane grey stane" at the foot of the hill of Craigleauch.

On the Continent also, we find some old sacred stone associated with the place of the witches' Sabbat. Pierre de Lancre quotes a confessing witch, Estebene de Cambrue, as saying in 1567: "The place of this great convocation is generally called throughout the countryside the *Lanne de Bouc*. Here they give themselves to dancing around a stone, which is planted in that place, and upon which is seated a tall black man." *Lanne de Bouc* means 'The Field of the Goat'; the "tall black man" was the Man in Black, the Devil of the coven.

Solitary menhirs, or blocks of stone—whether natural or artificial —which have a striking and impressive aspect, often attract some legend which associates them with the Devil. This provides another reason for connecting them with witches, in the popular mind at any rate. When there is a tradition of actual pagan worship associated with the stone, the connection may well go far back through the ages. Also, some modern witches have deliberately sought out ancient stones, in order to revive the powers latent in them or in the aura of the place.

Before people dismiss such an idea as 'primitive superstition', we should remember that in Britain there are some of the most wonderful stone monuments in the world. They are relics of an elder faith, about which very little is known, but which was capable of inspiring people, our own ancestors, to marvellous endeavours.

Stonehenge, the 'Hanging Stones', is absolutely unique. There is nothing like it anywhere else. It is also a mystery; we still do not know all the secrets of its construction, or precisely why it was built. For many years it was believed to have been the work of the Druids; but we know today that Stonehenge was already very old before any Druid ever set foot in Britain.

The Druids were priests and philosophers, who belonged to the Celtic people of the early Iron Age. They revered Britain as being the sacred island, which housed an older Mystery tradition than theirs and from which their own tradition was derived. Caesar tells us that the noble Celtic families of the Continent of Europe used to send their sons to Britain to be inducted into the Druidical mysteries, because here in Britain the traditions were preserved in their purest form.

Now, we know that the Druids Caesar encountered in Europe, the Druids classical writers refer to, came to Britain in the wake of Celtic immigrants. So the only way that the statement about the Druidic traditions being at their purest in Britain makes sense, as if Britain was the original treasure-house of arcane lore, which one could call Proto-Druidic. Such magnificent monuments as Stonehenge and Avebury are further evidence to support this theory. The people who built these were no ignorant, skin-clad savages.

We have had to wait for the day of the computer to arrive, to discover how wonderful Stonehenge really is. A British-born astronomer, Professor Gerald S. Hawkins of Boston University, U.S.A., decided to test out exhaustively the theory that, beside the well-known summer solstice alignment, Stonehenge has other astronomical alignments of importance. He therefore fed all available data about the possible alignments of Stonehenge into a computer. The results were amazing.

Professor Hawkins has given us the story of his work on Stonehenge, in his book *Stonehenge Decoded* (Souvenir Press, London, 1966). Briefly, the computer revealed significant alignments to the rising and setting of the sun and moon at the equinoxes and solstices; some of which had not previously been suspected. More than this, it showed that Stonehenge itself could have been used as a computer, for the purpose of predicting eclipses.

Professor Hawkins calculated the odds against these alignments being mere coincidence. They worked out at 10 millions to one. In any other country but phlegmatic Britain, his book would have created a sensation. As it is, those who have read it with an open mind have realised that its conclusions mean a complete reappraisal of our ideas about the people of Ancient Britain.

Another revolutionary thinker about Britain's past history, as shown in its stone monuments, is Professor Alexander Thom. Professor Thom has approached the problem from the viewpoint of mathematics, as applied to the measurements of the stone circles. He gives his conclusions in his book *Megalithic Sites in Britain* (Clarendon Press, Oxford, 1967).

Professor Thom has discovered that the people who built Britain's stone circles, about 4,000 years ago, had a far profounder knowledge of mathematics than has hitherto been believed possible. Perhaps his most striking discovery is the fact that they used a standard unit of length for their work, throughout Britain. This unit of length Professor Thom has called the megalithic yard, because it is just a little shorter than the yard now in use. The megalithic yard works out at 2.72 feet; and the builders of the stone circles liked to get as many measurements as possible which were integral multiples of this unit.

The existence of this megalithic yard, and its use throughout Britain, immediately suggests a far greater degree of organisation in Ancient Britain than was previously imagined. The country's prehistoric past is an enigma; a dark treasure cave, lit by a few beams of light.

Present-day British witches believe that their Old Religion, the Craft of the Wise, has its roots in the very ancient past, going back to the Stone Age, in which these megalithic monuments were built. As we have noted above, the observances of the Old Religion continued long after this country was officially converted to Christianity. They were associated with trees, rivers, sunlight, moonlight, ritual fire—all the things still associated with witch rites; and also with the enduring mystery of the massive, silent stones, left by those races who had vanished into the past.

SUMMERS, MONTAGUE

A remarkable figure in the modern history of witchcraft is the late Montague Summers. He was a man almost as mysterious, strange and picturesque as the witches he wrote about.

A devout Roman Catholic, Montague Summers accepted com-

352 SUMMERS, MONTAGUE

pletely the proposition that the Devil, or Satan, is a real and fearfully dangerous entity, and that witches are Satan's servitors. All his books about witchcraft, brilliant and readable though they are, are written from this standpoint. Nevertheless, his contribution to the literature of witchcraft is a most valuable one, on account of the wide and meticulous scholarship which he brought to the subject.

He was generally known as the Reverend Montague Summers, or even as Father Summers; though precisely what kind of Holy Orders he was in is not clear.

Charles Richard Cammell, in his book *Aleister Crowley* (New English Library, 1969), has given us one of the few intimate descriptions of Montague Summers that we possess. Mr. Cammell reveals a very curious detail; namely that Crowley and Summers not only knew each other, but shared a mutual admiration! At one time both Crowley and Summers were living at Richmond, in Surrey, as was Mr. Cammell; and he tells us that they met in his flat and discussed their many interests in an atmosphere of friendliness and wit. One would give much to have heard their conversation; as they seem such complete opposites, though both men of truly singular brilliance.

Such a curious acquaintance would not, perhaps, surprise Mr. Dennis Wheatley, because in his brief account of Montague Summers, in the chapter on black magic in his *Gunmen, Gallants and Ghosts* (Arrow Books, London, 1963), he states frankly that Summers inspired him with fear. He also tells us that he used Montague Summers' physical appearance as a model for the sinister Canon Copely-Syle in his black magic story, *To the Devil—a Daughter* (Arrow Books, London, 1960).

It seems that Montague Summers had a private chapel in his home, which some people regarded as being rather strange and possibly dubious. However, the writer would personally take a lot of convincing that Montague Summers was secretly devoted to black magic.

That Summers had an enormous fund of knowledge about the occult, especially on its darker side, is indubitable; but he devoted a great deal of his literary career to writing against what he regarded as the black international conspiracy of Satanism. To him, witchcraft and Spiritualism were branches of this conspiracy. He defended the role of the Catholic Church in persecuting witches, whom he regarded as heretics and anarchists, as well as Satanists.

One story told about him was that he had a kind of special brief from high quarters in the Catholic hierarchy, to write about witchcraft and the occult; because in general Roman Catholic writers were not encouraged to deal with this subject, especially in such detail as Summers did. For this reason, the story went, although in Holy Orders Summers was not attached to any particular church or religious foundation, but lived apparently as a private citizen. How much truth, if any, there is in this assertion, I cannot tell.

Summers certainly wore clerical garb, in which he made a distinguished and striking figure, with his rather long silver hair, and fine soft hands sparkling with jewelled rings. Although not tall, his presence was very dignified; people stood somewhat in awe of him.

As well as living at Oxford and at Richmond, Montague Summers at one time resided in Brighton (my own town of residence). He always insisted that Brighton had a secret centre of black magic, and that the black mass had been celebrated at this hideout, which was somewhere in the tangle of old streets near Brighton Station.

From local enquiries, it appears that in fact there was an occult group in Brighton some years ago, which practised what Summers would certainly have described as black magic. The sacrifice of a cockerel was involved in some of the rites. Their meeting place was in the area Summers mentions.

As well as writing about witchcraft, Montague Summers had a great knowledge of the theatre and its dramatists. On one occasion, in 1921, his two interests were combined. He directed a revival of the seventeenth-century play, *The Witch of Edmonton,* at the Lyric Theatre, Hammersmith, with Sybil Thorndike playing the part of the witch. That must have been a remarkable theatrical event.

Montague Summers was responsible not only for his own original books on witchcraft, but for a whole series of translations and editings of older works on the subject, which were thus made available to students in the English language. Particularly valuable among these is his translation of the notorious *Malleus Maleficarum.*

Outstanding among Montague Summers' own writings are his *History of Witchcraft and Demonology* (first published in 1926, and reprinted by Routledge and Kegan Paul in 1969); *The Geography of Witchcraft* (London, 1927); *A Popular History of Witchcraft* (Kegan Paul, London, 1937); and *Witchcraft and Black Magic* (Riders, London, 1946). He also wrote with similar verve, colour, and total belief about vampires and werewolves—phenomena which he regarded as being allied to witchcraft, or associated with the activities of witches.

T

TAROT CARDS

These mysterious cards are today popular with occultists of many schools for the purpose of divination. They are also regarded as containing mystical and magical secrets, for those who can discern them. However, before the Tarot reached its present-day level of general interest, it was preserved among the gypsies, and also among their frequent companions in hardship and misfortune, the witches.

Grillot de Givry, in his *Pictorial Anthology of Witchcraft, Magic and Alchemy* (University Books, New York, 1958), bears witness to the fact that, in France at any rate, and probably elsewhere on the Continent, the Tarot cards were part of the magical armoury of the village witch. Before the days of fashionable Society clairvoyants, ladies of rank and wealth who wanted their fortunes told would go secretly to consult the wise woman in her tumbledown cottage. Later, her place was taken by such elegant practitioners as Mademoiselle Le Normand and Julia Orsini. The former lady is famous for the consultations she gave to Napoleon and Josephine by means of the divining cards.

When the Tarots arrived in England is not known, but there are records to prove that cards were imported here from Europe before 1463.

As for the Gypsies, they had for so long borne the Tarot pack with them in their wanderings that many people believed the Tarot to be of gypsy origin. Hence it was sometimes called 'The Tarot of the Bohemians'. Others have cast doubt on this, saying that the cards were known in Europe before the gypsies arrived here from the East. The generally accepted date for the gypsies' first appearance in Europe is 1417; and Tarot cards were known before then. However, some experts on gypsy lore would dispute this date also, saying that gypsies were in Europe before that time; so the enigma remains. No one really knows the origin of the Tarot.

The gypsies themselves claim to see in some of the pictures on the cards, the sad history of their wanderings and persecutions. They derive originally from India, and their language, Romany, has links with the Hindu tongue. Now, it is certainly true that playing cards, and very elaborate and beautiful ones, are known in India and the East generally, and in Tibet. In the latter country, before it came under Chinese Communist rule, cards were produced which were not only intended for gaming, but bore pictures associated with the Tibetan religion. Even so, although the Tarot cards can be used to play games, and were so used sometimes in olden days, their significance is obviously deeper than this.

Records exist of artists being paid to execute beautiful hand-painted Tarot packs for the diversion of kings and the nobility; and a few examples of such cards remain in museums. Also, we find very crude and quaint-looking old packs, produced in the early days of printing, for sale among the poorer classes. These cards, printed from wood blocks, often have a good deal of charm. In order to keep them flat, such old-fashioned packs of cards were kept in a little miniature press, when not in use.

The Tarot cards are the ancestors of our playing cards. Like them, the Tarots have four suits; but they also have a fifth suit the Trumps, or Major Arcana, and it is these latter which are the cards bearing the mystic pictures. There are twenty-two of the Major Arcana; and each of the four suits has fourteen cards, namely the ace to ten, and a mounted figure, the Knight, in addition to the usual court cards of King, Queen and Knave. Thus the Tarot pack consists of seventy-eight cards. This is the usual number; though there are found examples of augmented Tarots, like the *Minchiate* of Florence, which has 97 cards; and also of shortened Tarots, such as the Tarot of Bologna, which has only sixty-two cards.

Our pack of playing cards has discarded all the Trumps except one, The Fool, which has survived as the Joker. Also, it has lost the four Knights from among the court cards; and it has made the cards double-headed, so that they look the same either way up, for convenience in playing games. The Tarot cards, and many of the old playing-cards, are not like this, but are actual little pictures.

The playing-card suit symbols also have been simplified from the grander emblems of the Tarot. The four suits of the Tarot cards are Wands, Cups, Swords, and Coins or Pentacles (the latter in this sense meaning a round disc with a magical sigil upon it).

The gypsies have their own names for the four suits. They call them *Pal* (the Wand), *Pohara* (the Cup), *Spathi* (the Sword), and *Rup* (the Coin). *Pal* could be from the same Sanskrit origin as 'phallus'. *Pohara* is reminiscent of the Celtic *pair* and the English gypsy *pirry*, both meaning a cauldron. *Spathi* is possibly from the same root as *espada* (Spanish) and *epée* (French), meaning a sword. *Rup* is like English gypsy *ruppeny*, meaning silver, and, of course, the Hindu *rupee*.

What is particularly significant about these suit symbols is that they are the four Elemental Weapons or tools of magic. The Wand, the Cup, the Sword and the Pentacle, or their equivalents, lie upon the altar of every practising magician. Their usual elemental attributions are fire for the Wand, water for the Cup, air for the Sword, and earth for the Pentacle.

Moreover, a correspondence may be found between these four Tarot emblems and the Four Treasures of the Tuatha De Danann, the divine race of the Gaels, who arrived in ancient Eire untold centuries ago, as Celtic legend tells us. This race of gods had dwelt in four mystic cities, Findias, Gorias, Murias and Falias; and from each city they had brought a treasure. There was the fiery Spear of Lugh; the Cauldron of the Dagda; the Sword of Nuada; and the Stone of Fal, which became known as the Stone of Destiny, because the ancient Irish kings were crowned upon it. The story goes that this is that very Stone of Destiny which now forms part of the Coronation Chair in Westminster Abbey. The whereabouts of the other three treasures is unknown.

In the later Grail romances, the Four Talismans appear again, in another guise of myth. They become the blood-dripping Lance, the Grail Cup itself, and the Sword and Shield bestowed upon the knight who set out in quest of it.

To the student of the Qabalah, they are the four letters of the Divine Name, the Tetragrammaton. The whole Tarot can, in fact, be arranged to form the figure of the Qabalistic Tree of Life. The real Qabalistic attributions of the Tarot cards were long kept a profound secret, in the occult fraternity known as the Order of the Golden Dawn; and it has been only in comparatively recent years that Dr. Francis Israel Regardie has published this information fully and accurately. (*The Golden Dawn* by Israel Regardie. Second Edition, Hazel Hills Corporation, U.S.A., 1969.)

Aleister Crowley published a most elaborate volume upon the

Tarot, entitled *The Book of Thoth* (privately printed by the Ordo Templi Orientis, London, 1944). His version, however, is an individual one, many of the old designs of the cards being adapted to suit his own magical ideas.

A popular version of the Tarot pack is that which was drawn by Pamela Coleman Smith to the designs of A. E. Waite. The figures of this Tarot have something of the air of Art Nouveau. Waite was a member of the Golden Dawn, and although sworn to secrecy, he introduced many subtleties into the designs which accord with the attributions given to the cards by that famous magical Order.

Many, however, prefer the older version of the Tarot cards, of which probably the best example is the Tarot de Marseilles. This can still be obtained today.

The numbered series of the Major Arcana or Trumps of the Tarot runs as follows: the Juggler; the Priestess (or Female Pope); the Empress; the Emperor; the Pope; the Lovers; the Chariot; Justice; the Hermit; the Wheel of Fortune; Strength; the Hanged Man; Death; Temperance; the Devil; the Tower; the Star; the Moon; the Sun; Judgment; the World; and the unnumbered card, the Fool.

The pictures and personages they show are strange and enigmatic. Occultists of various schools have written thousands of words in their interpretation; some wise and some otherwise. The Tarot is a book without words. It speaks in the universal language of symbolism. It is equally at home in the gypsy caravan, the witch's cottage, or the splendidly-appointed private temple of the ceremonial magician. It can be used upon the level of fortune telling, or upon that of the High Mysteries. Some derive its origin from Ancient Egypt; it remains one of the real wonders and secrets of the world.

Witches see in the Tarot a relationship at any rate with their own traditions. Their Horned God is shown (especially in the older versions) upon the card called the Devil. The Goddess of the Moon appears as the Priestess. The Hermit can be interpreted as the Master Witch, passing on his way unknown, carrying the lantern of knowledge. The Wheel of Fortune is also the wheel of the year, equally divided by the Greater and Lesser Sabbats. The Hanged Man can be understood by the witch as he is by the gypsy, as the symbol of suffering and persecution. Nature in perfection, naked and joyous, is pictured upon the card called the World; and so on.

As a means of divination, the Tarot can often be startlingly accurate; on other occasions it may refuse to speak at all. As in all psychic matters, much depends upon the individual gifts of the diviner, and the conditions prevailing at the time.

TORTURE USED ON WITCHES

The above entry in this book is one that the writer has approached with reluctance. Were I to tell the full and detailed story of how the supposed followers of the Christian God of Love have smeared their bloodstained hands over the pages of human history, I would be accused of anti-Christian prejudice. Yet every detail of such an accusation could be supported by documentary evidence, in sickening abundance. Its cumulative effect would be to prove that Christianity has inflicted far more martyrdoms than paganism ever did.

Such documentation has been admirably done, sometimes with photographed copies of the originals, by Rossell Hope Robbins, in in his *Encyclopedia of Witchcraft and Demonology* (Crown Publishers, Inc., New York, 1959). This book is surely one of the most damning indictments of the Christian Church ever penned; the more so as it is not written for any such purpose, but simply as an historical review of the facts.

I disagree with Mr Hope Robbins' opinion of witchcraft itself; but his contribution to the history of this subject is of prime importance.

The origin of torture and execution in the name of religion is the certainty that your religion is true, and therefore any other religion must be false. This being so, you must regard people who profess a different religion from your own as heretics, and as inevitably damned (as Saint Augustine did). It is your religious duty to persecute them; and because their crime is against God, no cruelty is too great to use towards them. Indeed, anyone who urges mercy towards heretics is suspect himself. The evidence of history shows overwhelmingly that witches were persecuted, not because they had done harm, but because their crime was *heresy*. Hence the heavy involvement, from the beginning, of the Church in witchcraft trials.

The extirpation of witchcraft was a religious duty. So we read of a witch being flogged to the sound of bells ringing the Angelus; of the torture chamber being censed with Church incense, and the instruments of torture blessed, before the proceedings commenced. We find documents, recording questions put to a woman under torture, which are headed with the letters "A.M.D.G.", *Ad majorem Dei gloriam*, "To the greater glory of God".

Nor were the Protestants any less cruel and fanatical than the

Catholics. In fact, some of the most abominable stories come from the Protestant countries, particularly Scotland. The laws of Scotland with regard to witchcraft were different from those of England. Under Scottish law, torture was legal; under English law, after the Reformation, it was not.

Consequently, we may read such stories as that recorded of the trial of Alison Balfour, in Scotland in 1596. A confession of witchcraft was extorted from this woman by means of the 'boots', the 'claspie-claws', and the 'pilnie-winks'. These were instruments of torture for causing agony to the legs, the arms, and the fingers, respectively; and could be applied with such violence that the blood spurted from the limbs.

Before Alison Balfour confessed what was required of her, she was put in the claspie-claws and kept so for forty-eight hours. Not content with this, the pious and God-fearing agents of the Kirk put her husband into heavy irons, and tortured her son with the boots; and as a final touch they took her daughter, a little girl of 7, and screwed the child's fingers into the pilnie-winks, in the mother's presence. At this juncture, Alison Balfour confessed; and upon the strength of this confession she was subsequently executed.

No mercy was shown, by either Protestant or Catholic, to children, if they were involved in witchcraft. That godly Puritan, Cotton Mather, in his account of the witchcraft trial at Mohra, in Sweden, in 1669, tells us with the utmost complacency how, after a good deal of praying, preaching and psalm-singing, "Fifteen children which likewise confessed that they were engaged in this witchery, died as the rest"; that is, by burning at the stake.

At other times, children of witch families were sentenced to be flogged while their relatives burned. The witch-hunter Nicholas Remy recorded this fact with regret; he felt that the children should have been burned as well.

The sentences of death in Scotland were sometimes carried out in a particularly horrible manner, and a relic of this survives today. It is the Witches' Stone, near Forres, in Moray, Scotland. Beside the stone is an inscription, which says: "From Clust Hill witches were rolled in stout barrels through which knives were driven. When the barrels stopped they were burned with their mangled contents. This stone marks the site of one such burning".

That this method of execution was carried out elsewhere in Scotland also, is attested by two Scottish writers, J. Mitchell and John

Dickie, who published their book *The Philosophy of Witchcraft* in Paisley, Scotland, in 1839. They tell us:

> There is a hill in Perthshire which bears the name of the Witches' Crag to this day, and tradition still tells how it acquired the appellation. An old woman, who had been *found guilty* of Witchcraft, was taken to the top of it, and there put into a barrel, the sides and ends of which were stuck full of sharp-pointed nails. The barrel was then fitted up tightly, and suffered to roll down the steep declivity amid the rejoicings of the infuriated demons who had gathered together to witness the poor old woman's tortures!! Where the barrel rested a bonfire was kindled, and it, and all that it contained, were consumed to ashes.

By "infuriated demons", the authors mean, not evil spirits, but the witch-hunters and those who supported them, who had gathered together to enjoy the fun. Indeed, though they regarded themselves as acting from the highest and most *religious* motives, it seems that it was quite usual for the magistrates of a Scottish town to hold a public dinner after a witch-burning, as a form of celebration. There is a record of this being done at Paisley, in 1697, after seven people had been burned there as witches, in the presence of a vast crowd that had gathered to witness the scene.

It was on the Continent of Europe, however, and particularly in Germany, that the horrors of torture and cruelty raged most fiercely. Indeed, torture seems sometimes to have been indulged in for its own sake, even when the person had already confessed. The justification for this was, that a confession could not be fully true unless it was made under torture.

There were several degrees of torture practised in Germany in the seventeenth century, the blackest period of the whole history of witchcraft persecution. The first degree was called preparatory torture. It began with taking the prisoner to the torture chamber, and showing her the instruments, explaining in detail the particular agonies that each could inflict. Then the prisoner was stripped and made ready. Women prisoners were supposed to be stripped by respectable matrons; but in practice they were roughly handled and sometimes raped by the torturer's assistants.

Then some preliminary taste of torture was inflicted on them, such as whipping, or an application of the thumb-screws. This preparatory examination was not officially reckoned as torture; so those who confessed anything under it were stated in the court records to have confessed voluntarily, without torture.

If, however, the prisoner did not confess, the jailers proceeded to the final torture. This was not supposed to be repeated more than three times; but again in practice there were no safeguards for the prisoner, and the tortures could be varied at will by the sadistic ingenuity of witch-judges. One of the worst of these was Judge Heinrich von Schultheis, who is recorded to have cut open a woman's feet and poured boiling oil into the wounds. He wrote a book of instructions on how to proceed in witch trials, which was printed with the approbation of the Prince-Archbishop of Mainz. In this frightful volume, Schultheis declares that torture is a work pleasing in God's sight, because by means of it witches are brought to confession. It is therefore good, both for the torturer and the one who is tortured.

A portrait of this monster has survived to us. It shows a handsomely-dressed gentleman, plump and well-groomed, with the wide lace-trimmed collar and neat beard and moustache that were worn at that period. Only the closely-set eyes betray the gloating cruelty of the sadistic killer; but this they do so completely that one cannot look at the face without a shudder. It may well be that his successors realised what Schultheis was; because only one copy of his book is known to exist, and that is in Cornell University Library. A book seldom disappears as completely as that, unless copies of it have been deliberately destroyed.

The final torture, therefore, had innumerable means of inflicting agony upon the human flesh—the thumb-screws, the rack, the rawhide whip, the iron chair (which was heated while the prisoner was held fastened in it), spiked metal chains which were tightened around the forehead, and so on. But the favourite method was that known as the strappado, from the Latin *strappare,* to pull. This was a means of dislocating the prisoner's limbs, especially the shoulders. The victim's hands were tied behind his back, and fastened to a rope with a pulley. Then, with a sudden pull, he was hoisted into the air. While he hung thus, heavy weights were tied to his feet to increase the pain.

While the prisoners were thus hanging, they were interrogated with questions, and the results written down as a 'confession'. If they subsequently tried to deny or retract anything, they were tortured again. Sometimes they were tortured again, in any case, with particular severity, in order to force them to name 'accomplices'. Names were suggested to them, of persons the authorities wished to implicate.

By this means, more and more people could be drawn into the net of the witch-hunters.

For this purpose, a particularly agonising torture, known as squassation, was often employed. It was a further development of the strappado. The victim was hoisted in the same way, and kept hanging, with weights attached to the feet; but his body was then suddenly and violently dropped, nearly but not quite to the ground. The effect of this was to dislocate every joint of the body. Under this form of torture, prisoners sometimes collapsed and died. It was then given out that "The Devil had strangled them, to stop them revealing too much", or some such story. They were regarded as guilty, and their bodies burned.

The worst period at Bamberg was under the rule of Prince-Bishop Gottfried Johann Georg II Fuchs von Dornheim, who came to be known as the Witch-Bishop. His reign lasted from 1623 to 1633, and in it he burned at least 600 people as witches. His cousin, the Prince-Bishop of Wurzberg, burned 900 alleged witches during his reign; but Bamberg became the more notorious, as being the very home of torture of the most atrocious kind.

Of particular interest is the Hexenhaus, or special prison for witches, that was built at Bamberg in 1627 by order of the Witch-Bishop. The building no longer exists, having been destroyed when witch-hunting went out of fashion and the Bishop's successors became ashamed of it. In its day, however, it was considered a very handsome edifice, and a plan and picture of it remain. Besides two chapels and a torture-chamber, it had accommodation for the imprisonment, in separate cells, of twenty-six witches—two covens. On the front of the Hexenhaus were two stone tablets, bearing versions in Latin and German of a significant text from I Kings, Chap. IX, vs. 7, 8, and 9: "This house . . . shall be . . . a byword. Everyone that passeth by it shall be astonished, and shall hiss, and they shall say, Why hath the Lord done this unto this land, and to this house? And they shall answer, Because they forsook the Lord their God . . . and have taken hold upon other gods, and have worshipped them, and served them; therefore hath the Lord brought upon them all this evil."

This seems clearly to indicate that the witches were accused of having their own gods, instead of the Christian God.

Eventually, the reign of terror in Bamberg grew so scandalous that the Emperor himself took firm action to stop it. He was urged thereto by his Jesuit confessor, Father Lamormaini; a fact that should be recorded, to show that not all Christian priests approved of the proceedings against witches. Another Jesuit who spoke out against the torture of witches, with the utmost bravery, was Father Friedrich Von Spee, whose book *Cautio Criminalis* was published in Rinteln in 1631. He was imprisoned and disgraced for his boldness, and was probably lucky to escape execution.

From the worst of these manifestations of cruelty, England was mercifully free; mainly because English law is fundamentally different from Continental law, in that here the onus is on the prosecution to prove guilt, rather than on the prisoner to prove innocence, and that torture was not officially permitted. Such torture as did take place in England was unofficial and outside the law. It was administered by such rogues as Matthew Hopkins the notorious Witch-Finder General (*See* HOPKINS, MATTHEW), who found means to torment prisoners while still keeping within the letter of the law.

However, an influential Puritan divine, William Perkins, wrote in approval of subjecting witches to torture, in his *Discourse of Witchcraft*, published in Cambridge in 1608. Perkins says of torture that it might "no doubt lawfully and with good conscience be used, howbeit not in every case, but only upon strong and great presumptions going before, and when the party is obstinate".

Sometimes such pious sentiments were unofficially acted upon. In 1603, at Catton in Suffolk, a mob got together to torture an 80-year-old woman Agnes Fenn, who was accused of witchcraft. She was punched with the handles of daggers, tossed up into the air, and terrorised by having a flash of gunpowder exploded in her face. Then someone prepared a rough instrument of torture almost worthy of Bamberg.

This consisted of a stool, through which sharp daggers and knives had been stuck, with the points protruding upwards. Then, says a contemporary account, "they often times struck her down upon the same stool whereby she was sore pricked and grievously hurt".

TREES AND WITCHCRAFT

The late Elliott O'Donnell, author of so many volumes of ghost stories, also wrote a fascinating book called *Strange Cults and Secret Societies of Modern London* (Philip Allan, London, 1934). In this book, O'Donnell gives some very curious particulars of what he calls the tree cult. He relates how certain people, usually with something of the Celt in their ancestry, find a peculiar kinship with trees, and have some remarkable beliefs concerning them.

This tree cult is still in existence, and has a good deal in common with the Craft of the Wise. (It is not called 'the tree cult' by those who follow it; but it is convenient to follow O'Donnell's example in naming it thus.)

Beliefs concerning trees, their magical properties and the spirits that are thought to indwell them, are so old and so widespread that it is impossible to do more here than give a glimpse into tree lore and its connections with witchcraft.

Trees not only have distinct personalities of their own, for those who are sensitive to such things; but many trees are the abodes of spirits, which may be friendly towards humans, or sometimes very much otherwise. Elliott O'Donnell had a curious word, 'stichimonious', to describe such spirit-haunted trees, which I have not seen elsewhere than in his works. He found so many stories of an uncanny or ghostly nature connected with trees that he later wrote a volume of such tales, entitled *Trees of Ghostly Dread* (Riders, London, 1958).

A haunted wood in Sussex, particularly connected with the ghost of a witch, is Tuck's Wood near Buxted. The story behind this haunting is that, many years ago, a beautiful young girl called Nan Tuck somehow acquired the reputation of being a witch. One day an angry mob set about her and threatened to 'swim' her in the pond at Tickerage Mill. She fled, with the mob in pursuit, and made for Buxted Church to ask for sanctuary. She managed to reach the church, and tried to grasp the 'sanctuary ring' (the big ring of iron on many old-fashioned church doors). But the parson pushed her away, quoting the text about "not suffering a witch"; and presumably she was abandoned to the mob.

She subsequently hanged herself from a tree in Tuck's Wood; and ever afterwards her ghost has haunted the wood and its neighbourhood. Her burial place is marked by an old grave slab outside the churchyard wall, near the lych gate.

It is not so inexplicable that there are many stories of ghostly phenomena connected with woods and with trees in general, when one realises that so old and powerful a living thing as a tree must have a strong aura, or field of force, surrounding it. Some sensitive people can see the auras of trees, as a faint silvery light against the sky. By leaning their back against a tree, they can attune themselves to its vitality, drawn deep from the earth and nourished by sunshine and rain. Many trees have a healing influence upon humans, when their life-force is contacted in this way.

The world's oldest living things are trees—the ancient redwoods of California, estimated to be about 4,000 years old, and still producing buds and leaves. One of the world's greatest pieces of music, Handel's "Largo," is a melody in praise of the beauty of a tree. There is far more in trees than merely wood and leaves.

A conspicuous tree has often been used as a trysting-place for many purposes, including those of the Old Religion. Solitary thorn trees, with their strange gnarled shapes, somehow suggest witchcraft and the Kingdom of Faerie; and few more so than the fantastic tree known as the Witch of Hethel.

This very old thorn tree stands in the village of Hethel, south-west of Norwich, in Norfolk. How old it is, no one knows. A previous owner of the land, the first Sir Thomas Beavor, was said to have had a deed, dated early in the thirteenth century, which referred to the tree as "the old thorn". Another scrap of tradition states that the tree was a meeting place for discontented peasants, when they staged a revolt in the troubled reign of King John (1199-1216).

Today, the trunk of the thorn is cloven, and its twisting branches have spread to become like a miniature wood in themselves. In several places, they are supported by props. Yet in spite of its amazing age, the Witch of Hethel still manages to produce a few bunches of sweet-smelling blossom each May. Happily, this historic tree is today cared for by the Norfolk Naturalists' Trust.

But why is it called the Witch of Hethel? No one seems exactly to know. There is one significant pointer; the tree stands near to the village church, and although the latter is old, the thorn is thought to be older. We know that early churches were often built upon pagan sacred sites; so this church may have been deliberately built near a sacred tree. The Witch of Hethel may once have been the Goddess of Hethel, under the form of her sacred tree.

That hawthorn was once a sacred tree is shown by the fact that it is considered unlucky to bring its blossoms indoors. The only time when it was lawful to break the branches of the White Goddess's tree was on May Eve, when they were used in the May Day celebrations. There are many folk tales of people who have suffered injury or misfortune, through cutting down or uprooting some venerable old thorn tree.

The oak, the ash and the thorn are the Fairy Triad; and where they grow together, you may expect fairies to haunt. There is a popular rhyme in the New Forest:

> Turn your cloaks,
> For fairy folks
> Are in old oaks.

Turning your cloak inside out, and wearing it like that, was a remedy for being 'pixy-led', or made to lose one's way by fairy glamour.

The oak is the old British tree of magic, reverenced by the Druids; one of the mightiest and longest-lived of trees, and yet lying potentially within the smallness of the acorn. This is the probable origin of the old Sussex belief that to carry an acorn in one's purse or pocket will preserve health and vitality and keep one youthful.

Also, the acorn in its cup is phallic in shape, and hence an emblem of life and luck. For this reason, the heads of gateposts at the entrance to a house were in olden times often carved in the shape of an acorn.

This is the reason, too, why old-fashioned roller blinds at windows often have a carved wooden acorn at the end of their cords. The acorn hung at the window originally to bring good luck, and keep away evil influences. Its real meaning tended gradually to be forgotten; but the custom of decorating window blinds with an acorn remained.

It has been suggested that the old nonsense-words, 'Hob a derry down-O', which sometimes occur in folk-songs, are actually the worn-down remains of a Celtic phrase, meaning 'Dance around the oak-tree'. *Derw* is the old British word for oak; and it seems fairly sure that *Derwydd,* meaning 'oak-seer', is the origin of 'Druid'. Present-day witches sometimes dance around an oak or a thorn-tree and pour a libation of red wine at its root. The tree is an emblem of the power of life and fertility, which they worship by this act.

Fragments of traditional lore about trees often bear witness to their ancient importance in pagan religion. For instance, there is a curious passage in John Evelyn's book, *Sylva, or a Discourse of Forest Trees* (London, 1664). Writing of a certain very old and venerable oak-tree in Staffordshire, he tells us: "Upon oath of a bastard's being begotten within reach of the shade of its boughs (which I can assure you at the rising and declining of the sun is very ample), the offence was not obnoxious to the censure of either ecclesiastical or civil magistrate."

This seems certainly to hark back to the fertility rites of olden times, beneath the sacred oak. The same old custom lies concealed in a certain Sussex place-name, Wappingthorn Wood, just north of Steyning. 'Wap' or 'wape' is an old word meaning to have sexual intercourse, in this case beneath the sacred thorn tree.

The elder is a tree of rather sinister repute, and much associated with witchcraft. No careful countryman of olden days would burn logs of elder in his fireplace, because to do so would bring the Devil into the house. The berries of the elder make potent wine, and its strongly-scented white flowers are valued by the herbalist, to make elder-flower and peppermint mixture, a remedy for colds and chills. Yet there is something disturbing about the heavy perfume of elder flowers in the warm air of summer. Arthur Machen described it in a telling phrase, as "a vapour of incense and corruption". Some regard it as noxious, while others believe it to be an aphrodisiac.

The elder tree is notoriously a dwelling place of spirits; so much so that an old belief says you should never cut or break a piece from an elder tree, without asking leave of any unseen presences. An elder tree that grows in an old churchyard is particularly potent for magical purposes. For instance, it can be used to charm warts, if you cut a small stick of green wood from it in the waning moon, rub the warts with the elder stick and then bury it somewhere where it will be undisturbed and rot away. As the stick decays, so the warts will disappear.

Some people believed the elder to be a protection against witch-craft; perhaps because it was thought to be the tree of which the Cross was made, and also the tree on which Judas hanged himself. Others regarded solitary elder bushes with suspicion, especially if they encountered one in the twilight where they could not remember seeing a bush before. It might be a witch in disguise, changed by magical glamour into the appearance of an elder tree. Some old stories said that witches could do this. There are so many legends about the elder tree that its association with magic and witchcraft is almost certainly pre-Christian.

A continuing cult of magical beliefs connected with trees is shown by a curious incident that happened in Sussex in 1966. In March of that year the *Brighton Evening Argus* reported that a curse had been publicly laid upon whoever cut down an ancient elm tree near

Steyning, Sussex. The tree was threatened with destruction to make way for housing development; and a notice had been found pinned to it, which read:

> Hear ye, hear ye, that any fool,
> Who upon this tree shall lay a tool,
> Will have upon him a curse laid,
> Until for that sin he has paid.

The notice was adorned with magical symbols. The police investigated the matter; but so far as I know the author of the mysterious threat was never discovered.

The expression 'Touch wood' is a relic of the ancient worship of trees. (I once had a man say to me, in all seriousness, "I don't believe in superstition; and, touch wood, I never shall!") The concepts of the World Tree or the Tree of Life occur again and again in pagan mythology and symbolism. Our Christmas tree, with its bright baubles and the star on the top, is a miniature version of the World Tree of our pagan ancestors, with its roots deep in earth, the sun, moon and stars hung on its spreading branches, and the Pole Star on its topmost point. Sometimes the star is replaced by a fairy doll, who represents the goddess of Nature ruling over the world.

A sign that a tree is the home of uncanny influences, is the presence upon it of the peculiar growth that country people call witches' brooms. This appearance is actually caused by a kind of fungus, which has the effect of stimulating certain branches of the tree into unnaturally thick growth, dense and bushy like a broom. The broom-like cluster of branches also tends to come into leaf before the rest of the tree. A tree that had the sign of the witches' broom upon it was certain to have something strange and magical about it, in old country lore.

U

U.F.O.s

The U.F.O., or Unidentified Flying Object, was known long before Kenneth Arnold's famous sighting on Mount Rainier, which started the modern investigation into so-called 'flying saucers'.

The Roman author Pliny, in his *Natural History,* mentions a "flying shield" that appeared in the sky; and there is a wealth of strange tales, scattered through ancient writings, that students of the subject are re-examining today, with fresh interest.

In olden days, strange appearances in the sky were often ascribed to witchcraft. An interesting legend from this point of view is that of the Kingdom of Magonia, told of in old stories from France and Italy.

Magonia was supposed to be a beautiful, unearthly city, somewhere in the clouds. From it, mysterious cloudships sailed over the earth, and sometimes landed. However, the Church regarded Magonia as a wicked heathen place, and said that it was either built by witches, or else the witches were in league with its inhabitants, to rain hail upon the earth and destroy the crops.

A man of more liberal and less superstitious views than many of his time, was the tenth-century Archbishop Agobard of Lyons. He did not share the popular fears about witches and sorcery; and he wrote about the belief in the sky-ships of Magonia in terms which could have a bearing on present-day studies of U.F.O.s. He denounced the idea "that the sorcerers who cause the storms are in connection with the ship-people, and are paid by them", and said such a belief was "stupid".

The bishop also related how once he himself had saved the lives of four people, three men and a woman. For some reason the mob believed these people to have landed from a sky-ship, and they were in danger of being stoned to death, when the bishop intervened and rescued them. Unfortunately, Bishop Agobard gives no description of these beings, nor does he say what became of them.

Writers in past centuries have sometimes referred to a strange appearance in the sky which they call a 'fire-drake.' It seems to have been a kind of fiery cloud, which flew rapidly across the heavens. Such "flying dragons" were seen over various countries in 1532, according to an old book, *The Contemplation of Mysteries* (quoted in *The World of Wonders,* Cassell and Co., London, 1884), which was published in the reign of Queen Elizabeth I. It ascribes them to the "pollicie of devils and inchantments of the wicked". In the eighteenth century such appearances were reasoned about, rather unconvincingly, as being caused by differences of temperature in the atmosphere. But the flying 'fire-drake' sounds remarkably like the twentieth century U.F.O.

UNITED STATES OF AMERICA, WITCHCRAFT IN PRESENT-DAY

Witchcraft is active and widespread in the United States at the present day. There are also historical and traditional links with European witchcraft.

America has a great inheritance of old-world lore, brought to its shores by pioneer ancestors from all over Europe. In some parts of the United States, these beliefs have been intermingled with voodoo as practised by American negroes. The result is that a good deal of what is called voodoo in America today owes at least as much to European origins as it does to Africa or the Caribbean.

For over thirty years, the late Roy Heist ran a business on San Francisco's Mission Street, which combined taxidermy with a trade in the requisites of witchcraft and voodoo, extending to all parts of the United States. In 1962 he was quoted as saying that business was particularly good with New York, Chicago, New Orleans and Los Angeles, as well as locally in San Francisco—proof that the present-day interest in witchcraft is not really new, only more open than it used to be.

Heist was a remarkable man, with piercing eyes and a shock of white hair. He looked the part of a wizard, and he prided himself on the genuineness of his wares; if a customer asked for dried bat's wing or mummy dust, then that was just what they got. But his customers had to be genuine magical practitioners, who knew what they wanted. Heist would not prescribe for them. That way, he kept within the law.

Other testimony to the fact of witchcraft practices in the United States which are not simply done for kicks by moderns who have been seeing sensational films, is provided by the work of an American authority on folklore, Vance Randolph.

Mr Randolph has made a close study of witchcraft lore in the Ozark Mountains district of Missouri and Arkansas. This is a rural and relatively isolated region, the real backwoods, where old customs and beliefs lingered long; though the mountain folk were clannish and reserved, and would not discuss their private affairs with any curious outsider. In his book *Ozark Superstitions* (Columbia University Press, 1947), it was stated that the belief in witchcraft among hillfolk was still strong, and there were many people still reputed to be witches.

It is evident from Vance Randolph's work that witchcraft in the Ozarks is the remains at any rate of an organised cult. The secret doctrines and teachings must pass only between blood relatives, or between people who have been united in sexual intercourse. The words of charms must be learned from a person of the opposite sex, to be fully powerful. Witches are initiated by a solemn ceremony. Randolph was told, by women who claimed to have experienced both, that being initiated as a witch was a profound spiritual crisis, even more moving than what the Christians call conversion.

A very interesting article on "Nakedness in Ozark Folk Belief" by Vance Randolph, appeared in *The Journal of American Folklore* in 1953. He tells of naked rites to aid the growing of crops, which he himself had witnessed in Missouri. For instance, he saw a man and two women rolling naked on ground freshly prepared for sowing turnips, and was told that it was "their religion". Randolph stated in this article his opinion that, although ceremonies connected with witchcraft were secret, the old nature worship was not dead; and he believed that in certain well-hidden places in American backwoods, men and women still danced naked, in celebration of ancient rites.

Another part of the United States in which old beliefs have lingered, is south-eastern Pennsylvania, among the farming communities called the Pennsylvania Dutch. These people are famous for their brightly-painted barns, decorated with what are known as hex signs. This term is derived from the old German word *hexe,* meaning a witch. The purpose of these signs was originally to protect against black witchcraft and evil spirits.

Though many variations appear, the basis of the design is a circle with a geometrical figure inside it, usually a five-pointed, six-pointed, or eight-pointed star. Hex signs are usually painted in brilliant primary colours: red, blue, yellow, white and black. They appear not only on barns, but as general motifs of decoration in folk art, for all kinds of things; though the brightly-coloured barn decorations have attracted most attention.

The real hex sign has been described as a painted prayer. The outer circle represents God, or the Infinite. The centre of the circle is the human being, reaching out to God. The design represents harmony and beauty, a right relationship to God and the Universe. Formalised drawings of hearts and flowers sometimes occur in the design also. They represent life, love, beauty and prosperity.

Among the Pennsylvania Dutch, *hex* or *hexerai* means witchcraft. There is white hexerai and black hexerai, and both kinds make use of drawn symbols. A famous book of hexerai is *John George Hohman's Pow-Wows, or The Long-Lost Friend*. This very curious book first appeared in 1820, and still circulates in the United States, usually without a printer's or publisher's name. Most of its spells and charms have a Christian appearance; but their essential nature is of traditional European magic. The book contains directions: "To prevent witches from bewitching cattle," "How to relieve persons or animals bewitched," "Against evil spirits and all manner of witchcraft," and so on. Its author, John George Hohman, was a resident of Berks County, Pennsylvania, and a noted practitioner of white hexerai.

The outbreak of witchcraft persecution in Salem, Massachusetts, in 1692, as a result of which twenty people were executed, is the most notorious witchcraft episode in American history; but by no means the only one. The first person to be hanged as a witch in New England was Alse Young, in 1647; and in succeeding years a number of others were executed on the same charge.

The fact that the Salem trials were based upon the hysterical accusations of a group of neurotic young women, has often been taken to mean that there was no witchcraft actually existing in Massachusetts at that time. However, a detailed examination of the evidence casts some doubt upon this view. Here and there, things are said which make it seem at least possible that an underground cult existed in seventeenth-century Massachusetts, with doctrine which was not that of the dour Puritans.

For instance, a man called William Barker, of Andover, Massachusetts (a town which already possessed a reputation for sorcery), made a very strange and lengthy confession, the record of which contains the following: "He saith the Devil promised that all his people should be equal, that there should be no day of resurrection or of judgment, and neither punishment nor shame for sin."

There occur also some detailed descriptions of Sabbats, upon which the Reverend Cotton Mather, one of the leading figures in the witch-trials, remarked: "The Witches do say, that they form themselves much after the manner of Congregational Churches; and that they have a Baptism and a Supper, and Officers among them, abominably resembling those of our Lord." This is, in fact, quite a good way to describe coven organisation.

In present-day Salem, Massachusetts, poignant relics of the witch-craft trials are now preserved on public display, in Essex County Superior Court House and at the Essex Institute.

When Raymond Buckland, an English witch who has settled in New York, recently published the statement: "In only recent years did the Craft come to America . . . there is no long background of true Witchcraft in the United States," his temerity raised a good deal of wrath among American witches. From the facts given above, it will be seen that their indignation was justified. It has been suggested that Mr Buckland derived this view from the late Gerald Gardner; but this can hardly be so, because it was Gerald Gardner who first introduced me to the writings of Vance Randolph about American witch lore.

Raymond Buckland is the holder of a Ph.D. in anthropology, and the director of the Buckland Museum of Witchcraft and Magick at Long Island, New York. He and his wife were initiated as witches in the Isle of Man, at the famous Witches Mill where the late Gerald Gardner's coven met; so his presentation of witchcraft is naturally very much that of Gerald Gardner, with its insistence that witchcraft is essentially an ancient religion, and should be used for good and not evil.

Other witches in USA agree with this view; but they discount the Gardnerian insistence upon ritual nudity. They say that if witch power cannot penetrate through the moderate layer of clothing that most people wear today, then it must be pretty feeble power.

They also dislike the system of witch aristocracy, involving 'high priestesses', 'witch queens', and so on, that the Bucklands have sought to establish. They say that there have been covens of witches, and individual witches, in America, ever since the country was first colonised from Europe. The fact that until recent times witches had to keep very quiet, with the memory of Salem ever-present at the back of their minds, does not mean they had died out. Indeed, some American witches have been none too polite about the Bucklands, describing them as 'Johnny-come-latelies', and their version of witchcraft as 'artsy-fartsy'.

Nevertheless, Dr Buckland and his wife (whose witch name is Lady Rowen), have 'seeded' quite a number of new covens throughout the United States; and Dr Buckland is the author of several popular books upon the occult, including *Witchcraft from the Inside* (Llewellyn Publications, Minnesota, 1971), and *Ancient and Modern Witchcraft* (H.C. Publishers Inc., New York, 1970).

Yet the memory of Salem is not dead; in some minds, the terror and hysteria of the witch-hunt only sleeps, and is capable of waking from its slumber, even in the modern world. This is proved by a frightening incident which happened in Cincinnati. The October 1968 issue of a magazine called *Eye* carried an article called "The Magic Explosion", dealing with present-day interest in witchcraft and the occult, and mentioning meetings in Cincinnati. Soon afterwards, some witches who live in that city had their apartment broken into and wrecked by vandals. Valuable paintings were slashed to ribbons. If the witches had been there at the time, would they have been slashed too?

The expression 'magic explosion' is, however, not too sensational to describe what has happened recently in the United States. Everywhere, people are eager to learn about the occult, and interest in witchcraft is particularly lively. Witches themselves regard this as the beginning of the new Aquarian Age. Sometimes this is a healthy new freedom of the mind—sometimes something far otherwise.

For one thing, the commercialisers have not been slow to cash in. Shops purporting to sell witchcraft and magic supplies have now opened up all over the country, on a scale that would have amazed old Roy Heist. You can buy everything from statues of 'the horned god of the witches' (modelled on Eliphas Levi's picture of Baphomet), through candles, incense, anointing oils and herbs, to 'authentic witches athames' and luxuriously-bound books of blank leaves for recording spells. The sound of the pipes of Pan can scarcely be heard, for the rustle of dollar bills and the clang of the cash register!

There are also books purporting to teach their readers do-it-yourself witchcraft. Some of these books sneer at the idea of any standard of occult right and wrong, and present witchcraft simply as a means of 'getting on' in a materialistic society, of grabbing more dollars, and of bending others to your will; in other words, the gratification of greed and lust, no matter how squalid. As one who has studied and practised the occult for nearly a quarter of a century, I warn the readers—and the writers—of these books. By approaching any sort of occultism in this spirit, they are laying up trouble for themselves. The power of karma is very real, and none can escape it.

A more serious, and sadder, development is the number of mushroom 'Satanist' cults which have sprung up. These insist upon identifying witchcraft with devil-worship and Satanism. Their rituals are as synthetic as the plastic horns their flamboyant leaders delight to be photographed wearing; as any experienced occultist would immediately recognise. But to the frustrated and sexually repressed, and to young people looking for kicks, these cults are attractive.

What is sad about them is the way in which they show that there are many people today who can only understand sexual satisfaction as being the work of the Devil. Hence such people can only achieve the fulfilment of their natural instincts in a context of 'wickedness'. In the surroundings of what they conceive of as a 'Black Mass' or a 'witches' Sabbat'—the more lurid the better—they find at last the orgasmic release that has hitherto been denied them.

People of this mentality have been sexually crippled by life-denying negative morality, phoney 'purity' and hypocritical prudery. The sadism and blood-lust which often go hand-in-hand with Satanism, are further symptoms of what Wilhelm Reich has truly called the emotional plague, which is the result of centuries of 'Churchianity'. People have been indoctrinated with the idea that nearly all their natural feelings and desires are evil; and the old gods have been hidden behind the ugly mask of Satan.

Some of the leaders of these cults believe in what they are doing, and are a classic example in the occult world of the saying that a little learning is a dangerous thing. Others are simply clever psychologists, whose only real belief in Satanism is that they've found a devilish good racket. In my opinion, all are dangerous; not because they can evoke a non-existent 'Satan', but because they invite their followers to attune themselves to unseen forces of evil, and to the lowest planes of the astral world.

One of the influences which have brought about the craze for delving into the darker regions of the occult, is the sensational film *Rosemary's Baby*, which deals with Satanism. Was it more than a cruel coincidence that the producer of this film, Roman Polanski, lost his wife and their unborn child in the horrific murders carried out by Charles Manson and his followers, who called themselves Satan's Slaves? (*See* MANSON, CHARLES.)

American witches who are serious followers of the Craft of the

Wise have, like their brothers and sisters in Britain, been coming forward publicly in an effort to combat misrepresentation, and clear themselves of the stigma of Satanism. Many of them have talked to writers like Susan Roberts, who found them to be a fair cross-section of American citizens. Not *quite* ordinary people, truly—but people just the same.

Her book *Witches, U.S.A.* (Dell Publishing Co., Inc., New York, 1971) reveals that there are many men and women in America today who are using the old witchcraft lore to evolve a basic philosophy of life. They regard this as being as legitimate a way of searching for truth as any other, in a world in which the authority of established religion, science and politics is being more and more deeply questioned.

On Lammas Day (1st August) 1971, a number of California covens joined together in an attempt to end the war in Vietnam. A letter was sent to a leading occult magazine in advance of this date, inviting other people to join with them in this collective use of the power of thought, which was reminiscent of English witches' efforts against Hitler. According to the writer of the letter, Ken Nahigian of Sacramento, California, their feeling was that if a large enough number of witches and other occultists were united in working for this aim at one time, they would be able to "harness enormous fields of collective psychic power for peace".

At the time of writing, it is too early to estimate the result of this magical effort; but it opens up interesting possibilities for the future.

UPRIGHT MAN, THE

The vagabonds and sturdy beggars of olden time had among themselves certain organisations, with rules and orders of precedence, which had considerable power. These organisations were called the Beggars' Brotherhoods. They were presided over by an elected King of the Beggars, one of the most famous of whom was Cock Lorell, known as "the most notorious rogue that ever lived".

Cock Lorell ruled his picaresque kingdom for about twenty-two years, until 1533. He is said to have first drawn up the Five-and-Twenty Orders of Knaves, according to their precedence. One of these Orders, the 'Upright Man', has a very curious connection with the Old Religion of the witches.

The vagabonds were known as the 'Canting Crew', because for purposes of secrecy they spoke among themselves the jargon which is still known as thieves' cant. Much of the cant language was evolved from the tongue of the gypsies, with whom the vagabonds mingled as they travelled the roads together.

In the case of the Witches of Warboys, Huntingdonshire, in 1593, Alice Samuel, one of the accused, confessed that "an upright man" gave her six spirits as familiars, "which had reward of her by sucking of her blood".

The witches' familiar in this sense is simply a small animal, reptile or bird, used for divining. It is quite possible that in the old days witches used to give the familiar a spot of their blood—or drop of their milk, in the case of a nursing mother—in order to establish a psychic link between the familiar and the witch. There are many instances of such familiars being given by one witch to another.

Alice Samuel swore at first that she did not know the name of the "upright man"; but it came out during the trial that his name was William Langley or Langland, and it was suggested that he was "the devil in man's clothing".

Now, the male leader of a coven was known in olden times among the witches as 'The Devil'. He was regarded as the representative of the Horned God, and sometimes dressed in animal skins and a horned head-dress on important ritual occasions.

As such, he presided over those rites of fertility which so upset Puritans, because of their sexual emphasis. Being regarded as the incarnation of the male source of life, in a spiritual sense his embraces were sought in ritual intercourse by his female followers.

From the records that have come down to us about the role of the Upright Man in the old beggars' brotherhoods, it is evident that it has strong connections with that of the Devil in the witch covens.

He was not the first rank of the Canting Crew. That distinction belonged to the 'Rufflers', or 'notorious rogues'. The Upright Man came second, and third were the 'Roberds-men', defined as "mighty Thieves, like Robin Hood". Yet the Upright Man enjoyed certain peculiar privileges, which belonged to no one else. This is his description, from *The Fraternitye of Vacabonds,* printed in London by John Awdeley, and originally published about 1561:

> An Upright Man is one that goeth with the truncheon of a staff, which staff they call a Filtchman. This man is of so much authority, that meeting with any of his profession, he may call them to account, and command a share or snap unto himself, of all that they have gained by their trade in one month. And if he do them wrong, they have no remedy against him,

no though he beats them as he useth commonly to do. He may also command any of their women, which they call Doxies, to serve his turn. He hath ye chief place at any market walk, and other assemblies, and is not of any to be controlled.

It would seem that his office was something altogether apart, and that he was regarded with a kind of religious respect. His rights over all the women are particularly curious. Further details of them are given in *A New Dictionary of the Terms, Ancient and Modern, of the Canting Crew,* by "B. E., Gent", published in London in 1640. "Upright-men: the second rank of the Canting Tribes, having sole right to the first night's lodging with the Dells."

The "Dells" were "the twenty-sixth order of the Canting tribe; young bucksome Wenches, ripe and prone to Venery, but have not lost their Virginity, which the *upright man* pretends to, and seizes. Then she is free for any of the Fraternity."

Moreover, it was the Upright Man who performed the ceremony of initiation called 'Stalling to the Rogue', by which a newcomer was admitted to the brotherhood. Thomas Harman, who compiled the first dictionary of English cant terms in 1566, tells us that when the Upright Man

> mete any beggar, whether he be sturdy or impotent, he will demand of him whether ever he was 'stalled to the roge', or no. If he says he was, he will know of whom, and his name yt stalled him. And if he be not learnedly, able to shew him the whole circumstance thereof he will spoyle him of his money, either of his best garment, if it be worth any money, and have him to the bowsing-ken: which is, to some typling house next adjoyninge, and layth there to gage the best thing that he hath for twenty pence or two shillings; this man obeyeth for feare of beatinge. Then dooth this upright man call for a gage of bowse, which is a quarte potte of drink, and powres the same upon his peld pate, adding these words,—'I G.P., do stalle thee, W. T., to the Roge, and that from henceforth it shall be lawful for thee to cant, that is, to ask for begge for thi living, in all-places.'

(A Caveat for Common Cursetors, Vulgarly Called Vagabones).

The strange and secret office of the Upright Man, in the underworld of old England, seems to have no other purpose but one derived from a deeply-believed tradition. He is the clear descendant of the Old Religion, surviving among the outcasts of society.

V

VAMPIRES

The word 'vampire' is from the Slavonic *wampyr;* and since the famous novel *Dracula,* by Bram Stoker (Constable and Co, London, 1897), and the many films and plays based upon it, people usually associate the belief in vampires with the Balkan countries. It is not generally realised that this belief was formerly just as strongly held in Britain.

Nevertheless, it is the real origin of the old custom of burying the unhallowed dead at a crossroads, with a stake through the corpse's heart. The object of this practice, which was not abolished by law until 1823, was to prevent the corpse becoming a vampire.

Vampirism has always been associated with black magic. Those who practised black magic in their lifetime were particularly likely to become vampires after their death. Some occultists today believe vampirism to be a fact, although fortunately a rare one.

Opinions differ as to what precisely a vampire is. Some believe it to be an evil spirit, which animates the newly-dead body of a person wicked enough to have some affinity with it. Others say that the vampire is the soul of the dead person, who because of his or her bad conscience, is afraid to pass on to the Other World, and so remains earthbound. The soul clings desperately to its link with earth; that is, its mortal body. It prevents this from decaying by sending a ghostly simulacrum of itself, formed of etheric material, to attack the living and feed upon their blood, which is the vital stream of life. This dangerous ghost feeds not so much upon the actual blood, as upon the vitality of its victim, whose very life may be slowly drained away by such a visitation.

A third theory is the more crude one, that the vampire is actually a living corpse, which sleeps in its tomb by day, and leaves it at night to prowl in search of blood, by which means it sustains its unholy life. The Slavs call such hideous creatures of darkness *Nosferatu*, "the Undead".

It is a vampire of this kind that is described in the famous and horrible story of the Vampire of Croglin Grange, recorded by Augustus Hare in his memoirs. Augustus Hare was a Victorian clergyman with a *penchant* for collecting ghost stories, and he set this one down as if it were fact. Later researchers, however, think it may be fictional; as, although there is a place called Croglin in Cumberland, they cannot trace the 'Hall' or 'Grange' where this frightful tale is supposed to have happened.

In brief, a young lady living at Croglin Grange was supposed to have been attacked by a terrible, corpse-like being which got in through her bedroom window and bit her in the throat. The men of the house pursued the horror, and shot at it; but it escaped in the darkness, and made its way towards the churchyard. The next day, they renewed the search, and eventually discovered the creature lying in a coffin, within a vault. In its leg was the mark of the bullet that had been fired at it the previous night. The body was destroyed, and the haunting ceased.

However, if there is any truth in the legend of the vampire, the second of the theories detailed above seems the most likely one.

In the days when witches were hanged in England, it is probable that their bodies were often buried at a crossroads, with a stake through the heart, because witches were believed to be likely to become vampires after their death. There are many stories of haunted crossroads in lonely places in the English countryside, which probably have their origin in this old custom. Suicides, too, and anyone who died under the Church's ban, were often buried in this way.

Some interesting particulars of very old English vampire stories are given by Thomas Wright, in his *Essays on Subjects Connected with the Literature, Popular Superstitions, and History of England in the Middle Ages* (2 vols, John Russell Smith, London, 1846). He tells us:

> Several stories of the English vampyres of the twelfth century are given in the twenty-second and twenty-third chapters of the fifth book of William of Newbury's History. The body of a man in Buckinghamshire left his grave, and wandered about both by night and day, to the terror and danger of the neighbourhood. Application was made to the bishop of Lincoln, then at London, who held a consultation with his friends on the subject; and in the course of the inquiry some of them told him that it was a thing of

no uncommon occurrence in England, and that the only remedy was to dig up the body and burn it. However, another method of getting rid of the monster was suggested. The bishop made out a chartula of absolution, the grave was opened, and the body was found without any signs of corruption: the chartula was placed on its breast, and, after the grave had been again closed up, it was never more seen or heard of. Another such body caused a pestilence at Berwick-upon-Tweed. The body of a priest of Mailros, which wandered about in the same manner, was wounded in the shoulder by a man who was watching to drive it away; and when, immediately afterwards, the grave to which it had been traced was opened, it was found full of blood. Another had been so destructive, that some of the young men of the village agreed to go together to dig him up and burn him. They found the body but slightly covered with earth, 'swoln out with an enormous corpulency, and its face red and chubby'; and so much blood flowed from it when pierced with a sharp weapon, that it might thereby be known to have been a 'sucker of the blood of many'.

Walter Map, in his treatise *De Nugis Curialium,* also gives some curious stories of English vampires in the twelfth century, which shows how prevalent this belief was among our forefathers at that period.

The correct wood for the stake which was driven through the corpse's heart is generally said to be ash; though some accounts give whitethorn or rowan. Garlic, either the flowers or the bulb, is also recommended as a protection against evil influences. It should be used fresh; when it has dried up and become stale it should be burned, and replaced with fresh flowers or root, as necessary. The wild dog rose is another flower which has the virtue of repelling vampires.

The probable reason why we connect the Balkan countries of Transylvania, as that region used to be called, with vampirism, is that so great a terror of vampires prevailed there in the early eighteenth century that a government enquiry took place, and was reported in the contemporary press.

At Meduegya in Servia in 1732 the case occurred which prompted the official investigation referred to above. There had been previous reported cases; but this was the first one to be investigated in such a way, and it seemed to bear out the old belief that vampirism is contagious. Those who die of the vampire's assaults become vampires themselves.

It appears that five years previously a man called Arnod Paole had been killed by falling from a wagon. During his lifetime, Paole often recounted how he had once been bitten by a vampire. The people of Meduegya soon had good reason to remember these tales, when an outbreak of vampirism began to terrorise the neighborhood. As a result of it, four people died.

It was decided to open Paole's grave, and forty days after his burial this was done. The body was found to be quite fresh, and shockingly stained with blood. The vampire corpse was burnt at once; but the epidemic continued to spread. Eventually, the trouble reached such proportions that it came to the ears of the government, and official action was taken.

A detachment of soldiers, including three army surgeons, together with their commanding officer, were sent to Meduegya. Their orders were to open the graves of those who had died recently, examine the bodies, and if necessary, burn those which appeared to be in the vampire condition.

They made a detailed report of what they found, dated 7th January 1732. It makes one of the most amazing and grisly stories ever to find its way into official records. Thirteen graves were opened in all; and of these, ten were found to contain corpses that were fresh and rosy-cheeked, and which when dissected proved to contain fresh blood. The other three bodies, although exhumed from the same cemetery, and in some cases more recently interred than the suspect corpses, were undergoing the normal process of decomposition.

All the bodies which were found to be in the vampire condition were beheaded and then burnt to ashes.

The lore of vampires tells us that they are only active between sunset and sunrise. They are things of darkness, and cannot bear the clean light of the sun. Dogs, which are psychically sensitive animals, can perceive the approach of a vampire, and will become unusually disturbed, barking and howling, if such a fearful entity is abroad in the night. The Buckinghamshire vampire, written of by William of Newbury, was unusual in being active "both by night and day".

I have not touched here upon the subject of vampirism by the living; to do so in full would make this entry excessively long. It should be said, however, that apart from such psychopathic cases as that of the murderer John George Haigh, who drank the blood of his victims, there is a very dangerous kind of vampirism which consists of draining the vitality of another person. When done deliberately, this is a form of black magic. It is sometimes done, however, more or less unconsciously, by selfish and possessive people, and the results for the victim can be serious.

W

WEREWOLVES

The hideous transformation of man (and sometimes woman) into wolf is a traditional power of black witchcraft. Its usual means are by stripping naked, anointing oneself with a magical unguent, and then girding on an enchanted belt, sometimes said to be of wolf's skin and sometimes of human skin. This causes the transformation to take place—according to legend, at any rate.

Is such an awful thing really possible? Or is it simply a foolish superstition, reduced to its ultimate absurdity by the makers of cheap horror films?

Some occultists believe that in a certain sense, werewolfery *is* possible. What is transformed, however, is not the physical body, but the astral body of the human being. There can be circumstances in which this astral entity can partly or wholly materialise, if it can draw sufficient substance from the physical body to do so. The physical body will in the meantime be lying in a state of deep trance.

Algernon Blackwood, that brilliant writer upon occult themes, has described in detail the precise mechanism of werewolfery in his story 'The Camp of the Dog', one of the tales in his book *John Silence* (Eveleigh Nash, London), which first appeared in 1908. In the nineteenth century, the famous French occultist, Eliphas Lévi, also attributed werewolfery to the transformation of the astral body. Lévi added the detail that if the astral body of the sorcerer was struck at or wounded, while it was abroad in its wolf shape, the wounds or blows would manifest themselves upon the sorcerer's material body. This phenomenon is well-known to occultists in connection with astral travelling, and is called 'repercussion'.

The Old Norse language has a significant word, *'ham-farir'*, the meaning of which demonstrates the age of this belief. In the *Icelandic-English Dictionary* by Gudbrand Vigfusson (Oxford, 1874), this word is defined as "the 'faring' or travelling in the assumed shape of an animal, fowl, or deer, fish or serpent, with magical speed over land and sea, the wizard's own body meantime lying lifeless and motionless."

A number of the more astute writers of ancient days also explained werewolfery in this way, notably Gaspar Peucer in 1553; but later, as the witchcraft persecution grew more intense, the anti-witch writers insisted upon the actual, crude physical change of man into wolf and back again. Writers of olden times also recognised a form of mental sickness called lycanthropy, in which the afflicted person imagined himself to be a wolf, and tried to run on all fours, howling in a horrible manner. This was originally regarded as a kind of madness, but later ascribed to the power of Satan, along with most things that were strange and inexplicable.

Why, however, should the wolf be the favourite shape for these manifestations? Probably because this beast of prey was for so long a lively source of fear to our ancestors, in the days when the land was lonelier than it is now, the forests thicker, and the population much less. The last wolves in England were killed in the reign of King Henry VIII; but in Scotland and Ireland they were not exterminated until the eighteenth century. In other European countries, the danger of actual wolves remains to this day; and with it, very probably, the lingering belief in the wolf that may not be always a wolf, and the man that may not be unchangeably a man, especially on nights of the full moon.

Gervase of Tilbury, writing in about 1212, said in his book *Otia Imperialia* (quoted by Montague Summers in *The Werewolf,* Kegan Paul, London, 1933); "Certainly, we have often seen in England men who are turned into wolves at the changes of the moon." He adds that these men were called *'gerulfos'* by the French, but that the English word for them was *'werewolf', 'were'* meaning 'man'. (The modern French term is *'loup-garou'*.) In Ireland, the people of Ossory were known in ancient times as 'the Children of the Wolf', because of their reputed ability to become werewolves.

The werewolf belief is not something that arose merely in the Middle Ages. Pre-Christian writers also tell stories of werewolves; and there was an actual cult of werewolfery connected with the worship of Zeus Lycaeus, 'Wolfish Zeus' or 'Zeus of the Wolves.' This cult goes back to the very early days of Ancient Greece; but it was still being secretly carried on when Pausanius wrote his *Description of Greece* in about A.D. 176 (quoted by Montague Summers in *The Werewolf*).

The tradition of the werewolf in Europe goes back a very long way, and there may be a number of different sources from which it has evolved: cannibalistic rites of primitive totemism; dancers in animal skins; depraved blood-lust and sadism; the madness known as lycanthropy; and the projection of the astral body in animal form, aided by trance-inducing unguents and magical processes.

The chief recorded trials for werewolfery are all from the continent of Europe. In most cases, it was alleged by the prosecution that the werewolf gained his or her powers of transformation through witchcraft.

In December, 1521, three men were tried as werewolves at Poligny, in France, and in due course found guilty and executed. All three confessed to a number of killings while they were in the form of wolves, and also to coupling with she-wolves, which they preferred to normal intercourse with women.

In 1573 Gilles Garnier was executed at Dôle in France, for having in the form of a werewolf devoured several children. A contemporary account says that Garnier was a solitary man who lived with his wife among lonely woods. They were poor, hungry people, and because of this Garnier had been tempted to make a pact with an evil spirit, which he met while wandering one evening in the woods. The spirit gave him an unguent or salve, by which means he was able to transform himself into a wolf and get meat to satisfy his hunger; but the meat he came to enjoy most was human flesh.

A very famous werewolf trial, that of Peter Stubbe or Stumpf, took place in Germany in 1589. It is well-known because a pamphlet account of it was printed in London in 1590, entitled "A True Discourse Declaring the damnable life and death of one Stubbe Peeter, a most wicked Sorcerer, who in the likeness of a Wolf, committed many murders, continuing this devilish practice 25 years, killing and devouring Men, Women and Children. Who for the same fact was taken and executed the 31 of October last past in the Town of Bedburg near the City of Cologne in Germany." There is a copy of this black-letter pamphlet in the British Museum.

In 1598, several big trials for werewolfery took place in France. One of them, in Paris, concerned a tailor of Chalons who enticed children into his shop, and then killed and ate them. At night, he was said to have roamed the woods as a werewolf. Among other things, barrels of human bones were found in the cellars of his house; and the details of the case were so frightful that the court ordered the records of it to be burned. The tailor, too, was burned at the stake.

In this year also, a whole family called Gandillon were found guilty of werewolfery at St.-Claude. An unusual feature of this case was that two of the accused were women. But the woman werewolf has been alleged to exist in other instances, though the charge is more frequently made against men.

Another trial of the same year was at Angers, where a beggar named Jacques Roulet was found guilty of killing children in the form of a werewolf. In his case, however, in spite of his confession of having been "devoted to the Devil" by his parents, and of having received from them the unguent that made him a werewolf, the sentence of death was remitted. He was sent to a hospital, which in those days would have been run by monks.

Similar mercy was shown to Jean Grenier, a lad of 14 or so who boasted of being a werewolf in 1603. His case is recorded in detail by Pierre De Lancre, the judge from Bordeaux who saw and questioned him. De Lancre describes Grenier's strange and frightening appearance, with teeth that were unusually large and long, as also were his blackened nails, while his haggard eyes glittered like those of a wolf. He had marvellous agility, and could run on all fours and leap like an animal.

Grenier was a homeless, runaway lad, who seemed to like telling wild stories. But apparently he genuinely believed himself to be a werewolf; and several children in the district had been killed by a wolf.

Grenier confessed that he had been taken by another youth into the depths of a wood, and presented to a tall, dark man, whom he called the Lord of the Forest. The stranger was dressed all in black, and rode upon a black horse. He dismounted and conversed with the two lads, saluting Jean with a kiss; but his lips were colder than ice. At a subsequent meeting, Jean had agreed to bind himself to the service of the Lord of the Forest, who had marked him with a small dagger.

Then they had drunk wine together, and the Lord of the Forest had presented him with a wolf-skin and a pot of magical unguent, and instructed him in werewolfery. On several occasions, he said, he had seen meetings in the forest, where men whom he knew had bowed down before its mysterious lord.

Jean Grenier was at first sentenced to death; but this was commuted to life imprisonment in a monastery at Bordeaux. Here De Lancre visited him in 1610, and talked to him. Grenier seems to have been treated more as a sick lad victimised by an evil spirit, than as a criminal; though he was told that if he tried to escape from the monastery he would be hanged. He died in 1611, aged about 21 or 22.

It is possible to see in such tales as that of Jean Grenier the remains of a cult, which resembles those of the Leopard Men and Panther Men of Africa. We know that the cult of Zeus Lycaeus, which involved werewolfery, existed in ancient pagan Greece; and the Norse followers of Odin, who were called *berserks* because they wore the skin of bears or wolves, may be relevant also. On the other hand, the grisly feature of cannibalism that appears in accounts of werewolfery, could perhaps have arisen from sheer hunger for flesh meat among poor, half-starved peasants.

WITCH BALLS

The term 'witch ball' is given most frequently to those bright reflecting balls of glass that one often sees hanging up in antique shops. They look like larger and more durable versions of the shining balls that are sold to decorate Christmas trees.

Their use in old houses and cottages was to hang suspended in a window, or in some dark corner; or sometimes a standing version was made, to be placed where it would reflect the light. They are often quite large and heavy, and need a chain to hang them by. A particularly huge silver witch ball used to hang in an old shop in the Brighton Lanes, nearly filling the little dark window, and surrounded with all kinds of small antiques and Victoriana.

One finds, however, that not many antique dealers can tell you what a witch ball really is. In fact, a good deal of curious lore surrounds these mysterious globes. Their main purpose as house decorations was to avert the much-feared influence of the Evil Eye. (*See* EVIL EYE.)

The shiny, reflecting globe cast back the influence of the malign glance of the Evil Eye, upon the person who sent it forth. Hence the popularity of witch balls hung in windows. However, their attractiveness as ornaments in themselves and their ability to lighten a dark corner by reflecting a cheerful ray of sunlight, has given witch balls continued popularity after their original use has been forgotten.

There are other kinds of witch balls, beside the mirror-bright reflecting ones. A very attractive variety was made of Nailsea glass. This consists of a ball of many colours, semi-transparent when the light shines through it, and presenting a swirl of different hues, somewhat like the patterns which have come to be called 'psychedelic'. These Nailsea glass balls are generally smaller than the reflecting ones.

These in their turn are probably an imitation in glass of a still older type of witch ball. I have one of this earlier type in my own collection. It came from an old house in a Sussex village, and consists of a hollow sphere of thick glass, slightly greenish in colour. It has a small hole, plugged with a cork; and inside is a mass of teased-out threads of different colours. It must have taken someone long ago a great deal of patience, to introduce thread after thread through the little hole, until the ball was filled.

The effect of these many threads, which were probably bright-coloured originally, though faded now with age, was that of an intertwining, mazy pattern. In my opinion, when the Nailsea glass-makers started their famous manufacture in 1788, this is the pattern they copied in making witch balls of coloured glass.

The object of the bright swirl and maze of different colours, like many other forms of decoration which involve a pattern of twisting lines, was again to counteract the glance of the Evil Eye. The idea was, that instead of falling directly upon some person, the dangerous glance would be diverted to follow the twisting pattern, and thus its power would be dissipated.

From late in the seventeenth century glassmakers had been producing hollow glass globes, or globular bottles, for people to hang up in their houses as a protection against evil influences. Devout Christians filled the bottles with holy water; but others preferred the older device of the mazy threads and twining colours.

It was believed that the glass ball would attract to itself all the influences of ill luck and ill wishing that would otherwise have fallen upon the household. Hence every so often the witch-ball would be wiped clean. The same belief and treatment was accorded in the West Country to the glass 'walking sticks' made with a swirl of bright colours in them, or hollow and filled with tiny coloured beads. These too were originally hung up in houses as an amulet against the Evil

Eye, and wiped clean by careful housewives to wipe the bad luck away. They were called 'witches' sticks', and many of them were also a product of Nailsea glass.

The Nailsea glassmakers produced all kinds of fancy articles, which were sold at country markets and fairs. People bought the many-coloured witch balls to give their friends and relatives as presents. They were regarded as luck-bringers as well as protective amulets; and some people call them 'wish balls', because they were given with a wish for good luck and prosperity.

Returning to the bright mirror globes, these were also sometimes called 'watch balls'; the idea being that if you watched them long enough the mirrored scene in them would fade out, and change into a visionary picture. Some authorities consider these names to have been corrupted into 'witch balls'; but in my opinion they are merely variants of the term 'witch ball', as the ideas behind them are basically connected with witchcraft.

The brighter mirror globes were originally imported from the Continent. They are often depicted in old Dutch paintings. However, from about 1690 English glassmakers started producing them, and their products were less fragile than the Continental ones. The early silvered witch balls were coated inside with an amalgam containing bismuth, lead, tin and mercury. They were not very durable, as the reflection was liable to damage by damp; nor was their reflection very clear. (Incidentally, damp is still an enemy to the brightness of any reflecting witch ball, if it gets inside the glass; and anyone who owns an antique of this kind should *wipe* it clean, not wash it.)

Later, in the early nineteenth century, improved methods of manufacture were evolved, including one of coating the glass inside with real silver; and in this period very fine reflecting globes were made, of mirror-like perfection. Coloured witch balls of this type began to be made also. In my own collection are witch balls of both dark and pale green, and of gold colour, as well as silver; and a very beautiful blue is sometimes seen also.

In the early nineteenth century the witch ball began to be more of a decoration, and its old magical significance faded into the background. Witch balls were made with everything on them from Scriptural texts to hunting scenes.

But their original significance was not entirely forgotten. In 1930 *The Times* had some interesting correspondence on the survival of belief in witchcraft; so much, in fact, that on 20th September 1930 it published a leading article on the subject, saying it was plain that this belief had by no means died out. In the course of this correspondence, one writer mentioned that she had seen witch balls for sale in a shop near the British Museum, and had been told that there was a ready sale for them. They were believed to turn aside the effects of hostile witchcraft.

Today, with the renewed popularity of all sorts of bric-a-brac and Victoriana among collectors, one now and again sees attempts at making modern reproductions of the old-fashioned witch balls; though so far these are by no means as pleasing as those with the real patina of age upon them. What is not certain is whether their purchasers only want them for decoration, or whether they realise the time-honoured magical significance of the witch ball.

WITCHCRAFT

The subject of this entry could equally well, perhaps better, be called 'Wisecraft'; but witchcraft is the more familiar and time-honoured word. Even so, it is no older than Anglo-Saxon days, and there were witches long before the Angles and Saxons came to Britain.

The Old English forms of the word 'witch' were *wicca* (masculine) and *wicce* (feminine). This shows that a witch could be either a man or a woman. The old plural form was *wiccan*. Later, the Middle English form of the word was *wicche,* for both masculine and feminine.

The word *wiccan* for 'witches' occurs in the Laws of King Alfred, circa A.D. 890. It is found again in Aldhelm's *Glossary* in 1100. The verb 'to bewitch' was *wiccian;* and an Old English word for 'witchcraft' was *wiccedom,* a word that evolved into 'witchdom'.

Dr. Henry More (1614-1687), in his letter which was printed in Joseph Glanvill's *Sadducismus Triumphatus* (London, 1726), had this to say about the derivation of 'witch':

> As for the words *Witch* and *Wizzard,* from the notation of them, they signify no more than a wise man, or a wise woman. In the word *Wizzard,* it is plain at the very sight. And, I think, the most plain, at least operose, deduction of the name *Witch,* is from *Wit,* whose derived adjective might be *Wittigh,* or *Wittich,* and by contraction afterwards, *Witch;* as the noun *Wit* is from the verb to *weet,* which is to know. So that a *Witch,* thus far, is no more than a knowing woman; which answers exactly to the Latin word *Saga,* according to that of Festus, *Sagae dictae anus quae multa sciunt.* Thus, in general; but use, questionless, had appropriated the word to such a kind of skill and knowledge, as was out of the common road, or

extraordinary. Nor did this peculiarity imply in it any unlawfulness. But there was after a further restriction, and most proper of all, and in which alone, nowadays, the words *Witch* and *Wizzard* are used. And that is, for one that has the knowledge or skill of doing, or telling things in an extraordinary way, and that in virtue of either an express or implicit sociation or confederacy with some evil spirit. This is a true and adequate definition of a *Witch,* or *Wizzard,* which, to whomsoever it belongs, is such, and vice versa.

At the time when Henry More wrote this, witchcraft was still a capital crime in Britain, and the punishment was death by hanging. This quotation illustrates the way in which anyone, up to comparatively recent years, who demonstrated any psychic or mediumistic ability, was likely to be accused of being in league with Satan, or at least with evil spirits; even though Dr. More notes that this was not originally implied at all by the word 'witch'.

So ingrained in some followers of the Christian denominations is this idea that we still sometimes see condemnations of Spiritualism on these grounds; namely, that it is 'dealing with the Devil'. When the famous medium, Daniel Dunglas Home, was travelling in European countries where the Catholic Church was predominant, he was quite seriously accused of having a pact with Satan! The Witchcraft Act was persistently used to harass Spiritualist mediums. In fact, the last big trial under this Act was that of the medium Helen Duncan, in 1944; and it was not until 1951 that the Act was finally removed from the Statute Book. (*See* LAWS AGAINST WITCHCRAFT.)

The word 'warlock' is sometimes used for a male witch; but as will be seen from the foregoing passages, this is a modern innovation. 'Warlock' is actually a Scottish term. 'Wizard', as Henry More observed, is simply 'wise-ard', a wise man.

Charles Godfrey Leland regarded the alleged 'Satanic' side of witchcraft as being the creation of the Churches, and grafted by them on to the old paganism. The darker hues of witchcraft, where they existed in the Middle Ages, he saw as being shadowed upon it by the misery and oppression prevalent in society at that time. In his *Legends of Florence* (David Nutt, London, 1896), he has this to say of the history of witchcraft:

> The witches and sorcerers of early times were a widely spread class who had retained the beliefs and traditions of heathenism with all its license and romance and charm of the forbidden. At their head were the Promethean Templars, at their tail all the ignorance and superstition of the

time, and in their ranks every one who was oppressed or injured either by
the nobility or the Church. They were treated with indescribable cruelty,
in most cases worse than beasts of burden, for they were outraged in all
their feelings, not at intervals for punishment, but habitually by custom,
and they revenged themselves by secret orgies and fancied devil-worship,
and occult ties, and stupendous sins, or what they fancied were such. I
can seriously conceive—what no writer seems to have considered—that there
must have been an immense satisfaction in selling or giving one's self to
the devil, or to any power which was at war with their oppressors. So they
went by night, at the full moon, and sacrificed to Diana, or 'later on' to
Satan, and danced and rebelled. It is very well worth noting that we have
all our accounts of sorcerers and heretics from Catholic priests, who had
every earthly reason for misrepresenting them, and did so. In the vast
amount of ancient witchcraft still surviving in Italy, there is not much
anti-Christianity, but a great deal of early heathenism. Diana, not Satan,
is still the real head of the witches. The Italian witch, as the priest Gril-
landus said, stole oil to make a love-charm. But she did not, and does not
say, as he declared, in doing so, 'I renounce Christ'. There the priest plainly
lied. The whole history of the witch mania is an ecclesiastical falsehood, in
which such lies were subtly grafted on the truth. But in due time the Church,
and the Protestants with them, created a Satanic witchcraft of their own,
and it is this aftergrowth which is now regarded as witchcraft in truth.

I agree with Leland's view, because it makes sense and can be
supported by the evidence of history and folklore. If any witch ever
'renounced Christ', it was in blazing resentment against a Church
that supported the oppressors and stifled human liberty. If he or she
ever indulged in 'devil worship', it was because the Church had declared the ancient gods to be devils, and invested the Devil with the
attributes of Pan.

In the second volume of the same work, Leland declares: "I could,
indeed, fill many pages with citations from classic and medieval
authors which prove the ancient belief that Diana was queen of the
witches."

Further on, he says:

It is worth noting that sundry old writers trace back the witch sabbats,
or wild orgies, worshipping of Satan, and full-moon frolics to the festivals
of Diana. Thus Despina declares:

"It was customary of old to celebrate the nightly rites of Diana with
mad rejoicing and the wildest or most delirious dancing and sound (*ordine
contrario sen praepostero*), and all kinds of licentuousness, and with these

rites as partakers were popularly identified the Dryads of the forests, the Napaeoe of the fountains, the Oreads of the mountains, nymphs, and all false gods."

If we add to this that all kinds of outlaws and children of the night, such as robbers and prostitutes, worshipped Diana-Hecate as their patron saint and protectress, we can well believe that this was the true cause and origin of the belief still extremely current or at least known even among the people in Florence, that Diana was the queen of the witches.

In a fresco of the fourteenth century in the Palazzo Publico in Siena, Diana is represented with a bat flying under her, to indicate night and sorcery.

There is no reason to believe that the witchcraft of Italy is *basically* any different from that of the remainder of Western Europe; though the more Celtic regions will naturally show an admixture of their own traditions, as will those where Norse ancestry is prevalent, and so on.

Witchcraft was not only the secret religion of the outcasts of society such as those mentioned above, however. It was also the cult of *people who did not conform,* in whatever walk of life they found themselves.

Because of its connection with moon magic, the number three is much associated with witchcraft. There are traditionally three kinds of witchcraft: white, black and grey. White witchcraft is used solely for constructive purposes. Black witchcraft is used for anti-social or destructive purposes. Grey witchcraft can be adapted either to good or to evil.

Again, there are three degrees of witchcraft, which somewhat resemble those of Entered Apprentice, Fellow Craftsman, and Master Mason, as used by the Masonic fraternity. The existence of these three degrees is seldom mentioned in old literature dealing with witchcraft, as very little of real information was allowed to transpire. Nevertheless, there are some references.

One is to be found in an old French book about witchcraft, *Receuil de Lettres au Sujet des Malefices et du Sortilege . . . par le Sieur Boissier* (Paris, 1731). Boissier tells us that there were three 'marks' which were bestowed upon witches, at three different times; but only the older ones had all three, and this made them magicians.

Another and earlier reference to this point comes from Portugal, in the days of the Inquisition. In the *Confession of certain Witches who were burnt in the city of Lisbon, A.D. 1559,* preserved in the Sentences of the Inquisition, it is recorded that "no one can be a witch (*bruja*) without going through the degrees of *feiticeyra* and *alcoviteyra*".

The fact that these secret degrees existed shows that the society of the witches had knowledge to impart. So also does the wide-spread tradition (it is found in the countryside of England and among the peasants of Italy), that witches cannot die until they have passed on their witchcraft to someone else. What is passed on is the traditional knowledge and lore.

The number three crops up again significantly in the record of an English witch trial in 1672. An accused woman named Anne Tilling, of Malmesbury, Wiltshire, confessed that three witches acted together, and "each three with other threes". This sounds like the breaking-down of the old coven structure into smaller cells, under the pressure of persecution, which was severe in the seventeenth century. If to every group of four threes, or twelve, there was appointed a leader, this would make the traditional thirteen.

There is no doubt that the old organisation of the witch cult has become fragmented by the years of persecution. There are pockets of witchcraft surviving all over Britain; indeed, all over Western Europe. Some retain one part of the old tradition, while others conserve other parts. My task has been to contact as many different sources as I can, and then to piece together what I have been able to learn from them.

There are regional differences of ritual and of ideas. Nevertheless, it is just these differences, this dovetailing of one fact with another, which to me makes this research interesting and authentic. If everything were smooth and uniform, it would probably be modern; but there are fragmentary traditions and rituals, hints, loose ends, that puzzle and intrigue.

Although in the old days people of all classes belonged to the witch cult, probably the greater number of its followers could hardly read or write. Also, written documents were dangerous evidence; so the traditions of the cult were transmitted by word of mouth from generation to generation.

When more of the common people acquired a little book learning, some of them started writing things down in private books of their own. They would allow their trusted friends to copy what they would from such writings; but the rule was that when a member of the cult died his written book must be secured and burned.

There was a practical reason for this, as with most witch traditions.

It was done to protect the family of the deceased from persecution. The witch-hunters knew that witchcraft tended to be handed down in families. Hence all the relatives of a proven witch were suspect. And what clearer proof than a hand-written book?

Even after witchcraft ceased to be a capital offence, suspected witches often got rough treatment. They might be slashed or stabbed to draw blood on them, as a means of breaking their spells. They might be 'swum' in the village pond, to see if they floated. Even if they were only shunned and whispered about, this was not pleasant in a small community; at any time it could break out into mob violence. So the traditional destruction of all written records is frustrating but understandable.

When the organisation of the Old Religion became very broken up, many witches ceased to be organised into covens at all. They worked alone; though they generally knew other witches, and sometimes joined forces with them for some special purpose.

Such lone witches still exist, shrinking from all contact with modern covens that seek publicity. They usually have a little secret shrine in their home, where they invoke the old powers and give thanks for work successfully accomplished.

The contents of such a shrine will vary considerably, according to the taste of the individual witch. They may include things handed down, either in the family or by older witches now passed away. There are almost sure to be some curious candlesticks, an incense burner and either a crystal or a magic mirror for clairvoyance. Some magic symbols, such as the pentagram, will be in evidence; and so will the old black-hilted knife, or Athame. Probably a pack of Tarot cards will be there, too.

Along with these things will be any objects, weird or exotic, that take the individual's fancy. Witches have always liked to use strange and striking things, that would excite the imagination of those who saw them. They well know that the generation of atmosphere, the aura of the uncanny, is one of the most important secrets of magic. It contributes to "the willing suspension of disbelief", the feeling that, within the magic circle, or in the presence of the magical shrine, anything may happen.

Witchcraft is not only a religion and a system of magic. It is a philosophy, a way of life, a way of looking at things. It is not an intellectual affair; a witch seeks to develop intelligence and perception, rather than intellectualism. He or she does not despise emotions and feelings, as many intellectuals do. On the contrary, a witch recognises that emotions and feelings may come from a deeper level of the mind than intellectual reasoning, and therefore seeks to develop and make use of them.

Nor does a witch despise the physical senses; because these, too, are gateways which can lead to inner realisation. So again, he or she seeks to make use of the physical perceptions, as a means of attaining psychic and spiritual perception. There are many misconceptions about what psychic and spiritual experiences really consist of. They are not states of dreamy credulity; on the contrary, they are states of heightened awareness, in which for a while we awaken out of the condition that we have come to accept as 'normal'. Some occultists will tell you that there are actually five states of human consciousness, corresponding to the five-pointed star, the witches' pentagram. These are:

1) Deep, dreamless sleep.
2) Sleep in which dreams occur.
3) What we regard as normal waking consciousness.
4) True self-awareness.
5) Illumination.

An important point about witchcraft is that it *is* a craft, in the old sense of the word, the Anglo-Saxon *craeft,* implying art, skill, knowledge. The word 'witch' means 'wise one'; and a person cannot be *made* wise, they have to *become* wise. There are arts and skills and traditional knowledge which, used in the right way, will help you to become a 'wise one'. This is the real meaning of witchcraft.

It should by now be superfluous to say that modern witches do not make pacts with Satan or celebrate the Black Mass. But nor are they followers of the rather shallow and sugary philosophies that so often pass for 'higher teachings' in the more popular forms of occultism. Witches are not 'do-gooders', or purveyors of 'uplift'. They are practical people interested in the serious study of occult powers and the exploration of the Unknown—remembering that 'occult' only means 'hidden'.

Although they accept gifts, they do not work for hire. Nor will they very often undertake to do the many things people write and ask them to do, such as enabling someone to win sporting bets, or to gain the love of some particular person, or to compel an errant husband or wife to return.

Sometimes, even darker requests are received. I myself have on more than one occasion been asked if I would harm or 'get rid of' somebody. One woman wrote to me saying that she did not want a certain relative *killed,* only made fairly ill!

The unpalatable truth, which people do not care to hear, is that they can only change their lives by changing themselves. This the study and practice of witchcraft can undoubtedly do. But the concept of modern witches that many people have, as a sort of combination of Universal Aunts and Murder Incorporated, is a false one.

Nevertheless, I have seen some remarkable results achieved by witches' magic. Sceptics, of course, may dismiss such things as coincidence, when a ritual is done to achieve a certain result and that result follows. Nothing can be proved either way, as the event happens apparently by a fortuitous combination of circumstances; but the point is that it happens.

Rituals are not always successful, of course. The technique employed may be wrong. The operators may have misjudged the situation. The conditions prevailing at the time of the ritual may be adverse. However, I have seen a sufficient number of successes scored, to believe in the power of witchcraft.

I have seen, too, enough happenings to give grounds for belief that witches are 'kittle cattle to meddle with'. People who commit acts of aggression against the Old Religion or its followers, or deliberately set out to harm them, always have such behaviour followed by ill luck to themselves.

The situation for witchcraft today is in many respects very different from what it was in centuries past. Now that medical services take care of the less wealthy and privileged people, they no longer go to the village witch for her services as a midwife, or for herbal remedies. Many of the arts that she practised have now become quite respectable, and are known as hypnotism, psychology and so on. At the same time, the witches' persecutors have had their powers severely curtailed. Apart from smear campaigns in the sensational press, the witch-hunter's occupation is gone, too.

When Gerald Gardner wrote *Witchcraft Today,* he regarded witchcraft as something that was dying. However, subsequent events have proved him wrong. We have seen in the last twenty years an amazing renaissance of public interest, not only in witchcraft, but in the occult generally. Formerly forbidden subjects are now freely discussed— very often with the use of forbidden words! Times are changing at a rate which alarms and bewilders the older generation. And witchcraft is changing with them, and coming into its own as a popular form of pagan religion, based on sympathy with Nature; while its creed of "Do what you will, so long as it harms no one", has become widely and seriously accepted as being more truly moral than lists of "Thou shalt nots".

Nevertheless, witches do not seek for converts. They ask only acceptance and freedom to be what they want to be and to do what they want to do. They know that a pendulum which swings one way will swing back. They have had the swing of the pendulum against them, and seen the horrors of the years of persecution. Now, the swing is in the opposite direction—for the time being.

But even so, the Craft of the Wise keeps itself a little apart. Nor does it tell all of its secrets. It guards the flame of the lantern, like the Hermit in the Tarot cards, so that those who are able to will and know, and can dare and be silent, may go their way by its light.

WITCHES' LADDER, THE

The *Folklore Journal* in 1886 carried a story of a remarkable find in an old house in Wellington, Somerset. Some builders who were working on the house discovered a secret room in the space between the upper room and the roof. Judging by the contents of this hidey-hole it seems to have been a meeting-place for witches.

Six broomsticks were discovered there, together with an old arm-chair; perhaps a seat for whoever presided over the meeting. There was also another very curious object, which at first the finders were baffled to account for.

This consisted of a piece of rope, about 5 feet long and half an inch in thickness. It was composed of three strands, and had a loop at one end. Inserted in this rope, crossways, were a number of feathers. They were mostly goose feathers, though with some black plumes from a crow or rook, sticking out from the rope at irregular intervals. The feathers had not been merely knotted into the rope, but seemed to have been twisted into it between the strands at the time when it was made.

Some old Somerset people who saw this strange find regarded it with disfavour, and were reticent when asked what it was. The work-men called it "a witches' ladder", and suggested that it was "for getting across the roof", which was obviously absurd. One old lady, when asked if she knew what it was, replied that she knew of the use of the candle with pins in it, of the onion with pins in it, and of the rope and feathers. She refused to tell any more; but as the spells of sticking a candle or an onion with pins were known to be means of cursing someone, it became evident to the students of folklore who interested themselves in this find, that the witches' ladder was another means of placing a curse.

Further enquiry brought to light a few more details. The rope and the feathers had to be new, and the feathers had to be from a male bird. Nor was this spell confined to Somerset. It was also known in other parts of the West Country, and was evidently considered a dangerous and secret form of witchcraft.

When the copy of the *Folklore Journal* which contained a description and engraving of the witches' ladder reached Charles Godfrey Leland in Italy, he investigated and found that the curse of the rope and feathers was known in that country, too. Among Italian witches, it was called *la guirlanda delle streghe*, 'the witches' garland'. It took a very similar form, namely that of a cord with knots tied in it, and with a black hen's feather in each knot. The malediction was uttered repeatedly, as each knot was tied; and then the finished charm was hidden in the victim's bed to bring misfortune upon him.

The Reverend Sabine Baring-Gould, who had an extensive knowledge of the folklore of the West Country, introduced the spell of the witches' ladder into his novel *Curgenven,* published in 1893. According to his account of it, the witch ladder was made of black wool, white and brown thread, entwined together; and at every two inches this cord was tied round a bunch of cock's feathers, or pheasant's or moorhen's feathers, set alternately. The old grandmother who made it wove and knotted into the witches' ladder every kind of ache and pain she could think of, to light upon the enemy she intended it for. Then she tied a stone to the end of it, and sank the charm in Dozmary Pool, a legend-haunted water on Bodmin Moor. She believed that as the bubbles rose to the top of the pool, so the power of the curse would be released to do its work.

It is a remarkable tribute to the widespread nature of witches' secret practices, that practically the same charm should be known and used in places as far apart as Somerset and Italy, by people who were in those days not sufficiently literate to have got it from books; even if any description of it had been published before, which in view of the puzzlement of leading folklorists when confronted with this find seems unlikely.

It will be noted that the magical number three enters into the making of the spell, as it so often does. It has to be a triple cord into which the feathers are knotted. The feathers themselves are possibly symbolic of sending the spell flying invisibly towards the person it is meant for.

WITCH OF SCRAPFAGGOT GREEN, THE

One of the strangest witch stories of modern times occurred in Essex, towards the end of the Second World War.

For many years the village of Great Leighs had known that a witch lay buried at the crossroads called Scrapfaggot Green. There was no green left there now; only a great stone that marked the witch's grave. The story went that she had been burned at the stake upon Scrapfaggot Green, some 200 years ago. Her remains had been buried on the spot, with the ashes of the fire that consumed her, and the great stone had been laid there to keep her down.

Actually, as we know, after the Reformation in England death sentences on witches were carried out by hanging, not burning at the stake. (*See* BURNING AT THE STAKE.) The latter, however, was the means of execution for treason, and for a woman found guilty of killing her husband, which was regarded as 'petty treason'. If a witch was found guilty of either of these things, she could be executed by burning at the stake; but recorded instances are few. The last certainly recorded case of a witch being executed in England was that of Alice Molland, who was hanged at Exeter in 1685.

It seems more likely, therefore, that the detail of 'burning at the stake' is a later romantic addition, and that the time when this nameless unfortunate was executed was earlier than '200 years ago'. But though unfortunate, she was by no means powerless, as will be seen as the story unfolds.

Great Leighs is not far from Chelmsford, which actually was the place of execution of many witches; and the practice of burial at a crossroads was general in times past, for those who had died a death accursed.

However, the Witch of Scrapfaggot Green lay quietly in her grave until the turmoil of the Second World War. Then the rural peace of Great Leighs was rudely interrupted by the coming of the army. Military traffic rumbled along its leafy lanes and rattled the windows of its farms and cottages. The narrow winding road called Drachett Lane, which led over the crossroads, could scarcely admit the passage of army vehicles. So the order went out, given by an outsider who knew nothing of local tradition, to send an army bulldozer along and widen the road.

The order was carried out; and in the course of the road-widening, the lumbering bulldozer pushed aside the Witch's Stone.

From that day onwards, a series of events took place which might be regarded as fantastic, were it not for the fact that nearly everyone in the village was witness to one or another of them. Nor were the strange happenings trivial. Apparently senseless they might be; but the force required to carry some of them out was truly extraordinary.

For instance, a local builder found his heavy scaffolding poles scattered about his yard one morning as if they were matchsticks. Like the majority of these queer happenings, it took place overnight, and no human agency could be found to account for it.

The same builder was employing some painters at work on a cottage. Overnight, a dozen heavy paint pots, together with the rest of the painters' tools, disappeared. The workmen searched the house, and eventually found the pots and the other missing articles hidden under a bed in an attic.

Other strange overnight persecutions were visited on a local farmer. After a perfectly calm and windless night, he found his straw ricks tumbled down and scattered. Moreover, his wagons had been turned round in their sheds, so that it took his men half an hour to get them out.

Daily, the tale of mischief grew. Sheep were found outside fields in which they had apparently been safely penned; yet there were no displaced hurdles or gaps in hedges to show how they had escaped. Three geese completely disappeared from a man's garden, with no tell-tale feather remaining to show the work of a fox or other predator. And a chicken that no one owned turned up dead in a water butt.

The bells of the village church were heard to ring at midnight, when no human hands were pulling their ropes; and something interfered with the works of the church clock, and made it two hours slow.

The bewitching of Great Leighs caused so much talk and speculation in the countryside, as one crazy event followed another, each without any normal explanation, that eventually the story got into the National Press. On October 8th 1944 the *Sunday Pictorial* printed a full-page article, "The Witch Walks at Scrapfaggot Green", by its reporter, St. John Cooper.

Mr Cooper was himself a witness to the astonishment of the landlord of the village pub, the 'Dog and Gun', when a huge stone was discovered outside his front door. The landlord declared that the stone had not been there before; nor did anyone know where it had come from. The reporter helped to lift it out of the way, and gave his opinion that it would have taken three strong men to carry it any distance. As usual, there was no explanation; that is, no normal or material one.

By this time, however, the view was being freely expressed in the village that the cause of all these eldritch happenings was the disturbance of the witch's grave. The late Harry Price, who was then head of the London University Council for Psychical Investigation, was consulted about the case, and gave his opinion that the events were being caused by a poltergeist.

This left no one much the wiser; nor did it offer any remedy. Apparently, however, Mr Price suggested that the stone which had marked the witch's grave should be replaced in its old position. Why this action should have stopped the activities of a poltergeist is not clear. However, it was certainly in accord with public feeling in the village.

During the next week the villagers got together, headed by the Chairman of the local Council, and manhandled the Witch's Stone back into place. As the monument weighed about two tons, it was hard work; but they had seen enough to convince them that it was a good idea. Moreover, it was not long to Halloween; and what might that night of witchery bring forth?

The *Sunday Pictorial* published a photograph of the scene of the replacement of the stone, in its issue of 15th October 1944. Apparently, on the very last day before the stone was replaced, the witch's restless ghost had performed a final prank. A villager who kept rabbits found the animals had somehow been put into the hen house, and were sharing it with the chickens! There is a touch of humour about this, in contrast with the malice of some of the previous happenings. *Was* someone—or something—placated?

At any rate, as the queer happenings had started with the moving of the stone, so with its replacement they stopped. Great Leighs was left again to its rural peace—a quiet intensified by the wartime blackout. A crazy, fantastic story; but a true one.

X

X—THE SIGN OF THE CROSS

The sign of the cross, although generally regarded as the emblem of Christianity, is in reality much older. Its significance as a religious symbol goes back far into prehistoric times.

Being so ancient, the cross has acquired a variety of forms. There is the Latin Cross, the form usually seen on the altars of Christian churches; the Greek Cross or equal-armed cross; the St. Andrew's Cross or X-shaped cross; the Swastika or Fylfot Cross; the Tau or T-shaped cross; the *Crux Ansata* or looped cross; and the Celtic or wheel-shaped cross. There are also local variations of these, such as the Cross of Lorraine or three-barred cross; the Russian Cross, which is the same as the Latin but with a third slanting bar on the lower part; and the Maltese Cross, which is equal-armed but with bifurcated ends to the arms.

Of these many varieties of crosses, the simplest forms are most probably the oldest. Certainly the equal-armed cross, the Tau Cross, the wheel cross, the Fylfot Cross, and the looped cross, can all be traced back to times of great antiquity. They have always been regarded as sacred and fortunate symbols. Even the Latin Cross has been found plainly represented on the pre-Columbian monuments of Central America, notably at Palenque.

There is therefore evidence that the idea of the sign of the cross serving to keep away evil is common to both Christian and pagan. Hence the idea so beloved of sensational thriller writers, that witches abhor and fear the sign of the cross, is without foundation.

In fact, in Minoan Crete the worshippers of the Great Mother adorned the goddess's altars with an equal-armed cross. When Sir Arthur Evans uncovered the buried splendours of the Cretan city of Knossos, he found many examples of the cross. He used one of them, a beautiful equal-armed cross of marble, as the centrepiece in a reconstruction he made of an altar to the Minoan Mother Goddess. On either side of the cross, in a photograph of this reconstruction, are two figurines of the goddess, bare-breasted but otherwise in the elaborate dress of Minoan ladies. There are also cups for libations of wine; hollowed blocks of stone to receive offerings, or perhaps to burn incense; and an ornamentation of a great many sea shells and some phallic-shaped objects, representing the powers of male and female.

This is the essential significance of the equal-armed cross. It represents the union of the two great complementary forces which by their interplay bring forth the manifested universe. The upright bar of the cross represents the male, and it interpenetrates the horizontal bar which represents the female.

In Chinese philosophy, these principles are called the Yang (masculine) and the Yin (feminine). The Yang is a single bar, the Yin a divided bar; so that if one were placed across the other, the figure of the equal-armed cross would appear.

In Ancient Egypt, the looped Cross, or *Crux Ansata*, was the Key of Life, and the symbol of immortality. The Egyptian name for it was the 'Ankh'. It repeats the idea of the union of masculine and feminine in another form; because the Ankh consists of a T-shape, with a loop or O-shape above it. The T-shape represents the masculine principle, and the loop the feminine.

The Fylfot Cross or Swastika has in recent years been besmirched by its association with Hitler and his Nazis. This is a pity, because its origins are so ancient as to make it one of the most widespread and venerable religious signs. Forms of it are found in Ancient Mexico, among the American Indians, in China, in Tibet, in Ancient Crete, in the prehistoric civilisations of the Mediterranean area and among our Scandinavian ancestors. It was the latter who called it the Fylfot, or Hammer of Thor. 'Swastika' is actually the Sanskrit name for it; and it has been the sign of light and beneficence in the East for thousands of years. Some occultists believe that Hitler brought destruction upon himself by appropriating and desecrating an emblem so potent and venerated.

The Rev. S. Baring-Gould, M.A., who should be a reliable authority upon ecclesiastical matters, tells us in his *Curious Myths of the Middle Ages* (London, 1869), that the Fylfot, or Hammer of Thor, found its way into a good many English churches, as a mark upon the church bells. The reason is that church bells used to be thought to dispel storms when they were rung. Hence they were marked with the sign of Thor, the god of thunder, who had authority over the powers of the air. This is yet another instance of the way in which Christian and pagan beliefs and customs continued side by side long after this country was officially Christian.

The Fylfot Cross is found in those parts of England where the Norse immigrants settled; particularly in Lincolnshire and Yorkshire. Baring-Gould states that this sign was found upon church bells in Appleby, Scotherne, Waddingham, Bishop's Norton, West Barkwith, Hathersage, Mexborough "and many more".

The wheel cross, or Celtic Cross, of which a number of very old and beautiful examples are to be found in Cornwall, is definitely pre-Christian. The coins of ancient Gaul had an equal-armed cross on them; in fact, actual little wheel-crosses have been found in Gallic territory, and presumed to be a very early type of coinage. Celtic jewellery, too, sometimes shows this basic design, of the equal-armed cross in the circle.

The wheel cross, like the Swastika, has also been found upon prehistoric remains in Mexico. The world-wide distribution of such emblems, across sea and continents, has led students of ancient traditions to suspect that their real place of origin is the lost civilisation of Atlantis, or the even more remote and shadowy realm of Lemuria, or Mu.

The equal-armed cross has another hidden meaning. It not only represents the union of masculine and feminine forces; it also symbolises the Four Cardinal Points, the Four Winds, and the Four Elements. The point of union at the centre is the hidden Fifth Element, the Quintessence, or Spirit.

The equal-armed cross, when it is surrounded with a circle to make it the wheel cross, or Celtic Cross, thus shows the representation of the manifested universe surrounded by the circle of infinity and eternity. The wheel cross is also called the rose cross, and may be the real emblem of that mysterious occult brotherhood, the Rosicrucians. It was the badge of the Grand Master of the Knights Templars.

The cross is therefore a sign common to both pagan and Christian, and its meaning is much older and grander than merely that of a Roman instrument of execution.

Y

YULE

Yule is the Anglo-Saxon word for the festival of the winter solstice. Our celebration of Christmas is compounded of several different traditions, Celtic, Roman and Saxon, with the whole adapted later to Christianity.

The Celtic festival of the winter solstice was called by the Druids Alban Arthan, according to Bardic tradition. It was then that the Chief Druid cut the sacred mistletoe from the oak, a custom that still lingers, with our use of mistletoe as a Christmas decoration. Mistletoe is usually banned from churches at Christmas, owing to its pagan associations. However, at York Minster there used to be a different custom, which Stukeley, the eighteenth-century writer on Druidism, notes: "On the Eve of Christmas Day they carry Mistletoe to the high Altar of the Cathedral and proclaim a public and universal liberty, pardon, and freedom to all sorts of inferior and even wicked people at the gates of the city, towards the four quarters of Heaven."

This custom was undoubtedly a relic of Druidry. York is a very old city, known to the Romans as Eboracum.

The idea of holding festival at the winter solstice, to celebrate the rebirth of the sun, was so universal in the ancient world that the Christians adapted the popular feast into the celebration of the birth of Christ. No one really knows when Christ's birthday was; but by holding this feast at midwinter, Christ was mystically identified with the sun.

The Romans celebrated the winter solstice with a merry festival called the Saturnalia. The winter solstice takes place when the sun enters the sign of Capricorn; and Saturn, the ruler of Capricorn, was supposed to have been the ruler also of the far-off Golden Age of the past, when the earth was peaceful and fruitful, and everyone was happy. So at this time of year the houses were decked with the boughs of evergreen trees and bushes, all normal business was suspended, and social distinctions were temporarily forgotten in the atmosphere of festival. The servants and slaves were given a feast, and the masters waited on them at table. People gave each other presents, and the Saturnalia became a byword for riotous fun and merriment.

The pagan Saxons celebrated the feast of Yule, with plenty of ale and with blazing fires, of which our Yule Log is the last relic. The latter is the midwinter, indoor equivalent of the outdoor bonfires on Midsummer Eve. Its ritual nature is made evident by the fact that there was an old custom, 'for luck', of saving a piece of the Yule Log to kindle the next year's Christmas blaze.

The word *Yule,* according to Bede and various other authorities of the olden time, is derived from an old Norse word *Iul,* meaning a wheel. In the old Clog Almanacs, the symbol of a wheel was used to mark Yuletide. The idea behind this is that the year turns like a wheel, the Great Wheel of the Zodiac, the Wheel of Life, of which the spokes are the old ritual occasions, the equinoxes and solstices, and the four 'cross-quarter-days' of Candlemas, May Eve, Lammas and Halloween. The winter solstice, the rebirth of the sun, is a particularly important turning point.

Hence modern witches celebrate Christmas with a will; only they recognise it as Yule, one of the great Nature festivals of old. They deplore the money-grabbing materialism which is taking all the old-fashioned happiness out of Chirstmas, and turning it into a commercialised racket.

Alban Arthan, the Saturnalia, Yuletide or Christmas, the mid-winter festival was traditionally a happy time. With the rebirth of the sun, the giver of warmth, light and life, people had something to be genuinely happy about; and all kinds of merry old customs, rooted in the distant pagan past, thrived in the English countryside.

People in those days had no mechanical entertainment, such as the cinema, radio or television. They made their own fun, and kept up old customs because they enjoyed them. Christmas lasted a full twelve days, and work did not start again until Plough Monday. In many places, to make sure that all the winter festivities were duly observed, a Lord of Misrule was elected, a kind of make-believe king of merriment.

It is significant that the reign of the Lord of Misrule was said to begin on Halloween and to end at Candlemas. Both of these dates are Great Sabbats; at Halloween the Horned God, the principle of death and resurrection, comes into his own at the beginning of the

Celtic winter season; while at Candlemas the first signs of spring appear.

The evergreens for Yuletide decorations were holly, ivy, mistletoe, the sweet-smelling bay and rosemary, and green branches of the box tree. By Candlemas, all had to be gathered up and burnt, or hobgoblins would haunt the house. In other words, by that time a new tide of life had started to flow through the world of nature, and people had to get rid of the past and look to the future. Spring-cleaning was originally a nature ritual.

The old mumming plays, which were and in some places still are part of English Yuletide festivities, are linked with the rebirth of the sun. Saint George in shining armour comes forth to do battle with the dark-faced 'Turkish Knight'. Saint George is the sun, slaying the powers of darkness. They fight, and the dark knight falls. But the victor immediately cries that he has slain his brother; darkness and light, winter and summer, are complementary to each other. So on comes the mysterious 'Doctor', with his magical bottle, who revives the slain man, and all ends with music and rejoicing. There are many local variations of this play, but the action is substantially the same throughout.

Z

ZODIAC, THE

It has already been suggested that the source of the mystic power of the witches' number, thirteen, is the thirteen lunar months of the year. There is, however, another important source, namely the twelve signs of the zodiac plus one of the luminaries, the sun by day and the moon by night, which rule over them. The Sun makes his journey round the magic circle of the zodiac in the course of a year; the moon travels through the twelve signs in a lunar month.

No one really knows how old the zodiac is, or who invented it. Our word 'zodiac' is derived from the Greek *zoidiakos;* meaning 'figures of animals', according to the usual dictionary interpretation. It is akin to *zoe* 'life' and *zoidion,* a figure of some living thing. As not all the figures of the zodiac *are* animals, one may at least speculate that a better interpretation would be 'a figure of Life', or 'an image of the course of Life', for all things, human and cosmic.

The zodiac is a circle, divided, as all circles may be, into 360 degrees, or twelve signs of 30 degrees each. This circle is the course in the heavens of the *apparent* path of the sun, moon and planets; it is about 18 degrees wide. Its twelve signs are named after the adjacent constellations, which symbolically depict the characteristics of the many things including human beings, which the signs govern. The zodiac of the sun's path, or ecliptic, is *not* the same thing as the zodiac of the starry constellations; a fact critics of astrology do not always realise. (*See* ASTROLOGY.)

There is a story that in very far-off days the zodiac was reckoned to consist, not of twelve signs of 30 degrees each, but of ten signs of 36 degrees each; the sign Libra being omitted, and the signs Virgo and Scorpio being reckoned as one. This, says an obscure occult legend, referred to the time when the human race was androgynous, having both sexes in one. But when the separation into male and female took place, it was signified by altering the signs of the Great

Wheel of Life. Virgo, the female, was separated from Scorpio, the male; and between them was placed Libra, the sign of marriage.

The zodiac, with its patterns of relationships between the planets and the signs they rule, its triplicities of the Four Elements and so on, is a wonderful design of beauty and harmony, like a great mandala. It is truly a magical circle; hence the popularity of zodiac bracelets, and zodiac rings, with the signs represented upon them, as 'lucky charms'. They are emblems of infinity and eternity, of ever-becoming life. To wear one's own zodiacal sign, as an emblematical piece of jewellery, is to express the wish of putting oneself in harmony with the best qualities inherent in one's own sign. All of the zodiacal signs have their own good and bad qualities; all are necessary parts of the Great Pattern.

The signs of the zodiac have often formed a motif for decorative art. A fine representation of the zodiac was carved in the Temple of Isis at Denderah; and passing down the centuries, the zodiac reappeared again as a decoration in many old Christian churches and cathedrals.

Perhaps the most wonderful zodiac of all, however, is that which is claimed to exist among the green hills and winding rivers of Somerset, in the neighbourhood of Glastonbury. I say "claimed to exist", because some sceptics deny its actuality; and it is of course not recognised by any orthodox antiquaries. Nevertheless, anyone who will examine the evidence, particularly of aerial photography, must surely concede that coincidence has to be stretched a very long way to account for it.

In brief, the Glastonbury Zodiac, as it has come to be called, is formed by the natural configurations of the countryside hills, rivers, etc., aided by prehistoric earthworks, the lines of old roads, lynchets, and the patterns of fields. It forms a great circle, some 10 miles in diameter and about 30 miles in circumference. The centre of the circle is at Butleigh; Glastonbury, the ancient Isle of Avalon, is on its northern boundary; and below it, to the south-east, lies Cadbury Castle, believed to be the site of King Arthur's 'Camelot'.

The great Zodiacal figures were first discovered in modern times by Mrs. K. E. Maltwood, F.R.S.A., in about 1925, as a result of making maps to illustrate the twelfth-century Arthurian romance called *The High History of the Holy Grail* (translated by Sebastian Evans, J. M. Dent, Everyman's Library Edition, London, 1913). In surveying and studying the ground covered by King Arthur's questing knights, Mrs. Maltwood realised that the mythical 'Kingdom of Logres', with its various strange adventures, was actually a veiled description of this great planisphere, of pre-Christian origin, as the Arthurian Romances themselves are. This was the *real* Round Table of King Arthur.

Mrs. Maltwood has described her discoveries in *A Guide to Glastonbury's Temple of the Stars* (James Clarke and Co., London, 1964), together with *An Air View Supplement to Glastonbury's Temple of the Stars,* and *The Enchantments of Britain* (Victoria Printing and Publishing Co., British Columbia, 1944). Since the publication of these books, many other students of Britain's antiquities have taken up the quest for further information and proof of this wonder of Ancient Britain.

More clues have emerged; in particular, a striking and cryptic passage from the diaries of Doctor John Dee, who was occult adviser to the first Queen Elizabeth. (*See* DEE, DR. JOHN.) Dr. Dee and his colleague Edward Kelley were very interested in the Glastonbury area; and his mention of "the starres which agree with their reproductions on the ground" shows that he knew of the Great Zodiac's existence, though he refrained from describing it plainly. (Dee knew the value of the virtue of silence upon occult matters, having himself been persecuted in those less tolerant days.)

This passage from Dr. Dee's diary is reproduced in Richard Deacon's recent biography, *John Dee,* published by Mullers, London, in 1968. It should give people who scoff at the existence of secret traditions something to think about.

The implications of the existence of these great effigies, like those of the alignments of Stonehenge and the mathematics of the stone circles, are tremendous and far-reaching. The Old Religion of our ancestors, call it Wise Craft or what you will, is worthy of study, and cannot be dismissed as superstition.

Index

The main subject entries of this book will be found listed in alphabetical order in the table of Contents at the beginning of the book, on pages 5-8. This index is intended as a supplement to the table of Contents serving to indicate subjects, places and people mentioned in the articles, in addition to those actually named in the article headings.